Contents

I know nothing except the fact of my ignorance.

Socrates (469-399BC)

CONTENTS

Many thanks to the following people and organisations for their editorial contributions: Chris Woodhead of Cognita ; Go4It; Northwood College; Simon Clegg CBE of Ipswich Town Football Club; Edward Elliott, Head of The Perse School; David Boddy, Headmaster of St James Independent School for Senior Boys; Mumsnet; Liam Butler of the Independent Schools Council; the British Accreditation Council; and Chris Proctor and colleagues, SFIA.

We are very grateful to Brighton College; Regent College; Dulwich College Preparatory School; The Lady Eleanor Holles School; and the Olympic Development Authority, for allowing us to use their images on the cover and in the editorial front of this book.

Thanks also go to the many individuals and organisations who have helped update information for this edition. We are particularly grateful to the schools for ensuring that we continue to receive information from them with such promptness, efficiency and courtesy.

Introduction

Former HM Chief Inspector of Schools, Chris Woodhead, talks about the things to consider when choosing an independent school in London and the south-east.

More children are educated in independent schools in London and the south-east than in any other part of the country. Why? Because more parents in the south-east can afford to educate their children privately, but equally, because in London in particular, demand for a good education outstrips supply.

Your guess about the continuing affordability of private education is as good as mine. We may or may not be escaping the recession and those responsible for setting fees in independent schools may or may not have realised that the annual above-inflation hike is unsustainable. What I do know is that demand for private schooling will continue. In the south-east, as in every other region of England, there are some wonderful state schools, but there are not nearly enough of them. If you live within spitting distance of the front gates, you might stand a chance of securing a place in a successful and therefore over-subscribed school. Otherwise, forget it.

The Labour Government would, of course, like us all to believe that the number of failing schools has been reduced, that the Academy and Specialist Schools initiatives have resulted in many more highly effective schools, and that you only have to look at each year's record GCSE and A level statistics to realise that all is rosy in the world of state education. In real terms we spend two thirds more on education than we did in 1997. As the Public Accounts Committee has pointed out, there has not been a commensurate improvement in educational standards. The truth is that billions of pounds of public money have been poured down the drain and many parents have and will continue to have no option other than to dig deep into their pockets and go private.

In principle, the Conservatives' plan to enable parents to set up their own schools is excellent. The more schools we have competing with one another to meet the aspirations of parents as consumers the better. Any initiative which undermines state monopoly provision must be good. But, in practice, how independent will these so called 'independent state schools' be? They will still have to teach the discredited National Curriculum. They will still be inspected by a discredited Ofsted. They will not, crucially, be allowed to set their own admissions policy. So, if you want your academically-able child to attend an academically-selective school, a change of Government will leave you no better off than you are now. And how many parents have the time, energy and knowledge to set up their own school? The jury is, I am afraid, very much out on Mr Cameron's flagship education reforms.

Where does this leave the many thousands of parents in the south-east of England who want to give their children the best possible start in life? How do you ensure that you choose the independent school that is right for your child?

It is a statement of the obvious, but first and foremost you need to know your child. As parents we all run the risk of imposing our own dreams on the actual abilities and personalities of our children. A child who has high academic intelligence may well benefit from the intensity of a prep and pre-prep education designed to gain entry to a top London day school. Those who have not are going to flounder. Every parent says they want their children to be happy at school. Some, in my experience, pursue this goal in very peculiar ways.

Second, find out as much as you can about every school which seems a possibility. Research the examination results, but remember that a high league table position may say more about the academic ability of the intake than the quality of the teaching. Look at the inspection reports, though, sadly, these days they will tell you more about whether the school complies with the latest health and safety edict than the excellence of the education it offers. Above all, visit. Thirty years ago, Sir Keith (as he then was) Joseph said that 'the nearest thing we have to a magic wand in education is a good headteacher'. He was right. The Head sets the tone in his or her school, defines the values which inspire staff and pupils, walks the corridors and classrooms and touchlines – or not, as the case may be. A few months ago I went round a school with its Headmistress. She did not address a word to a child or introduce me to a single member of staff. This was not a school I would have wanted my grandchildren to attend.

Ask if you can visit a few lessons. Ask yourself, if the answer is no, what the school has to hide. Is there an excitement in the lessons you observe? Are the pupils concentrating and involved? Are you interested in what the teachers are saying? The crucial test is whether you would have liked to stay longer. Browse through a few exercise books to establish the quality of the children's work and, what is equally important, the frequency and thoroughness of the teacher's marking.

The academic side of school life is, of course, not everything. Good independent schools really do know their pupils. They care about each child as an individual and ensure that problems are identified and solved before they become intractable. Your visit therefore needs to involve discussions with the pastoral staff. I would also want to find out as much as possible about the extracurricular activities in order to see whether there is a good fit between the interests of my child and what the school has to offer.

Finally, unless you are one of the fortunate and very wealthy few, a quick internet search to identify a financial consultant who specialises in planning for school fees might be half an hour very well spent.

This article was written before the General Election of May 6 2010.

How to use this guide

Are you looking for:

Help and advice? Take a look at our editorial section (pages v to xliv) for articles written by experts in their field covering issues you are likely to come across when choosing a school for your child.

A school or college in a certain geographical region? Look first in the directories for basic information about all the schools in London and the south-east of England complete with contact details. Schools are listed in alphabetical order within each county or, for schools in central London, in postcode order. From this section you will be directed to more detailed information in the guide where this is available.

A certain type of school or college in your local area? Look in the directories for your local area. Underneath each school you will find icons that denote different types of schools or qualifications that they offer. You can find a key to these icons below or at the front of each section of the directory.

A specific school or college? If you know the name of the school or college but are unsure of its location, simply go to the index at the back of the guide where you will find all the school listed alphabetically. Page numbers prefixed with the letter D denote the directory section; those without, the listings.

Maps? See pp 2, 4, 48 and 62 for maps of London, Greater London, and the south-east.

More information on relevant educational organisations and examinations? Look in the examinations and qualifications section and the useful organisations section, both located towards the back of the guide.

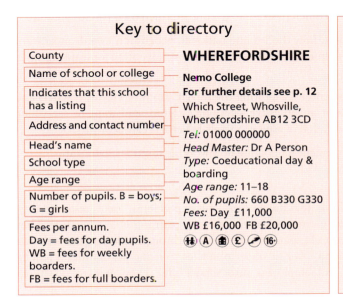

Key to directory

County	WHEREFORDSHIRE
Name of school or college	Nemo College
Indicates that this school has a listing	For further details see p. 12
Address and contact number	Which Street, Whosville, Wherefordshire AB12 3CD
	Tel: 01000 000000
Head's name	Head Master: Dr A Person
School type	Type: Coeducational day & boarding
Age range	Age range: 11–18
Number of pupils. B = boys; G = girls	No. of pupils: 660 B330 G330
Fees per annum. Day = fees for day pupils. WB = fees for weekly boarders. FB = fees for full boarders.	Fees: Day £11,000 WB £16,000 FB £20,000

Key to directory icons

- Boys' school
- Coeducational school
- Girls' school
- International school
- Tutorial/sixth form college
- A levels
- Boarding accommodation
- Bursaries
- International Baccalaureate
- Learning support
- Entrance at 16+
- Vocational qualifications

Go4it: celebrating an education for life

The national Go4it Award is given to schools who demonstrate they are creating, developing and enhancing a culture of creativity, positive risk-taking, innovation, a can-do attitude and above all, a real adventure for learning.

"I believe teachers know instinctively that children need to experience a sense of adventure through their learning. Instead, too many children are growing up scared – they know how to pass a test, but to succeed in life they need also to learn about life experiences, including taking risks and sometimes failing."

Simon Woodroffe, entrepreneur, founder of Yo! Sushi and Go4it Champion.

Today's young people need good qualifications but equally, if not more, important are the attitudes and behaviours they take with them into adult life. Our education system spends a lot of time testing and measuring young people's academic achievement, but how do you measure their level of 'get up and go'?

Educational leadership charity HTI (Heads, Teachers and Industry) created the Go4it awards scheme as the benchmark for a can-do ethos in schools.

Now in its third year, the origins of Go4it lay in a hard-hitting Issues Paper written by HTI's former President Digby, Lord Jones of Birmingham.

In *Cotton Wool Kids*, Lord Jones explained why excessive risk aversion is damaging society and the economy and why schools should be a focal point for promoting an enterprise culture. He urged schools to give young people more opportunities to experience and practise risk-related skills because today's pupils are tomorrow's innovators, not just in the workplace, but also in society. They are growing up in a very different world to the one in which their parents grew up.

HTI's response was to launch Go4it, now the leading national recognition awards process for UK schools which demonstrate a culture of creativity, innovation, adventure for learning and a positive attitude towards risk.

Go4it is gaining phenomenal momentum, capturing the imaginations of Heads, teachers and employers who have had enough of an obsessive safety-first culture and want to see young people liberated to become life-savvy, full of aspiration, self-belief and can-do attitudes.

Almost a thousand state and independent schools are now working towards Go4it status.

So what do Go4it schools do?

They encourage children to think for themselves, solve problems, take responsibility, understand that failure is part of the journey to success and view learning as an adventure. They empower teachers to be innovative and expand pupils' horizons through wide-ranging activities in and out of school. They go round, over or under obstacles to make possibilities a reality. They welcome the community and employers into school life. They dare to do things differently.

Go4it gives schools the opportunity to showcase and celebrate the bigger picture achievements beyond the academic. For many, it is an affirmation of all the things they are doing already, but as one Go4it Head teacher said the award acts as a "unifying symbol for all our endeavours".

How it works

Assessment is against eight criteria and follows a number of stages after registration:

- The establishment of a Go4it steering group drawn from across the school community

- A written submission, providing a portfolio of evidence against each of the criteria, including a section that needs to be written and evidenced by students

- A half-day assessment, including presentation of examples to support the portfolio of evidence, a targeted tour of the school to witness activities that demonstrate a Go4it ethos and three sets of interviews involving staff and students

- An assessment review day to determine whether the school has successfully met the Go4it criteria

- Celebration!

It is a rigorous process, which not only surprises and delights because it often reveals the hidden extent to which many school go to encourage Go4it behaviours in their pupils, but also spurs ambitions to achieve even more.

Every good school knows that academic achievement is only part of the equation in preparing young people for adulthood. Go4it provides the framework and recognition for schools that aspire to give young people an education for life and work, not just qualifications.

For further information or an application pack, please contact Tracey Maude on 024 7641 0104; email: t.maude@hti.co.uk; or visit: www.hti.org.uk.

Northwood College Goes 4 It

Unique Thinking Skills Programme in north-west London looks wider than exam success.

Northwood College, a girls' school in north-west London, has always been about more than preparing pupils to pass exams (which it does very well, of course). Head Mistress Jacqualyn Pain says, "the school takes a holistic approach to developing pupils as 'active thinkers', ready to face a fast-changing world, in which many of the jobs they will end up doing probably don't even exist today".

It's an obvious fit with the Go4it philosophy, and when Jane Simister, who heads Northwood College's unique Thinking Skills Programme, came across the Go4it award in 2007, she instantly saw how it could benefit the school. "We felt Go4it chimed with the ethos we were developing and could help us to embed this more thoroughly. Achieving the award would be a great way to celebrate our successes," says Mrs Simister.

When you are doing something innovative, like putting thinking skills at the heart of a school, it is motivating to have external recognition, she adds. Some of Go4it's assessment criteria were areas that the school had already decided it wanted to focus on – like developing a culture of positive risk-taking.

"Research shows that bright girls, in particular, can often tend to be risk averse, because they fear they'll lose their 'clever label' if they don't excel at everything they do," says Mrs Simister.

At Northwood College the brightest girls are encouraged to try new activities that don't necessarily play to their academic strengths – creating complex wire sculptures, learning to dance the Cha-Cha-Cha or doing cryptic crosswords. They learn what it feels like not to be immediately brilliant at something – and that you can stick with it and enjoy it anyway. "It's one way of building a tougher, more resilient intellectual character," says Mrs Simister.

Other activities and initiatives put forward as part of the award assessment included 'INVENT', an annual Dragons' Den-style competition in which girls invent a new product, and then present their ideas on stage to a panel of guest judges. INVENT has seen girls come up with ideas that have even attracted commercial interest – like Vanish Varnish, a nail-varnish remover in a pen-shaped dispenser, aimed at schoolgirls who are prone to getting caught out in class on a Monday morning with coloured nails.

Go4it assessors were also very impressed by the amount of charity work done by pupils, usually on their own initiative. One group of eight girls in Year 11 – named 'The Acht' – was interviewed about their fundraising for the Wings of Hope children's charity. They went on to win the 'Most Funds Raised' category in the Wings of Hope Achievement Awards, which recognises fundraising efforts, and to come second out of 1,400 participants in the overall award.

Since getting Go4it status girls at Northwood College have continued to demonstrate their commitment to its values. Mrs Simister recalls the recent Junior School Music Competition, where one group took the unusual and brave step of entering with a composition of their own.

"One of the Go4it assessment criteria is about encouraging students to learn to work together collaboratively in teams. What impressed me was that the girls tackled this task by dividing up roles – for instance, choosing a creative thinker to generate lots of ideas and a critical thinker to point out what would work best and where improvements could be made. That's something we've done as an exercise in our Thinking Skills lessons in the Junior School, but it was lovely to see the girls picking it up themselves and using it entirely independently," says Mrs Simister. The girls went on to win the ensemble section of the contest.

There are plenty of other examples. Girls demonstrate their spirit of adventure with activities like the Duke of Edinburgh's Award and World Challenge, in which a group of girls recently took on the entire organisation, planning and funding of a trip to Brazil. Alternatively, they take a standard requirement – like doing work experience – but then add an extra element of adventure, like doing it abroad in Germany or Spain.

In sport, the Go4it judges saw Sky Draper, a talented triathlete who is preparing for the 2012 Olympics as part of the Dame Kelly Holmes Talent Squad. Instead of focusing only on her own training, she has set up a running club to encourage her schoolmates to compete at a higher level – demonstrating the Go4it values of a can-do attitude, as well as enterprise and competitiveness.

The Go4it award has been good for Northwood College. It has created greater awareness inside the school of the value of fostering certain very important qualities, says Miss Pain, and acted as a celebration of the many exciting things that go on. The school will be reapplying for the award next year – and is confident that there will be no shortage of evidence and enthusiasm from the girls to prove their Go4it status.

For more information about Northwood College, see page 54

Olympic legacy should change young people's lives

Simon Clegg, the former chief executive of the British Olympic Association, talks about young people, independent education and sport.

Within the British Olympic Association, the basis of the bid to bring the Olympics to London in 2012 was a very clear understanding that nothing had the potential to move sport higher and more quickly up both the political and social agendas in this country.

We have undoubtedly achieved the former: sport has never had such a place at the high table of government. The massive investment in the regeneration of the East End of London, the additional £300 million that the government have made available for high performance sport to help achieve success in 2012, means that we have achieved our political goals - although we do also need to recognise that sport will fall down the political agenda after 2012 when there will be more important things that we as a nation need to address and that the government will need to address on our behalf.

But the real challenge is how we move sport up the social agenda. If the closest the kids in Glasgow and Belfast get to the Olympic Games in 2012 is watching it on a television screen then I think we have failed a whole generation. I think we really do need to use this vehicle that we have got over the next two years to ensure that there is proper engagement to drive sport up the social agenda - because that is the real legacy of the Olympic Games. It is not about the infrastructure that we leave down in one part of London, the legacy should be how we have changed people's lives in a way that would otherwise take generations to achieve.

I am passionate about the benefit that sport can bring to society. Not only through exercise but also in terms of the camaraderie and the building of *esprit de corps*, and the ability of young people to learn that it is important to play by the rules and the whole principles of fair play. Sport also educates young people in experiencing failure and victory, and plays an important role in teaching young people about acting in an appropriate manner on a sports field. Our high-level sports people in this country do need to be seen as role models for society and it is quite important that young children aspire to be like these role models: sport is a very powerful vehicle for achieving that.

I went first of all to Haslemere Prep School in Surrey and then, after Common Entrance, I went on to Stowe. Sport is not the exclusive domain of the independent education sector, but I think that sport and extracurricular activities in general play a much more important part in independent schools than they do in state schools. I was very lucky in that both schools I went to took their sport very seriously and had great facilities. The independent sector has increasingly been conscious of the need to provide quality sports facilities, particularly over recent decades as they find themselves in an increasingly competitive market.

Sporting facilities are one of those additional areas that can influence people when they come to make a decision where to send their children. I was recently invited back up to Stowe for the opening of the new athletics track with Sebastian Coe. They have now got the most fantastic facilities, state-of-the-art facilities which upgraded the track that they had there for many decades. This constant development of facilities in independent schools is striking.

There are some important factors in this disparity between the independent and state sectors. First of all, the financial independence that the independent sector enjoys is key: they are able to spend their own money on developing not only their own academic facilities, but also their extracurricular facilities as well. Of course in the public sector that is much more constrained; any funding that is available is spent mainly on academic facilities. There is also a very clear understanding in the independent sector that the schools operate in a highly competitive environment and they need to attract custom. One of the ways of doing that is improving the facilities at the school from a holistic point of view.

The physical development of the individual is a major part of the holistic approach that I have to education. I take a very broad view about education, in which I see the development of the whole individual as more important than just academic qualifications. Education should be about preparing children for life after academia and therefore one needs to think about not only their academic development but also their physical and social development as well.

To me, sport is a factor when it comes to choosing an independent school. Considering the career path that I have enjoyed, where sport played an important part first of all when I was in the Army, then when I was on the national ski teams in the mid 1980s, through to my involvement with the British Olympic Association and now with my role at Ipswich Town Football Club, that perhaps is not surprising.

But I have always looked at education from a holistic approach, where one needs to balance not only the academic aspects but also the sporting aspects, social aspects, and the pastoral aspects. When all those areas come together, a child is sure to have an excellent education. It is impossible to look at any one area in isolation, and of course different parents will have different priorities to myself, but from my point of view sport is an integral part of the holistic approach, and independent schools in this country should be applauded for the importance they place on the benefits associated with kids getting active.

2010 and beyond

Edward Elliott, Head at The Perse School, Cambridge, predicts the next decade in independent education.

It is a sign of our recessionary times, when anxious parents question the financial durability of independent schools. A handful of small prep school closures, and some scaremongering by the popular press, can quickly create the impression of a sector in economic trouble. Add to this concerns that the Charity Commission will act against independent schools who do not demonstrate sufficient public benefit, together with fears of excessive government regulations stifling the very independence of independent schools, and it is possible to conclude that the sector is heading for difficult times.

I take a longer view. My school was founded in 1615, and in the Perse's first one hundred years, it survived and even thrived against a backdrop of Bubonic Plague, Civil War, and financial depression. In 1941 the school was subject to a direct hit by the Luftwaffe (which did disrupt teaching for four days) so whatever the future brings I am confident that we will emerge as successful as ever.

The next decade will be a challenging one for independent schools. The current recession will affect pupil numbers, particularly when interest rates and taxation start to rise and disposable incomes fall. Parents of children already in independent schools make huge sacrifices to keep their children here (witness the increasingly elderly collection of parental Volvos in the school car park), but those considering independent education for the first time can be put off altogether or delay purchasing it until their children reach secondary age. Although economically understandable, such a move can be educationally disadvantageous. An excellent prep school is exactly that – a wonderful preparation for secondary and higher education. Good foundations are vital for future educational success and attainment gaps can open up very quickly between children in different school environments.

In such an economic climate, independent schools will have to work harder to persuade parents to part with their money. Schools will redouble their efforts and demonstrate the academic and extracurricular advantages of an independent education, but will need to do so in ways that don't involve huge capital expenditure. The days of 'facilities races' between independent schools are over, and instead of building multi-million pound swimming pools, independent schools will demonstrate their competitive advantage through less glamorous but arguably pound-for-pound more educationally effective measures, such as specialist university entrance preparation classes, vibrant programmes of extracurricular activity, and an explosion in online virtual support for learning. Over the next decade, all independent schools will develop impressive web based virtual learning environments (VLES) where pupils and their parents can access learning resources, homework details, the latest assessment scores, and online learning communities 24/7. Pupils who have mastered all their school based assignments will be able to pit their wits against students from elsewhere in the world through e-competitions such as 'Mathletics'.

Recession may also help independent schools. Heads are currently enjoying a bumper recruitment year, as highly talented graduates move into teaching as other career areas, most notably the City, are closed off. Even in shortage subjects such as the sciences, economics, and maths, independent schools are quietly recruiting some of the best new talent to enter the profession in decades.

Whatever the aspirations and rhetoric of political leaders, the poor state of public finances will mean that budgets will be under pressure in the maintained sector. It is difficult to see how the state will close the funding gap with the independent sector and pupils in the independent schools will continue to benefit from the lower-than average class sizes, better resourced campuses, and more highly qualified staff.

Budget cuts will also have a negative impact on higher education, and universities will reduce the number of undergraduate places available to cut costs. A combination of continuing A level grade inflation, (no self-respecting educational minister will want to preside over the first fall in A level grades in 20 years), and fewer undergraduate places will make it even more difficult to get into the top British universities. Independent schools will react by spending even more time and resources, assiduously preparing their pupils for university admissions tests and interviews, and gathering intelligence on how university selection processes really work. This skilful student preparation will more than offset any social engineering which the government may require admissions tutors to carry out, and when coupled with the higher examinations grades achieved in the independent sector will ensure that the majority of independently educated pupils get into their first choice university. This said, an increasing number of independent pupils may look at the British university sector and decide to apply to North American institutions instead (where costs can be similar and arguably the education better). Independent school students are by definition sophisticated consumers of education, and they will want to select the best undergraduate courses on offer wherever that may be. The globalisation of higher education for undergraduates is here to stay.

Independent schools will continue to use their independence from government control to innovate in the best interests of their pupils. The steady expansion in wellbeing classes will continue as schools teach pupils about stress management, the need for relaxation, and the importance of positive thinking to cope with the demands of twenty first century living. Forward thinking Heads will introduce additional modern foreign languages such as Arabic, Mandarin and Portuguese, to prepare pupils for a world where the Middle East, China and Brazil are economically and culturally more important. The same Heads will also seek out rigorous qualifications in maths and the separate sciences to ensure that independent school pupils have the mathematical and scientific skills needed to cope with an ever more technological world.

Although independent schools will change in the next ten years, much will stay the same. In particular the emphasis that the independent sector places on all-round education and giving children life skills such as self confidence, creativity, team work, and leadership through music, sport, art and drama, will remain. The sector has never taken the narrow view that education = exam results, and as a consequence its pupils have benefitted from a wonderfully diverse educational diet with GCSE lessons being interspersed with debating competitions, music performances, local sporting derbies, overseas trips, and even that most under-rated of school occasions, the assembly. The latter remains important, as independent schools have a duty to shape the morality and ethics of the next generation.

With their long histories, independent schools are past masters of adapting to change and keeping ahead of the game. Free from the bureaucracy of state control, they can respond to parental demands and the changing nature of higher education and the work place. It is that very independence which will ensure the future success of independent schools.

Edward Elliott is Head of The Perse School, Cambridge

London boarding – a solution to many family problems

David Boddy, Head of St James Independent School for Boys in Twickenham, says weekday boarding is helping to relieve the stresses of modern family life.

Sitting in front of me, Christopher's mother was distraught. Her employers were demanding early morning meetings to add to the burden of several late night meetings. Being a single mum, the one who suffered most was Christopher. What was the solution?

The London-based weekly-boarding option at St James Senior Boys School is an increasingly popular way for very hard-pressed parents to find a practical solution to the problems of contemporary working life. It is too easy to moralise and say it should not happen. The reality, however, is that high earning parents always have demanding work lives. Having a son living in a family boarding environment during the week relieves acres of anxiety for the parents and provides much needed stability for the boy.

For nearly two decades now the school has operated a small boarding facility of up to 20 pupils, around 7.5% of the school roll. There has been a good balance between Lower School pupils, aged 11-12 and Upper School pupils, aged 13-18. The boarding house is overseen by a schoolmaster and his wife, who are both enthusiastic about the virtues of the boarding house. They create a warm and disciplined atmosphere. Boys always need to know what is expected of them and they need to be confident that they will be praised when they do their duties and treated with dignity and maturity at all times. Boys are given daily duties to make sure the boarding house is kept tidy and clean and the older ones have special responsibilities ensuring

the care of the younger pupils. Every boy is treated like a brother and the ethos established is that service to all is the expected norm. No selfish activity is allowed but boys within their small dormitories or individual rooms are encouraged to express their own creativity and individuality.

Of real benefit to all pupils is the fixed time for homework and additional study. Our particular ethos embodies daily periods of Quiet Time and meditation. The golden rule here is that no boy should disturb the peace of another pupil during the ten minutes of Quiet Time. It also provides a time where more substantial pastoral issues can be dealt with by the boarding master and mistress. Conversations about human respect and what it means to live well naturally unfold after these quiet times and often carry on at the dinner table after meditation. In many ways these issues sound like old-fashioned family virtues, but during a recent Ofsted inspection they were the very things that many of the boarders commented upon as being reasons why they so loved being there. Sadly, perhaps, some also commented on the fact that it would be lovely to do the same thing at home, but because mum and/or dad are too busy, it doesn't seem able to happen. They are deeply grateful they can experience it during their lives as boarders.

At the end of this academic year, St James Senior Boys will be moving to a new site in Ashford, Middlesex. Our medium term plans include doubling the amount of boarding provision on the new site. We know that our philosophically-inspired approach to education has wide appeal. But we also know that for London-based families, the stress of daily living and caring for adolescent boys is very great indeed. For these two reasons we plan to nearly double our boarding provision over the next few years. We aim to introduce flexi-boarding with some pupils on site for seven days per week, others for four nights per week and still others on a very short term basis, to help parents cope with business travel *etc*. It is important that the boarding house does not get to be seen as a transitory environment, and so those who come will have to agree to a 'social contract' of behaviour and contribution to boarding life in the form of regular service and duties.

I believe the future of boarding at our edge of London school is very bright. Apart from meeting the needs of anxious parents, whose lives are far too busy, the boarding option importantly meets the needs of the boys as they grow into young men who are inwardly confident, outwardly sociable and emotionally stable. The boarding option lets them become the real men they want to be and gives more confidence to their families than would otherwise be possible.

David Boddy is Headmaster of St James Independent School for Senior Boys
in Twickenham, Middlesex.

Your school run survival guide

Finding the right school for your children can be a something of a challenge but it's nothing next to the patience-of-a-saint-testing daily grind that is actually getting them there every morning. De-stress those term-time starts to the day with these tips from the school-run-hardy parents who post on Mumsnet.

Get 'em up, get 'em dressed, get 'em fed, and off you go to school. Oh, if only it were so. In (bitter, strength-sapping) truth, the school run is a daily struggle against the mighty forces of dawdling, prevarication and delay. And that's before you factor in the havoc-wreaking, vital-minutes-stealing potential of squabbling siblings, crying babies, doorbell-ringing boiler-repair men and inevitably disappearing PE kit.

So, to help save you sanity of a weekday morning, here's the pick of the school-run tips posted on Mumsnet by parents the nation over. As ever in parenting life, there's nothing to beat the hard-won advice of those who've been there and torn their hair out searching for book bags before you...

Get ready

Fail to prepare and you prepare to fail, as your own mother probably told you many a tedious time. But, when it comes to the school run, never has a nagger's pet phrase been so true. If you want to stand even the slightest chance of making it out of the house on time in the morning, you need to be Mrs Tick the Preparation Boxes the night before. That means laying out everyone's schoolclothes at bedtime (including your own!), and checking that games kits, swimming stuff, homework and textbooks are present and correct in the right bags and satchels. It also means checking well before midnight that tomorrow isn't dress-up-as-a-Victorian day or bake-a-cake Friday and that you've found, filled in and signed all the umpteen school-trip slips, homework diaries and consent forms that come home in school bags and can moulder there unseen for weeks. "You can save yourself serious amounts of angst on this front," adds Mumsnetter *spidermum*, "if you drill your children to put unpack, unload and put everything in its rightful place before they do anything else when they return from school."

For extra school-run prep points, make sure you've got a hairbrush in the car (for last-minute detangling) and a full set of raincoats for those days that start off fine but are tipping it down by the time you turn up at the school gate. "It's also worth keeping a stash of muesli bars, juice cartons, bananas in the glovebox," says *Mrs Badger*, "for the really ghastly mornings when, even if the kids have had breakfast, you haven't."

Most important of all, put your kids to bed early. "Those who stay up till all hours will be tired and grotty in the morning," says *fortyplus*. "And that's a surefire recipe for pre-school-run conflict." Though you might not want to go as far as one Mumsnetters *ledodgy* and *shimmy21*, who recommend, respectively, saving time the next day by 'putting them to bed in their uniform' and 'feeding them breakfast the evening before'.

Get set

Right, so school-run morning dawns. "Get yourself dressed before getting the kids up," advises *Mrs Badger*. "If you're telling them off for being in their pyjamas when you're still in yours, you're fighting a losing battle " Insist that everyone is fully uniformed up before eating breakfast (supply messy eaters with napkins or aprons to stave off milk-and-marmalade stain situations). Letting them get changed after breakfast means they'll disappear back into their bedrooms in a trance-like state and become absorbed in all manner of absolutely-not-dressing activities. To this end, *Perigine* recommends "keeping toothbrushes and flannels in the kitchen or downstairs loo to stop trips upstairs. I've found what goes up doesn't necessarily come down, at least not without a fight!"

To avoid post-breakfast momentum-droop, put the clocks forward ten minutes ("it'll mean the kids get a move on but you're not rushing about like a looney," says *whatkatydidntdo*) and resolutely ban morning TV ("small children cannot watch telly and do anything else at the same time. Not putting it on is much easier than turning it off after a screaming row," sighs a battle-for-the-remote-weary *exbury*). Meet all resistance to getting ready with disinterest and the words, "I don't care whether you put your shoes on/get in the car/whatever. But if we're late, I'll tell your teacher why." This works perfectly, reports *Issymum*, "providing a) you really don't care and will live out the threat and b) your child doesn't reply 'I don't care either', in which case you're stuffed."

Go

Once you've opened the front door, keep walking forwards. "Do NOT go back for ANYTHING they've forgotten and make sure they know that," says *CocoLoco*. But don't open the door without doing a quick check that all members of your family are actually clothed and booted and coated. Which includes you, of course. "Never go out in your pyjamas, however late you are," warns *Calijrau* with a shudder. "That'll be the morning you get a flat tyre (as heard on Mumsnet), have a minor collision (as heard on Mumsnet) or forget your house keys (as heard on Mumsnet)."

And if you walk out of the front door but find no one small is following? "Try singing," says *tigermoth*. "I make up random, cringingly rubbish songs on the spot, sing deliberately badly, and threaten to rank it up at top volume if they don't hurry up. Don't stop until they're in the car and ready to go."

Finding the fees

Chris Procter, joint managing director of SFIA, outlines the planned approach to funding school fees.

The census produced by the Independent Schools Council showed school fees inflation at 5.7% for 2008. Despite the fact that boarding fees averaged £7,353 per term and day fees £3,193 per term, pupil numbers are the highest ever. Even though the cost of educating a child at an independent school continues to outstrip inflation year on year, parents still believe that an independent education represents real value for money.

The overall cost (including university fees) might seem daunting: the cost of educating one child privately could well be very similar to that of buying a house but, as with house buying, the school fee commitment for the majority of parents can be made possible by spreading it over a long period rather than funding it all from current resources. It is vital that parents do their financial homework, plan ahead, start to save early and regularly. Grandparents who have access to capital could be beneficial; by contributing to school fees they could help to reduce any inheritance tax liability.

Parents would be well-advised to consult a specialist independent financial adviser (IFA) as early as possible, since a long-term plan for the payment of fees – possibly university as well as school – can prove very attractive from a financial point of view and thus offer greater peace of mind.

Funding fees is neither science nor magic, nor is there any panacea. It is quite simply a question of planning and using whatever resources are available, such as income, capital, or tax reduction opportunities.

Case study - The Nemo family

A case study of how the Nemo family managed, over the relatively short period of three years, to increase their level of savings and investments, clarify and improve their pension benefits, remain on track to repay their mortgage early and achieve their original goal, of planning ahead for their son's school fees.

Mr and Mrs Nemo wanted to plan for, and manage, the costs of school fees. SFIA recommended that they do this via equity release for the first four years and thereafter via an ISA investment. This they did and all was fine until Mrs Nemo was made redundant the following year.

She decided to become a self-employed consultant and, as her income was now less certain, this change in the family's circumstances raised question marks over the level of funding of the ISA. To complicate matters further, Mr Nemo's employment as a pilot was put in jeopardy later that year, due to the sudden decline in bookings.

At that time, a falling stock market meant that using investments was not an attractive solution and so, given their situation, this led to Mr and Mrs Nemo deciding to suspend their monthly investments and concentrate instead on the mortgage repayments.

Over the following months SFIA had several meetings with the clients to ensure that the family's finances remained on track and that the school fees would not present an issue.

Happily, Mrs Nemo's self-employment proved more successful than originally anticipated and Mr Nemo's employment no longer looked to be in threat. This being the case, their investments were continually monitored with re-allocations being carried out to protect the capital from further falls; this led to there being no loss to the original capital invested.

A new mortgage was arranged to provide for the provision of the school fees on a firmer basis. It was decided to cap the cost of school fees at £550 per month, even though their actual cost would be, on average, £912 per month once their son began at senior school.

Additionally, since Mr Nemo intended to retire whilst his son was still in private education, the new mortgage was set up so that it would be fully repaid in time for his retirement.

SFIA's planning not only managed to cap the cost of the school fees and arrange for the mortgage to be repaid early, the net expenditure to Mr and Mrs Nemo increased by only £50 per month. With good advice and careful financial management the Nemo family improved their overall financial position and they increased their level of monthly savings, even though, for a time, their income fell. A review of the client's pension provision also resulted in an improvement of benefits, without any additional contributions.

The fundamental point to recognise is that you, your circumstances and your wishes or ambitions for your children or grandchildren are unique. They might well be similar to those of other people but they will still be uniquely different. There will, therefore, be no single solution to your problem. Indeed, after a review of all your circumstances, there might not be a problem at all.

So, what are the reasons for seeking advice about educational expenses?

- To reduce the overall cost?
- To get some tax benefit?
- To reduce your cash outflow?
- To invest capital to ensure that future fees are paid?
- To set aside money now for future fees?
- To provide protection for school fees?
- Or just to make sure that as well as educating your children you can still have a life!

Any, some or all of the above – or others not listed – could be on your agenda. The important thing is to develop a strategy.

At this stage, it really does not help to get hung up on which financial product is the most suitable. The composition of a school fee plan will differ for each individual depending on a number of factors. That is why there is no one school fee plan on offer.

The simplest strategy, and in most cases the most expensive option its to write out a cheque for the whole bill when it arrives and post it back. Like most simple plans that works very well, if you have the money. Even if you do have the money, is that really the best way of doing things? Do you know that to fund £1000 of school fees as a higher rate taxpayer paying 40% income tax, you currently need to earn £1667, this rises to £2,000 under the new higher rate of 50%?

How then do you start to develop your strategy? As with most things in life, if you can define your objective, then you will know what you are aiming at. Your objective in this case will be (a) to determine how much money is needed and (b) when it will be required. You need to draw up a school fees schedule or what others would term a cash flow forecast.

So:

- How many children?
- Which schools? (or use an average school fee)
- When?
- Any special needs?
- Inflation guesstimate?
- Include university costs?

With this basic information, the school fees schedule/cash flow forecast can be calculated and you will have defined what it is you are trying to achieve.

Remember though that senior school fees are typically more than prep school fees – this needs to be factored in. Also be aware that the cost of university is not restricted to the fees alone; there are a lot of maintenance and other costs involved: accommodation, books, food, to name a few.

You now have one side of an equation, the relatively simple side. The other side is you and your resources. This also needs to be defined, but this is a much more difficult exercise. The reason that it is more difficult, of course, is that school fees are not the only drain on your resources. You probably have a mortgage, you want to have holidays, you need to buy food and clothes, you may be concerned that you should be funding a pension.

This is the key area of expertise, since your financial commitments are unique. A specialist in the area of school fees planning knows how to get at these commitments, to record them and help you to distribute your resources according to priority.

The options open to you as parents depend completely upon your adviser's knowledge of these complex personal financial issues. (Did I forget to mention your tax position, capital gains tax allowance, other tax allowances including those of your children and a lower or zero rate tax paying spouse or partner? These could well be used to your advantage.)

A typical school fees plan can incorporate many elements to fund short-, medium- and long-term fees. Each plan is designed according to individual circumstances and usually there is a special emphasis on what parents are looking to achieve, for example, to maximise overall savings and to minimise the outflow of cash. Additionally it is possible to protect the payment of the fees in the event of unforeseen circumstances that could lead to a significant or total loss of earnings.

Short-term fees

Short-term fees are typically the termly amounts needed within five years: these are usually funded from such things as guaranteed investments, liquid capital, loan plans (if no savings are available) or maturing insurance policies, investments etc. Alternatively they can be funded from disposable income.

Medium-term fees

Once the short-term plan expires, the medium-term funding is invoked to fund the education costs for a further five to ten years. Monthly amounts can be invested in a low-risk, regular premium investment ranging from a building society account to a friendly society savings plan to equity ISAs. It is important to understand the pattern of the future fees and to be aware of the timing of withdrawals.

Long-term fees

Longer term funding can incorporate a higher element of risk (as long as this is acceptable to the investor) which will offer higher potential returns. Investing in UK and overseas equities could be considered. Products may be the same as those for medium-term fees, but will have the flexibility to utilise investments which may have an increased 'equity based' content.

Finally, it is important to remember that most investments or financial products either mature with a single payment or provide for regular withdrawals; rarely do they provide timed termly payments. Additionally, the overall risk profile of the portfolio should lean towards the side of caution (for obvious reasons).

There are any number of IFAs in the country but few who specialise in the area of planning to meet school and university fees.

SFIA are the largest Independent Financial Adviser who specialise in school fees planning in the UK.

This article has been contributed by SFIA and edited by Chris Procter, Joint Managing Director. He can be contacted at:

SFIA Ltd,
41 London Road,
Twyford,
Berkshire RG10 9EJ
Tel: 0845 458 3690
Fax: 0118 934 4609
Email: enquiries@sfia.co.uk
Web: www.sfia.co.uk

A well-rounded education

Liam Butler, of the Independent Schools Council, tells us why independent education should be considered a necessity, rather than a luxury.

As the credit crunch bites it seems that many parents are cutting down on 'luxuries'. This should mean a sharp downturn in pupils entering the independent sector and an increase in people moving into the state sector shouldn't it? Perhaps not, as more and more parents consider their child's independent education to be a necessity rather than a luxury.

Over 500,000 children benefit from an independent education in one of ISC's 1276 member schools. Independent schools offer a wealth of facilities and high teaching standards that enable students to achieve great results year after year. Independent schools are in the unique position to provide a truly bespoke education for your child.

Results

One of the reasons parents continue to choose an independent education for their child is thanks to high teaching standards and this is clearly reflected in the grades that independent schools post year after year. In 2008 over half of A level entries from pupils at ISC schools were awarded a grade A. Also, pupil/teacher ratios continue to fall in ISC schools, reflecting many schools' commitment to teaching a wide range of subjects even if class sizes are small. There is now one teacher to every ten pupils allowing children to receive a uniquely supported and bespoke education. Independent schools are excellent at providing breadth of education as well as flexibility.

More than one in three pupils at ISC schools receives assistance with fee costs, with four out of five of these awards coming directly from the school itself.

There are now over 40 ISC schools that offer the International Baccalaureate, allowing parents to pick the style of education that best suits their child. Thanks to the flexibility of not being tied to the National Curriculum or Local Authorities, ISC schools are also some of the first to adopt the new Pre-U exam which is a 16+ course designed to prepare students for university. Independent schools offer an array of choices for parents when it comes to curricula and qualifications and it's up to parents to do the research and pick the one that will best suit their child. The one-size-fits-all approach to education is long gone in the independent sector and it's now up to the parent to choose the right school for their child.

Facilities and Extracurricular

In 2007/08 ISC schools spent nearly £300million on new buildings demonstrating their commitment to constant improvement of facilities for pupils. Total spending on facilities and equipment stood at nearly £700million, roughly equating to £1400 per pupil. However, it's not just academic facilities such as ICT centres, science laboratories and state-of-the-art classrooms that schools are committed to improving. With great sporting facilities too, schools can offer everything from athletics, rugby and football to squash, tennis and lacrosse. Independent schools are committed to providing children with a rounded education filled with both sporting and academic successes. Indeed many ISC schools have produced some of the best sportsmen and women in recent memory. The 2008 Beijing Olympics was dominated by independent school educated stars such as Chris Hoy and Ben Ainslie. The England rugby team also boasts a hoard of independent school alumni, Jonny Wilkinson, Matthew Tait and Lewis Moody to name but a few.

A recent survey by Ipsos MORI found independent education to be more popular than ever. Nearly three in five of all parents would send their child to independent school if they could…

Many children also take advantage of various Cadet Force initiatives, such as Combined Cadet Force, which teach leadership and teamwork. Many schools even offer a BTEC in leadership as a result of pupils' participation in CCF. The school day doesn't have to begin at nine and end at five and many parents choose a weekly or flexible boarding option, allowing their children to take full advantage of the after school activities that are on offer. Students are not confined to the school premises either, as schools are very keen to organise trips abroad for history, geography and modern foreign language purposes. Pick up any school's newsletter and you'll find details of groups of students trekking off to some far flung destination.

IPSOS Mori

A recent survey by Ipsos MORI found independent education to be more popular than ever. Nearly three in five of all parents would send their child to independent school if they could afford it. This is the highest level since the survey began in 1997, up 20% on the last survey in 2004. While 'better standards of education' continues to be the prime factor for parents wanting to send their children to independent schools, 'better discipline' more than doubled in popularity rising to second place above 'smaller class sizes'.

Is there help with fees?

More than one in three pupils at ISC schools receives assistance with fee costs, with four out of five of these awards coming directly from the school itself. Indeed, most ISC schools offer bursaries, scholarships or both.

Scholarships tend to be linked to the ability of the child whether it is academic, sporting, music or drama. The best way to ascertain availability and eligibility is to contact the school directly. They are more than happy to discuss with you the options available.

Bursaries, on the other hand, tend to be means-assessed on a financial basis and will require the parent or guardian to fill out a financial declaration to establish whether the student meets the necessary criteria.

So why choose an independent school?

Education isn't a one-size-fits-all affair and thankfully independent schools come in all shapes and sizes. The independent sector gives parents the opportunity to choose a school that is right for their child. Whether it is the breadth and flexibility of the curriculum that appeals or perhaps the extracurricular activities, you can be assured that your child will receive a well-rounded education helping them to achieve their full potential.

Further information about the Independent Schools Council can be found on their website: www.isc.co.uk

Independent Schools Council
St Vincent House
30 Orange Street
London WC2H 7HH

Telephone: 020 7766 7070
Fax: 020 7766 7071

See also page xlii

The questions you should ask

However much a school may appeal at first sight, you still need sound information to form your judgement.

Schools attract pupils by their reputations, so most go to considerable lengths to ensure that parents are presented with an attractive image. Modern marketing techniques try to promote good points and play down (without totally obscuring) bad ones. But every Head knows that, however good the school prospectus is, it only serves to attract parents through the school gates. Thereafter the decision depends on what they see and hear.

Research we have carried out over the years suggests that in many cases the most important factor in choosing a school is the impression given by the Head. As well as finding out what goes on in a school, parents need to be reassured by the aura of confidence that they expect from a Head. How they judge the latter may help them form their opinion of the former. In other words, how a Head answers questions is important in itself and, to get you started, we have drawn up a list of points on which you may need to be satisfied. Some can be posed as questions and some are points you'll only want to check in your mind. They are not listed in any particular order and their significance will vary from family to family, but they should be useful in helping you to form an opinion.

If you never get to see the Head, but deal with an admissions person of some sort, it may not mean you should rule the school out, but it certainly tells you something about the school's view of pupil recruitment.

Before visiting and asking questions, **check the facts** - such as which association the school belongs to, how big it is, how many staff *etc*. Is there any form of financial pie chart showing how the school's resources are used? The answers to questions like this should be in the promotional material you've been sent. If they aren't, you've really got a good question to ask!

Check the website. Is it up-to-date? Almost certainly not 100% because that's just about impossible, but it shouldn't be obsolete. A useful win/win for the parent probably!

When you get to the school you will want to judge the overall atmosphere and decide whether it will suit you and your child. Are any other members of the family going to help to pay the fees? If so, their views are important and the school's attitude towards them may be instructive.

When you make it to the inner sanctum, **what do you make of the Head as a person?** Age? Family? Staying? Moving on? Retiring? Busted flush? Accessible to children, parents and staff? If you never get to see the Head, but deal with an admissions person of some sort, it may not mean you should rule the school out, but it certainly tells you something about the school's view of pupil recruitment.

Academic priorities - attitude towards league tables? This is a forked question. If the answer is 'We're most concerned with doing the best for the child', you pitch them a late-developer; if the answer is, 'Well, frankly, we have a very high entry threshold', then you say 'So we have to give you a foolproof academic winner, do we?'

Supplementary questions:

- What is the ratio of teachers to pupils?
- What are the professional qualifications of the teaching staff?
- How many AS levels are offered and required?
- What mix - *ie* three arts and a balancing science - and, of course, *vice versa*?
- Or does the school aim for a creative fourth/fifth option such as IT/DT/music/drama?

What is the school's retention rate? In prep schools this means how many pupils do they lose at eleven when the school goes on to thirteen. In senior schools this is really about the sixth form intake/exit rate. Is there a 'flight to the country' or to sixth form colleges? Larger lower classes and smaller upper classes may reflect a school's inability to hang on to pupils.

Supplementary questions:

- What are the school's exam results?
- What are the criteria for presenting them?
- Were they consistent over the years?
- Is progress accelerated for the academically bright?
- How does the school cope with pupils who do not work?
- Where do pupils go when they leave?

How important and well resourced are **sports, extracurricular and after school activities, music and drama?** How long is the school day - and week?

Supplementary questions:

- What is the attitude to physical fitness and games?
- What sports are offered and what are the facilities?
- What are the extracurricular activities?
- What cultural or other visits are arranged away from the school?
- What steps are taken to encourage specific talent in music, the arts or sport?

Other topics to cover:

- What is the school's mission?
- What is its attitude to religion?
- How well is the school integrated into the local community?
- How have they responded to the recent Charities Act initiatives?
- What are the responsibilities and obligations at weekends for parents, pupils and the school?
- Does the school keep a watching brief or reserve the option to get involved after a weekend incident?

EDITORIAL - The questions you should ask

- What is the school's attitude to discipline?
- Have there been problems with drugs, drink or sex?
- How have they been dealt with?
- What is the school's bullying policy?
- How does the school cope with pupils' problems?
- What sort of academic and pastoral advice is available?
- What positive steps are taken to encourage good manners, behaviour and sportsmanship?
- What is the uniform?
- What steps are taken to ensure that pupils take pride in their personal appearance?
- How often does the school communicate with parents through reports, parent/teacher meetings or other visits?
- What level of parental involvement is encouraged both in terms of keeping in touch with staff about your own child and more generally, *eg* a Parents' Association?
- Is it possible to have the names and addresses of parents with children at the school to approach them for an opinion?

And finally - and perhaps most importantly - what does your child make of the school, the adults met, the other kids met, pupils at the school in other contexts and the website?

The British Accreditation Council for independent further and higher education

Beyond school, beyond university, beyond the World of Education As We Know It, there is a world that many people never see: a world of horse-riding and jewellery, of film and music, of dance and art; and many more things besides. This is the world of independent further and higher education, or FE and HE to the initiated. Join us now, as we lift the veil…

There are tutorial colleges, there are specialist colleges offering A levels which are not widely available. There are vocational institutions, and those offering university foundation years. There are institutions for the study of everything that the human mind could devise - or so, sometimes, it seems.

In June 2009 the British Accreditation Council (BAC) will celebrate its 25th anniversary as the principal non-EFL (English as a Foreign Language) regulatory body for the independent further and higher education sector. BAC-accredited colleges in the UK now number more than 330 and offer courses in everything from website design to yoga to equine dentistry, alongside more standard qualifications in subjects such as business and law.

One colourful and internationally-renowned example is the unique and very successful Istituto Marangoni in London, which is a branch of the long-established fashion design school in Milan. Istituto Marangoni offers courses ranging from one year to three years in fashion business, fashion design, fashion styling, graphic design, and interior design along with a Master programme in brand management. By offering a range of courses covering both artistic and business aspects of the fashion industry the school is helping more students to access a very competitive industry. The school itself is ideally placed in the centre of London, allowing students ample opportunity to source garments and accessories for projects (a requirement of the fashion styling course). Contrary to the common view of design or art schools much work at Istituto Marangoni is carried out on computers and during a recent BAC inspection the lack of 'messy' activities such as painting was commented on; clearly the school is preparing students for the future world of work.

Chiltern College in Reading is also accredited by BAC, and specialises in childcare training; courses offered at the college include the Cache Level 3 Diploma in childcare and education, the Cache NVQ Level 3 in children's care, learning and development and the Stage II Certificate in Montessori theory and methodology. The vast majority of students at Chiltern are UK students, some of whom are under 18. Those students carrying out full-time study have accommodation and food provided by the college and are able to train at the on-campus nursery and primary school. As well as providing a convenient and comfortable working environment the college also maintains a high staff-to-student ratio and helps students to settle in with their own 'freshers week'. Towards the end of training, individual careers support is provided.

It's clear from examples such as these that high-quality study, both of a practical and academic nature, is no longer confined to the familiar world of schools and universities. Both of the colleges mentioned above provide a tailored and comfortable environment for study without compromising on standards; whilst the environment may be different from that of a school, it is no more lenient, with both colleges monitoring attendance rigorously and achieving good exam results. For anyone who is having doubts about taking on Post-16 education, it is worth considering the wealth and diversity of courses and institutions that are available, and the benefits that you may be missing out on.

BAC-accredited colleges in the UK now number more than 330 and offer courses in everything from website design to yoga to equine dentistry, alongside more standard qualifications in subjects such as business and law.

All institutions applying for BAC accreditation undergo a rigorous three-stage process of inspections and background checks which scrutinise their premises, the management and staffing of their organisation, their commitment to student welfare, the quality of the actual teaching and academic resources on offer, and how well they manage and monitor the quality of their own provision. Each college will repeat this process every four years and submits to additional annual monitoring by BAC to check that standards are being maintained. This comprehensive approach to accreditation helps BAC to remain the best and most respected mark of quality in the private FE and HE sectors.

A directory of BAC-accredited colleges can be found on our website and if you would like to find out more about our work please contact us.

The British Accreditation Council
44 Bedford Row
Bloomsbury,
London WC1R 4LL

Telephone: 020 7447 2584.

Email: info@the-bac.org
Website: www.the-bac.org

British Accreditation Council
for independent further and higher education

Choosing a school initially

Educational institutions often belong to organisations which guarantee their standards. Here we give a brief alphabetical guide to what all the initials mean.

BSA

The Boarding Schools' Association

Since its foundation in 1966, the Boarding Schools' Association (BSA) has had the twin objectives of the promotion of boarding education and the development of quality boarding through high standards of pastoral care and boarding accommodation. Parents and prospective pupils choosing a boarding school can, therefore, be assured that the 500 schools in membership of the BSA are committed to providing the best possible boarding environment for their pupils.

A school can only join the BSA if it is in membership of one of the ISC (Independent Schools Council) constituent associations or in membership of SBSA (State Boarding Schools' Association). These two bodies require member schools to be regularly inspected by the Independent Schools' Inspectorate (ISI) or Ofsted. Since April 2007, all boarding schools, whether independent or state schools, have been inspected for their boarding provision by Ofsted, using the National Minimum Standards for Boarding Schools and reporting under the heading of Every Child Matters. Reports are published on the Ofsted website.

Relationship with government

The BSA is in regular communication with the Department for Children, Schools, and Families (DCSF) on all boarding matters. The Children Act (1989) and the Care Standards Act (2001) require boarding schools to conform to national legislation and the promotion of this legislation and the training required to carry it out are matters on which the DCSF and the BSA work closely. The key area is in training.

Boarding training

The programme of training for boarding staff whose schools are in membership of the BSA is supported and sponsored by the DCSF. The Utting Report on the Safeguards for Children Living Away from Home highlighted the importance of the development of 'policy, practice and training for services for children who live away from home'. It focuses on the right of parents to expect that staff looking after children are competent to do so, and points out the responsibility of central government to secure consistent national standards in promoting the welfare of children away from home. The Singleton Review (March 2009) reiterated the importance of rigorous safeguarding of such children.

In addition the BSA organises 50 conferences and seminars a year for governors, heads, deputies, housemasters and housemistresses, and matrons and medical staff where further training takes place in formal sessions and in sharing good practice. The BSA works with the DCSF in providing the following range of training and information:

- Professional qualifications for both teaching and non-teaching staff in boarding schools. The BSA has been responsible for the development of courses leading to university validated Certificates of Professional Practice in Boarding Education. These certificates, the result of at least two years' study, are awarded by the University of Roehampton.

- A rolling programme of day seminars on current boarding legislation and good practice.

How can the BSA further help parents when they are choosing a boarding school?

Advice

Parents are invited to contact the BSA for information on:

- choosing a boarding school

- why boarding might at some stage benefit your child

- details on the 500 member schools of the BSA

Parents are also invited to contact the BSA for useful publications:

- Choosing a Boarding School – what parents and their children should look for and ask about when choosing a boarding school;

- Parenting the Boarder by Libby Purves; and

- Being a Boarder by Rose Heiney.

SBSA

The BSA issues information on the 35 state boarding schools in England and Wales and the BSA should be contacted for details of these schools. In these schools parents pay for boarding but not for education, so fees are substantially lower than in an independent boarding school.

In conclusion

Today's quality boarding schools provide each of their pupils with a safe and challenging environment, where communication with home is easy and where the boarding facilities and the pastoral care are of the highest order. The Boarding Schools' Association and its members are committed to this vision for boarding.

National Director: Hilary Moriarty BA(Hons), MA, PGCE
Director of Training: Alex Thomson OBE, BSc(Hons), PGCE, DipEd, FCIPD

Boarding Schools' Association
Grosvenor Gardens House
35-37, Grosvenor Gardens
London SW1W 0BS

Tel: 020 7798 1580
Fax: 020 7798 1581
Email: bsa@boarding.org.uk
Website: www.boarding.org.uk

GSA

The Girls' Schools Association, to which Heads of leading girls-only schools belong.

The Girls' Schools Association (GSA) is the professional association of the Heads of 200 leading independent schools for girls in the UK, educating some 110,000 girls. Schools in the Association offer a choice of day, boarding, weekly, and flexi-boarding education, and range in type from large urban schools of 1000 pupils to small rural schools of around 200. Many schools have junior and pre-prep departments, and can offer a complete education from four to 18. A significant proportion of schools also have religious affiliations. All the schools in the Girls' Day School Trust (GDST) are in membership of GSA.

GSA schools are widely recognised for their exceptional record of examination achievements. Education is, however, not only about success in exams. Girls' schools offer wider development opportunities, and are special for a number of reasons. They provide an environment in which girls can learn to grow in confidence and ability. In a girls' school, the needs and aspirations of girls are the main focus and the staff are experts in the teaching of girls. Girls hold all the senior positions in the school, and are encouraged by positive role models in the schools' teaching staff and management. Expectations are high. In GSA schools, girls do not just have equal opportunities, they have *every* opportunity. Members of GSA share a commitment to the values and benefits of single-sex schools for girls, and a belief that all girls, regardless of educational setting, deserve the opportunity to realise their potential, to be active and equal, confident and competent leaders, participants and contributors.

The Girls' Schools Association plays a vital role in advising and lobbying educational policy makers on issues relating to girls' schools and the education of girls. As the specialist organisation for the education of girls, the Association is regularly consulted by the Department for Children, Schools and Families, the Office for Standards in Education, the Qualifications and Curriculum Authority and other bodies. However, GSA is not only a 'single-issue' organisation, and is a powerful and well respected voice within the educational establishment. GSA is one of the constituent bodies of the Independent Schools' Council. The Independent Schools Council (ISC) operates, on behalf of GSA, a strict accreditation scheme for schools wishing to join the Association. Once in membership, schools are required to undergo a regular cycle of inspections to ensure that these rigorous standards are being maintained. Schools must also belong to the Association of Governing Bodies of Independent Schools, and Heads must be in membership of the Association of School and College Leaders (ASCL).

A programme of professional development for members ensures that the Heads of all GSA schools are highly trained, and are fully up-to-date with all aspects of their profession. Courses are also regularly held for staff and opportunities are available for subject teachers to meet together on curriculum issues.

The Association's secretariat is accommodated in Leicester in premises shared with the ASCL. 130 Regent Road, Leicester LE1 7PG; Tel: 0116 254 1619; Email: office@gsa.uk.com; Website: www.gsa.uk.com

President: Gillian Low, The Lady Eleanor Holles School
Executive Director: Ms Sheila Cooper

HMC

The Headmasters' and Headmistresses' Conference, to which the Heads of leading independent schools belong.

Founded in 1869 the HMC exists to enable members to discuss matters of common interest and to influence important developments in education. It looks after the professional interests of members, central to which is their wish to provide the best possible educational opportunities for their pupils.

The Heads of some 250 leading independent schools are members of The Headmasters' and Headmistresses' Conference, whose membership now includes Heads of boys', girls' and coeducational schools. There are up to 30 additional members who are Heads of maintained schools. International membership includes the Heads of around 60 schools throughout the world.

The great variety of these schools is one of the strengths of HMC but all must exhibit high quality in the education provided. While day schools are the largest group, about a third of HMC schools consist mainly of boarders and others have a smaller boarding element including weekly boarders.

All schools are noted for their academic excellence and achieve good results, including those with pupils from a broad ability band. Members believe that good education consists of more than academic results and schools provide a wide range of educational activities.

Only those schools which meet with the rigorous membership criteria are admitted and this helps ensure that HMC is synonymous with high quality in education. There is a set of Membership Requirements and a Code of Practice to which members must subscribe. Those who want the intimate atmosphere of a small school will find some with around 350 pupils. Others who want a wide range of facilities and specialisations will find these offered in large day or boarding schools. Some have over 1000 pupils. About 50 schools are for boys only, others are coeducational throughout or only in the sixth form. The first girls-only schools joined HMC in 2006.

Within HMC there are schools with continuous histories as long as any in the world and many others trace their origins to Tudor times, but HMC continues to admit to membership recently-founded schools which have achieved great success. The facilities in all HMC schools will be good but some have magnificent buildings and grounds which are the result of the generosity of benefactors over many years. Some have attractive rural settings, others are sited in the centres of cities.

Pupils come from all sorts of backgrounds. Bursaries and scholarships provided by the schools give about a third of the 190,000 pupils in HMC schools help with their fees. These average about £22,000 per annum for boarding schools and £9000 for day schools. About 152,000 are day pupils and 38,000 boarders.

Entry into some schools is highly selective but others are well suited to a wide ability range. Senior boarding schools usually admit pupils after the Common Entrance examination taken when they are 13.

Most day schools select their pupils by 11+ examination. Many HMC schools have junior schools, some with nursery and pre-prep departments. The growing number of boarders from overseas is evidence of the high reputation of the schools worldwide.

The independent sector has always been fortunate in attracting very good teachers. Higher salary scales, excellent conditions of employment, exciting educational opportunities and good pupil/teacher ratios bring rewards commensurate with the demanding expectations. Schools expect teachers to have a good education culminating in a good honours degree and a professional qualification, though some do not insist on the latter especially if relevant experience is offered. Willingness to participate in the whole life of the school is essential.

Parents expect the school to provide not only good teaching which helps their children achieve the best possible examination results but also the dedicated pastoral care and valuable educational experiences outside the classroom in music, drama, games, outdoor pursuits and community service. Over 90% of pupils go on to Higher Education, many of them winning places on the most highly-subscribed university courses.

All members attend the Annual Meeting, usually held in a large conference centre in September/October. There are ten divisions covering England, Wales, Scotland and Ireland where members meet once a term on a regional basis.

The chairman and committee, with the advice of the secretary and membership secretary, make decisions on matters referred by sub-committees (such as education and academic policy, professional development, universities, junior schools, membership and sports), steering groups (such as inspection and finance) and working parties set up to deal with ad hoc issues. Close links are maintained with other professional associations in membership of the Independent Schools Council and with the Association of School and College Leaders, which represents Heads of both maintained and independent schools.

Membership Secretary: Ian G Power.   Tel: 01858 465260
The Secretary: Geoff H Lucas.   Tel: 01858 469059

12 The Point, Rockingham Road
Market Harborough, Leicestershire LE16 7QU
Email: hmc@hmc.org.uk
Website: www.hmc.org.uk

IAPS

The Independent Association of Preparatory Schools maintains the standards of Independent Preparatory and Junior schools.

The Independent Association of Preparatory Schools is the main professional association for headmasters and headmistresses of independent preparatory and junior schools throughout the British Isles and overseas.

There are more than 560 UK schools represented, in cities, towns and the countryside. They offer more than 130,000 boys and girls a choice of day, boarding, weekly and flexible boarding education, in both single sex and coeducational schools.

Some are free standing prep schools, while others are junior schools linked to senior boys' and girls' schools. There are also choir schools, schools offering special educational provision or facilities, and schools with particular religious affiliations.

Parents are assured of high professional standards in IAPS schools, maintained by regular inspection and a comprehensive and up-to-date programme of professional development.

Pupils, who may start as young as four, are offered a rich and varied school life in which high academic standards and traditionally strong pastoral care have a firm moral and spiritual base. Cultural and sporting opportunities, from music, art and drama to more than 30 recreational games, are keenly fostered by IAPS.

In addition IAPS organises holiday and term-time sporting competitions, games coaching courses, skiing activities at home and abroad, and a chess congress.

The targets of the National Curriculum are regarded as a basic foundation, which is greatly extended by the wider programmes of study offered in IAPS prep schools. Teaching groups are small and specialist subject teaching begins at an early age.

IAPS has well-established links with senior independent schools, and great experience in methods of transfer and entry to them. It also represents the views of independent primary and junior schools to the Department for Children, Schools and Families, and plays an active part in national educational planning.

IAPS
11 Waterloo Place, Leamington Spa, Warwickshire CV32 5LA

Tel: 01926 887833   Fax: 01926 888014
Email: iaps@iaps.org.uk; Website: www.iaps.org.uk

promoting
excellence
in education
*The Independent
Association
of Prep Schools*

ISA

The Independent School's Association, with membership across all types of school.

The Independent Schools Association, which celebrated its centenary in 1979, is one of the oldest of the various organisations of independent schools. It differs from most of the others in that it is not confined to any one type of school, but includes senior, preparatory, junior, nursery, coeducational, single sex, boarding and day schools. The only criterion is that it should be good of its kind.

The association began as the Association of Principals of Private Schools, and it was the first attempt to encourage high standards in private schools and to foster friendliness and cooperation among Heads who had previously worked in isolation. In 1895 it was incorporated as The Private Schools Association. In 1927 the word 'private' was replaced by 'independent', since by then many of the schools were no longer 'private' in the sense of being owned by private individuals. At present, although a number of the smaller schools are still privately owned, most are controlled by Boards of Governors constituted as Educational Trusts or Companies. The Association currently has 300 schools with approximately 70,000 pupils.

Membership is confined to heads of schools that are not under the control of the DCFS or LAs. Principals of such schools are eligible provided the Executive Council is satisfied as to their suitability and the efficiency of the school. In addition the school must fulfil the accreditation requirements of the Independent Schools Council. The ISA Executive Council monitors all developments through its national network of Area Coordinators and Committees and arranges for Accreditation of member schools to be reviewed at intervals of six years.

The Association exists to:

- promote friendship and fellowship among members nationally and through area meetings;

- provide opportunities for pupils in ISA schools to take part in area and national competitions in sport and the arts;

- provide information and advice from the ISA office and from area co-ordinators which will help and support individual members;

- arrange conferences and professional development courses which will foster excellence in education; and

- influence educational debate and promote independence and choice and to work actively with other associations as appropriate.

ISA, Boys' British School, East Street, Saffron Walden, Essex CB10 1LS
Tel: 01799 523619; Fax: 01799 524892
Email: isa@isaschools.org.uk; Website: www.isaschools.org.uk

The Independent Schools Council

David Lyscom, chief executive of the ISC, explains how this umbrella organisation works with its members to promote and preserve the quality, diversity and excellence of UK independent education, both at home and abroad.

What is the ISC?

The Independent Schools Council (ISC) is a politically independent, not-for-profit organisation representing over 1300 schools which collectively educate more than half a million pupils in the UK and overseas. ISC is constituted by eight member organisations: five associations representing Heads of independent schools, and associations representing school bursars, governors and British schools overseas. ISC has a permanent staff based in London.

What do we do for schools?

ISC carries out a number of important functions for schools.

First and foremost, ISC has a key role in representing and promoting the interests of the independent school sector. Increasingly this is through a vigorous public affairs agenda: tracking nascent policy ideas as they emerge from government and other political parties; seeking to inform and influence the debate; contributing to formal consultations run by government and other policy-making bodies; and lobbying for change where change is required. The flipside of this representational work is advice and guidance to schools on changes that may be required to how schools operate, whether that change is driven by new legislation, regulation or simply new ideas on what constitutes best practice.

Two key areas over the last year have been charitable status and ContactPoint. The sector is currently waiting to hear the Charity Commission's views on five independent schools, all ISC members, who have undergone the first public benefit reviews. ISC has worked both with the Commission and with the schools to seek to ensure that the reviews are properly conducted and informed.

On ContactPoint, we continue to campaign on the principle that a national database containing details of 11 million children will only divert resources away from more effective child safeguarding measures. But in the face of government insistence that ContactPoint should go ahead we are highlighting problems with the system and the regulatory regime that must be fixed if the database is to have any validity. In addition, we spent much time working to eliminate anomalies in policy guidance, first published in July 2008 by the UK Border Agency (UKBA), which set out how they saw new immigration rules applying to schools recruiting students from outside the EEA. Now that the policy is in force, we continue to raise concerns with UKBA on poor implementation. Representing a sector that brings more than 20,000 pupils into the UK from overseas, we cannot afford to get this wrong.

Secondly, ISC collects and analyses school and pupil data in three large-scale annual projects - the census, public examination results and university admissions - and conducts other tailored research. The sector increasingly relies on accurate statistical data so that policy debates can proceed on a sure footing. ISC not only collects that data it also provides insightful analysis into trends. For example, we are able to dispel some of the myths about the diversity of independent schoolchildren by showing that over 20% come from ethnic minority backgrounds. We have also been able to show that ISC pupil numbers are holding up as the recession bites, countering the media's obsession with falling roll calls.

Thirdly, ISC is responsible for inducting more trainee teachers than any other single organisation in the UK, through the ISC teacher induction panel, ISCtip. Induction was introduced in England in 1999 (2003 in Wales). From these dates all teachers gaining qualified teacher status (QTS) have been required to undertake induction if they wish to teach in the maintained sector and to register with the General Teaching Council. This also applies to those experienced teachers who are currently seeking QTS, or will seek QTS in the future, via the Graduate Teaching Programme.

ISC puts on a range of annual and one-off conferences and events for the sector, ranging from the annual conference in June each year to issue-specific workshop sessions for schools. This year we are covering partnerships, legal affairs, SEN, marketing and ICT strategic issues. ISC also offers bespoke catchment area and parent satisfaction research services for schools.

We have developed a range of important services for schools, which can be found on our website (www.isco.co.uk) where we provide: information on current legal and public affairs issues in our MemberZone (by free subscription, only for school staff and governors); information for teachers in our TeacherZone; a free job advert service in our JobZone; a service to schools to publicise their open days; information for the press; and all our publications.

In addition to our web-based service, ISC runs an information and advisory service for parents called ISCias. Completely free to parents, it is an invaluable source of advice and information for anyone thinking about independent education for their children. Please do call us on our national helpline: 0845 SCHOOLS (724 6657). Our helpline staff has full access in real time to a comprehensive information database and also reference material on a range of topics related to independent schools.

The Independent Schools Council can be contacted at:
St Vincent House, 30 Orange Street, London WC2H 7HH

Telephone: 020 7766 7070
Fax: 020 7766 7071
Website: www.isc.co.uk

SHMIS

The Society of Headmasters and Headmistresses of Independent Schools, founded in 1961, represents the interests of the smaller independent schools.

SHMIS has as its members some 100 Heads of well-established secondary schools, many with a boarding element, meeting a wide range of educational needs. All member schools provide education up to 18, with sixth forms offering both A and AS levels and vocational courses. Many also have junior schools attached to the foundation. A number cater for pupils with special educational needs, whilst others offer places to gifted dancers and musicians. All the schools provide education appropriate to their pupils' individual requirements together with the best in pastoral care.

The average size of the schools is about 350, and all aim to provide small classes ensuring favourable pupil:teacher ratios. The majority are coeducational and offer facilities for both boarding and day pupils. Many of the schools are non-denominational, whilst others have specific religious foundations.

The Society believes that independent schools are an important part of Britain's national education system. Given their independence, the schools can either introduce new developments ahead of their state colleagues or maintain certain courses appropriate to the pupils in their schools. They are able to respond quickly to the needs of parents and pupils alike.

Schools are admitted to membership of the Society only after a strict inspection procedure carried out by the Independent Schools Inspectorate. Regular inspection visits thereafter ensure that standards are maintained. The Society is a constituent member of the Independent Schools Council and every Full Member in the Society has been accredited to it. All the Society's Heads belong to the Association of School and College Leaders (ASCL – formerly the Secondary Heads Association) and their schools are members of AGBIS.

The Society's policy is: to maintain high standards of education, acting as a guarantee of quality to parents who choose a SHMIS school for their children; to ensure the genuine independence of member schools; to provide an opportunity for Heads to share ideas and common concerns for the benefit of the children in their care; to provide training opportunities for Heads and staff in order to keep them abreast of new educational initiatives; to promote links with higher and further education and the professions, so that pupils leaving the Society's schools are given the best advice and opportunities for their future careers; and to help Heads strengthen relations with their local communities.

SHMIS office, 12 The Point, Rockingham Road, Market Harborough, Leicestershire LE16 7QU; Tel: 01858 433760; Fax: 01858 461413; Email: gensec@shmis.org.uk; Website: www.shmis.org.uk

Glossary of abbreviations

AASAP	Association of American Study Abroad Programmes
AEB	Associated Examining Board for the General Certificate of Education
AEGIS	Association for the Education and Guardianship of International Students
AGBIS	Association of Governing Bodies of Independent Schools
AHIS	Association of Heads of Independent Schools
AJIS	Association of Junior Independent Schools
ALP	Association of Learning Providers
ANTC	The Association of Nursery Training Colleges
AOC	Association of Colleges
AP	Advanced Placement
ARELS	Association of Recognised English Language Schools/Federation of English Language Course Organisers
ASCL	Association of School & College Leaders
AQA	Assessment and Qualification Alliance/Northern Examinations and Assessment Board
BA	Bachelor of Arts
BAC	British Accreditation Council for Independent Further and Higher Education
BAECE	The British Association for Early Childhood Education
BD	Bachelor of Divinity
BEA	Boarding Educational Alliance
BEd	Bachelor of Education
BLitt	Bachelor of Letters
BSA	Boarding Schools' Association
BSc	Bachelor of Science
BTEC	Range of work-related, practical programmes leading to qualifications equivalent to GCSEs and A levels awarded by Edexcel
Cantab	Cambridge University

CE	Common Entrance Examination
CEE	Council for Environmental Education
CES	Catholic Education Service
C & G	City & Guilds Examination
CertEd	Certificate of Education
CIFE	Conference for Independent Education
CIS	Council of International Schools
CISC	Catholic Independent Schools' Conference
COBIS	Council of British International Schools
CSA	The Choir Schools' Association
DCFS	Department for Children, Schools and Families (formerly DfES)
DipEd	Diploma of Education
EAIE	European Association for International Education
ECIS	European Council of International Schools
Edexcel	GCSE Examining group, incorporating Business and Technology Education Council (BTEC) and University of London Examinations and Assessment Council (ULEAC)
FRSA	Fellow of the Royal Society of Arts
GCE	General Certificate of Education
GCSE	General Certificate of Secondary Education
GDST	Girls' Day School Trust
GNVQ	General National Vocational Qualifications
GSA	Girls' Schools Association
HMC	Headmasters' and Headmistresses' Conference
HMCJ	Headmasters' and Headmistresses' Conference Junior Schools
HSE	Human Scale Education
IAPS	Independent Association of Preparatory Schools
IB	International Baccalaureate
IBSCA	International Baccalaureate Schools and Colleges Association

IFF	Inspiring Futures Foundation (formerly ISCO)
ISA	Independent Schools Association
ISBA	Independent Schools' Bursars' Association
ISCis	Independent Schools Council information service
ISC	Independent Schools Council
ISEB	Independent Schools Examination Board
ISST	International Schools Sports Tournament
ISTA	International Schools Theatre Association
ITEC	International Examination Council
JET	Joint Educational Trust
LA	Local Authority (formerly LEA - Local Educational Authority)
LISA	London International Schools Association
MA	Master of Arts
MEd	Master of Education
MLitt	Master of Letters
MMI	Maria Montessori Institute
MSc	Master of Science
NAGC	National Association for Gifted Children
NAHT	National Association of Head Teachers
NASS	National Association of Independent Schools & Non-maintained Special Schools
NDNA	National Day Nurseries Association
NEASC	New England Association of Schools and Colleges
NFER	National Federation of Educational Research
OCR	Oxford, Cambridge and RSA Examinations
Oxon	Oxford
PGCE	Post Graduate Certificate in Education
PhD	Doctor of Philosophy
PNEU	Parents' National Education Union

GLOSSARY

QCA	Qualifications and Curriculum Authority
RSIS	The Round Square Schools
S Level	GCE Special Paper
SAT	Scholastic Aptitude Test (USA)
SATIPS	Support & Training in Prep Schools
SBSA	The State Boarding Schools Association
SEC	The Society of Educational Consultants
SEN	Special Educational Needs
SFIA	School Fees Insurance Agency Limited
SFIAET	SFIA Educational Trust
SHMIS	Society of Headmasters and Headmistresses of Independent Schools
SMA	Schools Music Association
SWSF	Steiner Waldorf Schools Fellowship
UCAS	Universities and Colleges Admissions Service for the UK
UKCISA	The UK Council for International Education
UWC	United World Colleges
VB	Verbal Reasoning

Listings

©MAPS IN MINUTES™ 2010
©Crown Copyright, Ordnance Survey 2010

Cambridgeshire

Buckinghamshire

Hertfordshire

Essex

London

Berkshire

Surrey

Kent

Hampshire

West Sussex

East Sussex

The following unitary authorities are also within the counties listed:

Thurrock and Southend-on-Sea	Essex
Medway	Kent
Brighton & Hove	East Sussex
Portsmouth and Southampton	Hampshire
Bracknell Forest, Reading, Slough, Windsor & Maidenhead and Wokingham	Berkshire
Milton Keynes	Buckinghamshire
Peterborough	Cambridgeshire

Central London

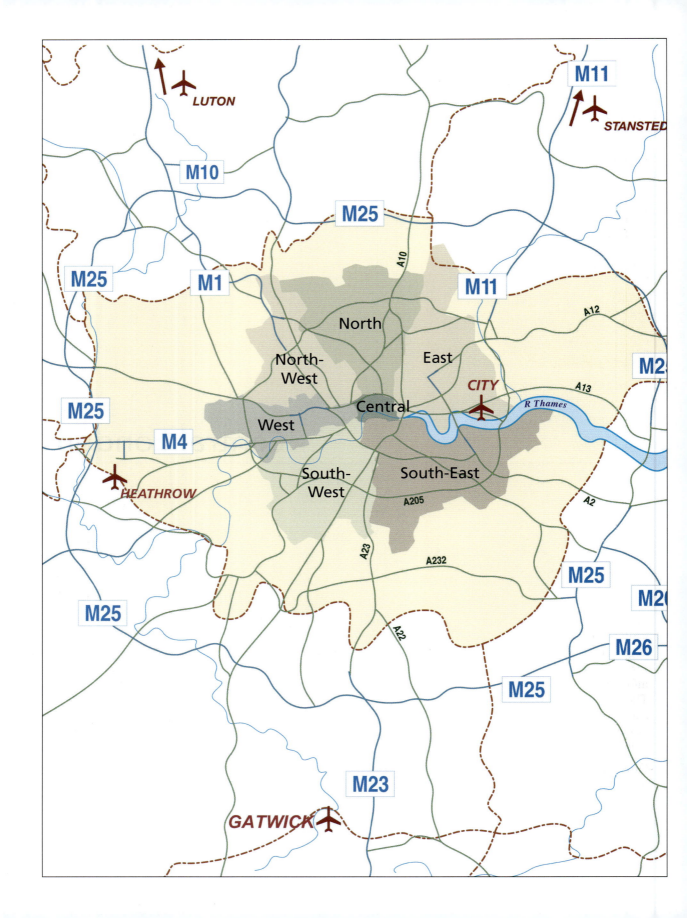

Blackheath High School GDST

(Founded 1880)

Vanbrugh Park, Blackheath, London SE3 7AG
Tel: 020 8853 2929   Email: info@bla.gdst.net
Fax: 020 8853 3663   Website: www.blackheathhighschool.gdst.net

Head: Mrs Elizabeth Laws BA(Hons), PGCE
Appointed: 2000
School type: Girls' Day
Age range of pupils: 3–18
No. of pupils enrolled as at 1.4.10: 650
Fees per annum as at 1.4.10: Day: £6966–£11,601
Teacher/pupil ratio: 1:12

Blackheath High School (which opened in 1880) is a selective, independent day school for girls aged three to 18. Situated in Blackheath, south-east London, it is a member of the Girls' Day School Trust (GDST). As a registered charity (No.306983), we aim to advance the education of girls or young women.

Girls benefit from all the advantages of a small school in terms of care, support and positive relationships, while having the opportunities and facilities of a far larger school. Students enjoy small teaching groups with teaching based on giving the girls exciting, informative and well-structured lessons and projects. The school provides a broad and interesting curriculum, enriched by a strong and varied programme of extracurricular activities with the use of ICT incorporated throughout.

Girls learn Mandarin and Latin, perform in the 345-seat theatre and play tennis on one of the 13 tennis courts. The school holds many national awards including the prestigious ICT Mark, recognising the school as being in the forefront of using information and communications technology (ICT) to enhance all aspects of pupil's work, including providing personal laptops for every sixth former, and a virtual learning environment.

Students flourish in an all-girl environment and the school's distinctive, holistic, forward-thinking approach to girls' education lays a strong emphasis on their health and welfare. Pupils can join one of the school's many clubs, including wellbeing activities. Many girls participate in the Duke of Edinburgh's Award Scheme and enjoy activities such as debating, film club, junior gardening club, the editorial team of the school magazine and exciting trips abroad to places like Russia, USA, China and across Europe. Girls in Year 2 and Year 7 receive a musical instrument and free tuition for a year.

Rated 'outstanding' in the most recent ISI inspection (February 2008) and Ofsted inspection (June 2008), the 650 pupils enjoy considerable success in gaining places at prestigious universities including Oxford and Cambridge, while achieving standards well above the national average. In 2009, the pass rate at A level was 100% with 80% of students gaining grades A or B. Over one third of the candidates achieved at least three grade As each and nearly two thirds gained pass grades in at least one maths or science subject. At GCSE, 100% of Year 11 students attained at least five GCSEs graded A* to C, 98% at grade A* - C and 68% at A* or A.

The school provides an educational experience described as 'stimulating and extraordinarily supportive, conducive to the highest standards of teaching and learning' in the Inspection Report prepared by the ISI.

Cameron House

(Founded 1980)

4 The Vale, Chelsea, London SW3 6AH
Tel: 020 7352 4040   Email: info@cameronhouseschool.org
Fax: 020 7352 2349   Website: www.cameronhouseschool.org www.gabbitas.co.uk

Headmistress: Mrs Lucie Moore BEd(Hons)
School type: Coeducational Day
Member of: IAPS, CReSTeD, NAHT, SATIPS
Accredited by: IAPS, ISC
Age range of pupils: 4–11
No. of pupils enrolled as at 1.4.10: 115
Boys: 52 Girls: 63
(Pre-prep 59, Prep 56)
Fees per annum as at 1.4.10: Day: £13,170
Average size of class: 18
Teacher/pupil ratio: 1:11
Religious denomination: Non-denominational

Cameron House is a vibrant, creative school whose confident pupils shine both academically and socially. Its nurturing and caring ethos ensures the talents and strengths of each individual are identified, extended and celebrated. High staff:pupil ratios allow the dedicated, highly-qualified teachers to provide the children with a stimulating, tailored learning environment. While emphasis is placed on the core curriculum, the school's teaching goes far beyond. French is taught from reception, singing, speech and drama are popular, as is debating. The IT room, interactive whiteboards in every classroom and bank of laptops, provide access to online learning, and each class has its own library. A varied and dynamic physical education programme gives the children opportunities to take part in lessons, matches and tournaments several times a week. Numerous after-school clubs foster interests including: fencing, karate, ballet, chess and Latin to name just a few. Both boys and girls are thoroughly prepared for entrance exams and scholarships at 11 for prestigious London day and boarding schools.

Channing School

(Founded 1885)

Highgate, London N6 5HF
Tel: 020 8340 2328   Email: info@channing.co.uk
Fax: 020 8341 5698   Website: www.channing.co.uk

Head: Mrs B Elliott MA(Cantab)
Appointed: September 2005
School type: Girls' Day
Age range of pupils: 4–18
No. of pupils enrolled as at 1.5.10: 600
Sixth Form: 80
Fees per annum as at 1.5.10: Day: £11,430–£12,390

Founded in 1885, Channing is a happy and successful school where the sense of community is strong. Though large enough to ensure academic rigour and excellent facilities, the school is small enough for the Head and members of staff to know each girl personally.

The school is in an attractive part of Highgate, in spacious and open grounds, and offers a balanced education that aims to develop lively, well-stocked minds. Teaching groups are small in size, which allows a friendly relationship between girls and staff. Academic results are excellent, with 100% pass rates, 87% A and B grades at A level in 2009 and 86% A and A* at GCSE. Girls usually take nine or ten subjects at GCSE and there is a wide range of A and AS level choices, including ancient Greek, further maths, economics, theatre studies and critical thinking. The junior school (Fairseat) has its own building - the elegant and gracious family home of Sir Sydney Waterlow, one-time Lord Mayor of London - set in spacious gardens, is notable for its happy and secure atmosphere and has its own hall and music wing.

Art, drama, music and sport are all strong, with frequent concerts and theatrical productions. The school is fortunate in its gardens and open space (there are seven tennis courts on site) and in its facilities. Recent developments include a new sixth form centre, a well-equipped performing arts studio, a fitness area and further extension of excellent IT facilities. Extracurricular activities are considered an important and integral part of education: most girls learn an instrument, and the Duke of Edinburgh's Award Scheme, Young Enterprise and Community Service are all well subscribed.

Family tradition is strong at Channing and there is an energetic parents' association. The atmosphere is friendly, happy and purposeful, with strong pastoral care. We set high standards of courtesy, concern and respect for others and aim to develop in each girl the personal confidence that will enable her to make the most of whatever opportunities her life may bring.

Channing School is a registered charity No. 312766. Its objectives are to provide instruction of the highest standard together with moral and religious training.

City of London School
A rounded education in the Square Mile
(Founded 1442)

CITY OF **LONDON SCHOOL**

Queen Victoria Street, London EC4V 3AL
Tel: 020 7489 0291   Email: admissions@clsb.org.uk
Fax: 020 7329 6887   Website: www.clsb.org.uk

Headmaster: Mr D Levin MA
Appointed: 1999
School type: Boys' Day
Age range of pupils: 10–18
No. of pupils enrolled as at 1.9.10: 900
Sixth Form: 250
Fees per annum as at 1.9.10: Day: £13,050

"There is no such thing as a typical City boy. What characterises the education offered at the school is a true preparation for life."

City of London is a truly unique independent school not least because of its unrivalled location on the banks of the Thames, between St Paul's Cathedral and the Tate Modern. We are at the heart of the capital and our pupils benefit enormously from all that is on offer on our doorstep.

We are a modern and forward-looking institution drawing on clever boys from all social, economic and ethnic backgrounds and in so doing truly reflect the diversity of the capital in the 21st century. Boys travel to City from all over London and come from a huge number of both state primary and independent preparatory schools and, once here, receive an academic yet liberal education.

Our examination results are excellent, but, more importantly, boys leave us with a sense of identity and an independence of thought and action which are rare among leavers from private schools; it is significant that the vast majority of boys go on to their first choice of university.

Facilities are outstanding (the school moved downstream to its new buildings in 1986) and are continually updated.

Access to the school is not restricted by money, and we are generously endowed with academic, music and sport scholarships (for academic merit) and also academic and livery bursaries for families who may not be able to afford the full fees. In addition, the City-Asquith Campaign has raised significant funding for several full-fee bursaries to be awarded each year to those who could not otherwise afford even a proportion of fees. In this way, the school seeks to maintain the socio-economic mix which has always been its tradition and strength.

For a prospectus and to book onto one of our numerous parental visits, please contact:

Mrs J Brown, the Admissions Secretary,

Tel: 020 7489 0291

Or email: admissions@clsb.org.uk

Or write to: City of London School, Queen Victoria Street, London EC4V 3AL

Colfe's

(Founded 1652)

Horn Park Lane, Greenwich, London SE12 8AW
Tel: 020 8852 2283   Email: head@colfes.com
Fax: 020 8297 1216   Website: www.colfes.com

COLFE'S
S C H O O L

Head: Mr R F Russell MA(Cantab)
School type: Coeducational
Member of: HMC
Age range of pupils: 3–18
No. of pupils enrolled as at 1.1.10: 1020
Fees per annum as at 1.6.10:
Nursery: £8478 (includes lunch)
Pre-Prep: £9288 (includes lunch)
Preparatory: £9846
Senior School: £12,132
Average size of class: 22

Colfe's is one of the oldest schools in the capital with a reputation for academic excellence within a friendly, caring atmosphere. We aim to provide teaching of the highest calibre, and want our boys and girls to be creative and flexible thinkers - ready to meet the challenges of the 21st century.

The curriculum follows the spirit of the National Curriculum in both preparatory and senior schools. Fast-tracked pupils are entered for the separate sciences at GCSE and follow the IGCSE maths course. A total of 27 subjects are available at A level, including government & politics, drama, psychology, physical education and classical civilisation.

We place considerable emphasis on our pastoral care, providing pupils with a supportive environment in which they can develop their talents to the full. The school became fully coeducational in 2003, and pupils are actively encouraged to participate in sports, music, drama and the arts. PE/games are compulsory for all pupils up to and including Year 11. Specialist on-site facilities include a sports hall swimming pool and fitness suite, plus extensive playing fields and an all-weather pitch (opened 2006). Main sports are rugby, football and cricket (boys) and hockey, netball, tennis and athletics (girls). A new centre for the performing arts was opened in 2003, and provides outstanding facilities for drama, art and music.

Academic scholarships are awarded to those who demonstrate an outstanding performance in the Entrance Examination. Means-tested bursaries are also available. In addition, a limited number of music and sports scholarships are available at 11+, together with a number of other scholarships, bursaries and awards to those entering the school at 16+.

Colfe's is a registered charity (No. 1109650) which exists to provide education for boys and girls.

Devonshire House Preparatory School

(Founded 1989)

2 Arkwright Road, Hampstead, London NW3 6AE
Tel: 020 7435 1916   Email: enquiries@devonshirehouseprepschool.co.uk
Fax: 020 7431 4787   Website: www.devonshirehouseschool.co.uk

Headmistress: Mrs S Alexander BA(Hons)
School type: Preparatory, Pre-preparatory &
Nursery Day School
(The Oak Tree Nursery)
Age range of pupils:
Boys: 2½–13
Girls: 2½–11
No. of pupils enrolled as at 1.3.10: 560
Boys: 319 Girls: 241
Fees per annum as at 1.3.10: Day: £6750–£12,855
Religious denomination: Non denominational

Curriculum

The central themes of the curriculum are the
traditional subjects of literacy and numeracy.
Specialist teaching of subjects and the combined
sciences form an increasingly important part of the
curriculum as the children grow older. Expression in
all forms of communication is encouraged with
classes having lessons in art, music, drama,
information and design technology, physical exercise
and games. Much encouragement is given to pupils to
help to widen their horizons and broaden their
interests. The school fosters a sense of personal
responsibility amongst the pupils.

Entry requirements

The offer of places is subject to availability and to an
assessment. Children wishing to enter the school
over the age of six will be required to sit a more
formal test.

Academic & leisure facilities

The school is situated in lovely premises in the heart
of Hampstead with their own walled grounds. The
aim is to achieve high academic standards whilst
developing enthusiasm and initiative throughout a
wide range of interests. It is considered essential to
encourage pupils to develop their own individual
personalities and a good sense of personal
responsibility.

Dolphin School
(incorporating Noah's Ark Nursery Schools)
(Founded 1986)

106 Northcote Road, London SW11 6QW
Tel: 020 7924 3472   Email: admissions@dolphinschool.org.uk
Fax: 020 8265 8700   Website: www.dolphinschool.org.uk

Principal: Mrs Jo Glen BA(Hons)
Appointed: September 2006
School type: Coeducational Day and Nursery
Member of: TISCA
Age range of pupils: 2¹/₂–11
No. of pupils enrolled as at 21.4.10: 245
Fees per annum as at 1.4.10: Day: £7485–£8070
Nursery School: £4290
Average size of class: 18 in school: 8 in Nursery
Teacher/pupil ratio: 1:18 (KS2), 1:9 (KS1), 1:8
Nursery
Religious denomination: Christian Foundation

Curriculum
Our small class sizes enable us to get to know your child extremely well so that we can not only set specific individualised academic targets, but also discover how he or she learns best. We give priority to English and maths as well as hands-on science, colourful geography, history (with outings to the real thing) and whole-school Spanish.

Games and the arts
We train pupils in the arts with fantastic specialist teaching and a plethora of performing and exhibiting opportunities. We also coach children in a wide range of sports through dynamic teaching and a superb fixture list.

Pastoral care
We are committed to giving both time and care to grow your child's character on his or her journey from Reception to Year 6. Our Christian ethos leads us to believe that personal growth ultimately matters more than anything. So while we are thrilled that our leavers win academic or sporting scholarships to a range of excellent secondary schools, we are even more excited about who they are - and pleased that they enjoyed the journey.

Entry requirements
Reception class: appointment with the Principal. Years 1-6: interview, assessment day and past school reports.

Principal's philosophy
If we want children to be the best they can be, academically, artistically, in sport or as people, we must start by valuing them for who they are.

Outstanding characteristics
The combination of nurture and dynamism. The passionate commitment of the staff. A fantastic all-round education.

Examinations offered
11+ entry examinations.

Senior exit schools: Alleyn's, Dulwich College, JAGS, Streatham & Clapham High, St Mary's Ascot, Tring Park Arts Educational, Oakham, Emanuel, TCC, Trinity, Lady Margaret's Fulham.

Dolphin School Trust is a registered charity (No. 29664) and exists to promote a high quality of education for all its children based upon Christian principles.

Dulwich College Preparatory School

(Founded 1885)

42 Alleyn Park, Dulwich, London SE21 7AA
Tel: 020 8670 3217   Email: registrar@dcpslondon.org
Fax: 020 8766 7586   Website: www.dcpslondon.org

Headmaster: Mr M W Roulston
Appointed: 2009
School type: Independent Preparatory Boys' School
(Day and Weekly Boarding from 8 years)
Age range of pupils:
Boys: 3–13
Girls: 3–5
No. of pupils enrolled as at 1.1.10: 817
Boys: 793 Girls: 24
No. of boarders: 20
Fees per annum as at 1.1.10: Day: £4350–£13,542
Weekly Boarding: £18,213–£19,662
Average size of class: 18
Religious denomination: Church of England

We are an independent prep school with a national reputation for academic, musical, artistic and sporting excellence.

In recent years our boys have gone on to succeed at more than 50 excellent day and boarding schools throughout the country. Alleyn's, Charterhouse, Dulwich College, Eton College, Marlborough, Tonbridge, St Paul's, Wellington College, Westminster and Winchester College are just a selection of our leavers' destination schools.

While DCPS is essentially a boys' school, with 817 pupils aged between three and 13, we start with the nursery which also caters for girls. There are three other distinct sections of the school: the Annexe, the Lower School and the Upper School. In addition we have a well equipped boarding house and are delighted to offer weekly boarding. Our ongoing programme of building work ensures that we have the very best facilities.

It is difficult to summarise the school's aims and ethos in just a few words. Nevertheless, the following points outline our guiding philosophy.

- We provide the boys with opportunities. Opportunity leads to enthusiasm, enthusiasm to understanding, and understanding to choice.

- We provide each child with the opportunity to be the best possible version of himself.

Some of these opportunities are listed below.

- Around 35% of our leavers win scholarships each year.

- We run more than 25 sports teams each term with the top teams regularly doing well in national competitions. Recent sports tours include cricket to South Africa, football to Dubai, rugby to Portugal and swimming in the USA.

- More than 700 individual music lessons take place every week.

- Approaching 30 groups perform in our concert hall. Many also appear on the programme for our gala concerts at prestigious venues such as The Royal Festival Hall and The London Palladium. Last year the Big Band played at the Royal Albert Hall in the Schools Prom

- Pupils experience at least four residential trips within the curriculum. 12 more are offered as optional holiday trips.

- Drama productions are staged annually from reception to Year 6 as well as an Upper School play in the spring.

In conclusion - DCPS is a boys' school FOR the boys.

Dulwich College Preparatory School Trust Ltd is a registered charity which aims to promote standards of excellence. (Charity No. 312715)

Eaton Square School

(Founded 1981)

79 Eccleston Square, London SW1V 1PP
Tel: 020 7931 9469   Email: admissions@eatonsquareschool.com
Fax: 020 7828 0164   Website: www.eatonsquareschool.com

Headmaster: Mr Sebastian Hepher BEd(Hons)
Appointed: 2002
School type: Coeducational Day
Age range of pupils: 2½–13
No. of pupils enrolled as at 1.9.10: 529
Boys: 280 Girls: 249
Fees per annum as at 1.9.10: Day: £2550–£14,610
Religious denomination: Non-denominational

Sebastian Hepher joined Eaton Square School as Headmaster in September 2010 from Eaton House, The Manor School. The Headmaster is a member of the Independent Association of Preparatory Schools.

Eaton Square School is one of the few coeducational day schools in the heart of London offering nursery, pre-preparatory and preparatory education for children from 2½ to 13 years of age. The school maintains high academic standards and encourages in every child an enthusiasm for learning, good manners, self-discipline and, in all things, a determination to do their best and realise their full potential. Small classes, coupled with a large number of highly qualified teaching staff, are an integral part of the school's success and allow personal supervision of each child. The school offers a stretching, challenging approach to learning that emphasises achievement and builds confidence.

Curriculum

The form teacher teaches general subjects to their class up to the age of eight. Thereafter, specialist subject teachers continue the curriculum in preparation for the Common Entrance examinations for senior English public schools, for girls at age 11 and boys at age 13. A wide range of subjects is encompassed in the curriculum, including English, mathematics, science, history, geography, French, Latin, art, drama, music and physical education. Information and communication technology (ICT) is introduced from the age of three and it is an integral part of the syllabus. The various parts of the school are served by a school-wide network, allowing pupils and staff to access their work from any computer. There is a computer suite in each of the three school buildings. In addition, all classrooms are equipped with interactive whiteboards and data projectors.

The school also benefits from an art and science block with separate science laboratory and a wonderfully equipped art, design and technology studio. A new music department has just been completed featuring five sound-proofed practice rooms and a state-of-the-art performance and composing classroom, with keyboards linked to computers and interactive facilities, allowing children to both rehearse individually and collaboratively share their compositions. Eaton Square encourages art along with music and drama, all of which are flourishing departments within the school.

Sports and clubs

Sport and physical education include swimming, fencing, gymnastics, football, rugby, cricket and tennis and the school has successful teams competing against other London schools. After-school clubs offer an ever-increasing variety, from drama workshops to sailing. The school takes full advantage of the rich variety London has to offer and numerous visits to museums, exhibitions and theatres are arranged. Whole year group trips are regularly organised. An annual ski trip, a classical trip to Rome and Pompeii and various adventure/field study weeks are stimulating, valuable educational experiences.

Entry requirements

Entry to the reception classes is by assessment in November of the year prior to entry. For older children there are 8+ and 11+ entry examinations.

Examinations offered

Children are prepared for entrance examinations to top London day schools and boarding schools.

Francis Holland School, Regent's Park, NW1

(Founded 1878)

Clarence Gate, Ivor Place, Regent's Park, London NW1 6XR
Tel: 020 7723 0176   Email: registrar@fhs-nw1.org.uk
Fax: 020 7706 1522   Website: www.francisholland.org.uk

Head: Mrs Vivienne Durham MA(Oxon)
School type: Independent Girls' Day
Member of: GSA, GBA, ISC
Age range of pupils: 11–18
No. of pupils enrolled as at 1.1.10: 445
Sixth Form: 110
Fees per annum as at 1.9.10: Day: £13,890
Average size of class: 18 (GCSE) and 8 (Sixth Form)
Religious denomination: Church of England

Curriculum

Girls on arrival are placed in one of three parallel forms and taught a broad curriculum. In the second year they start a second language - Italian, German or Spanish. Girls usually take nine or ten subjects for GCSE, eleven in some cases. All girls take at least four AS levels and three A2s. They proceed to university, art or music college. The curriculum is kept under constant review, and there is regular consultation with parents about each girl's programme of study. Many sixth formers successfully complete the Extended Project, a qualification designed to challenge the most able students beyond A level.

Entry requirements

Entry at 11 is by means of written tests in English and mathematics, together with an interview. A few girls are accepted into the sixth form each year and into other years as vacancies occur.

Examinations offered

GCSE subjects offered: art, classical civilisation, English, English literature, French, German, geography, Greek, history, Italian, Latin, mathematics, music, PE, religious studies, Spanish, physics, chemistry and biology. Additional subjects at A level include history of art, economics, politics, psychology and theatre studies.

Academic & leisure facilities

The school has its own swimming pool and gymnasium and uses Regent's Park for tennis, hockey, rounders and netball. The new Gloucester Wing, opened by HRH The Duke of Gloucester in May 2009, provides additional classrooms and seminar rooms, a fourth art studio and a performance area for music, drama and theatre studies. There are two school orchestras, several choirs and a jazz band.

Music, drama, art and sport play an important part in the school. Individual instrumental lessons and lessons in speech and drama are popular.

The school seeks to foster a happy atmosphere in which pupils will thrive academically and enjoy a wide range of extracurricular clubs, activities and excursions.

Scholarships and bursaries

Academic scholarships and music scholarships available at Year 7 and sixth form. Entry bursaries up to 100% of fees.

Francis Holland School Charitable Trust exists to provide high quality education for girls and religious instruction in accordance with the principles of the Church of England. Registered charity no. 312745.

Francis Holland School, Sloane Square, SW1

(Founded 1881)

39 Graham Terrace, London SW1W 8JF
Tel: 020 7730 2971   Email: registrar@fhs-sw1.org.uk
Fax: 020 7823 4066   Website: www.francisholland.org.uk

Head: Miss Stephanie Pattenden BSc
Appointed: September 1997
School type: Independent Girls' Day
Member of: GSA, GBA, ISC
Age range of pupils: 4–18
No. of pupils enrolled as at 1.1.10: 450
Sixth Form: 70
Fees per annum as at 1.9.10: Day: £12,060–£14,205
Average size of class: 12 (GCSE) and 6 (Sixth Form)
Religious denomination: Church of England

Academic and pastoral

Girls throughout the school follow a strong academic curriculum including a compulsory modern language, Latin, separate sciences and drama. At GCSE three subjects are added to a core of six or seven subjects and in the sixth form four ASs leading to three or four A levels is the norm. On leaving school all girls proceed to higher education, sometimes following a gap-year. Destinations include art or music colleges, Oxford, Cambridge and other traditional UK universities as well as newer universities in the UK or abroad. Consistently high A level results and best ever GCSE results (46% A* and 76% A*/A) in 2009. Pastoral care was highly praised in the last ISI inspection report: "Excellent pastoral care in a friendly, supportive community..." Girls are known as individuals and encouraged and supported in a happy and purposeful environment.

Entry requirements

Entry at 4+ is by means of a school-based assessment and at 11+ there are written tests in English and mathematics, and a further half-day school assessment including an interview. A few girls are accepted into the sixth form each year and into other years as vacancies occur.

Examinations offered

GCSE subjects offered: art, classical civilisation, English, English literature, French, German, geography, Greek, history, drama, Latin, mathematics, music, PE, religious studies, Spanish, physics, chemistry and biology. Additional subjects at A level include history of art, economics, politics and psychology.

Extracurricular

The extensive extracurricular programme, comprising music, drama, art and sport, will be further strengthened by brand new facilities opening in autumn 2010. Charitable activities are strongly encouraged and girls undertake ambitious projects which not only raise thousands of pounds, but also develop leadership and team working skills. Duke of Edinburgh's Award Scheme is also popular. Ballet, drama and instrumental lessons are popular and all girls have numerous opportunities to go on day and residential trips at home and abroad.

Scholarships and bursaries

Academic scholarships and music scholarships are available at Year 7 and sixth form. Entry bursaries up to 100% of fees.

Francis Holland School Charitable Trust exists to provide high quality education for girls and religious instruction in accordance with the principles of the Church of England. Registered charity no. 312745.

GEMS Hampshire School

(Founded 1928) ISC Accredited

15 Manresa Road, Chelsea, London SW3 6NB
Tel: 020 7352 7077   Email: hampshire@indschool.org
Fax: 020 7351 3960   Website: www.ths.westminster.sch.uk

Principal: Mr A G Bray MISA, CertEd
School type: Coeducational Day
Member of: GEMS, ISA
Age range of pupils: 3–13
No. of pupils enrolled as at 1.1.10:
Boys: 132 Girls: 79
Early Years: 80
Pre-Preparatory: 80
Preparatory: 80
Fees per annum as at 1.1.10: Day: £8970–£12,990
Average size of class: 15
Teacher/pupil ratio: 1:6.4
Religious denomination: Interdenominational

Locations
Early Years Section:
5 Wetherby Place, London SW7 4NX
Pre-Preparatory and Preparatory Sections:
15 Manresa Road, London SW3 6NB

Change of location
In January 2009, the pre-preparatory and preparatory sections made a successful move to a new site at 15 Manresa Road, London SW3. The school had spent three years working on the refurbishment of the Grade 2* listed building, which was originally built as a library in 1890. The building has state-of-the-art facilities for the children which are sympathetically integrated with its original architectural features.

Curriculum
A broad-based and balanced curriculum is provided. Children are given every opportunity to develop individual talents as fully as possible - a broad range of academic subjects being supported by a high level of instruction in music, art, physical education and drama. Children are encouraged to study the history and development of their environment by means of regular visits to museums, art galleries, exhibitions and places of interest.

All children begin to learn French at the age of three. As an integral part of the syllabus, Year 4 and above are accompanied by members of staff on an annual study visit to France where the staff combine with French teachers to provide a fully integrated programme of lessons, educational visits and outdoor pursuits and activities.

The school also offers the *Maths Whizz* online home tuition system as an integral part of both the curriculum and fees.

In the 11+, 12+ and 13+ examination classes, more advanced instruction is given in all subjects and extra opportunities are provided in further areas of study to reinforce maturity and readiness for children to move into their next school. The school operates an Extended School Activities Programme, which includes: door to door bus service; Early Bird Club from 08.00 hours; Stay and Study/Play until 18.00 hours; Multi Activity Camps during half terms and holidays.

Entry requirements
Three to five: interview with the Principal. Five to eight: interview with the Principal, plus a report from previous school. 8+: test, interview with the Principal, plus possibly a day spent in the school.

Examinations offered
Scholarship plus Common Entrance and other entrance examinations to senior day and boarding schools.

Academic & leisure facilities
On site: form and school libraries, purpose built science laboratory, ICT suite, art/DT studio, music/drama studio and fully equipped stage.

Off site: extensive facilities for a full physical education curriculum, plus a wealth of cultural venues for educational visits.

Glendower School

(Founded 1895)

87 Queen's Gate, London SW7 5JX
Tel: 020 7370 1927   Email: office@glendower.kensington.sch.uk
Fax: 020 7244 8308   Website: www.glendowerprep.org

Headmistress: Mrs R E Bowman BA, PGCE
Appointed: April 2004
School type: Girls' Preparatory Day
Member of: IAPS. Accredited by ISC.
Age range of pupils: 4–11+
No. of pupils enrolled as at 10.2.10: 90
Fees per annum as at 10.2.10: Day: £12,555
Average size of class: 17 max
Religious denomination: None

Curriculum

In the lower school, girls aged four to seven years are taught general subjects by a class teacher, who frequently has an assistant but music, drama, swimming, physical education, French and ICT are taught by specialist staff.

Girls enter the upper school at the age of seven years and are taught mainly by specialist teachers. Subjects included in the curriculum are: mathematics, English, French, science, history, geography, religious education, current affairs, Latin (at ten years), ICT, art, CDT, music, drama and physical education.

The recently acquired adjoining building facilitates two form entry from 4+ so that class sizes do not exceed 17.

Entry requirements

Interviews at four years. Test and interview thereafter as vacancies occur at any other age.

Examinations offered

Girls are prepared for the entrance examinations for the London independent day schools at 11+ and for various boarding schools at 11+.

Academic & leisure facilities

The girls use excellent sports facilities off site but the school has its own art/CDT room, a recently refurbished school hall with stage, an ICT room and a well-equipped science laboratory. All classrooms have at least one computer, a printer and a plasma screen.

From September 2010 there will be new catering/dining, ICT and cloakroom facilities, as well as three additional classrooms.

Visits to the museums, galleries, theatres, as well as ecology trips and visits to the Royal Institute form an essential part of the school curriculum. Various club activities take place from four to five pm most evenings.

Glendower School Trust Ltd is a registered charity which exists to provide high quality education for local girls. (Charity No. 312717)

Hawkesdown House School Kensington

(Founded 2001)

27 Edge Street, Kensington, London W8 7PN
Tel: 020 7727 9090   Email: admin@hawkesdown.co.uk
Fax: 020 7727 9988   Website: www.hawkesdown.co.uk

Head: Mrs C Bourne MA(Cantab)
School type: Boys' Independent Pre-prep Day
Age range of pupils: 3–8
No. of pupils enrolled as at 1.9.09: 130
Fees per annum as at 1.9.09: Day: £11,325–£12,975
Average size of class: 15-18
Teacher/pupil ratio: 1:8
Religious denomination: Non-denominational;
Christian ethos

Hawkesdown House is an independent school for boys from the ages of three to eight. The school was the first free standing pre-preparatory school to be elected to IAPS (Independent Association of Preparatory Schools) and it has continued to remain in IAPS under the leadership of a new Head, Mrs Claire Bourne. Early literacy and numeracy are of prime importance and the traditional academic subjects form the core curriculum. A balanced education helps all aspects of learning and a wide range of interests is encouraged. The school finds and fosters individual talents in each pupil. Boys are prepared for entry at eight to the main London and other preparatory schools. The Head places the greatest importance on matching boys happily and successfully to potential schools and spends time with parents ensuring that the transition is smooth and free of stress.

Sound and thorough early education is important for success, and also for self-confidence. The thoughtful and thorough teaching and care at Hawkesdown House ensures high academic standards and promotes initiative, kindness and courtesy. Hawkesdown is a school with fun and laughter, where boys develop their own personalities together with a sense of personal responsibility.

The school provides an excellent traditional education, with the benefits of modern technology, in a safe, happy and caring atmosphere. Many of the boys coming to the school live within walking distance and the school is an important part of the Kensington community.

There are clear expectations and the boys are encouraged by positive motivation and by the recognition and praise of their achievements, progress and effort. Individual attention and pastoral care for each of the boys is of great importance.

Hawkesdown House has a fine building in Edge Street, off Kensington Church Street.

Parents who would like further information or to visit the school and meet the Head, should contact the School Office for a prospectus or an appointment.

Herne Hill School

(Founded 1976)

The Old Vicarage, 127 Herne Hill, London SE24 9LY
Tel: 020 7274 6336   Email: enquiries@hernehillschool.co.uk
Fax: 020 7924 9510   Website: www.hernehillschool.co.uk

Head: Mrs Jane Beales
Director: Mr Dominik Magyar
School type: Coeducational Day
Member of: ISA
Age range of pupils: 3–7
No. of pupils enrolled as at 1.1.10: 240
Fees per annum as at 1.1.10: Day: £3840–£9570
Religious denomination: Christian foundation, welcomes all faiths

Herne Hill School has much to offer - caring and enthusiastic staff, happy and confident children, and excellent results at 7+ years. Main entry is into the nursery at 2+ years, the kindergarten at 3+ (both in order of registration, with priority given to siblings) and the reception at 4+ (after an informal interview).

The school is well known as an oasis of happy learning and as the largest feeder into the Dulwich Foundation Schools. Its open and friendly atmosphere makes it particularly well suited for families new to the area. It is situated in an Old Vicarage and a spacious new building. The half acre grounds include a bark playground in the old orchard.

By focusing on early years education, Herne Hill School has developed a strong expertise in making the critical transition from nursery to school seamless. Children joining the nursery or kindergarten can avoid the disruption of a 4+ change and have continuity for up to five years in what are arguably their most important formative years. Children joining in reception also benefit from the smooth progression from a play-based learning approach to more structured lessons.

Herne Hill School for love, care and an excellent education, encapsulates the school philosophy that love, nurture and a caring environment foster the children's self-confidence, sense of achievement and happiness, thereby stimulating their curiosity and desire to learn.

The curriculum is finely balanced to take account of each child's individual needs as well as the requirements of the 7+ entry tests - and to make learning fun! It is designed to develop the skills of independent learning and to sustain the children's innate joy of learning. Music, drama, gym, dancing and French are emphasised and taught by specialists.

The latest ISI inspection report delivered a strong endorsement of the school's ethos, staff, curriculum, *modus operandi* and infrastructure. The inspectors summarised their findings as follows: "High-quality teaching effectively supports pupils' very good personal development and enables them to achieve results which are far above national standards." The full report can be found on: www.isinspect.org.uk.

The school holds two open mornings a year, typically on a Saturday in March and September. Prospective parents may also see the school 'in action' by joining one of the regular tours held during usual school hours.

Highgate School

(Founded 1565)

North Road, Highgate, London N6 4AY
Tel: 020 8340 1524   Email: office@highgateschool.org.uk
Fax: 020 8340 7674   Website: www.highgateschool.org.uk

Head Master: Mr A S Pettitt MA
Appointed: September 2006
School type: Coeducational Day
Member of: HMC, ISC
Age range of pupils: 3–18
No. of pupils enrolled as at 1.3.10:
Boys: 917 Girls: 490 Sixth Form: 327
Fees per annum as at 1.9.10: Day: £13,095–£15,120
Average size of class: 8-22
Teacher/pupil ratio: 1:8
Religious denomination: Church of England

Curriculum
GCSE, AS and A2 levels. 18 GCSE subjects offered, 24 at AS and A2 level.

Vocational
Work experience available.

Computing facilities
Extensive Pentium PC network, computer-aided design and desktop publishing.

Languages
French, German, Mandarin, Russian, Spanish, Latin and ancient Greek at GCSE and A level.

Entry requirements
Total age range three to 18. Senior department 11-18. Main entry at seven, 11, 13 and 16. Interview and own exam used at seven, 11 and 13. Sixth form entry by interview (A grades preferred in AS level subjects). Scholarships and bursaries available.

Sir Roger Cholmeley's School at Highgate is a registered charity that exists to provide excellent education. (Registered No. 312765)

Hill House International Junior School

(Founded 1949)

17 Hans Place, Chelsea, London SW1X 0EP
Tel: 020 7584 1331   Email: info@hillhouseschool.co.uk
Fax: 020 7591 3938   Website: www.hillhouseschool.co.uk

Headmaster: Richard Townend FLSM(Chm)
Appointed: 2002
Governors: Richard Townend, Mrs Janet Townend, William Townend, Edmund Townend
Second Master: Edmund Townend BSc(Hons), PGCE
School type: Coeducational Day
Age range of pupils: 4–13
No. of pupils enrolled as at 1.3.10: 980
Boys: 560 Girls: 420
Fees per annum as at 1.3.10: Day: £9000–£12,300 inclusive
Average size of class: 12-14
Teacher/pupil ratio: 1:7
Religious denomination: Christian Ecumenical

Motto

A child's mind is not a vessel to be filled but a fire to be kindled.

Hill House was founded by Colonel and Mrs Stuart Townend at La Tour-de-Peilz in Switzerland in 1949 and at Hans Place in London in 1951 with the intention that children from all over the world should have the opportunity to follow an English curriculum while learning that every nation is equal but different and that peaceful co-existence comes from mutual respect, understanding and consideration for others. Over fifty years later we still hold true to those founding principles and the day-to-day administration of every aspect of the school remains in the care and control of the founding family.

To us every child has a talent to be discovered and nurtured whether it be academic, artistic or sporting and each is equally valuable and important in the creation of the unique character of every child. So at Hill House we provide specialist teaching in all academic subjects complemented by a music staff of twenty six specialist instrumental and choral teachers who give individual tuition in orchestral instruments to over 500 children every week with orchestras, chamber music ensembles and nine choirs. Twenty specialist sports instructors provide instruction in twenty team and individual sporting activities. Painting, drawing and design all flourish in a strong art department led by specialist staff. Classes are small and, though the school is large, the pastoral and academic care of the pupils is constantly monitored by senior tutors who look after no more than 50-60 children each.

Hill House has always had an annex in Switzerland. The purpose-built house in Glion, 700 metres above Lac Léman, hosts special courses for selected pupils from London, providing experience of a boarding school environment in the setting of a mountain village in the French-speaking canton of Vaud.

Prospective parents are welcome to visit Hans Place any morning of the week during term time between 8.30-9.00am, without appointment, for a tour of the school.

Entry is non selective but admission is only by personal application to a Governor at Hans Place.

Hornsby House School

(Founded 1988)

Hearnville Road, Balham, London SW12 8RS
Tel: 020 8673 7573   Email: school@hornsby-house.co.uk
Fax: 020 8673 6722   Website: www.hornsby-house.co.uk

Head: Mr Jon Gray
Appointed: September 2006
School type: Coeducational Day
Age range of pupils: 4–11
No. of pupils enrolled as at 1.5.10:
Boys: 202 Girls: 183
Fees per annum as at 1.9.10: Day: £11,130–£11,940
Average size of class: 18
Religious denomination: Christian based, Non-denominational

Curriculum

Hornsby House School provides high academic standards within a wide and creative curriculum. Excellent facilities enhance the teaching of ICT, art, music, science and sport, all of which play a central part in the children's education. Before School Club, Homework Club and an extensive range of extracurricular activities are available.

Entry requirements

Entry to reception is on a 'first-come-first-served' basis, with priority for siblings. Places in other year groups are offered following an assessment and meeting with the Headmaster.

The Hornsby House Educational Trust, a registered charity, exists to provide education for boys and girls. (No. 800284)

HOUSE SCHOOLS GROUP

Bassett House School
Kensington

Orchard House School
Chiswick

Prospect House School
Putney/Wandsworth

Bassett House School
60 Bassett Road, London W10 6JP
Tel 020 8969 0313, info@bassetths.org.uk
www.bassetths.org.uk

Orchard House School
16 Newton Grove, Bedford Park, London W4 1LB
Tel 020 8742 8544, info@orchardhs.org.uk
www.orchardhs.org.uk

Prospect House School
75 Putney Hill, London SW15 3NT
Tel 020 8780 0456, info@prospecths.org.uk
www.prospecths.org.uk

Bassett House in Kensington, **Orchard House** in Chiswick and **Prospect House** in Putney are prep schools for children aged three and above. All are member schools of the prestigious IAPS association for prep schools and each participates in the Early Years Grant scheme, which reduces fees charged for children aged under five years old. All three schools are coeducational to age 11 when the children sit competitive entrance exams for their senior schools (although some children occasionally sit entrance exams to other schools at age seven or eight).

The schools are non-selective for younger children, yet the academic expectations are high and the achievement distinguished. We believe this is for two principal reasons. First, we provide at each of our schools a nurturing, positive and happy yet structured environment. We know that happiness and success go hand in hand and we celebrate success at every level and in every sphere of school life, be it in academic work, sport, music or the arts. Secondly we have a low pupil-to-teacher ratio and an abundance of resources. Together these bring out the best in each and every child.

Examination results both at age eight and for senior schools have consistently been excellent: the schools are proud of their hard-won and long-lasting reputations.

Parents usually register their children early to secure places in each school's nursery or reception classes but vacancies in other year groups arise from time to time. It you wish to consider one of these schools for your child, we strongly encourage you to visit us. Please call the school secretary of the relevant school, who will be happy to arrange for you to visit the school and see it in action. In addition, there are occasional open days which give an even greater opportunity to speak to our strongest supporters, namely the children!

L'Ecole de Battersea

Trott Street, Battersea, London SW11 3DS

Head: Mrs F Brisset

Deputy Head: Mr L Balerdi

Principal: Mrs M Otten

School type: Independent Bilingual Pre-Primary and Primary (Ecole Homologuée)

Age range of pupils:
3–11 years, boys and girls

No of pupils enrolled as at 1.9.10:
230 pupils

Fees per annum as at 1.9.10:
£8,730–£8,910

Religious denomination:
All denominations welcome

Entry requirements:
Interview with parents and school tour

L'Ecole de Battersea opened in 2005 following on from the success of its sister school, L'Ecole des Petits. The school is unique in that it offers a **continuous bilingual education from age three through until age eleven** at the end of primary, where both the French and English educational systems operate together. The teaching emphasis throughout the school is fundamentally based on the French system, into which aspects of the English curriculum and methodology are integrated.

The highly motivated bilingual team of teachers are qualified in both the English and French educational systems.

This bilingual facility enables children and parents to choose to progress on to either the English private school system or on to the French Lycée system, and is also ideal for the increasingly popular International Baccalaureate.

The school welcomes bilingual pupils from a range of cultures, and so aims to generate a **truly international atmosphere**.

Partnership with the family is paramount in the school's ethos, and the school successfully seeks **to develop confident and balanced children** with experience of a wide range of activities, an appreciation of artistic and cultural heritage and a thoughtful and considerate attitude towards others.

Class sizes are small and the school occupies a recently refurbished building with **top quality facilities**, and with good outside spaces for a Central London school. The school is only **five minutes drive from Chelsea** and operates a twice daily school bus service between South Kensington and Battersea, as well as a link to its sister school in Fulham, ten minutes distance.

The school is inspected by both the French Inspectorate and Ofsted and achieves excellent academic results. **Ofsted 2008 report said the school offered "*Outstanding quality*"** and it was selected as one of the top private schools in the country in *The Tatler Education Guide 2009*.

TEL 020 7371 8350   admin@lecoledespetits.co.uk   www.lecoledespetits.co.uk

Founded in 1977

L'Ecole des Petits

2 Hazlebury Road, Fulham, London SW6 2NB

Head: Mrs F Brisset

Principal: Mrs M Otten

School type: Independent Bilingual Pre-Primary (Ecole Homologuée)

Age range of pupils:
3–6 years, boys and girls

No of pupils enrolled as at 1.9.10:
136 pupils

Fees per annum as at 1.9.10:
Full day £8,610–£8,910, part day £5,250

Religious denomination:
All denominations welcome

Entry requirements:
Interview with parents and school tour

L'Ecole des Petits is a flourishing pre-primary school situated in Fulham, just **ten minutes from Chelsea**, with easy access by public transport. The school also runs its own daily morning and afternoon **bus service between South Kensington and Fulham**, and between its sister school in Battersea.

The school was founded in 1977 to cater for English and French families who want their children to **grow up in a bilingual environment**. By combining the Early Years curriculum with the French National curriculum, the school provides all aspects of education in both French and English,

and today has a wonderfully **international flavour with children from 22 different countries** attending.

Children are taught by qualified and highly-motivated bilingual teachers. The school aims to provide **an education that enhances early learning skills in the controlled environment of small classes**.

The school has a warm and friendly atmosphere which encourages children to express themselves whilst following the structured bilingual curriculum. We consider maintaining **traditional family values** a very important aspect of our approach.

Our philosophy is to develop confident and happy children by providing **the best possible all-round education and care**, with an abundance of sports, drama, clubs, school outings and events as well as academic lessons.

We prepare our children to move onto both English and French schools, and many also continue their primary education at our sister school, L'Ecole de Battersea.

According to one of our parents, *"This is an exceptional school that provides a nurturing environment, as well as good discipline and a wonderful education, and my child could not be happier and more confident about going to school."*

OFSTED 2009: *"Outstanding School"*.

TEL 020 7371 8350   **admin@lecoledespetits.co.uk**   **www.lecoledespetits.co.uk**

Lion House School

(Founded 1984)

The Old Methodist Hall, Gwendolen Avenue, London SW15 6EH
Tel: 020 8780 9446　　Email: office@lionhouseschool.co.uk
Fax: 020 8789 3331　　Website: www.lionhouseschool.co.uk

Head: Miss H J Luard MontDip
School type: Coeducational Day
Age range of pupils: 2$\frac{1}{2}$–7$\frac{1}{2}$
No. of pupils enrolled as at 1.4.10: 115
Fees per annum as at 1.9.10:
on application
Average size of class: 16-20
Teacher/pupil ratio: 1:8
Religious denomination: Non-denominational

Lion House School is a combined nursery and pre-preparatory situated in the heart of Putney. It is a small, happy school where the children are offered a broad and varied curriculum within a creative environment, preparing them for entrance into a range of preparatory schools. Nursery sessions are flexible and parents may choose a mix of morning, afternoon or full school days. Lion House also offers supervised After School Clubs to assist busy parents who may wish to collect their children later.

Lyndhurst House Prep School

(Founded 1952)

24 Lyndhurst Gardens, Hampstead, London NW3 5NW
Tel: 020 7435 4936   Email: pmg@lyndhursthouse.co.uk
Fax: 020 7794 7124   Website: www.lyndhursthouse.co.uk

**LYNDHURST HOUSE
PREPARATORY SCHOOL**

Headmaster: Andrew Reid MA(Oxon)
Appointed: September 2008
School type: Boys' Day
Age range of pupils: 4–13
No. of pupils enrolled as at 1.4.10: 150
Fees per annum as at 1.4.10: Day: £12,660–£14,160
Average size of class: 14
Teacher/pupil ratio: 1:8

Lyndhurst House Pre-Prep & Prep School for boys was founded by Vernon Davies in 1952, in a tall, handsome Willett-style building in leafy Lyndhurst Gardens, Hampstead.

For the past 58 years Lyndhurst has played a full part in the range of local independent educational provision, sending on its thirteen year olds to the many renowned senior schools in London, and some to boarding further afield with an excellent record of academic success and achievement, matched by a strong participation in sports, music and art.

One of the smaller prep schools in the area, Lyndhurst provides a structured but individually responsive education from reception at four-plus up to Common Entrance and scholarship at 13, delivered by an experienced, well-qualified, and stable staff team, and the abiding characteristics of its pupils seem to be a lively enthusiasm and sense of engagement and belonging. Lyndhurst House is a non-denominational school.

Headmaster Andrew Reid MA(Oxon) looks forward to the school's Diamond Jubilee in 2012, when it will celebrate 60 years of producing happy, confident, well-rounded pupils.

For all enquiries, please contact

Mrs P M Green

Lyndhurst House Preparatory

24 Lyndhurst Gardens

Hampstead

London NW3 5NW

Tel: 020 7435 4936

Email: pmg@lyndhursthouse.co.uk

Website: www.lyndhursthouse.co.uk

We look forward to meeting you.

Newton Prep

(Founded 1991)

149 Battersea Park Road, London SW8 4BX
Tel: 020 7720 4091   Email: admin@newtonprep.co.uk
Fax: 020 7498 9052   Website: www.newtonprep.co.uk

Headmaster: Mr Nicholas M Allen BA, PGCE
Appointed: September 2006
School type: Coeducational Pre-preparatory &
Preparatory Day
Member of: IAPS
Age range of pupils: 3–13
No. of pupils enrolled as at 1.2.10: 517
Boys: 279 Girls: 238
Fees per annum as at 1.2.10: Day: £6420–£12,960
Average size of class: 17
Teacher/pupil ratio: 1:10
Religious denomination: Non-denominational

Newton Prep is a vibrant school which offers a
challenging education for inquisitive children who are
eager to engage fully with the world in which they are
growing up. The school aims to:

- Inspire children to be adventurous and committed in
  their learning.

- Provide balance and breadth in all aspects of a child's
  education: intellectual, aesthetic, physical, moral and
  spiritual.

- Encourage initiative, individuality, independence,
  creativity and enquiry.

- Promote responsible behaviour and respect for others
  in a happy, safe and caring environment.

Entry requirements

Children joining the school in the nursery are assessed
in groups; children joining reception are assessed
individually. Older children spend up to three days in
school, joining regular classes as well as undertaking
tests.

Examinations offered

Entrance examinations to senior schools, Common
Entrance and scholarships at 11 and 13.

Accommodation

The premises are bright and spacious. The school has
expanded above and around the original Victorian
building. The modern extension comprises a further 16
classrooms, a multispace area, two gyms, a dining room,
two art studios and an auditorium. The school has an
all weather pitch and tennis courts as well as a school
garden, all within the one and a half acres that adjoin
the school. Newton Prep has fully equipped science
and ICT suites and a computerised library of over
15,000 books. The extracurricular activities available
include: judo, fencing, yoga, ballet, modern dance,
Mandarin, and speech and drama.

Parkgate House School

(Founded 1987)

80 Clapham Common North Side, London SW4 9SD
Tel: 020 7350 2461   Email: admissions@parkgate-school.co.uk
Fax: 020 7738 1633   Website: www.parkgate-school.co.uk

Principal: Miss C M Shanley
School type: Coeducational Day
Age range of pupils: 2–11 years
No. of pupils enrolled as at 7.1.10: 233
Fees per annum as at 7.1.10: Day: £3960–£10,920
Religious denomination: Non-denominational

Parkgate House School is an independent school educating over 200 children aged from two to 11 years. Residing in a historic Georgian Grade II listed building overlooking Clapham Common, the school is supported by an impressive staff of over forty teaching professionals. Children receive focused attention in one of three specialised areas: the Montessori Nursery for two to four year olds; the Pre-Preparatory Department for those aged four to seven and the Preparatory Department for the seven to 11 age range. At any age, children enjoy an expansive, high quality curriculum, which is further enhanced by an established after-school programme including choir, IT, drama, French, sport and horse riding. A recent Ofsted report praised Parkgate House: 'The quality of the curriculum provided by Parkgate House School is outstanding for pupils of all ages. Pupils thrive as they move through the school.'

Parkgate House School believes that happy, confident children will realise their full potential. The school has high academic expectations of its pupils and is extremely proud of its impressive record of academic success over the years. Pupils are fully prepared for entry into leading senior schools in the London area and beyond. The school has an established record of excellent 11+ examination results where first choice senior school places are achieved, and where art, music and academic scholarships are annually awarded from top London day schools and country boarding schools.

Parkgate House School celebrates success at every level and in every sphere of school life, be it academic, sport, music or the arts. Parents' assemblies provide the school with an excellent opportunity for this, as do annual music recitals, art exhibitions, award ceremonies and drama productions.

For all these reasons you will find Parkgate House a very special and unique school, providing your child with the very best education has to offer.

Queen's College

(Founded 1848)

43-49 Harley Street, London W1G 8BT
Tel: 020 7291 7000   Email: queens@qcl.org.uk
Fax: 020 7291 7099   Website: www.qcl.org.uk

Head: Dr F M R Ramsey MA, DPhil(Oxon)
School type: Girls' Day
Member of: GSA
Age range of pupils: 11–18
No. of pupils enrolled as at 1.3.10: 360
Sixth Form: 90
Fees per term as at 1.3.10: £4470
Average size of class: 15-20 (6-10 in sixth form)
Religious denomination: Church of England

Queen's educates about 360 girls between the ages of 11 and 18 and occupies four large houses in Harley Street. We are academically selective, but not narrowly so, and we place very great importance on the nurture and development of the talents of each individual girl. This is not a school to force anyone into a mould, and we are very proud of that. Our size allows for small classes and close relations between the well-qualified staff and pupils, but we are large enough to be able to offer a wide range of subjects.

Curriculum

The aim at Queen's College is to provide a broad and balanced curriculum. In the second year, girls are given the chance to try each of German, Italian, Japanese, Spanish and Russian; and in the third year they choose one of these to study as their second modern language. Games, gym and dance are also part of the curriculum at this stage. In Year 12 girls usually select four A level subjects. Most then take three subjects in Year 13.

A level subjects offered

Mathematics, further mathematics, physics, chemistry, biology, psychology, English literature, French, German, Italian, Spanish, Russian, Latin, Greek, classical civilisation, economics, geography, government and politics, history, history of art, religious studies, art, textiles, music, theatre studies.

Entry requirements

The main points of admission are at 11+ and 16+. Vacancies may occur at other stages. Admission at 11+ is on the basis of an interview, a reference from the candidate's school, and examinations in mathematics and English. Admission at 16+ is on the basis of an interview and a reference from the candidate's current school, and good performance at GCSE.

Scholarships and bursaries

Academic, music and art scholarships are available at 11+ and 16+. A means-tested bursary can provide up to 100% remission of fees, depending on financial circumstances.

Redcliffe School Trust Ltd

(Founded 1948)

47 Redcliffe Gardens, Chelsea, London SW10 9JH
Tel: 020 7352 9247   Email: admissions@redcliffeschool.com
Fax: 020 7352 6936   Website: www.redcliffeschool.com

Head: Mrs Susan Bourne BSc, PGCE
School type: Coeducational Day
Member of: IAPS
Age range of pupils:
Boys: 2½–8
Girls: 2½–11
No. of pupils enrolled as at 1.5.10:
Boys: 43 Girls: 92
Fees per annum as at 1.5.10: Day: £11,280
Nursery: £6480 morning class–£4320 afternoon class
Teacher/pupil ratio: 1:16

Easily accessible from all parts of central and West London, Redcliffe is a small, friendly school with highly motivated, confident and happy children. In September 2007 Redcliffe School expanded and now occupies both number 47 Redcliffe Gardens and the under croft of St Luke's Church in Redcliffe Square, where the classrooms for the lower school are situated. Emphasis is placed on a good combination of hard work and plenty of fun within a framework of discipline and good manners. The balanced curriculum includes mathematics, English, history, geography, science, IT, art and craft, scripture, current affairs, music, physical education and drama. French is taught throughout the school. Individual attention encourages the pursuit of high academic standards and we are proud that our children gain places at their first choice of senior or prep school, including Colet Court, Sussex House, St Philip's, Downe House, Benenden, Queen's Gate, Godolphin and Latymer and Francis Holland. Every class has some form of physical education each day; in the gym or playground, local netball court or park. A varied programme of sporting activities is available; changing each term and taught by a specialist sports teacher. Current activities include football, gymnastics, swimming and netball. After school activities include swimming, ballet and drama. Music is a strength of the school with visiting instrumental staff and a high standard of performance. Parents are encouraged to be involved with the school through open assemblies, parents' discussion groups, the Parents' Committee and regular meetings with the teachers.

Redcliffe School Trust is a registered charity and provides a high standard of education for children within a caring environment. (Charity No: 312716).

Montessori Nursery and Pre-Preparatory School
For Boys and Girls between 2 and 11 years

- Small School
- Small Classes
- Academic Excellence
- Catholic Ethos
- French CNED Curriculum
- Extra Curricular Activities
- Breakfast Clubs
  & After School Clubs

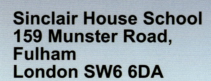

Sinclair House School
159 Munster Road,
Fulham
London SW6 6DA

Telephone: 020 7736 9182
Facsimile: 020 7371 0295
Website: www.sinclairhouseschool.co.uk
Email: info@sinclairhouseschool.co.uk

Principal: Mrs Carlotta TM O'Sullivan

St Mary's School Hampstead

(Founded 1926)

47 Fitzjohn's Avenue, Hampstead, London NW3 6PG
Tel: 020 7435 1868   Email: enquiries@stmh.co.uk
Fax: 020 7794 7922   Website: www.stmh.co.uk

Head: Miss Angela Rawlinson BA, MA(1st Class Honours), DipTchng, NPQH
Appointed: April 2004
School type: Coeducational Day
Member of: IAPS, AGBIS, CISC, ISBA
Age range of pupils: 2 years 9 months–11 years
No. of pupils enrolled as at 1.1.10: 287
Boys: 27 Girls: 260
Fees per annum as at 1.1.10: Day: £5550–£10,920
Average size of class: 20 max
Teacher/pupil ratio: 1:16
Religious denomination: Roman Catholic

We have a thriving nursery. The boys are prepared for transference to popular London boys' preparatory schools.

The girls are prepared for the Common Entrance and the entrance examinations for the London senior schools at the age of 11 years. Pupils enjoy a broad curriculum and also benefit from a wider range of activities which is seen as essential to the rounded development of a healthy child. Importance is attached to physical education, drama and the arts. Extracurriculum classes include speech and drama, ballet, violin, recorder and piano. School trips abroad are arranged for older children.

This Roman Catholic School is a registered charity (No. 1006411) which exists to provide a high standard of preparatory education for girls and boys, and is managed by a majority of Lay Trustees and Governors.

ST MARY S SCHOOL HAMPSTEAD

St Benedict's School

(Founded 1902)

54 Eaton Rise, Ealing, London W5 2ES
Tel: 020 8862 2000   Email: enquiries@stbenedicts.org.uk
Fax: 020 8862 2199   Website: www.stbenedicts.org.uk

Headmaster: Mr C J Cleugh BSc, MSc
Appointed: January 2002
School type: Coeducational Day
Age range of pupils: 3–18
No. of pupils enrolled as at 1.1.10: 987
Boys: 786 Girls: 201 Sixth Form: 180
Fees per annum as at 1.1.10: Day: £10,320–£11,760
Average size of class: max 24 (sixth form max 14)
Teacher/pupil ratio: 1:10.8

Since its foundation in 1902 the name of St Benedict's has resonated with its distinctive blend of history, tradition and academic excellence. Its strengths and opportunities are now open to both girls and boys across all years. Our mission, *Teaching a way of living*, defines us uniquely as a Benedictine school. We respect the dignity of all and welcome pupils of other Christian denominations and, in the senior school, other faiths.

This is a new and exciting phase in the proud history of our school, one that has been facilitated by a £10 million rebuilding programme in which we fuse our heritage with state-of-the-art facilities and technology.

The school is now fully coeducational from three years through to 18.

The junior school and nursery provide a fun, friendly, vibrant coeducational environment. Your child's educational journey begins and the seeds of our Benedictine ethos are planted, nurtured and given every opportunity to flourish. In the nursery a carefully planned and child-centred programme based on the Early Years' Foundation Stage Curriculum, enables and extends learning. The junior school provides a broad and balanced curriculum based on a rigorous academic core and with extensive opportunities in music, art,

sport and drama. Sharing excellent facilities with the senior school and participating in cross-curricular activities helps ease the transition at 11+.

In the senior school pupils are encouraged to think and express themselves creatively, to work independently, to take pride in all their achievements and to enjoy the rewards that scholarship brings. High standards are expected, but our pupils are not just educated - they are given the tools with which to attain knowledge and wisdom. In the sixth form students are encouraged to take on leadership roles and all contribute to a variety of projects, which raise funds for communities across the world. We have a strong record of success at Oxbridge entrance.

The main sports for boys are rugby and cricket, while for girls it is netball and tennis in the senior school and netball and rounders in the junior school. The school's sports ground at Perivale boasts 14 acres of playing fields, supplemented by a magnificent pavilion opened in 2005. A new multi-purpose sports pitch was completed in 2008. St Benedict's enjoys a national reputation for rugby.

A rich and varied co-curricular programme is offered. The junior school runs a 'Hobbies' programme each evening, while in the senior school there are more than 70 clubs and societies. There are numerous excursions undertaken to places of interest in London and around the country and abroad. The school has a strong tradition in drama and music, with regular productions and concerts.

We invite you to come and visit our school and see for yourselves the many opportunities that exist here. You can be sure of a warm Benedictine welcome.

St Nicholas Preparatory School

23 Princes Gate, Kensington, London SW7 1PT
Tel: 020 7225 1277   Email: info@stnicholasprep.co.uk
Fax: 020 7823 7557   Website: www.stnicholasprep.co.uk

Head: Mr David Wilson MA, BEd, Dip TEFL
Appointed: September 1999
Deputy Head: Ms Clare Deighton BA Ed(Hons)
School type: Coeducational Pre-preparatory &
Preparatory Day
Age range of pupils: 2 years 9 months–11+ years
No. of pupils enrolled as at 1.5.10: 280
Fees per annum as at 1.5.10: Day: £11,055–£12,630

St Nicholas Preparatory School is a coeducational day school situated opposite Hyde Park. It has had a flourishing Montessori nursery, a pre-prep and a prep department since September 1999.

The school is equipped with first rate facilities for information technology and science with an extensive library and benefits from a large three acre communal garden with direct access from the school.

Pupils enjoy a balanced, modern, widely-based curriculum and are prepared for selective entry to senior schools. Creative subjects and a full range of sporting activities are offered.

If you would like further information please contact the School Secretary.

The school also benefits from its own gymnasium and ballet floor, and we are within walking distance of the Science Museum, the V & A Museum and other famous places of interest.

For French nationals the school is able to offer the CNED programme for children in CE1, CE2, CM1 and CM2.

Studio Day Nursery

91-93 Moore Park Road, Fulham, London SW6 2DA
Tel: 020 7736 9256

Head: Miss J M R Williams NNEB, RSH(Norlander)
School type: Coeducational Day
Age range of pupils: 2–5
No. of pupils enrolled as at 1.9.09:
Up to 50
Fees per annum as at 1.9.09:
per session: morning: £22
afternoon: £17
full day: £40

The Studio Day Nursery offers excellent all-round care combined with a strong educational programme including special needs.

Open 8am to 7pm all year, except between Christmas and New Year.

Activities include reading, writing, maths, cooking, project work, art, drama, natural studies and games during visits to the park.

Montessori and traditional methods taught by qualified teachers.

A happy stimulating environment for boys and girls.

Ofsted Inspected. Early Years Grant available.

The Cavendish School

(Founded 1875)

31 Inverness Street, Camden Town, London NW1 7HB
Tel: 020 7485 1958   Email: admissions@cavendish-school.co.uk
Fax: 020 7267 0098   Website: www.cavendishschool.co.uk

Headmistress: Mrs T Dunbar BSc(Hons), PGCE, NPQH
Appointed: April 2007
Chair of Governors: Mrs M Robey
School type: Girls' Day
Member of: IAPS
Age range of pupils: 3–11
No. of pupils enrolled as at 1.9.10: 190
Fees per annum as at 1.9.10: Day: £11,250
Nursery: £5700–£10,650

The Cavendish School is a small, friendly IAPS school for girls age three to 11 with limited places available for sibling boys in the ages three to seven. The school is situated near Regent's Park but still in the heart of Camden Town with its excellent public transport links. The Cavendish has a Christian ethos and welcomes pupils of all faiths.

Strong yet informal links between home and school are maintained and we pride ourselves on the high level of our pastoral care and attention to each child's individual needs.

The school is non-selective at entry. We provide manageable class sizes and high teacher-pupils ratios so that the foundations of a good education and effective study habits are laid from the beginning.

Through a broad and balanced curriculum we provide personalised learning and much specialised teaching which allows our pupils to flourish and many gain entry and scholarships to top senior schools at 11+.

There is an extensive programme of extracurricular activities, after-school care services and flexible arrangements for nursery-age pupils.

Our strengths in music and art are reflected in the renewal of our Artsmark Gold in 2009 by the Arts Council of England. Class music is taught by specialists, instruction is available in a wide variety of instruments and we have a thriving orchestra and choir.

The school is housed in well maintained Victorian buildings and a modern wing which houses purpose-built ICT facilities.

The school maintains close links with the local community in a variety of ways both charitable and educational.

Our most recent inspection report by the Independent School Inspectorate is very complimentary and is well worth reading.

The Cavendish School Charitable Trust, a registered charity, is proud of its recent interim ISC inspection. (No. 312727)

The Lloyd Williamson School

(Founded 2000)

12 Telford Road, London W10 5SH
Tel: 020 8962 0345   Email: lloydwilliamsonschools@yahoo.co.uk
Fax: 020 8962 0345   Website: www.lloydwilliamsonschools.co.uk

Co-Principals: Lucy Meyer & Aaron Williams
Appointed: April 2000 & Sept 2006
School type: Coeducational Day
Age range of pupils: 6 months–14 years
Fees per annum as at 1.1.10: Day: £9705
Average size of class: 12-16
Teacher/pupil ratio: 1:12

Over the past ten years, the Lloyd Williamson School has built an excellent reputation for being a school with high academic standards, personalised learning for individual children and a friendly, happy environment in which to learn. We foster initiative and a love for learning. 'Outstanding' (Ofsted).

We are pleased to offer parents important extras:

- Breakfast and after-school clubs at NO extra cost (the school and nurseries are open 7.30am - 6.00pm).
- Holiday clubs (we are open 50 weeks of the year).
- Small classes (maximum of 16).
- Competitive fees.
- Home-cooked meals freshly prepared every day by our in-house chefs.

We boast an outstanding playground with excellent facilities, a homely atmosphere with school pets, and dedicated teachers who support the children to be focused, positive and enthusiastic.

'Throughout the school, relationships between staff and children are excellent, which gives the pupils security and confidence to succeed.' (Ofsted)

In the words of our children:

"I'm really happy here - the teachers really listen and if I get stuck they help!"

"I really like the sports; we have a great football team!"

"There is always someone who listens to me."

"I like the way the big children look after the little children."

And the parents:

"You always know a Lloyd Williamson child - they're so polite!"

"I think the school is, beyond doubt, the best I could wish for."

"The best-kept secret in London!"

To visit the school or nurseries, please contact the school administrator, Emma Cole on: 020 8962 0345.

The North London International School

(Founded 1885)

6 Friern Barnet Lane, London N11 3LX
Tel: +44 (0)20 8920 0600 Email: admissions@nlis.org
Fax: +44 (0)20 8211 4605   Website: www.nlis.org

Head of School: Mr David Rose MA(Ed), BA, CertEd
School type: Coeducational International Day
Homestay available for students age 16-19
Member of: ISA, ECIS, IAPS, LISA, IB, ISCis
Age range of pupils: 2–19
No. of pupils enrolled as at 1.5.10: 400
Kindergarten (ages 2-4): 20 boys 17 girls
Lower School (ages 4-6): 26 boys 16 girls
Lower School (ages 6-11): 87 boys 52 girls
Upper School (ages 11-16): 109 boys 48 girls
Upper School (ages 16-19): 25 boys 15 girls
Fees per annum as at 1.5.10: Day: £3225–£15,480
Religious denomination: Inter-denominational

Curriculum

The North London International School aims to provide a secure, well-ordered and happy environment with the learning process at its core, offering the finest possible education for all pupils in order for them to reach their full potential. Serving a cosmopolitan and diverse north London community, great importance is attached to respect, understanding and empathy with everyone's cultures, religions and backgrounds.

Students follow the International Baccalaureate (IB) curriculum, starting at aged three with the Primary Years Programme, moving onto the Middle Years Programme at age 11 and the IB Diploma Programme at age 16. The programmes are designed to encourage the development of learning skills and to meet a child's academic, social, physical, emotional and cultural needs. Through enquiry-based learning and various disciplines, subject interrelatedness is accentuated, preparing students for the pre-university Diploma Programme.

The school recognises that students can have a variety of different learning styles. The Quest Programme is designed for students who need help developing strategies to assist them to study effectively. Through one-to-one tuition from specialist staff, students can reach their full potential, further enhanced by the school's teacher-student ratio.

Entry requirements

Students are accepted for entry at any time throughout the school year.

Kindergarten and Lower School (ages two to 11): students are invited to attend for half a day and may be asked to complete a basic assessment.

Upper School (ages 11-16): students attend an interview with the Head of the school, are invited to visit the school for a day and may be required to complete a basic assessment.

Entry to the upper school is automatic for students in the lower school.

Upper School (ages 16-19): Diploma Programme applicants are invited for interview with the programme coordinator. Students would be expected to have five or six GCSE passes, with B, A or A* grades for subjects to be studied at Higher Level.

Examinations offered

Key Stage 2, IBMYP and IB Diploma.

Facilities

The school has dedicated IT, music, art and design technology facilities for all students. The commitment to the use of ICT in all subject areas is highlighted by IT and graphics suites, individual student home drives and email accounts, student dedicated laptops and wireless network.

Students' physical development is considered as important as academic development and the school's sports fields provide excellent facilities for football, cricket, athletics, hockey, tennis and softball. The school's hall, playgrounds and local amenities are also utilised to offer further activities such as basketball, badminton, squash, swimming, table tennis, ice-skating and skiing. Matches and tournaments between local schools are regular fixtures.

The school is able to provide a bus service for students living in the local area in addition to the excellent bus, tube and train routes from the rest of London and the surrounding area.

The Roche School

(Founded 1988)

11 Frogmore, London SW18 1HW
Tel: 020 8877 0823 Email: office@therocheschool.co.uk
Fax: 020 8875 1156 Website: www.therocheschool.co.uk

Principal: J A Roche BSc, PhD
Head: Mrs Vania Adams BA(Hons), PGCE, MA
School type: Coeducational Day
Age range of pupils: 2–11
No. of pupils enrolled as at 1.1.10: 190
Boys: 95 Girls: 95
Fees per annum as at 1.1.10: Day: £9450–£10,230
Average size of class: 18
Teacher/pupil ratio: 1:9
Religious denomination: Christian

Curriculum

The Roche School aims to offer children good teaching and a wide variety of opportunities, academic, artistic and sporting, in a pleasant, homely atmosphere in which children feel free to express themselves. We take care that the styles of teaching should match the children's different levels of understanding and stimulate each child to make the best possible progress. The school is proud of its academic reputation and seeks to build on it.

French is taught throughout the school.

Entry requirements

Prospective pupils spend a morning in class during which their work is assessed. There is no testing at nursery and reception entry.

Examinations offered

Children are prepared for 7+, 8+ and 11+ examinations to other schools.

The Royal School, Hampstead

(Founded 1855)

65 Rosslyn Hill, Hampstead, London NW3 5UD
Tel: 020 7794 7708   Email: enquiries@royalschoolhampstead.net
Fax: 020 7431 6741   Website: www.royalschoolhampstead.net

Headmistress: Ms J Ebner BEd(Hons)(Cantab), MA(London), PGDipCouns, Cert FT, NPQH
Appointed: September 2006
School type: Girls' Day & Boarding
Age range of pupils: 3–16
No. of pupils enrolled as at 1.4.10: 210
No. of boarders: 25
Fees per annum as at 1.4.10: Day: £8940–£10,500
Weekly Boarding: £15,870
Boarding: £20,700
Average size of class: 16 average
Teacher/pupil ratio: 1:9

The Royal School is a small, friendly day and boarding school for girls set in a modern, safe and spacious campus conveniently located in the heart of Hampstead.

Founded by Queen Victoria in 1855 the school enjoys royal patronage from HRH The Duchess of Cornwall and provides a remarkable educational experience.

This unique girls-only education allows pupils to achieve their full potential academically, emotionally, creatively and physically whilst building friendships that last a lifetime.

The first school (age three to seven) lays the early years foundation teaching through play-based activities in a nurturing environment.

The lower school (seven to 11) encourages girls to gain independence and a love of learning. Music, French, drama, PE and ICT are taught by specialists. Girls also enjoy sewing, food technology and cooking in our excellent new design & technology facility.

The middle school (11-14) offers a broad, balanced curriculum. Whilst exploring traditional subjects girls are also allowed to pursue other areas that enrich their knowledge of the world around them. Extensive extracurricular activities are available including photography, drama, sports, music, nature and art clubs.

The upper school (14-16) encourages maturity and academic success through building responsibility and

confidence. A wide range of GCSE subjects are offered alongside tailor-made curriculums such as sociology GCSE. Many opportunities are open to girls including becoming prefects, or Childline Counsellors. Academic results are excellent and guidance is given for sixth form choices. We have alliances with excellent GSA schools and many colleges.

We welcome boarders from the UK and overseas alongside flexi-boarding; a boon for parents in today's busy world. Boarders enjoy a friendly atmosphere in spacious accommodation with superb views. Our dedicated boarding staff ensure the girls are safe and well cared for whilst enjoying enriching activities such as crafts, films, shopping, theatre trips and more.

Bursaries are available.

THE VILLAGE SCHOOL

2 Parkhill Road • Belsize Park • NW3 2YN • 020 7485 4673
www.thevillageschool.co.uk

Head: Miss C E F Gay BSc (Hons), PGCE
Appointed: September 2007
School type: Girl's Preparatory Day

Age range of pupils: 3-11
No of pupils enrolled as at 1.09.10: 98
Fees per annum as at 1.09.10: £11,430

We are an academic school in Belsize Park. We encourage individual achievement in a happy, creative environment.

Welcome to Pre-Preparatory

A caring, stimulating place for children aged 3+

- We believe in the individuality of each child and learning as a collaborative process tailored to their unique interests.
- We are committed to delivering the broadest curriculum.
- We believe learning should be fun.

All areas of development are delivered through planned, purposeful play situations with encouragement at all time towards spontaneous and independent activity.

- Academic success is achieved through a stimulating, inspiring curriculum and specialist subject teaching.
- Success continues to be gained in the entrance examinations to independent secondary schools, averaging 3 offers per pupil in 2010 and 100% first choice places attained.
- We offer an outstanding range of after-school activities.
- The sports curriculum includes netball and tennis on our own floodlit courts, with rounders, cricket and rugby on nearby Hampstead Heath.
- Easter and Summer holiday clubs.
- There is a school bus scheme.

Regular open afternoons, please contact the school secretary.
Come and find out what makes us so special.

Schools in Greater London

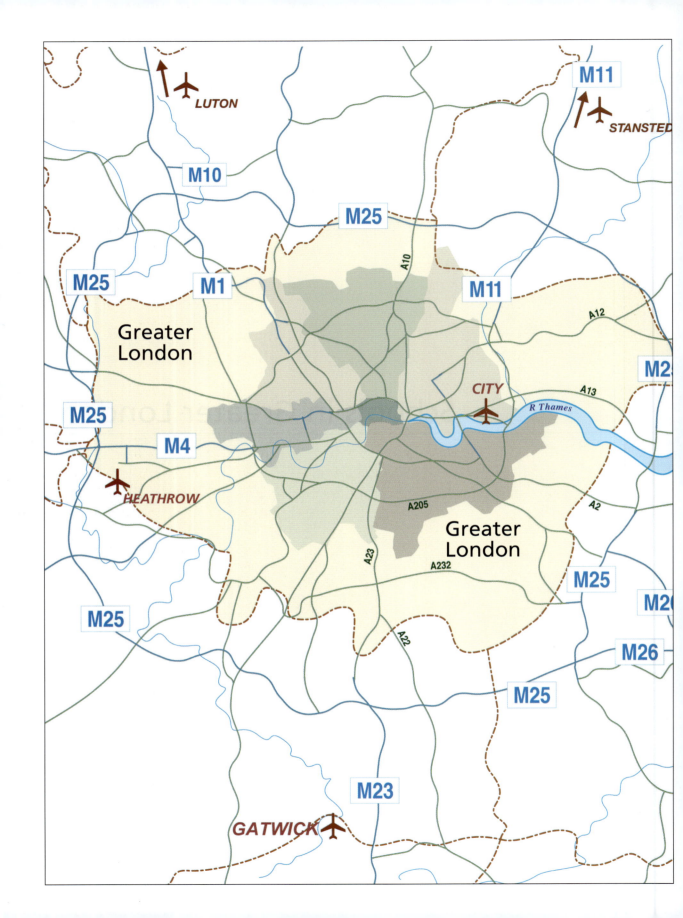

Bromley High School GDST

(Founded 1883)

Blackbrook Lane, Bickley, Bromley, Kent BR1 2TW
Tel: 020 8468 7000   Email: bhs@bro.gdst.net
Fax: 020 8295 1062   Website: www.bromleyhigh.gdst.net

FIDES et OPERA

Head: Mrs Louise Simpson BSc(UCW)
Appointed: January 2010
Head of Junior Department: Mrs Ellen Hill BEd(Sussex)
School type: Independent Selective Day School for Girls
Age range of pupils: 4–18
No. of pupils enrolled as at 1.4.10: 894
Sixth Form: 125
Senior School (ages 11-18): 600 (including the Sixth Form)
Junior School (ages 4-11): 312
Fees per annum as at 1.4.10: Day: £9027–£11,601
Average size of class: 20-25

When I ask parents why they chose Bromley High for their daughters they are unanimous in their response; because they want the best for her. We are proud that Bromley is able to offer such a high standard of education in so many fields but it's not just us that think this...

The ISI inspection report, published in February 2010 was clear in its judgements:

- Excellent attainment - with high A level and GCSE scores even when compared to pupils in highly selective schools.

- Excellent pastoral care for pupils, delivered by experienced staff who are specialists in the education of girls.

- Excellent personal development from pupils - encouraged by their involvement in a wide range of leadership opportunities and community projects.

- A school that is enhanced by a rich and diverse range of extracurricular activities that the girls participate in with energy and enthusiasm - our outstanding theatrical, musical and dance performances and our strength on the games pitches are clear indicators of this.

- Excellent leadership and management, supported by experienced and very effective teachers with the skills to teach lessons of outstanding quality.

- And judged as being outstanding in all areas for our Early Years Foundation Stage education.

The education that we provide is broad, balanced and, most important, personalised. Girls are guided, challenged and enthused by our teaching staff, they are supported and cared for by each other and by the school's high quality pastoral care and we as a school are supported by our membership of the Girls' Day School Trust - the largest group of independent schools in the country.

As a flagship member of the Trust we are lucky to have superb facilities to support all aspects of school life and as such our girls can achieve in any area that they are passionate about. Whether your daughter's skills lie in the swimming pool, an operating theatre, the drama studio, dance productions, a maths classroom or in a debating chamber, we will find out what makes her tick and will encourage her to be the best that she can be.

Please contact the school via our website; www.bromleyhigh.gdst.net or our admissions office on admissions@bro.gdst.net or Tel 020 8781 7000 for more information and to arrange a visit.

We look forward to meeting you.

ACS Hillingdon International School

Hillingdon Court, 108 Vine Lane, Hillingdon, Uxbridge, Middlesex UB10 0BE
Tel: 01895 259 771   Email: hillingdonadmissions@acs-england.co.uk
Fax: 01895 818 404   Website: www.acs-england.co.uk

Head of School: Ginger Apple
IB Co-ordinator: Chris Green
School type: Coeducational Day
Accredited by: NEASC
Authorised by: IB
Member of: ECIS, CIS, US College Board AP
Program, ISA
Age range of pupils: 4–18
Lower School: 4–9
Middle School: 10-13–High School: 14-18
No. of pupils enrolled as at 1.4.10: 539
Boys: 280 Girls: 259
Fees per annum as at 1.4.10: Day: £8820–£18,560
Average size of class: 20 max
Teacher/pupil ratio: 1:9

Enrolling students from over 40 countries, ACS Hillingdon International School is a school which strongly values partnerships among parents, teachers and students. Our philosophy actively encourages a sense of teamwork and aims to set a challenging yet achievable academic standard. We believe in meeting the developmental needs of our students by providing a balanced educational programme and preparing them to take their places in our ever-changing world. Although there is no formal entrance exam, ACS Hillingdon is a university-preparatory school, sending its students to some of the finest universities in the world. We are non-sectarian and located within easy commuting distance of central London.

Academic programme

- ACS Hillingdon is an International Baccalaureate (IB) World School, offering the IB Diploma Programme, and the IB Middle Years Programme (as a candidate school).

- ACS Hillingdon offers a traditional American High School Diploma, including prestigious Advanced Placement (AP) courses.

- ACS Hillingdon graduates attend leading universities around the world including: Cambridge, Imperial College, King's College, London School of Economics, Oxford, Royal Veterinary College and St George's Hospital

Medical School in the UK; Pennsylvania State University, Purdue, Texas A & M, Tufts University and the US Air Force Academy in the USA; and leading universities in other countries such as Canada, Japan, the Netherlands and Sweden.

- Small class sizes facilitate multi-level teaching academic challenge and a focus on individual student learning styles.

Faculty

- The faculty includes over 73 full-time teachers, all holding university degrees; approximately one-half have advanced degrees.

- All teachers have a minimum of two years' teaching experience.

- On average, teachers remain with ACS for eight years.

- The student to teacher ratio is approximately 9:1.

The campus

- ACS Hillingdon is located 15 miles west of central London with Underground rail access, on an 11-acre site set in parkland.

- The excellent facilities are augmented by a new music centre, complete with digital recording studio, rehearsal rooms, practice studios and a computer lab for music technology.

- The campus has on-site playing fields, tennis courts and playgrounds with additional off-site soccer, rugby, track, baseball, softball, swimming and golf facilities available.

- Door-to-door and shuttle bus services are available for much of central London, west London and Middlesex from Maidenhead to Westminster.

Student activities

- A full range of sports including basketball, tennis, soccer, rugby, swimming, baseball, softball, track and field, cross country and volleyball.

- Extracurricular activities include Student Council, Model United Nations, yearbook, music, art, drama, computers, languages and recycling.

Other campuses

ACS Hillingdon is one of the ACS International Schools which enrol over 2500 students aged between two and 18 from over 60 countries, speaking 30 languages. Based on international and American research, principles and educational practices, the schools are committed to maintaining the highest standards of scholarship and citizenship. The two additional campuses are located in Surrey:

- ACS Cobham International School is located on a 128-acre site 23 miles from central London. The school has a boarding programme, premier sports facilities, and purpose-built facilities for early childhood, lower, middle and high schools.

- ACS Egham International School is located on a 20-acre site 25 miles from central London. It is one of only three schools in the UK to offer the IB Primary Years Programme (ages three to 11) and the IB Middle Years Programme (ages 11-16) in addition to the International Baccalaureate Diploma Programme.

Admission

Admissions officers are available throughout the year to speak with you about possible enrolment. Visits can be arranged on weekdays or weekends to suit your schedule, and application for enrolment can now be made online, via our website.

- Applicants do not need to sit a formal entrance exam.

- New students are accepted in all grades throughout the year.

- Application forms, teacher references and previous school records are required for entry.

Heathfield School GDST

(Founded 1900)

Beaulieu Drive, Pinner, Middlesex HA5 1NB
Tel: 020 8868 2346   Email: enquiries@hea.gdst.net
Fax: 020 8868 4405   Website: www.heathfield.gdst.net

Head: Christine Juett BSc(Hons), PGCE, (Member of ASCL)
Appointed: January 1997
Head of Junior School: Carole McCulloch BA(Leeds), BSc(Hons), FRSC
School type: Girls' Day
Member of: GDST, GSA, AGBIS, ISCis, ACE, ISCO, ISDTA, ISC
Age range of pupils: 3–18
No. of pupils enrolled as at 1.1.10: 533
Sixth Form: 85
Fees per annum as at 1.1.10: Day: £6966–£11,601
Religious denomination: Non-denominational

Heathfield School, Pinner, is located in the exclusive suburbs of west London, with excellent transport links. The school is sited amongst extensive playing fields and has undertaken extensive building work to house new science laboratories; specialist music school; ICT suites; art, textiles and drama studios; learning resources centre; careers centre and sports centre with indoor swimming pool.

Our foundations date back to 1900 and we are a well-established independent school for girls forming part of the Girls' Day School Trust, existing to provide a fine academic education at a comparatively modest cost. Heathfield caters for girls from three to 18 years,

with an intake at three, four, 11 and 16 years of age. Study continues at university.

Our distinctive offer places a particular emphasis on preparing girls for the changing world of work and the global economy. Hence, there are many opportunities, both within and beyond the curriculum, to develop enterprise and leadership skills as well as developing an international outlook, including learning Mandarin. In 2008, the International School Award was given to the school.

Academic standards are well above national levels with 100% pass rates at A level and GCSE. Emphasis is placed on high academic standards, in addition to providing the girls with a sense of responsibility, self confidence and concern for others. Individual needs of each girl are met through tutorial systems and pastoral care.

There are high standards in sport, music, drama and art and Heathfield has achieved national recognition awards. Private tuition is offered in music, ballet, speech and drama, leading to recognized qualifications such as the Associated Board of the Royal Schools of Music with girls achieving high grades. The school has received both the Artsmark and Sportsmark Awards.

Curricular visits in Britain and abroad and an extensive range of extracurricular activities are on offer. Girls are encouraged to participate in the Duke of Edinburgh's Award Scheme, Young Enterprise and public speaking competitions.

As part of our service, coaches are arranged in the following pick-up areas: Ealing, Perivale, Greenford, Northolt, Wembley, Kingsbury, Kenton and Harrow.

Scholarships and bursaries are available within the senior school.

The Girls' Day School Trust is a registered charity which exists to provide a high quality education for girls of intellectual promise at a very competitive cost. (No. 306983)

Lyonsdown School Trust

(Founded 1906)

3 Richmond Road, New Barnet, Barnet, Hertfordshire EN5 1SA
Tel: 020 8449 0225   Email: enquiries@lyonsdownschool.co.uk
Fax: 020 8441 4690   Website: www.lyonsdownschool.co.uk

Head: Mrs L Maggs-Wellings BEd
Appointed: September 2005
School type: Independent Coeducational Day
Age range of pupils:
Boys: 3–7
Girls: 3–11
No. of pupils enrolled as at 1.9.09: 210
Boys: 43 Girls: 167
(inc pre-school)
Fees per annum as at 1.9.09: Day: £2835–£7206
Average size of class: 16-20
Teacher/pupil ratio: 1:15
Religious denomination: Christian Foundation (but all faiths welcome)

Curriculum

Pupils are nurtured by an experienced and caring staff who help them to maximise their potential. The school has a tradition of high academic standards and achievements within a broad and balanced curriculum.

Music tuition is available for a selection of instruments, as are speech, chess and drama lessons. There is a wide range of extracurricular clubs covering sports and creative activities and we also undertake numerous field trips and educational visits.

Entry requirements

Places in the pre-school are allocated from a waiting list at the age of three. Additional entry into reception is also non-selective. Early registration is recommended as pressure for places is high. There are occasional places available at other stages, when entry is by assessment and interview.

Lyonsdown School Trust Ltd, a registered charity (No. 312591), aims to keep fees low in order to make independent education available to a wider spectrum of children.

Northwood College

(Founded 1878)

Maxwell Road, Northwood, Middlesex HA6 2YE
Tel: 01923 825446   Email: admissions@northwoodcollege.co.uk
Fax: 01923 836526   Website: www.northwoodcollege.co.uk

discover > learn > succeed

discover   >   learn   >   succeed

Head: Miss Jacqualyn Pain MA, MA, MBA
Appointed: January 2009
School type: Girls' Day
Member of: GSA, IAPS
Age range of pupils: 3–18
No. of pupils enrolled as at 1.9.10: 820
Sixth Form: 125
Fees per annum as at 1.9.10: Day: £7650–£12,600

About us

Northwood College is an academic school for girls aged three to 18 in north-west London. We focus on raising young women who know their own minds and are creative and flexible thinkers, as well as being able to achieve outstanding exam results.

We are academically selective, but not narrowly exclusive. We value girls for more than simple academic performance, because our unique approach to advanced thinking skills means that we can develop, stretch and challenge every single one of them. We think that makes for a more interesting and vibrant school community - and it's what makes Northwood College special.

Thinking skills

Our approach to thinking skills is another one of our defining characteristics. It sets Northwood College apart, and gives our girls an edge in the way they approach any task or challenge. Our Thinking Skills Programme is led by C J Simister, who has taught at Northwood College for many years and is a renowned expert, author and consultant on cognitive development. Through the programme, we ensure our girls start to understand and develop the way they think from the day they join nursery through to the end of the sixth form. Over the years, they build up their reasoning skills, improve their creativity and acquire strategies for tackling complex problems and decisions. It gives them a life skill that will be as useful at university and in the workplace as it is at school.

Curriculum and results

All National Curriculum subjects are taught, plus Latin, classics and drama. In addition, girls in Year 7 study two modern foreign languages, chosen from French, German and Spanish.

Our girls achieve outstanding results: for the past six years the A level pass rate has been 100%, with nearly 80% at A & B grades in 2009. At GCSE our pass rate was 98.1% and more than three quarters of our girls achieved more than five A or A* grades. In recent years, Northwood College girls have achieved top five marks nationally in English Literature (AQA) and Drama (AQA) and top ten marks nationally in IGCSE Mathematics, English Literature (AQA), Biology and Physics (Edexcel).

Pupil wellbeing

It is a central tenet of Northwood College that girls achieve their best when they are happy. We look after the whole person in school life, helping girls stay healthy in body and mind, and develop a strong sense of self-esteem and responsibility towards others and the world around them. So for example we have well-developed buddying and peer mentoring schemes to make sure girls feel cared-for and look out for each other.

We were also recently awarded Healthy Schools status by our local Borough. Our catering department serves delicious, nutritious food that the girls love - and that helps them develop good eating habits. We also take care of the environment, recycling much of our waste, using recycled products and keeping our carbon footprint as low as we can.

Grounds and facilities

All sections of the college from nursery to junior school to senior school and sixth form, share the same 14-acre site. It's a beautiful green environment with many specialist facilities, including nine science labs, five IT rooms, three art studios, food technology and design technology rooms, a large sports hall, all weather surface, fitness suite, 25-metre indoor swimming pool and a fantastic Performing Arts Centre, comprising a recital room, drama studio, numerous practice and classrooms, a music technology suite, with the latest Apple Mac computers and a professional recording studio. The girls love it.

Our spectacular library, one of the learning hubs of the college, also deserves a special mention. Occupying the school's original vaulted gymnasium, the Centenary Library has more than 11,000 books and a wealth of other resources. Our passionate, full-time Chartered Librarian runs book clubs, arranges talks by well-known authors and inspires the girls with a love of reading.

Early Years Centre

The youngest Northwood College pupils (nursery and reception) have their own brand new Early Years Centre within the college grounds. Everything in the centre is designed with young children in mind, including low level windows so they can see out, a covered verandah for outside learning, a sensory garden and an adventure playground.

Entry requirements and scholarships

Entry to the college is by examination and interview, except for nursery, which uses a play-based assessment. At 11+ we use the North London Girls' Schools Consortium exam and offer academic scholarships to the highest performing girls in this exam. Girls also do an online test and group activity. We also offer Art, Music and Sport Scholarships at 11+ to girls with particular talent in these fields. Entry to the sixth form is by GCSE results, interview and online test. There are also a number of means-tested bursaries available, up to full fees, for girls at 11+ and 16+.

Transport links

The college is a few minutes walk from Northwood tube station (Metropolitan line) and close to several bus routes. An extensive series of school coaches cover areas including Edgware, Stanmore, Kenton, Gerrards Cross, Beaconsfield, Chorleywood, Kenton, Harrow, Borehamwood, Radlett, Bushey, Greenford, Uxbridge, Hillingdon and South Ruislip.

See for yourself

We enjoy showing parents and girls around Northwood College. On a tour you can explore our lovely site and above all, you can experience the atmosphere and see for yourself how our girls and teachers work together.

The Northwood College Educational Trust is a registered charity (No. 312646) which exists to provide high quality education for girls.

St Catherine's School

(Founded 1914)

Cross Deep, Twickenham, Middlesex TW1 4QJ
Tel: 020 8891 2898   Email: admissions@stcatherineschool.co.uk
Fax: 020 8744 9629   Website: www.stcatherineschool.co.uk

Headmistress: Sister Paula Thomas BEd(Hons), MA
Appointed: September 2007
School type: Girls' Day
Age range of pupils: 3–18
No. of pupils enrolled as at 1.2.10: 386
Fees per annum as at 1.2.10: Day: £7605–£10,515
Teacher/pupil ratio: 1:11

Focus on the individual.

St Catherine's combines nearly 100 years experience of Catholic girls' independent education with a modern curriculum that prepares girls for success in the 21st century. We are a Catholic school, in the ecumenical tradition, where every student is a valued member of a happy community. Emphasis is placed on providing a broad education and on responsibility and the importance of respect for others. We are a small school with a strong community spirit and as such are able to focus on the individual and help every girl achieve her personal best. High academic standards are maintained but without undue pressure.

In the most recent 2009 GCSE exam results the school achieved 100% A*-C grades, 58% A*/A grades and 88% A*-B grades. An extension for the prep department opened in December 2008. This included three new classrooms, a library and a practical base. Another new block to include a sixth form centre and other new facilities will be ready for use in September 2010.

The school is regularly in the top ten of the top 50 small schools for the last three years running in the *Sunday Times Parent Power* magazine.

The Lady Eleanor Holles School

(Founded 1711)

Hanworth Road, Hampton, Middlesex TW12 3HF
Tel: 020 8979 1601   Email: office@lehs.org.uk
Fax: 020 8941 8291   Website: www.lehs.org.uk

Head: Mrs Gillian Low MA(Oxon)
Appointed: September 2004
School type: Girls' Day
Age range of pupils: 7–18
No. of pupils enrolled as at 1.1.10: 875
Sixth Form: 177
Fees per annum as at 1.1.10: Day: £9960–£13 200
Average size of class: 22

Girls who come to The Lady Eleanor Holles School have exceptional opportunities that allow them to develop their individual characters and talents. The school, set within extensive playing fields and gardens and blessed with outstanding facilities provides an environment that is both inspirational and supportive.

Burlington House, an elegant, refurbished building adjacent to the main school, provides a happy, secure and stimulating environment for girls aged seven to 11. The junior department seeks to develop bright, happy and confident girls, the majority of whom proceed to the senior department at 11. The girls benefit from outstanding facilities on a 30-acre site which is shared with the senior department, including a heated indoor swimming pool.

The special characteristics of the senior department include not only the high academic standards for which it is nationally renowned, but a well-balanced, purposeful and productive environment. Girls enjoy their studies, but also relish the range of opportunities the school provides in sport, the creative arts and many extracurricular activities.

We are very proud of the girls' achievements at GCSE and A level, which not only mark a fitting end to their time at the school, but enable them to go on to a wide range of excellent universities to pursue the degree courses of their choice.

In its recently published inspection report, the ISI judged that: 'The quality of the educational experience provided throughout the school is *outstanding...*' and '...balances the successful attainment of outstanding public examination results with the pursuit of excellence in the extensive extracurricular programme.'

The Lady Eleanor Holles School is a Registered Charity (No 1130254) for the education of children.

St Helen's School

(Founded 1899)

Eastbury Road, Northwood, Middlesex HA6 3AS
Tel: +44 (0)1923 843210 Email: enquiries@sthn.co.uk
Fax: +44 (0)1923 843211 Website: www.sthn.co.uk

Head: Mrs Mary Morris BA
Appointed: June 2000
School type: Girls' Day
Age range of pupils:
Girls: 3–18
No. of pupils enrolled as at 1.1.10: 1122
Sixth Form: 160
Fees per annum as at 1.1.10: Day: £8343–£12,171

St Helen's School has a commitment to academic excellence that has given us an enviable reputation for over a hundred years. We provide a first-class academic education for able girls, developing personal integrity alongside intellectual, creative and sporting talents. The staff are highly qualified and enthusiastic and class sizes are small. Teaching is rigorous and stimulating throughout the school and public examination results are outstanding. Each girl is treated as a valued individual while great emphasis is placed on social responsibility and mutual respect.

Located on a beautiful 20-acre site approximately 30 minutes by Underground from central London, we offer excellent facilities including a state-of-the-art sports centre; specialist facilities for science, design and technology, art, drama, music and ICT; a digital, multi-media language laboratory; an excellent library housing an extensive collection of books, ICT facilities, newspapers and periodicals; and well-equipped teaching rooms.

The curriculum is designed to enable every girl to achieve intellectual and personal fulfilment and to develop her talents and interests to the full. We support the aims of the National Curriculum, but offer a wider range of subjects and teach to greater depth. The staff are specialists who aim to inspire a love of their subjects. Girls are encouraged to work independently and to develop good study habits. From Year 7 all girls study two modern foreign languages together with Latin, and science is taught throughout the senior school as three separate subjects. A broad range of options is available at GCSE, A level and IB diploma.

Music, art, drama and sport are integral parts of the life of the school and involve every girl. Many also take extra music, ballet and speech and drama lessons, as well as games coaching.

The use of information communication technology is a key element in teaching. We expect girls to use computers as part of their normal studies and provide ample facilities for them to do so. All girls follow a GCSE course in ICT which is also offered as an A level option.

St Helen's Sixth Form, where the International Baccalaureate is taught as well as A levels, is a flourishing community of approximately 160 girls who take an active role in the life of the school. Each year we welcome new students who join us from other schools. The sixth form is in many ways a new beginning and often the most enjoyable and challenging time of school life. Significant numbers each year go to Oxford and Cambridge. Almost every girl goes on to the university of her first choice

A large number of clubs and societies exist which cater for all interests. These change each year to reflect the particular interests of girls and staff. Work experience, both at home and abroad, foreign exchanges and visits are well supported.

In the Duke of Edinburgh's Award Scheme, girls are able to achieve bronze, silver and gold awards while at school. St Helen's is one of only eight girls' schools to offer a Combined Cadet Force, which is run jointly with Merchant Taylors' School. Debating is a highly successful activity from Years 6 to 13, with girls competing both in school and up to national level. Above all, we build the girls' confidence and encourage them to chase their dreams, ready to take their place in the adult world.

St Helen's School Northwood is a registered charity (No. 312762) which exists to provide high quality education for girls from the UK and overseas.

Twickenham Preparatory School

(Founded 1932)

Beveree, 43 High Street, Hampton, Middlesex TW12 2SA
Tel: 020 8979 6216   Email: office@twickenhamprep.co.uk
Fax: 020 8979 1596   Website: www.twickenhamprep.co.uk

Head: D Malam BA(Hons)(Southampton), PGCE(Winchester)
Appointed: September 2005
School type: Coeducational Day
Member of: IAPS
Age range of pupils:
Boys: 4–13
Girls: 4–11
No. of pupils enrolled as at 1.1.10: 265
Boys: 144 Girls: 121
Pre-prep: Boys 51 Girls 54
Prep: Boys 93 Girls 67
Fees per annum as at 1.1.10: Day: £8250–£8910
Teacher/pupil ratio: 1:12
Religious denomination: Christian

Entry requirements
Details in school prospectus.

Inspection reports on website.

A school which believes in praise and the celebration of success.

- Happy family coeducational environment.
- Strong academic tradition.
- Excellent results at 11+ and Common Entrance.
- Small class sizes.

- Outstanding pastoral care.
- Exciting thinking-skills programme throughout the curriculum working with international group Mind Lab.
- Subject specialist teaching throughout the school.
- 18th century mansion with purpose-built pre-prep.

At TPS we encourage a happy and purposeful family environment where every child is valued as an individual and every member of the school community is important. Each pupil has the opportunity to fully develop his or her talents in a wholly supportive environment. We really do have an inclusive approach to both work and play. There is a broad curriculum, excellent pupil/teacher ratio, good facilities and strong academic results. There are many activities to choose from outside the classroom and everyone has the chance to perform in music or drama or play for one of our school teams. The school plays a wide range of sports, with many team matches that involve all pupils, and all pupils are taught to swim. We are one of the foremost schools in the country for chess.

In addition to all National Curriculum subjects, French is taught from reception and Latin from age nine. Boys are prepared for 13+ Common Entrance and scholarship examinations to independent secondary schools and girls for 11+ entrance and scholarship exams, mainly to local independent day schools. The success rate is very high in entrance exams and National Curriculum tests.

A positive, Christian attitude prevails and that is reinforced by a strong pastoral care system where pupils are encouraged to play their part in looking after the needs of others in the school community.

Twickenham Preparatory School, a registered charity, (No. 1067572) exists to provide quality education for local children.

Schools in the South-East

Cambridgeshire

Buckinghamshire

Hertfordshire

Essex

Berkshire

London

Surrey

Kent

Hampshire

West Sussex

East Sussex

The following unitary authorities are also within the counties listed:

Thurrock and Southend-on-Sea	Essex
Medway	Kent
Brighton & Hove	East Sussex
Portsmouth and Southampton	Hampshire
Bracknell Forest, Reading, Slough, Windsor & Maidenhead and Wokingham	Berkshire
Milton Keynes	Buckinghamshire
Peterborough	Cambridgeshire

Ashford School

(Founded 1898)

East Hill, Ashford, Kent TN24 8PE
Tel: 01233 739030   Email: registrar@ashfordschool.co.uk
Fax: 01233 665215   Website: www.ashfordschool.co.uk

Head: Mr M R Buchanan BSc(Hons), CertEd, NPQH, CPhys
Appointed: August 2005
School type: Coeducational Day & Boarding
Boarding available from age 10
Age range of pupils: 3 months–18 years
No. of pupils enrolled as at 1.3.10: 724
Senior: 403
No. of boarders: 125
Fees per annum as at 1.3.10: Day: £5850–£13,530
Boarding: £21,810–£24,615
Average size of class: 16
Teacher/pupil ratio: 1:10
Religious denomination: Non-denominational

With Sweeney Todd, Haydnfest, African Sanctus, Maths Challenge, trips to Disneyland, CERN and LA in 2010, cadet training, lego robotics and art exhibitions to name just a few of the many activities to choose from, there is always adventure at Ashford School.

As a pupil at Ashford School, you will discover a bustling life full of opportunities for discovery and personal development. Whether you choose to join us as a day pupil or boarder you will be given the space and support to develop your individual interests and talents and you will have the chance to discover both the pleasures and responsibilities of living as a member of a community - a community that is friendly, homely, relaxed and caring. Should you choose to be a boarder with us, whilst learning to grow as a confident and responsible young person you will become a valued member of our boarding family; supporting others, developing lifelong friendships and discovering your talents through adventuring beyond your expectations.

Ashford School gives you the opportunity to engage in adventurous activities which will help you explore new experiences and develop your talent in music, sport, drama and leadership to name but a few. Living with young people from across the globe, you can aspire and succeed with other like-minded pupils to attend one of the world's top universities. Enjoying the family atmosphere and charm of our listed buildings and modern facilities located in Ashford town centre, you will be close to the leisure and shopping facilities of Canterbury and just a 35-minute train journey from bustling London.

Our focus is to ensure that every child enjoys an unending craving for learning and discovers themselves by having the opportunity to explore, to know, to do, to share and to be. We know we have succeeded when we say farewell to confident, versatile and capable young adults who have a good understanding of themselves and others. Come and join the adventure!

ACS Cobham International School

Heywood, Portsmouth Road, Cobham, Surrey KT11 1BL
Tel: 01932 867251   Email: cobhamadmissions@acs-england.co.uk
Fax: 01932 869789   Website: www.acs-england.co.uk

Head of School: Mr T Lehman
Academic Dean: Craig Worthington
School type: Coeducational Day & Boarding
Accredited by: NEASC
Authorised by: IB
Member of: The US College Board AP Program,
ECIS, CIS, ISA, BSA
Age range of pupils: 2–18
Lower School: 2–9
Middle School: 10-13–High School: 14-18
No. of pupils enrolled as at 1.4.10: 1352
Boys: 755 Girls: 597 Sixth Form: 471
No. of boarders: 96
Fees per annum as at 1.4.10: Day: £8840–£19,730
Boarding: £29,100–£32,960
Average size of class: 18
Teacher/pupil ratio: 1:9

ACS Cobham International School enrols students from 60 countries (American and British students represent well over half the population), speaking 30 languages, all seeking an education which prepares them for a global future. Our goal is to encourage critical thinkers, responsible global citizens and students who are prepared to achieve the highest standards, both in their subsequent education and throughout their careers. Although there is no formal entrance exam, ACS Cobham is a university-preparatory school, sending its students to some of the finest universities in the world. We are non-sectarian and located within easy commuting distance of central London.

Academic programme

- ACS Cobham is an International Baccalaureate (IB) World School, offering the IB Diploma.

- ACS Cobham offers a traditional American High School Diploma, including prestigious Advanced Placement (AP) courses.

- ACS Cobham graduates attend leading universities around the world including: Cambridge, Oxford, Imperial College London and London School of Economics in the UK; Stanford, Harvard, Princeton and Yale in the USA; and leading universities in other countries such as Canada, Japan, the Netherlands and Sweden.

- Small class sizes facilitate multi-level teaching, academic challenge and a focus on individual student learning styles.

Faculty

- The faculty includes over 128 full-time teachers, all holding university degrees; approximately one-half have advanced degrees.

- All teachers have a minimum of two years' teaching experience.

- On average, teachers remain with ACS for eight years.

- The student to teacher ratio is approximately 9:1.

Boarding

- The school offers coeducational boarding with separate-wing accommodation for 110 students aged between 12 (7th grade), and 18 (12th grade).

- Ergonomically designed two-person rooms have en suite facilities and internet connections.

The campus

- ACS Cobham is located 23 miles south of central London on a beautiful 128-acre site, giving students plenty of space and acting as a useful learning resource.

- In addition to superb purpose-built teaching facilities, the campus sports facilities include: on-site soccer and rugby fields, softball and baseball diamonds, an all-weather Olympic-sized track, tennis courts, six-hole golf course, and a new Sports Centre, which houses a basketball/volleyball show court, 25-metre competition-class swimming pool, dance studio and Fitness Suite.

- The Early Childhood expansion project has added additional purpose-built classrooms, creating a self-contained "village" for children ages two to five.

- Door-to-door and shuttle bus services are available for much of Surrey and South West London.

Student activities

- ACS Cobham offers extensive and varied extracurricular clubs, sports and community service activities both locally and internationally, which encourage students to participate in the richness of school life.

- Students also participate in international theatre art programmes, competitive sports tournaments, maths, literature and music competitions in the UK and across Europe.

Other campuses

ACS International Schools have two additional campuses, in the counties of Surrey and Middlesex:

- ACS Egham International School is located on a 20-acre site 25 miles from central London. It is one of only three schools in the UK to offer the IB Primary Years Programme (ages three to 11) and the IB Middle Years Programme (ages 11-16) in addition to the International Baccalaureate Diploma Programme.

- ACS Hillingdon International School is located on an 11-acre parkland site 15 miles west of central London. The school is housed in a restored Grade II listed building which is enhanced with a modern, purpose-built wing. The school also has a new music centre with a digital recording studio, rehearsal rooms, practice studios and a computer lab for music technology.

Admissions

Admissions officers are available throughout the year to speak with you about possible enrolment. Visits can be arranged on weekdays or weekends to suit your schedule, and application for enrolment can now be made online, via our website.

- Applicants do not need to sit a formal entrance exam.

- Students are accepted in all grades throughout the year.

- Application forms, previous school records and teacher references are required for entry.

ACS Egham International School

Woodlee, London Road, Egham, Surrey TW20 0HS
Tel: 01784 430 800   Email: eghamadmissions@acs-england.co.uk
Fax: 01784 430 626   Website: www.acs-england.co.uk

Head of School: Jeremy Lewis
School type: Coeducational Day
Accredited by: NEASC
Authorised by: IB
Member of: ECIS, CIS, ISA
Age range of pupils: 2–18
Lower School: 2–10
Middle School: 11-16–High School: 16-18
No. of pupils enrolled as at 1.4.10: 583
Boys: 304 Girls: 279
Fees per annum as at 1.4.10: Day: £8900–£19,240

Enrolling students from over 40 countries (American and British students represent well over half the population), ACS Egham International School is known as a friendly and caring international community which values a holistic approach to education. The school's philosophy is based on developing the individual potential of each student by providing an engaging and challenging educational programme. We promote high standards of scholarship, responsibility and citizenship through our International Baccalaureate (IB) Programmes so that all our students can be successful learners. Although there is no formal entrance exam, ACS Egham is a university-preparatory school, sending its students to some of the finest universities in the world. We are non-sectarian and located within easy commuting distance of London.

Academic programme

- ACS Egham is one of only three schools in the UK to offer the IB Primary Years Programme (three to 11), the IB Middle Years Programme (11-16) and the IB Diploma Programme (16-18).

- ACS Egham also offers a traditional American High School Diploma.

- ACS Egham graduates attend leading universities around the world including: University College London, King's College London, Royal Holloway, St Andrews Oxford and University of Warwick in the UK; American International College, Texas A&M, and Universities of Boston, Oklahoma, Purdue and Southern California in the USA; and other fine universities in Canada, Norway, Singapore and Holland.

- Small class sizes facilitate multi-level teaching, academic challenge and a focus on individual student learning styles.

Faculty

- The faculty includes over 73 full-time teachers, all holding university degrees, approximately one-half have advanced degrees.
- All teachers have a minimum of two years teaching experience.
- On average, teachers remain with ACS for eight years.
- The student to teacher ratio is approximately 9:1.

The campus

- ACS Egham is located 25 miles south-west of central London on a 20 acre site.
- The campus offers superb teaching, sports and extracurricular facilities including a newly refurbished cafeteria and kitchen and a new art, design technology and IT building.
- Door-to-door busing is available for much of Surrey from Farnborough to Heathrow.

Student activities

- Extensive and varied extracurricular clubs, sports, and community service activities both locally and internationally encourage students to participate in the richness of school life.
- Students also participate in international theatre art programmes, competitive sport tournaments, maths, literature, and music competitions in the UK and across Europe.

Other campuses

ACS International Schools have two additional campuses, in the counties of Surrey and Middlesex. Both ACS Cobham and ACS Hillingdon offer American Advanced Placement Courses and the International Baccalaureate (IB) Diploma Programme.

- ACS Cobham International School is located on a 128-acre site 23 miles from central London. The school has a boarding programme, premier sports facilities, and purpose-built facilities for early childhood, lower, middle and high schools.
- ACS Hillingdon International School is located on an 11-acre parkland site 15 miles west of central London. The school is housed in a restored Grade II listed building which is enhanced with a modern, purpose-built wing. The school also has a new music centre with a digital recording studio, rehearsal rooms, practice studios and a computer lab for music technology.

Admissions

Admissions officers are available throughout the year to speak with you about possible enrolment. Visits can be arranged on weekdays or weekends to suit your schedule, and application for enrolment can now be made online, via our website.

- Applicants do not need to sit a formal entrance exam.
- Students are accepted in all grades throughout the year.
- Application forms, teacher references and previous school records are required for entry.

Bradfield College

(Founded 1850)

Bradfield, Reading RG7 6AU
Tel: 0118 964 4510   Email: headmaster@bradfieldcollege.org.uk
Fax: 0118 964 4513   Website: www.bradfieldcollege.org.uk

Headmaster: Mr Peter Roberts
Appointed: September 2003
School type: Coeducational Boarding
Age range of pupils: 13–18
No. of pupils enrolled as at 1.4.10: 724
Boys: 484 Girls: 240 Sixth Form: 306
No. of boarders: 610
Fees per annum as at 1.4.10: Day: £21,900
Boarding: £27,375
Average size of class: Max 20
Teacher/pupil ratio: 1:9

A leading coeducational, independent boarding school, Bradfield College is secure and self-contained, enabling young people to mature into caring, contributing and confident citizens. Its all-inclusive ethos embraces the extended 'Bradfield family' which includes pupils past and present and extensive links with the wider community.

The modern college combines values and attributes essential to 21st century life with those of its founder, Thomas Stevens, who established St Andrew's College in 1850. The chapel at the heart of the college is central to spiritual life, reflection and serenity. Alongside an excellent academic education all partake of the 'Bradfield experience' which permits each individual to find his or her special niche. The classroom atmosphere engenders a love of learning for its own sake; the participatory culture ensures that expert and enthusiast alike thrive within the broad spectrum of extracurricular activities.

Pastoral care is paramount; boys and girls move on to senior houses after Faulkner's, a coeducational house in which all spend their first year at the college. Each house has a dedicated team of staff and every pupil benefits from the care of a housemaster or housemistress, a personal tutor and a matron.

The superb facilities at Bradfield include modern teaching and learning environments within the beautiful brick-and-flint original buildings. There is a music school, sports complex with indoor swimming pool, a tennis centre and two floodlit all-weather pitches. Alongside these a new state-of-the-art science centre will open its doors to pupils and the local community in September 2010. Set in its own medieval village in 250 acres of beautiful Berkshire countryside the college enjoys exceptional playing fields, golf course and stunning views across the Pang valley. All this is within 40 minutes of Heathrow and an hour from central London.

Admission to the college is at both 13+ and into the large and vibrant sixth form. Scholarships, exhibitions and awards are available at both levels of entry.

Bradfield College, Registered Charity No. 309089, is a college for the careful education of boys and girls.

Dame Bradbury's School

(Founded 1525)

Ashdon Road, Saffron Walden, Essex CB10 2AL
Tel: 01799 522348   Email: info@damebradburys.com
Fax: 01799 516762   Website: www.damebradburys.com

Headmistress: Mrs J Crouch
Appointed: September 2004
School type: Coeducational Day
Age range of pupils: 3–11
No. of pupils enrolled as at 1.4.10: 265
Fees per annum as at 1.4.10: Day: £1638–£8490
Average size of class: 20

Puppet-making, climbing Snowdon, stitching samplers and beating Japanese drums - these are just some of the activities packed into life at Dame Bradbury's School, a three-to-11 coeducational prep school and nursery based in Saffron Walden.

The school's key aims are for pupils to flourish and fulfil their potential, to be self-confident, imaginative and cultured, and to want to learn for the sheer joy of it. The children are encouraged to aim high, to be themselves and be kind.

Dame Bradbury's blends innovation with tradition: children are taught good manners in a caring community, but they also use Apple Macs, enjoy thinking skills classes and can study sound and lighting theatre techniques.

The school offers care from 8.15am to 6pm and runs more than 40 activities and clubs, including photography, Spanish, Latin, Warhammer, dance, squash, badminton and a range of other sports clubs. The facilities include a well-equipped theatre, science laboratory, art room, design technology room, sports hall, Astroturf, tennis courts and playing fields.

Dame Bradbury's also places great emphasis on the value of learning beyond the classroom, with day trips to places including Shakespeare's Globe, the Henry Moore Foundation, the Museum of London, the Fitzwilliam Museum, Ely Cathedral, Cambridge Arts Theatre and the Imperial War Museum at Duxford. Residential trips visit York (Year 4), Norfolk (Year 5) and Snowdonia (Year 6).

The school's Early Years (Nursery and Reception) and Late Stay provision was judged 'outstanding in every category' by Ofsted, while Independent Schools Inspectors praised the school's "joyful constructive atmosphere" and "supportive and vibrant environment".

Pupils progress to a wide range of schools including The Perse, Perse Girls', Saffron Walden County High, Bishop's Stortford College, Downe House, Cheltenham Ladies' College and Eton.

Dame Bradbury's can offer help with fees; bursaries may be awarded in the form of a discount of up to 100% of tuition fees.

Brighton College

(Founded 1845)

Eastern Road, Brighton, Brighton & Hove BN2 0AL
Tel: 01273 704200   Email: registrar@brightoncollege.net
Fax: 01273 704204   Website: www.brightoncollege.org.uk

Headmaster: Richard Cairns MA
Appointed: January 2006
Head of Prep School: Brian Melia MA(Cantab), PGCE
Head of Lower School: Miss Leah Hamblett MA
School type: Coeducational Pre-Prep, Prep and Senior
Member of: HMC
Age range of pupils: 3–18
No. of pupils enrolled as at 1.4.10: 730
Sixth Form: 300
No. of boarders: 255
Fees per annum as at 1.4.10: Day: £3747–£15,534
Boarding: £21,150–£24,078
Average size of class: 18
Teacher/pupil ratio: 1:9.5
Religious denomination: Church of England

Brighton College succeeds in combining academic excellence with a wealth of extracurricular opportunities, all underpinned by a deep commitment to the individual needs and enthusiasms of each child. Founded in 1845, it is the oldest independent school in Sussex, but also one of the most forward thinking and successful in the UK.

Attracting boys and girls from every part of the country and every social background, the school is a diverse and welcoming community with an international outlook. Behind the impressive gateway is an idyllic green campus, with some of the most modern facilities of any school. A healthy blend of tradition and modern ensure pupils are educated in a safe and secure environment but are prepared for the challenges of 'the real world'.

The school has an international reputation as a centre for the study of Mandarin Chinese language and culture, a compulsory subject for all pupils despite having only a small minority from Asia. As well as an

The youthful Headmaster, Richard Cairns, recently featured on the *London Evening Standard* '1000 Most Influential People in London' list. However, it is the list of speakers he regularly hosts at the college which is truly impressive - from government ministers to industrialists, inventors to explorers, each offering their experience and encouragement to pupils of all ages. Many visitors to the school are former pupils, such as former England Women's cricket captain Clare Connor, who led her country to Ashes victory, Lord Skidelsky, the distinguished politician and biographer of Keynes, or Sir John Chilcot the chairman of the Iraq Inquiry.

The school has a unique location, situated in the heart of the UK's youngest city with the sea to the front and the beautiful South Downs to the rear. Being close to London, the school attracts a high proportion of weekly boarders who take advantage of long weekends at home, leaving after school on Friday afternoon and not having to return until Monday morning class. A recent £1.5 million refurbishment of boarding facilities as well as a rich variety of evening and weekend activities for boarders ensures life after the school day has ended is anything but dull. *Tatler* magazine described the boarding accommodation as 'some of the smartest, most homely, we have seen'. An additional junior boarding house opens in 2010.

enviable record in sport, music, drama, art and dance, in summer 2009 the school received the best A level results of any coeducational school in England for the third year running, with a record 95% of entries awarded A or B grades. GCSE grades were the best in the county with 77% A*/A.

The college was described as 'Outstanding' in its most recent Ofsted report, with pastoral care singled out for special mention. Annually, 10-12% of pupils head to Oxford or Cambridge universities, with most other pupils entering their preferred universities. Six pupils have also received offers at the UK's top art schools.

Outside of the classroom, there are over 140 clubs and activities available to pupils, ranging from rugby and choir to juggling and ballroom dancing.

Recent innovations have included the introduction of life skills classes, covering everything from pitching a tent to boiling an egg, lessons in business etiquette and a specially written Story of Our Land course to ensure children understand the context of their own country's history. Since September 2009, the senior school has taken pupils from 11-18.

Every child has the chance to shine at Brighton College, whatever their interest. Whilst a call to represent England on the rugby pitch or the netball court is celebrated, so is a place in the regional heat of a debating competition, a performance in the school musical, or an improvement in an end-of-term effort grade.

Brighton College does not believe in 'types': it celebrates individuals.

Brighton College provides high quality education for girls and boys aged three to 18. Registered Charity No. 307061.

Danes Hill School

(Founded 1947)

Leatherhead Road, Oxshott, Surrey KT22 0JG
Tel: 01372 842509   Email: registrar@daneshillschool.co.uk
Fax: 01372 844452   Website: www.daneshillschool.co.uk

Headmaster: Mr W Murdock BA
Appointed: January 2007
School type: Coeducational Pre-preparatory &
Preparatory Day
Member of: IAPS, ISC
Age range of pupils: 3–13
No. of pupils enrolled as at 1.9.09: 872
Boys: 493 Girls: 379
Fees per annum as at 1.9.09: Day: £1589–£4405
Average size of class: 9-20
Teacher/pupil ratio: 1:10

Danes Hill is currently one of the largest day preparatory schools in the country, and its 870 boys and girls enjoy a broad and balanced curriculum in 55 acres of landscaped grounds.

Pupils up to the age of six are based in the pre-preparatory 'Bevendean' department which has just undergone a major rebuilding programme providing state-of-the-art classrooms and facilities. The emphasis at this early stage is on learning through play, laying down the key numeracy and literacy skills. All children enjoy specialist French teaching from age four, and Bevendean has its own swimming pool, library, ICT and brand new art and DT rooms.

In Year 2 pupils move to the main school, where the emphasis is on developing pupils' independence and self-motivation. All children now have specialist teaching in art, drama, design technology and music, and as they progress through the school their academic subjects are increasingly delivered by specialist staff too. In addition, subjects are 'setted' to provide smaller teaching groups and an excellent pupil-teacher ratio. Languages are a strength of the school, and those studied include French, German, Spanish, Latin, Greek and Mandarin Chinese.

Facilities at the main school include a new purpose-built art, DT and food technology classroom block, a theatre, floodlit all-weather Astroturf, two ICT suites and swimming pool. All classrooms have interactive whiteboards and the school's intranet allows staff and pupils to communicate throughout the campus.

Great emphasis is laid on pastoral care throughout the school, and older pupils have tutors as well as form teachers to monitor and encourage their progress. Good communications between home and school are seen as an essential part of the school's success, and parents are encouraged to be actively involved in all stages of their children's education.

Danes Hill has an outstanding record in external exams, achieving thirty or more academic and all-rounder scholarships to senior schools each year, as well as securing places for all pupils at their senior school of choice. In addition a number of children sit GCSE examinations in one or more languages at age 13, regularly securing A and A* grades.

Danes Hill School is a registered charity (No. 269433) to promote and provide for the advancement of education of children.

Deepdene School

(Founded 1948)

195 New Church Road, Hove, Brighton & Hove BN3 4ED
Tel: 01273 418984   Email: info@deepdeneschool.com
Fax: 01273 415543   Website: www.deepdeneschool.com

Heads: Mrs L V Clark-Darby BEd(Hons), CertFS &
Mrs N K Gane NNEB
School type: Coeducational Day
Age range of pupils: 1–11
No. of pupils enrolled as at 1.4.10:
Boys: 114 Girls: 106
Fees per annum as at 1.4.10: Day: £1800–£5760
Average size of class: 16
Teacher/pupil ratio: 1:8

The school was founded in 1948 as a privately owned and managed school. More than half a century later Deepdene remains a truly independent school. The co-principals own the school. They are experienced educational professionals who both manage and teach in the nursery and pre-prep departments.

Mrs Nicola Gane and Mrs Liza Clark-Darby take a personal interest in the development and well-being of every child in their care.

Although, it is a non-selective school, Deepdene pupils achieve consistently high academic results.

Deepdene is a non-denominational school and welcomes children from many different faiths and cultures, whilst continuing to maintain its traditional link with the Christian church.

The ethos of, and teaching at, Deepdene School help children to become confident, competent, considerate and courteous individuals.

Many pupils leaving Deepdene at the age of eleven years gain scholarships to their chosen preparatory schools.

Sport plays a significant part in the curriculum with coaching in cricket, rugby, football, netball, tennis and swimming.

Small classes ensure that all pupils benefit from individual attention in every lesson.

Caring, committed, qualified staff offer a stimulating and highly structured curriculum that places strong emphasis on the development of literacy and numeracy.

Academic study is balanced with an exciting programme of sport, music, languages, ICT, art, craft, dance and drama.

Throughout the school, teachers at Deepdene have both the time and resources to ensure that each, individual child fulfils his or her potential.

Emberhurst School

(Founded 1935)

94 Ember Lane, Esher, Surrey KT10 8EN
Tel: 020 8398 2933   Email: info@emberhurst-school.com
Fax: 020 8398 9492   Website: www.emberhurst-school.com

Headmistress: Mrs P Chadwick BEd
School type: Coeducational Day
Age range of pupils: $2\frac{1}{2}$+–7+
No. of pupils enrolled as at 1.4.10: 70
Boys: 40 Girls: 30
Fees per annum as at 1.4.10: Day: £2265–£6495
Average size of class: 12-16
Teacher/pupil ratio: 1:10

The selection of a good first school is a decision which will influence the whole of a child's future.

Many parents feel that the needs of their children are best met within the environment of a small friendly school such as Emberhurst. Our aim is to promote a stimulating atmosphere where learning is fun and a welcome part of everyday life.

We believe that education is the process of bringing out and developing the whole person.

History
Emberhurst School was established in 1935. After renovation in 1993, nursery facilities were opened, providing full pre-preparatory education for boys and girls $2\frac{1}{2}$+ to 7+ years.

Location
The school is situated in a residential area, close to Esher, Molesey, Thames Ditton, Claygate, Hinchley Wood and Kingston upon Thames.

Curriculum
Our approach is designed to help pupils:

- Enjoy a happy and secure learning environment, where they are valued.
- Develop lively enquiring minds, where they question, rather than merely accept.
- Acquire knowledge and understanding, which will equip them for future challenges.
- Obtain skills that they can transfer to other subjects and situations.

The acquisition of skill and knowledge is planned carefully to excite and stimulate young minds. Each day, exciting challenges and new areas of learning are presented to our eager pupils.

While the Nationional Curriculum is a useful starting point, our vibrant curriculum is developed through EYFS by our Early Years team. The six areas of learning are interconnected, so that we at Emberhurst develop motivated and happy learners who will progress smoothly into Key Stage One.

In Key Stage One, our teachers are trained to provide stimulating experiences in their lessons. Pupils need a variety of learning opportunities, if they are to achieve their learning potential.

Classes are small, to enable children to perform at the speed that suits them best and a very individual approach can be offered to every child.

Fosse Bank School

(Founded 1892)

Mountains, Noble Tree Road, Hildenborough, Tonbridge, Kent TN11 8ND
Tel: 01732 834212   Email: office@fossebankschool.co.uk
Fax: 01732 834884   Website: www.fossebankschool.co.uk

Headmistress: Mrs Lovatt-Young
Appointed: September 2005
School type: Coeducational Day
Age range of pupils: 3–11
No. of pupils enrolled as at 1.4.09: 124
Boys: 74 Girls: 50
Fees per annum as at 1.4.09: Day: £6300–£8655
Average size of class: max 18

Fosse Bank School offers an excellent academic education for children aged three to 11, combined with a truly supportive, friendly and stimulating environment in which your child can learn, grow and flourish. Our school has a positive caring ethos which celebrates success and encourages each child to be the best that they can be. The importance of good manners is emphasised and our children have a reputation for being confident, articulate and well-behaved. The school is located in a beautiful Grade II listed building, within 26 acres of parkland and boasting a range of wonderful facilities. There is ample, safe parking and a strong family community.

Academic studies

We follow and extend the National Curriculum, offering broad learning experiences. Music, PE and French are taught by specialists so that high standards are achieved in all subject areas. Our children achieve excellent academic results accepting offers of places at selective state and independent schools every year. Our Kent 11+ results have been outstanding in recent years with over 90% of children who sit the test being offered grammar school places at some of the best schools in Kent. Our Key Stage 2 SATs results are always well above the national standard of achievement.

Extracurricular

A wealth of activities are available both during and after school for all children, such as chess, sewing, cross-country running, ballet, football, fencing, construction and lego, and many others.

Entry procedure

Fosse Bank is not academically selective at entry. All children are required to attend a Taster Day before a place may be offered. Dance scholarships and means-tested bursaries are available. Children experiencing learning difficulties may be able to join small group sessions with a Learning Support Assistant. All enquiries are very welcome and should be directed to Miss Sarah O'Connor via email at: admissions@fossebankschool.co.uk or telephone: 01732 834212.

Fosse Bank School is a registered charity which exists to provide the advancement and promotion of education for children. Charity No. 1045435.

Kent College Pembury

(Founded 1886)

Old Church Road, Pembury, Tunbridge Wells, Kent TN2 4AX
Tel: 01892 822006   Email: admissions@kentcollege.kent.sch.uk
Fax: 01892 820221   Website: www.kent-college.co.uk

Headmistress: Mrs Sally-Anne Huang MA(Oxon), PGCE
School type: Girls' Day & Boarding
Boarders from 10
Member of: GSA, IAPS, ISA, BSA, AEGIS
Age range of pupils: 3–18
No. of pupils enrolled as at 1.1.10: 524
Sixth Form: 88
No. of boarders: 80
Fees per annum as at 1.9.10: Day: £7047–£15,474
Boarding: £19,182–£24,945
Average size of class: 16
Teacher/pupil ratio: 1:9
Religious denomination: Methodist - welcomes pupils of all faiths

When you arrive at Kent College your first impression is the beautiful, spacious setting and the superb views of the Kent countryside. Set in 75 acres of parkland, the school provides a safe, natural environment where girls enjoy living and learning. Kent College is a happy, caring home-from-home for boarders from over 20 different countries. Boarders can join from age ten onwards.

Exciting opportunities

Building self-esteem is at the heart of our ethos. All girls get a chance to shine, try something different, feel good about themselves and develop new and existing talents. Exciting opportunities to develop confidence are an integral part of school life: overseas music, drama and sports tours, an Australian exchange, 65 extracurricular activities, and Leith's Food & Wine Course to name a few. Our aim is to equip students with the confidence, skills and positive attitude to succeed in their examinations, at university, in their chosen career and in life ahead.

A broad and balanced approach

Academic standards are high with excellent GCSE and A level results and pupils have a record of success in gaining places at traditional universities to do a variety of courses, from medicine to engineering. The curriculum and approach to learning is broad and balanced.

Facilities & location

Modern, architect-designed facilities include homely boarding houses, a state-of-the-art theatre, large sports hall, music school and indoor swimming pool. There are modern IT suites around the campus and all students have email and broadband internet access. The school is only three miles from the town of Tunbridge Wells, 15 minutes from the M25 and 40 minutes from London by train.

Scholarships & bursaries

Academic, music, drama, sport and art scholarships are available. Means-tested bursaries are also available. A 20% discount is available for HM Forces families.

Kent College is a registered charity (No. 307920) and exists to provide quality education for girls.

Lancing College

(Founded 1848)

Lancing, West Sussex BN15 0RW
Tel: 01273 452213   Email: admissions@lancing.org.uk
Fax: 01273 464720   Website: www.lancingcollege.co.uk

LANCING COLLEGE

Headmaster: Mr Jonathan W J Gillespie MA
Appointed: September 2006
School type: Coeducational Boarding & Day
Age range of pupils: 13–18
No. of pupils enrolled as at 1.1.10: 523
Sixth Form: 241
No. of boarders: 329
Fees per annum as at 1.1.10: Day: £18,705
Boarding: £26,775
Average size of class: 15
Teacher/pupil ratio: 1:8

Set in 500 acres of spectacular South Downs countryside, Lancing College is a coeducational school for 13 to 18 year olds, with a strong reputation for academic, sporting and musical excellence. The school buildings are an architectural treasure and the magnificent Chapel provides a strong focus for the life of the college and the values it espouses. Although the site is rural, road and rail links are good and escorted transport is available from international airports at the start and finish of each term. A minibus service also operates to local stations with direct connections to London, which is 75 minutes away.

Facilities are outstanding and complement a well-qualified and dedicated teaching staff. Pastoral care is second-to-none, led by a team of experienced housemasters and housemistresses. In its latest Ofsted boarding inspection, Lancing was commended for offering exceptionally high quality and awarded an 'Outstanding' rating: "The College has a well thought through approach to providing its boarders with a wide range of support and opportunities that encourages them to achieve both educationally and socially and to their fullest potential. It welcomes and celebrates diversity."

In the last six years Lancing has been the most consistently high-performing coeducational school in Sussex, with its A and B grade percentage at A level exceeding 80%. Excellent examination results are coupled with exceptional extracurricular activities. The college's principal aim is to guide each pupil towards activities that excite them. In addition to the extensive playing fields and sports facilities, music and drama play important roles in school life and a strikingly modern art school opened in November 2008. A working farm provides practical experience for students wishing to develop their agricultural, veterinary and conservation interests and many pupils participate in the Duke of Edinburgh's Award Scheme or the Outreach Programme within the local community.

Lancing College is a Registered Charity (No. 1076483) to promote and extend education in accordance with the principles which govern the charitable foundation.

Queen Anne's School

(Founded 1894)

6 Henley Road, Caversham, Reading RG4 6DX
Tel: 0118 918 7333   Email: admissions@qas.org.uk
Fax: 0118 918 7310   Website: www.qas.org.uk

Queen Anne's
Caversham

Headmistress: Mrs Julia Harrington BA(Hons), PGCE, NPQH
Appointed: 2006
School type: Girls' Boarding & Day
Age range of pupils: 11–18
No. of pupils enrolled as at 1.4.10: 336
Sixth Form: 100
No. of boarders: 133
Fees per annum as at 1.4.10: Day: £5695
Weekly Boarding: £7545–£7975
Boarding: £8395
Average size of class: 18
Teacher/pupil ratio: 1:7

One of Queen Anne's greatest strengths is to discover and bring out the best in individuals. Maths and science are as strong as the arts and the girls have the support and encouragement to achieve their personal best in whichever field they choose.

QAS art students exhibit work at the Arlington Centre and the prestigious SW1 Gallery in London; drama students put on performances every term and girls regularly gain places at the National Youth Theatre. The school choir sings at Westminster Abbey and Winchester Cathedral and has toured Venice and Paris, performing at St Mark's and Notre Dame, and the music department runs a series of student workshops each year with world-renowned professional musicians. Sport is also strong and all abilities are catered for. Queen Anne's lacrosse teams are a force to be reckoned with and one student is the youngest to play lacrosse for the senior England squad.

The driving force behind the school's success is probably the enthusiastic can-do attitude of both pupils and teachers. It is a close community with a strong support network, which the school believes is integral to the development of happy, confident adults.

There is a huge range of extracurricular activities for the girls to choose from after school and an optional Saturday Morning Programme, which offers even more choice, ranging from fashion design and sailing to trampolining, photography and dog training.

Queen Anne's has outstanding facilities set in 35 acres of lovely grounds. There's a large sports centre with a 'rock' climbing wall, squash courts, fitness suite, dance studio and swimming pool; a Performing Arts Centre with a fabulous 250-seat theatre; a newly fitted language lab, a new three-storey seven-laboratory science centre and a new art & design centre, complete with an Artist in Residence. Planned developments include two new boarding houses. The new sixth form house is scheduled to open in September 2011 and a junior boarding house is due for completion in 2012.

Full, weekly and flexi boarding is available and there are excellent links to London and the south east. Buses operate over a widespread area and a minibus runs to and from Reading Station.

Application for entry can be made at 11+, 13+ and sixth form. Open Days and Taster Days take place throughout the year. These can be booked online at www.qas.org.uk/bookonline. Further information is available from Jane Gallie on 0118 918 7333, email admissions@qas.org.uk.

Tonbridge School

(Founded 1553)

Tonbridge, Kent TN9 1JP
Tel: 01732 365555   Email: hmsec@tonbridge-school.org
Fax: 01732 363424   Website: www.tonbridge-school.co.uk

TONBRIDGE
SCHOOL

Headmaster: T H P Haynes
Appointed: 2005
School type: Boys' Day & Boarding
Age range of pupils: 13–18
No. of pupils enrolled as at 1.4.10: 750
Sixth Form: 330
No. of boarders: 450
Fees per annum as at 1.4.10: Day: £20,910
Boarding: £28,140
Average size of class: GCSE 16, A level 9
Teacher/pupil ratio: 1:7.6

Tonbridge School is one of the leading boys' schools in the country. Boarders and day boys of varying backgrounds are offered an education remarkable both for its breadth of opportunity and the exceptional standards routinely achieved in all areas of school life.

Tonbridge School aims to provide a caring and enlightened environment in which the talents of each individual flourish. We encourage boys to be creative, tolerant and to strive for academic, sporting and cultural excellence. Respect for tradition and an openness to innovation are equally valued. A well-established house system at the heart of the school fosters a strong sense of belonging. Tonbridge seeks to celebrate its distinctive mixture of boarders and day boys; this helps to create a unique broadening and deepening of opportunity. We want boys to enjoy their time here, but also to be made aware of their social and moral responsibilities. Tonbridgians should enter into the adult world with the knowledge and self-belief to fulfil their own potential and, in many cases, to become leaders in their chosen field. Equally, we hope to foster a lifelong empathy for the needs and views of others.

The school is extremely successful in its university entrance (over 20% of leavers go to Oxbridge) and strives for excellence in all fields, yet the ethos of the school is one of strong participation and acceptance

of each others' strengths and weaknesses rather than blind concentration on results.

Tonbridge School is just off the M25, on the edge of the Kent/Surrey/Sussex borders and attracts families from all over southern England. It lies in about 150 acres of land on the edge of the town of Tonbridge, and thus provides a good balance between town and country living.

Families are warmly welcomed to come and see Tonbridge and to meet the Headmaster. We hope that a visit will leave you not only impressed by the facilities and the achievements of the boys, but also by the sense of fun and openness which the boys encounter here on a daily basis. Please contact our admissions department on 01732 304297 or admissions@tonbridge-school.org. For further information about Tonbridge please visit our website: www.tonbridge-school.co.uk.

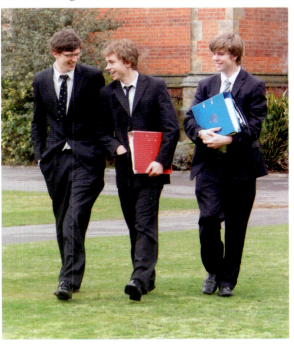

Wellesley House

(Founded 1898)

114 Ramsgate Road, Broadstairs, Kent CT10 2DG
Tel: 01843 862991   Email: hmsec@wellesleyhouse.net
Fax: 01843 602068   Website: www.wellesleyhouse.org

Headmaster: Mr S T P O'Malley MA(Hons), PGCE
Appointed: September 2006
School type: Coeducational Boarding & Day
Age range of pupils: 7–13
No. of pupils enrolled as at 21.4.10: 143
Boys: 87 Girls: 56
No. of boarders: 113
Fees per annum as at 21.4.10: Day: £15,300
Boarding: £19,080
Average size of class: 13
Teacher/pupil ratio: 1:8

Wellesley House aims to open up a world of opportunity for girls and boys aged from seven to 13. Our primary aim is to prepare pupils for entry to their senior schools via Common Entrance or scholarship by creating the ideal boarding and classroom environment in which to develop a love of learning and so excel.

Academic success is a priority and results are excellent. Wellesley's dedicated staff ensure this through their high expectations and support. Our ethos is that success follows success, whether in or outside the classroom, and occurs naturally in pupils who are happy and motivated. All pupils are encouraged to push themselves and made to feel secure enough to take risks. Additional educational need is identified and acted upon by trained learning support staff via individual education plans and extra tuition can be provided for those requiring help. Expert preparation and guidance for Common Entrance and the individual application procedure required for each senior school are tailored for each child. We aim to ensure their school of choice is the right choice, so that pupils continue to achieve long after they leave Wellesley.

A caring, family community where all children's strengths, not just the academic, are recognised and actively nurtured. Our goal is to produce confident, motivated, well informed and well mannered Welleslians fully prepared to thrive at their senior schools. A broad curriculum is enhanced by varied additional activities, visits and residential trips. Pupils are offered a comprehensive selection of competitive sport, whilst music, art and drama are central to life at Wellesley through the choir, individual and group instrumental performances, major theatrical productions and vibrant art displays.

A south-east coast position allows plenty of opportunity for beach walks and sailing, with easy access to London by car or high-speed rail link, and a bus transfer for pupils.

Worth School

(Founded 1959)

Paddockhurst Road, Turners Hill, Crawley, West Sussex RH10 4SD
Tel: 01342 710200   Email: registry@worth.org.uk
Fax: 01342 710230   Website: www.worthschool.co.uk

WORTH
S C H O O L

Headmaster: Mr Gino Carminati MA, FRSA
Appointed: April 2007
School type: Catholic coeducational 11-18
boarding & day
Member of: HMC, BSA, ASCL, ISCis, IB
Age range of pupils: 11–18
No. of pupils enrolled as at 1.3.10: 506
Sixth Form: 229
No. of boarders: 313
Fees per annum as at 1.9.09: Day: £16,026–£18,339
Boarding: £21,627–£24,756
Average size of class: 18 (in sixth form: 11)
Teacher/pupil ratio: 1:7

Worth is known for its strong community values, high academic standards, friendly atmosphere and the excellence of its all-round education. As a Benedictine school we encourage our pupils to develop their own individuality whilst living within a community that inspires learning, worship, friendship and service.

The school is set, alongside Worth Abbey, in 500 acres of rural Sussex yet only 12km from Gatwick airport and 50km from central London.

At Worth, we see our pupils as 'Lanterns to Light'. Inspiring pupils to think, learn, create, imagine and perform is pivotal if each individual is to develop their intellectual potential. This is achieved by the highest standards of teaching and also by the application of new approaches to learning and exciting opportunities in which to discover and learn. The school offers a broad curriculum at GCSE and in the sixth form, where students can opt for the International Baccalaureate Diploma (taught since 2002) or A levels. Examination results are high - IB scores are consistently significantly higher than the global average - and pupils enter the very best universities in the UK and abroad, including Oxbridge.

In September 2008, Worth welcomed sixth form girls into the school community and girls joined in Years 7 (11+) and 9 (13+) in September 2010. Investment in new facilities and teaching staff continues, including the opening of a new girls' boarding and day house.

Beyond the classroom, pupils benefit from a range of societies, lectures, trips and visits - enriching the academic life of the school whilst encouraging everyone to aim high. The school has a long tradition of community involvement, reaching out to others through an extensive voluntary service programme. A large proportion of pupils are involved in the Duke of Edinburgh's Award Scheme, for which the school is a centre of excellence. Sports facilities include extensive playing fields, an eight-hole golf course, fencing salle, dance studio and fitness suite. Stables are available on the site for students' horses. The drama and music departments are outstanding and benefit from a purpose-built Performing Arts Centre housing a theatre, recording studio, sound-proofed 'rock room', rehearsal rooms, recital room and music classrooms.

"Students here are keen, engaging, interesting people who will go to all sorts of lengths just to make your day that little bit better." Year 13 student.

Worth School is a registered charity (No. 1093914)

International Schools

Ashford School

(Founded 1898)

East Hill, Ashford, Kent TN24 8PB
Tel: 01233 739030   Email: registrar@ashfordschool.co.uk
Fax: 01233 665215   Website: www.ashfordschool.co.uk

Head: Mr M R Buchanan BSc(Hons), CertEd, NPQH, CPhys
Appointed: August 2005
School type: Coeducational Day & Boarding
Boarding available from age 10
Age range of pupils: 3 months–18 years
No. of pupils enrolled as at 1.3.10: 724
Senior: 403
No. of boarders: 125
Fees per annum as at 1.3.10: Day: £5850–£13,530
Boarding: £21,810–£24,615
Average size of class: 16
Teacher/pupil ratio: 1:10
Religious denomination: Non-denominationa

With Sweeney Todd, Haydnfest, African Sanctus, Maths Challenge, trips to Disneyland, CERN and LA in 2010, cadet training, lego robotics and art exhibitions to name just a few of the many activities to choose from, there is always adventure at Ashford School.

As a pupil at Ashford School, you will discover a bustling life full of opportunities for discovery and personal development. Whether you choose to join us as a day pupil or boarder you will be given the space and support to develop your individual interests and talents and you will have the chance to discover both the pleasures and responsibilities of living as a member of a community - a community that is friendly, homely, relaxed and caring. Should you choose to be a boarder with us, whilst learning to grow as a confident and responsible young person you will become a valued member of our boarding family; supporting others, developing lifelong friendships and discovering your talents through adventuring beyond your expectations.

Ashford School gives you the opportunity to engage in adventurous activities which will help you explore new experiences and develop your talent in music, sport, drama and leadership to name but a few. Living with young people from across the globe, you can aspire and succeed with other like-minded pupils to attend one of the world's top universities. Enjoying the family atmosphere and charm of our listed buildings and modern facilities located in Ashford town centre, you will be close to the leisure and shopping facilities of Canterbury and just a 35-minute train journey from bustling London.

Our focus is to ensure that every child enjoys an unending craving for learning and discovers themselves by having the opportunity to explore to know, to do, to share and to be. We know we have succeeded when we say farewell to confident, versatile and capable young adults who have a good understanding of themselves and others. Come and join the adventure!

Sue Registrar   TASIS.

ACS Cobham International School

Heywood, Portsmouth Road, Cobham, Surrey KT11 1BL
Tel: 01932 867251   Email: cobhamadmissions@acs-england.co.uk
Fax: 01932 869789   Website: www.acs-england.co.uk

Head of School: Mr T Lehman
Academic Dean: Craig Worthington
School type: Coeducational Day & Boarding
Accredited by: NEASC
Authorised by: IB
Member of: The US College Board AP Program,
ECIS, CIS, ISA, BSA
Age range of pupils: 2–18
Lower School: 2–9
Middle School: 10-13–High School: 14-18
No. of pupils enrolled as at 1.4.10: 1352
Boys: 755 Girls: 597 Sixth Form: 471
No. of boarders: 96
Fees per annum as at 1.4.10: Day: £8840–£19,730
Boarding: £29,100–£32,960
Average size of class: 18
Teacher/pupil ratio: 1:9

ACS Cobham International School enrols students from 60 countries (American and British students represent well over half the population), speaking 30 languages, all seeking an education which prepares them for a global future. Our goal is to encourage critical thinkers, responsible global citizens and students who are prepared to achieve the highest standards, both in their subsequent education and throughout their careers. Although there is no formal entrance exam, ACS Cobham is a university-preparatory school, sending its students to some of the finest universities in the world. We are non-sectarian and located within easy commuting distance of central London.

Academic programme

- ACS Cobham is an International Baccalaureate (IB) World School, offering the IB Diploma.

- ACS Cobham offers a traditional American High School Diploma, including prestigious Advanced Placement (AP) courses.

- ACS Cobham graduates attend leading universities around the world including: Cambridge, Oxford, Imperial College London and London School of Economics in the UK; Stanford, Harvard, Princeton and Yale in the USA; and leading universities in other countries such as Canada, Japan, the Netherlands and Sweden.

- Small class sizes facilitate multi-level teaching, academic challenge and a focus on individual student learning styles.

Faculty

- The faculty includes over 128 full-time teachers, all holding university degrees; approximately one-half have advanced degrees.

- All teachers have a minimum of two years' teaching experience.

- On average, teachers remain with ACS for eight years.

- The student to teacher ratio is approximately 9:1.

Boarding

- The school offers coeducational boarding with separate-wing accommodation for 110 students aged between 12 (7th grade), and 18 (12th grade).

- Ergonomically designed two-person rooms have en suite facilities and internet connections.

The campus

- ACS Cobham is located 23 miles south of central London on a beautiful 128-acre site, giving students plenty of space and acting as a useful learning resource.

- In addition to superb purpose-built teaching facilities, the campus sports facilities include: on-site soccer and rugby fields, softball and baseball diamonds, an all-weather Olympic-sized track, tennis courts, six-hole golf course, and a new Sports Centre, which houses a basketball/volleyball show court, 25-metre competition-class swimming pool, dance studio and Fitness Suite.

- The Early Childhood expansion project has added additional purpose-built classrooms, creating a self-contained "village" for children ages two to five.

- Door-to-door and shuttle bus services are available for much of Surrey and South West London.

Student activities

- ACS Cobham offers extensive and varied

extracurricular clubs, sports and community service activities both locally and internationally, which encourage students to participate in the richness of school life.

- Students also participate in international theatre art programmes, competitive sports tournaments, maths, literature and music competitions in the UK and across Europe.

Other campuses

ACS International Schools have two additional campuses, in the counties of Surrey and Middlesex:

- ACS Egham International School is located on a 20-acre site 25 miles from central London. It is one of only three schools in the UK to offer the IB Primary Years Programme (ages three to 11) and the IB Middle Years Programme (ages 11-16) in addition to the International Baccalaureate Diploma Programme.

- ACS Hillingdon International School is located on an 11-acre parkland site 15 miles west of central London. The school is housed in a restored Grade II listed building which is enhanced with a modern, purpose-built wing. The school also has a new music centre with a digital recording studio, rehearsal rooms, practice studios and a computer lab for music technology.

Admissions

Admissions officers are available throughout the year to speak with you about possible enrolment. Visits can be arranged on weekdays or weekends to suit your schedule, and application for enrolment can now be made online, via our website.

- Applicants do not need to sit a formal entrance exam.

- Students are accepted in all grades throughout the year.

- Application forms, previous school records and teacher references are required for entry.

ACS Egham International School

Woodlee, London Road, Egham, Surrey TW20 0HS
Tel: 01784 430 800   Email: eghamadmissions@acs-england.co.uk
Fax: 01784 430 626   Website: www.acs-england.co.uk

Head of School: Jeremy Lewis
School type: Coeducational Day
Accredited by: NEASC
Authorised by: IB
Member of: ECIS, CIS, ISA
Age range of pupils: 2–18
Lower School: 2–10
Middle School: 11-16–High School: 16-18
No. of pupils enrolled as at 1.4.10: 583
Boys: 304 Girls: 279
Fees per annum as at 1.4.10: Day: £8900–£19,240

Enrolling students from over 40 countries (American and British students represent well over half the population), ACS Egham International School is known as a friendly and caring international community which values a holistic approach to education. The school's philosophy is based on developing the individual potential of each student by providing an engaging and challenging educational programme. We promote high standards of scholarship, responsibility and citizenship through our International Baccalaureate (IB) Programmes so that all our students can be successful learners. Although there is no formal entrance exam, ACS Egham is a university-preparatory school, sending its students to some of the finest universities in the world. We are non-sectarian and located within easy commuting distance of London.

Academic programme

- ACS Egham is one of only three schools in the UK to offer the IB Primary Years Programme (three to 11), the IB Middle Years Programme (11-16) and the IB Diploma Programme (16-18).

- ACS Egham also offers a traditional American High School Diploma.

- ACS Egham graduates attend leading universities around the world including: University College London, King's College London, Royal Holloway, St Andrews Oxford and University of Warwick in the UK; American International College, Texas A&M, and Universities of Boston, Oklahoma, Purdue and Southern California in the USA; and other fine universities in Canada, Norway, Singapore and Holland.

- Small class sizes facilitate multi-level teaching, academic challenge and a focus on individual student learning styles.

Faculty

- The faculty includes over 73 full-time teachers, all holding university degrees, approximately one-half have advanced degrees.

- All teachers have a minimum of two years teaching experience.

- On average, teachers remain with ACS for eight years.

- The student to teacher ratio is approximately 9:1.

The campus

- ACS Egham is located 25 miles south-west of central London on a 20 acre site.

- The campus offers superb teaching, sports and extracurricular facilities including a newly refurbished cafeteria and kitchen and a new art, design technology and IT building.

- Door-to-door busing is available for much of Surrey from Farnborough to Heathrow.

Student activities

- Extensive and varied extracurricular clubs, sports, and community service activities both locally and internationally encourage students to participate in the richness of school life.

- Students also participate in international theatre art programmes, competitive sport tournaments, maths, literature, and music competitions in the UK and across Europe.

Other campuses

ACS International Schools have two additional campuses, in the counties of Surrey and Middlesex. Both ACS Cobham and ACS Hillingdon offer American Advanced Placement Courses and the International Baccalaureate (IB) Diploma Programme.

- ACS Cobham International School is located on a 128-acre site 23 miles from central London. The school has a boarding programme, premier sports facilities, and purpose-built facilities for early childhood, lower, middle and high schools.

- ACS Hillingdon International School is located on an 11-acre parkland site 15 miles west of central London. The school is housed in a restored Grade II listed building which is enhanced with a modern, purpose-built wing. The school also has a new music centre with a digital recording studio, rehearsal rooms, practice studios and a computer lab for music technology.

Admissions

Admissions officers are available throughout the year to speak with you about possible enrolment. Visits can be arranged on weekdays or weekends to suit your schedule, and application for enrolment can now be made online, via our website.

- Applicants do not need to sit a formal entrance exam.

- Students are accepted in all grades throughout the year.

- Application forms, teacher references and previous school records are required for entry.

ACS Hillingdon International School

Hillingdon Court, 108 Vine Lane, Hillingdon, Uxbridge, Middlesex UB10 0BE
Tel: 01895 259 771   Email: hillingdonadmissions@acs-england.co.uk
Fax: 01895 818 404   Website: www.acs-england.co.uk

Head of School: Ginger Apple
IB Co-ordinator: Chris Green
School type: Coeducational Day
Accredited by: NEASC
Authorised by: IB
Member of: ECIS, CIS, US College Board AP
Program, ISA
Age range of pupils: 4–18
Lower School: 4–9
Middle School: 10-13–High School: 14-18
No. of pupils enrolled as at 1.4.10: 539
Boys: 280 Girls: 259
Fees per annum as at 1.4.10: Day: £8820–£18,560
Average size of class: 20 max
Teacher/pupil ratio: 1:9

Enrolling students from over 40 countries, ACS Hillingdon International School is a school which strongly values partnerships among parents, teachers and students. Our philosophy actively encourages a sense of teamwork and aims to set a challenging yet achievable academic standard. We believe in meeting the developmental needs of our students by providing a balanced educational programme and preparing them to take their places in our ever-changing world. Although there is no formal entrance exam, ACS Hillingdon is a university-preparatory school, sending its students to some of the finest universities in the world. We are non-sectarian and located within easy commuting distance of central London.

Academic programme

- ACS Hillingdon is an International Baccalaureate (IB) World School, offering the IB Diploma Programme, and the IB Middle Years Programme (as a candidate school).

- ACS Hillingdon offers a traditional American High School Diploma, including prestigious Advanced Placement (AP) courses.

- ACS Hillingdon graduates attend leading universities around the world including: Cambridge, Imperial College, King's College, London School of Economics, Oxford, Royal Veterinary College and St George's Hospital

Medical School in the UK; Pennsylvania State University, Purdue, Texas A & M, Tufts University and the US Air Force Academy in the USA; and leading universities in other countries such as Canada, Japan, the Netherlands and Sweden.

- Small class sizes facilitate multi-level teaching, academic challenge and a focus on individual student learning styles.

Faculty

- The faculty includes over 73 full-time teachers, all holding university degrees; approximately one-half have advanced degrees.

- All teachers have a minimum of two years' teaching experience.

- On average, teachers remain with ACS for eight years.

- The student to teacher ratio is approximately 9:1.

The campus

- ACS Hillingdon is located 15 miles west of central London with Underground rail access, on an 11-acre site set in parkland.

- The excellent facilities are augmented by a new music centre, complete with digital recording studio, rehearsal rooms, practice studios and a computer lab for music technology.

- The campus has on-site playing fields, tennis courts and playgrounds with additional off-site soccer, rugby, track, baseball, softball, swimming and golf facilities available.

- Door-to-door and shuttle bus services are available for much of central London, west London and Middlesex from Maidenhead to Westminster

Student activities

- A full range of sports including basketball, tennis soccer, rugby, swimming, baseball, softball, track and field, cross country and volleyball.

- Extracurricular activities include Student Council, Model United Nations, yearbook, music, art, drama, computers, languages and recycling.

Other campuses

ACS Hillingdon is one of the ACS International Schools which enrol over 2500 students aged between two and 18 from over 60 countries, speaking 30 languages. Based on international and American research, principles and educational practices, the schools are committed to maintaining the highest standards of scholarship and citizenship. The two additional campuses are located in Surrey:

- ACS Cobham International School is located on a 128-acre site 23 miles from central London. The school has a boarding programme, premier sports facilities, and purpose-built facilities for early childhood, lower, middle and high schools.

- ACS Egham International School is located on a 20-acre site 25 miles from central London. It is one of only three schools in the UK to offer the IB Primary Years Programme (ages three to 11) and the IB Middle Years Programme (ages 11-16) in addition to the International Baccalaureate Diploma Programme.

Admission

Admissions officers are available throughout the year to speak with you about possible enrolment. Visits can be arranged on weekdays or weekends to suit your schedule, and application for enrolment can now be made online, via our website.

- Applicants do not need to sit a formal entrance exam.

- New students are accepted in all grades throughout the year.

- Application forms, teacher references and previous school records are required for entry.

Bradfield College

(Founded 1850)

Bradfield, Reading RG7 6AU
Tel: 0118 964 4510   Email: headmaster@bradfieldcollege.org.uk
Fax: 0118 964 4513   Website: www.bradfieldcollege.org.uk

Headmaster: Mr Peter Roberts
Appointed: September 2003
School type: Coeducational Boarding
Age range of pupils: 13–18
No. of pupils enrolled as at 1.4.10: 724
Boys: 484 Girls: 240 Sixth Form: 306
No. of boarders: 610
Fees per annum as at 1.4.10: Day: £21,900
Boarding: £27,375
Average size of class: Max 20
Teacher/pupil ratio: 1:9

A leading coeducational, independent boarding school, Bradfield College is secure and self-contained, enabling young people to mature into caring, contributing and confident citizens. Its all-inclusive ethos embraces the extended 'Bradfield family' which includes pupils past and present and extensive links with the wider community.

The modern college combines values and attributes essential to 21st century life with those of its founder, Thomas Stevens, who established St Andrew's College in 1850. The chapel at the heart of the college is central to spiritual life, reflection and serenity. Alongside an excellent academic education all partake of the 'Bradfield experience' which permits each individual to find his or her special niche. The classroom atmosphere engenders a love of learning for its own sake; the participatory culture ensures that expert and enthusiast alike thrive within the broad spectrum of extracurricular activities.

Pastoral care is paramount; boys and girls move on to senior houses after Faulkner's, a coeducational house in which all spend their first year at the college. Each house has a dedicated team of staff and every pupil benefits from the care of a housemaster or housemistress, a personal tutor and a matron.

The superb facilities at Bradfield include modern teaching and learning environments within the beautiful brick-and-flint original buildings. There is a music school, sports complex with indoor swimming pool, a tennis centre and two floodlit all-weather pitches. Alongside these a new state-of-the-art science centre will open its doors to pupils and the local community in September 2010. Set in its own medieval village in 250 acres of beautiful Berkshire countryside the college enjoys exceptional playing fields, golf course and stunning views across the Pang valley. All this is within 40 minutes of Heathrow and an hour from central London.

Admission to the college is at both 13+ and into the large and vibrant sixth form. Scholarships, exhibitions and awards are available at both levels of entry.

Bradfield College, Registered Charity No. 309089, is a college for the careful education of boys and girls.

Kent College Pembury

(Founded 1886)

Old Church Road, Pembury, Tunbridge Wells, Kent TN2 4AX
Tel: 01892 822006   Email: admissions@kentcollege.kent.sch.uk
Fax: 01892 820221   Website: www.kent-college.co.uk

Headmistress: Mrs Sally-Anne Huang MA(Oxon), PGCE
School type: Girls' Day & Boarding
Boarders from 10
Member of: GSA, IAPS, ISA, BSA, AEGIS
Age range of pupils: 3–18
No. of pupils enrolled as at 1.1.10: 524
Sixth Form: 88
No. of boarders: 80
Fees per annum as at 1.9.10: Day: £7047–£15,474
Boarding: £19,182–£24,945
Average size of class: 16
Teacher/pupil ratio: 1:9
Religious denomination: Methodist - welcomes pupils of all faiths

When you arrive at Kent College your first impression is the beautiful, spacious setting and the superb views of the Kent countryside. Set in 75 acres of parkland, the school provides a safe, natural environment where girls enjoy living and learning. Kent College is a happy, caring home-from-home for boarders from over 20 different countries. Boarders can join from age ten onwards.

Exciting opportunities

Building self-esteem is at the heart of our ethos. All girls get a chance to shine, try something different, feel good about themselves and develop new and existing talents. Exciting opportunities to develop confidence are an integral part of school life: overseas music, drama and sports tours, an Australian exchange, 65 extracurricular activities, and Leith's Food & Wine Course to name a few. Our aim is to equip students with the confidence, skills and positive attitude to succeed in their examinations, at university, in their chosen career and in life ahead.

A broad and balanced approach

Academic standards are high with excellent GCSE and A level results and pupils have a record of success in gaining places at traditional universities to do a variety of courses, from medicine to engineering. The curriculum and approach to learning is broad and balanced.

Facilities & location

Modern, architect-designed facilities include homely boarding houses, a state-of-the-art theatre, large sports hall, music school and indoor swimming pool. There are modern IT suites around the campus and all students have email and broadband internet access. The school is only three miles from the town of Tunbridge Wells, 15 minutes from the M25 and 40 minutes from London by train.

Scholarships & bursaries

Academic, music, drama, sport and art scholarships are available. Means-tested bursaries are also available. A 20% discount is available for HM Forces families.

Kent College is a registered charity (No. 307920) and exists to provide quality education for girls.

Brighton College

(Founded 1845)

Eastern Road, Brighton, Brighton & Hove BN2 0AL
Tel: 01273 704200   Email: registrar@brightoncollege.net
Fax: 01273 704204   Website: www.brightoncollege.org.uk

Headmaster: Richard Cairns MA
Appointed: January 2006
Head of Prep School: Brian Melia MA(Cantab), PGCE
Head of Lower School: Miss Leah Hamblett MA
School type: Coeducational Pre-Prep, Prep and Senior
Member of: HMC
Age range of pupils: 3–18
No. of pupils enrolled as at 1.4.10: 730
Sixth Form: 300
No. of boarders: 255
Fees per annum as at 1.4.10: Day: £3747–£15,534
Boarding: £21,150–£24,078
Average size of class: 18
Teacher/pupil ratio: 1:9.5
Religious denomination: Church of England

Brighton College succeeds in combining academic excellence with a wealth of extracurricular opportunities, all underpinned by a deep commitment to the individual needs and enthusiasms of each child. Founded in 1845, it is the oldest independent school in Sussex, but also one of the most forward thinking and successful in the UK.

Attracting boys and girls from every part of the country and every social background, the school is a diverse and welcoming community with an international outlook. Behind the impressive gateway is an idyllic green campus, with some of the most modern facilities of any school. A healthy blend of tradition and modern ensure pupils are educated in a safe and secure environment but are prepared for the challenges of 'the real world'.

The school has an international reputation as a centre for the study of Mandarin Chinese language and culture, a compulsory subject for all pupils despite having only a small minority from Asia. As well as an

The youthful Headmaster, Richard Cairns, recently featured on the *London Evening Standard* '1000 Most Influential People in London' list. However, it is the list of speakers he regularly hosts at the college which is truly impressive - from government ministers to industrialists, inventors to explorers, each offering their experience and encouragement to pupils of all ages. Many visitors to the school are former pupils, such as former England Women's cricket captain Clare Connor, who led her country to Ashes victory, Lord Skidelsky, the distinguished politician and biographer of Keynes, or Sir John Chilcot the chairman of the Iraq Inquiry.

The school has a unique location, situated in the heart of the UK's youngest city with the sea to the front and the beautiful South Downs to the rear. Being close to London, the school attracts a high proportion of weekly boarders who take advantage of long weekends at home, leaving after school on Friday afternoon and not having to return until Monday morning class. A recent £1.5 million refurbishment of boarding facilities as well as a rich variety of evening and weekend activities for boarders ensures life after the school day has ended is anything but dull. Tatler magazine described the boarding accommodation as "some of the smartest, most homely, we have seen". An additional junior boarding house opens in 2010.

Every child has the chance to shine at Brighton College, whatever their interest. Whilst a call to represent England on the rugby pitch or the netball court is celebrated, so is a place in the regional heat of a debating competition, a performance in the school musical, or an improvement in an end-of-term effort grade.

Brighton College does not believe in 'types': it celebrates individuals.

Brighton College provides high quality education for girls and boys aged three to 18. Registered Charity No. 307061.

enviable record in sport, music, drama, art and dance, in summer 2009 the school received the best A level results of any coeducational school in England for the third year running, with a record 95% of entries awarded A or B grades. GCSE grades were the best in the county with 77%A*/A.

The college was described as "Outstanding" in its most recent Ofsted report, with pastoral care singled out for special mention. Annually, 10-12% of pupils head to Oxford or Cambridge universities, with most other pupils entering their preferred universities. Six pupils have also received offers at the UK's top art schools.

Outside of the classroom, there are over 140 clubs and activities available to pupils, ranging from rugby and choir to juggling and ballroom dancing.

Recent innovations have included the introduction of life skills classes, covering everything from pitching a tent to boiling an egg, lessons in business etiquette and a specially written Story of Our Land course to ensure children understand the context of their own country's history. Since September 2009, the senior school has taken pupils from 11-18.

Lancing College

(Founded 1848)

Lancing, West Sussex BN15 0RW
Tel: 01273 452213   Email: admissions@lancing.org.uk
Fax: 01273 464720   Website: www.lancingcollege.co.uk

LANCING COLLEGE

Headmaster: Mr Jonathan W J Gillespie MA
Appointed: September 2006
School type: Coeducational Boarding & Day
Age range of pupils: 13–18
No. of pupils enrolled as at 1.1.10: 523
Sixth Form: 241
No. of boarders: 329
Fees per annum as at 1.1.10: Day: £18,705
Boarding: £26,775
Average size of class: 15
Teacher/pupil ratio: 1:8

Set in 500 acres of spectacular South Downs countryside, Lancing College is a coeducational school for 13 to 18 year olds, with a strong reputation for academic, sporting and musical excellence. The school buildings are an architectural treasure and the magnificent Chapel provides a strong focus for the life of the college and the values it espouses. Although the site is rural, road and rail links are good and escorted transport is available from international airports at the start and finish of each term. A minibus service also operates to local stations with direct connections to London, which is 75 minutes away.

Facilities are outstanding and complement a well-qualified and dedicated teaching staff. Pastoral care is second-to-none, led by a team of experienced housemasters and housemistresses. In its latest Ofsted boarding inspection, Lancing was commended for offering exceptionally high quality and awarded an 'Outstanding' rating: "The College has a well thought through approach to providing its boarders with a wide range of support and opportunities that encourages them to achieve both educationally and socially and to their fullest potential. It welcomes and celebrates diversity."

In the last six years Lancing has been the most consistently high-performing coeducational school in Sussex, with its A and B grade percentage at A level exceeding 80%. Excellent examination results are coupled with exceptional extracurricular activities. The college's principal aim is to guide each pupil towards activities that excite them. In addition to the extensive playing fields and sports facilities, music and drama play important roles in school life and a strikingly modern art school opened in November 2008. A working farm provides practical experience for students wishing to develop their agricultural, veterinary and conservation interests and many pupils participate in the Duke of Edinburgh's Award Scheme or the Outreach Programme within the local community.

Lancing College is a Registered Charity (No. 1076483) to promote and extend education in accordance with the principles which govern the charitable foundation.

Queen Anne's School

(Founded 1894)

6 Henley Road, Caversham, Reading RG4 6DX
Tel: 0118 918 7333   Email: admissions@qas.org.uk
Fax: 0118 918 7310   Website: www.qas.org.uk

Headmistress: Mrs Julia Harrington BA(Hons),
PGCE, NPQH
Appointed: 2006
School type: Girls' Boarding & Day
Age range of pupils: 11–18
No. of pupils enrolled as at 1.4.10: 336
Sixth Form: 100
No. of boarders: 133
Fees per annum as at 1.4.10: Day: £5695
Weekly Boarding: £7545–£7975
Boarding: £8395
Average size of class: 18
Teacher/pupil ratio: 1:7

One of Queen Anne's greatest strengths is to discover and bring out the best in individuals. Maths and science are as strong as the arts and the girls have the support and encouragement to achieve their personal best in whichever field they choose.

QAS art students exhibit work at the Arlington Centre and the prestigious SW1 Gallery in London; drama students put on performances every term and girls regularly gain places at the National Youth Theatre. The school choir sings at Westminster Abbey and Winchester Cathedral and has toured Venice and Paris, performing at St Mark's and Notre Dame, and the music department runs a series of student workshops each year with world-renowned professional musicians. Sport is also strong and all abilities are catered for. Queen Anne's lacrosse teams are a force to be reckoned with and one student is the youngest to play lacrosse for the senior England squad.

The driving force behind the school's success is probably the enthusiastic can-do attitude of both pupils and teachers. It is a close community with a strong support network, which the school believes is integral to the development of happy, confident adults.

There is a huge range of extracurricular activities for the girls to choose from after school and an optional Saturday Morning Programme, which offers even more choice, ranging from fashion design and sailing to trampolining, photography and dog training.

Queen Anne's has outstanding facilities set in 35 acres of lovely grounds. There's a large sports centre with a 'rock' climbing wall, squash courts, fitness suite, dance studio and swimming pool; a Performing Arts Centre with a fabulous 250-seat theatre; a newly fitted language lab, a new three-storey seven-laboratory science centre and a new art & design centre, complete with an Artist in Residence. Planned developments include two new boarding houses. The new sixth form house is scheduled to open in September 2011 and a junior boarding house is due for completion in 2012.

Full, weekly and flexi boarding is available and there are excellent links to London and the south east. Buses operate over a widespread area and a minibus runs to and from Reading Station.

Application for entry can be made at 11+, 13+ and sixth form. Open Days and Taster Days take place throughout the year. These can be booked online at www.qas.org.uk/bookonline. Further information is available from Jane Gallie on 0118 918 7333, email admissions@qas.org.uk.

St Helen's School

(Founded 1899)

Eastbury Road, Northwood, Middlesex HA6 3AS
Tel: +44 (0)1923 843210 Email: enquiries@sthn.co.uk
Fax: +44 (0)1923 843211 Website: www.sthn.co.uk

Head: Mrs Mary Morris BA
Appointed: June 2000
School type: Girls' Day
Age range of pupils:
Girls: 3–18
No. of pupils enrolled as at 1.1.10: 1122
Sixth Form: 160
Fees per annum as at 1.1.10: Day: £8343–£12,171

St Helen's School has a commitment to academic excellence that has given us an enviable reputation for over a hundred years. We provide a first-class academic education for able girls, developing personal integrity alongside intellectual, creative and sporting talents. The staff are highly qualified and enthusiastic and class sizes are small. Teaching is rigorous and stimulating throughout the school and public examination results are outstanding. Each girl

is treated as a valued individual while great emphasis is placed on social responsibility and mutual respect.

Located on a beautiful 20-acre site approximately 30 minutes by Underground from central London, we offer excellent facilities including a state-of-the-art sports centre; specialist facilities for science, design and technology, art, drama, music and ICT; a digital, multi-media language laboratory; an excellent library housing an extensive collection of books, ICT facilities, newspapers and periodicals; and well-equipped teaching rooms.

The curriculum is designed to enable every girl to achieve intellectual and personal fulfilment and to develop her talents and interests to the full. We support the aims of the National Curriculum, but offer a wider range of subjects and teach to greater depth. The staff are specialists who aim to inspire a love of their subjects. Girls are encouraged to work independently and to develop good study habits. From Year 7 all girls study two modern foreign languages together with Latin, and science is taught throughout the senior school as three separate subjects. A broad range of options is available at GCSE, A level and IB diploma.

Music, art, drama and sport are integral parts of the life of the school and involve every girl. Many also take extra music, ballet and speech and drama lessons, as well as games coaching.

The use of information communication technology is a key element in teaching. We expect girls to use computers as part of their normal studies and provide ample facilities for them to do so. All girls follow a GCSE course in ICT which is also offered as an A level option.

St Helen's Sixth Form, where the International Baccalaureate is taught as well as A levels, is a flourishing community of approximately 160 girls who take an active role in the life of the school. Each year we welcome new students who join us from other schools. The sixth form is in many ways a new beginning and often the most enjoyable and challenging time of school life. Significant numbers each year go to Oxford and Cambridge. Almost every girl goes on to the university of her first choice.

A large number of clubs and societies exist which cater for all interests. These change each year to reflect the particular interests of girls and staff. Work experience, both at home and abroad, foreign exchanges and visits are well supported.

In the Duke of Edinburgh's Award Scheme, girls are able to achieve bronze, silver and gold awards while at school. St Helen's is one of only eight girls' schools to offer a Combined Cadet Force, which is run jointly with Merchant Taylors' School. Debating is a highly successful activity from Years 6 to 13, with girls competing both in school and up to national level. Above all, we build the girls' confidence and encourage them to chase their dreams, ready to take their place in the adult world.

St Helen's School Northwood is a registered charity (No. 312762) which exists to provide high quality education for girls from the UK and overseas.

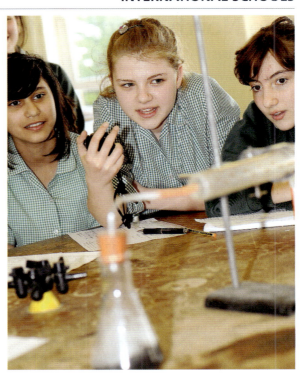

The North London International School

(Founded 1885)

6 Friern Barnet Lane, London N11 3LX
Tel: +44 (0)20 8920 0600 Email: admissions@nlis.org
Fax: +44 (0)20 8211 4605   Website: www.nlis.org

The North London
International School

Head of School: Mr David Rose MA(Ed), BA, CertEd
School type: Coeducational International Day
Homestay available for students age 16-19
Member of: ISA, ECIS, IAPS, LISA, IB, ISCis
Age range of pupils: 2–19
No. of pupils enrolled as at 1.5.10: 400
Kindergarten (ages 2-4): 20 boys 17 girls
Lower School (ages 4-6): 26 boys 16 girls
Lower School (ages 6-11): 87 boys 52 girls
Upper School (ages 11-16): 109 boys 48 girls
Upper School (ages 16-19): 25 boys 15 girls
Fees per annum as at 1.5.10: Day: £3225–£15,480
Religious denomination: Inter-denominational

Curriculum

The North London International School aims to provide a secure, well-ordered and happy environment with the learning process at its core, offering the finest possible education for all pupils in order for them to reach their full potential. Serving a cosmopolitan and diverse north London community, great importance is attached to respect, understanding and empathy with everyone's cultures, religions and backgrounds.

Students follow the International Baccalaureate (IB) curriculum, starting at aged three with the Primary Years Programme, moving onto the Middle Years Programme at age 11 and the IB Diploma Programme at age 16. The programmes are designed to encourage the development of learning skills and to meet a child's academic, social, physical, emotional and cultural needs. Through enquiry-based learning and various disciplines, subject interrelatedness is accentuated, preparing students for the pre-university Diploma Programme.

The school recognises that students can have a variety of different learning styles. The Quest Programme is designed for students who need help developing strategies to assist them to study effectively. Through one-to-one tuition from specialist staff, students can reach their full potential, further enhanced by the school's teacher-student ratio.

Entry requirements

Students are accepted for entry at any time throughout the school year.

Kindergarten and Lower School (ages two to 11): students are invited to attend for half a day and may be asked to complete a basic assessment.

Upper School (ages 11-16): students attend an interview with the Head of the school, are invited to visit the school for a day and may be required to complete a basic assessment.

Entry to the upper school is automatic for students in the lower school.

Upper School (ages 16-19): Diploma Programme applicants are invited for interview with the programme coordinator. Students would be expected to have five or six GCSE passes, with B, A or A* grades for subjects to be studied at Higher Level.

Examinations offered

Key Stage 2, IBMYP and IB Diploma.

Facilities

The school has dedicated IT, music, art and design technology facilities for all students. The commitment to the use of ICT in all subject areas is highlighted by IT and graphics suites, individual student home drives and email accounts, student dedicated laptops and wireless network.

Students' physical development is considered as important as academic development and the school's sports fields provide excellent facilities for football, cricket, athletics, hockey, tennis and softball. The school's hall, playgrounds and local amenities are also utilised to offer further activities such as basketball, badminton, squash, swimming, table tennis, ice-skating and skiing. Matches and tournaments between local schools are regular fixtures.

The school is able to provide a bus service for students living in the local area in addition to the excellent bus, tube and train routes from the rest of London and the surrounding area.

The Royal School, Hampstead

(Founded 1855)

65 Rosslyn Hill, Hampstead, London NW3 5UD
Tel: 020 7794 7708   Email: enquiries@royalschoolhampstead.net
Fax: 020 7431 6741   Website: www.royalschoolhampstead.net

Headmistress: Ms J Ebner BEd(Hons)(Cantab), MA(London), PGDipCouns, Cert FT, NPQH
Appointed: September 2006
School type: Girls' Day & Boarding
Age range of pupils: 3–16
No. of pupils enrolled as at 1.4.10: 210
No. of boarders: 25
Fees per annum as at 1.4.10: Day: £8940–£10,500
Weekly Boarding: £15,870
Boarding: £20,700
Average size of class: 16 average
Teacher/pupil ratio: 1:9

The Royal School is a small, friendly day and boarding school for girls set in a modern, safe and spacious campus conveniently located in the heart of Hampstead.

Founded by Queen Victoria in 1855 the school enjoys royal patronage from HRH The Duchess of Cornwall and provides a remarkable educational experience.

This unique girls-only education allows pupils to achieve their full potential academically, emotionally, creatively and physically whilst building friendships that last a lifetime.

The first school (age three to seven) lays the early years foundation teaching through play-based activities in a nurturing environment.

The lower school (seven to 11) encourages girls to gain independence and a love of learning. Music, French, drama, PE and ICT are taught by specialists. Girls also enjoy sewing, food technology and cooking in our excellent new design & technology facility.

The middle school (11-14) offers a broad, balanced curriculum. Whilst exploring traditional subjects girls are also allowed to pursue other areas that enrich their knowledge of the world around them. Extensive extracurricular activities are available including photography, drama, sports, music, nature and art clubs.

The upper school (14-16) encourages maturity and academic success through building responsibility and confidence. A wide range of GCSE subjects are offered alongside tailor-made curriculums such as sociology GCSE. Many opportunities are open to girls including becoming prefects, or Childline Counsellors. Academic results are excellent and guidance is given for sixth form choices. We have alliances with excellent GSA schools and many colleges.

We welcome boarders from the UK and overseas alongside flexi-boarding; a boon for parents in today's busy world. Boarders enjoy a friendly atmosphere in spacious accommodation with superb views. Our dedicated boarding staff ensure the girls are safe and well cared for whilst enjoying enriching activities such as crafts, films, shopping, theatre trips and more.

Bursaries are available.

Tonbridge School

(Founded 1553)

Tonbridge, Kent TN9 1JP
Tel: 01732 365555   Email: hmsec@tonbridge-school.org
Fax: 01732 363424   Website: www.tonbridge-school.co.uk

TONBRIDGE
SCHOOL

Headmaster: T H P Haynes
Appointed: 2005
School type: Boys' Day & Boarding
Age range of pupils: 13–18
No. of pupils enrolled as at 1.4.10: 750
Sixth Form: 330
No. of boarders: 450
Fees per annum as at 1.4.10: Day: £20,910
Boarding: £28,140
Average size of class: GCSE 16, A level 9
Teacher/pupil ratio: 1:7.6

Tonbridge School is one of the leading boys' schools in the country. Boarders and day boys of varying backgrounds are offered an education remarkable both for its breadth of opportunity and the exceptional standards routinely achieved in all areas of school life.

Tonbridge School aims to provide a caring and enlightened environment in which the talents of each individual flourish. We encourage boys to be creative, tolerant and to strive for academic, sporting and cultural excellence. Respect for tradition and an openness to innovation are equally valued. A well-established house system at the heart of the school fosters a strong sense of belonging. Tonbridge seeks to celebrate its distinctive mixture of boarders and day boys; this helps to create a unique broadening and deepening of opportunity. We want boys to enjoy their time here, but also to be made aware of their social and moral responsibilities. Tonbridgians should enter into the adult world with the knowledge and self-belief to fulfil their own potential and, in many cases, to become leaders in their chosen field. Equally, we hope to foster a life-long empathy for the needs and views of others.

The school is extremely successful in its university entrance (over 20% of leavers go to Oxbridge) and strives for excellence in all fields, yet the ethos of the school is one of strong participation and acceptance of each others' strengths and weaknesses rather than blind concentration on results.

Tonbridge School is just off the M25, on the edge of the Kent/Surrey/Sussex borders and attracts families from all over southern England. It lies in about 150 acres of land on the edge of the town of Tonbridge, and thus provides a good balance between town and country living.

Families are warmly welcomed to come and see Tonbridge and to meet the Headmaster. We hope that a visit will leave you not only impressed by the facilities and the achievements of the boys, but also by the sense of fun and openness which the boys encounter here on a daily basis. Please contact our admissions department on 01732 304297 or admissions@tonbridge-school.org. For further information about Tonbridge please visit our website: www.tonbridge-school.co.uk.

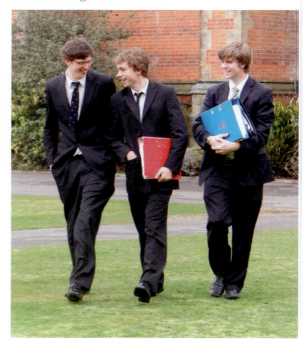

Worth School

(Founded 1959)

Paddockhurst Road, Turners Hill, Crawley, West Sussex RH10 4SD
Tel: 01342 710200   Email: registry@worth.org.uk
Fax: 01342 710230   Website: www.worthschool.co.uk

Headmaster: Mr Gino Carminati MA, FRSA
Appointed: April 2007
School type: Catholic coeducational 11-18
boarding & day
Member of: HMC, BSA, ASCL, ISCis, IB
Age range of pupils: 11–18
No. of pupils enrolled as at 1.3.10: 505
Sixth Form: 229
No. of boarders: 313
Fees per annum as at 1.9.09: Day: £16,026–£18,339
Boarding: £21,627–£24,756
Average size of class: 18 (in sixth form: 11)
Teacher/pupil ratio: 1:7

Worth is known for its strong community values, high academic standards, friendly atmosphere and the excellence of its all-round education. As a Benedictine school we encourage our pupils to develop their own individuality whilst living within a community that inspires learning, worship, friendship and service.

The school is set, alongside Worth Abbey, in 500 acres of rural Sussex yet only 12km from Gatwick airport and 50km from central London.

At Worth, we see our pupils as 'Lanterns to Light'. Inspiring pupils to think, learn, create, imagine and perform is pivotal if each individual is to develop their intellectual potential. This is achieved by the highest standards of teaching and also by the application of new approaches to learning and exciting opportunities in which to discover and learn. The school offers a broad curriculum at GCSE and in the sixth form, where students can opt for the International Baccalaureate Diploma (taught since 2002) or A levels. Examination results are high - IB scores are consistently significantly higher than the global average - and pupils enter the very best universities in the UK and abroad, including Oxbridge.

In September 2008, Worth welcomed sixth form girls into the school community and girls joined in Years 7 (11+) and 9 (13+) in September 2010. Investment in new facilities and teaching staff continues, including the opening of a new girls' boarding and day house.

Beyond the classroom, pupils benefit from a range of societies, lectures, trips and visits - enriching the academic life of the school whilst encouraging everyone to aim high. The school has a long tradition of community involvement, reaching out to others through an extensive voluntary service programme. A large proportion of pupils are involved in the Duke of Edinburgh's Award Scheme, for which the school is a centre of excellence. Sports facilities include extensive playing fields, an eight-hole golf course, fencing salle, dance studio and fitness suite. Stables are available on the site for students' horses. The drama and music departments are outstanding and benefit from a purpose-built Performing Arts Centre housing a theatre, recording studio, sound-proofed 'rock room', rehearsal rooms, recital room and music classrooms.

"Students here are keen, engaging, interesting people who will go to all sorts of lengths just to make your day that little bit better." Year 13 student.

Worth School is a registered charity (No. 1093914)

Specialist & Sixth Form Schools and Colleges

Ashbourne Independent Sixth Form College

(Founded 1981)

17 Old Court Place, Kensington, London W8 4PL
Tel: 020 7937 3858 Email: admin@ashbournecollege.co.uk
Fax: 020 7937 2207 Website: www.ashbournecollege.co.uk

Principal: M J Kirby MSc, BApSc
Appointed: 1/9/82
Director of Studies: John Wilson BA Hons (Oxon),
PGCE (Cantab)
School type: Independent Sixth Form College
Age range of pupils: 16–19
No. of pupils enrolled as at 1.4.10: 170
Boys: 80 Girls: 90
Fees per annum as at 1.4.10: Day: £19,725
Boarding: £21,500
Average size of class: Avg 7
Teacher/pupil ratio: 1:5

Ashbourne College is a highly successful private college. Located near Kensington Gardens and the Royal Albert Hall in central London, it offers outstanding teaching, which has seen its students secure places at some of the world's leading universities. It focuses primarily on offering one-year, eighteen-month and the standard two-year A level courses to pre-university students between the ages of 16-22. Start dates are available for both September and January (other dates can be discussed). Pre-GCSE and GCSE courses to 13-16 year olds are also available.

Ashbourne encourages students to enjoy their time at college with a wide range of extracurricular activities. This year students have had the opportunity to take part in the following events and clubs: The College Revue, ice-skating, go-karting, chess club, drama club, music club, trips to plays, two university visits, street dance, and a trip to Stratford-upon-Avon for English Literature students. Each year a cultural trip to a European city is organised, which is an excellent experience for all overseas students. In addition to this, the students have organised and run their own successful college newspaper, *'The Ashbourner'*.

Ashbourne College aims to send students to top UK universities, and in the past few years has sent scholars to all of the top universities within the UK. In certain cases, students have won scholarships to the best British universities including Oxford, Nottingham and LSE. Ashbourne College attracts high quality students wishing to obtain university placement at the UK's top ten universities. An Ashbourne student's university application process is developed through the personal tutoring system, where students meet with their personal tutor once a week in groups of up to 20 students.

Ashbourne College has achieved successful results this academic year with 39% of examinations resulting in A grades in the summer of 2009.

Bright Futures

(Founded 2002)

63-65 Portland Place, Westminster, London W1B 1QR
Tel: 020 7580 8096   Email: dawn@brightfuturesonline.co.uk
Website: www.brightfuturesonline.co.uk

Principal: Dawn Savage
School type: Online Sixth Form (a division of Southbank Int'l School, London)
Age range of pupils:

Have you ever considered a career change, gaining additional qualifications, or are you simply looking for an opportunity to better yourself? For nearly ten years, Bright Futures has been exploring the possibilities of online learning and developed innovative teaching and learning strategies to benefit students. Having taken what we had learnt we have, alongside our team of teaching and academic experts launched Bright Futures - the leading online A level course providers.

Studying for an A level qualification online with Bright Futures couldn't be easier. Enrolment dates are flexible and materials are available twenty four hours a day, seven days a week, ensuring each course fits in with your lifestyle.

Distance learning can often appear isolating. However with your own personal tutor, as well as the encouragement provided by the Bright Futures team, you will be provided with all of the support you will need to study at home. Communication with your tutor is the key to success with Bright Futures and they will help you to produce an individual plan, explain how to get the best out of the materials available and work with you to achieve your personal goals and exam targets.

All of our A level courses follow QCA specifications and if external examinations are required to complete the qualification, these can be taken at our own centre in Westminster or at a centre close to your home. Coursework may be required for some subjects and this will also be carried out at our site in Central London.

At Bright Futures, it is understood that previous achievement is not always the best indicator of likely success. Self motivation and a strong support structure are considered by us to be the right ingredients to help maximise student success. Learning with Bright Futures is an experience - just ask some of our previous students!

Duff Miller College

(Founded 1952)

59 Queen's Gate, South Kensington, London SW7 5JP
Tel: 020 7225 0577   Email: enqs@duffmiller.com
Fax: 020 7589 5155   Website: www.duffmiller.com

Principals: C Denning BSc, PGCE & C Kraft BSc, BPS
Appointed: 1989
School type: Coeducational Day
Member of: CIFE, BAC
Age range of pupils: 14–19
No. of pupils enrolled as at 1.4.10: 260
Fees per annum as at 1.4.10: Day: £10,000–£15,000
Average size of class: 7

At Duff Miller sixth form college we strive to create an environment that inspires our students and gives them the confidence and enthusiasm to achieve the highest possible results. The traditional values which have been crucial to Duff Miller's success as a sixth form college for more than half a century are complemented by the state-of-the-art technology which you would expect to find at one of the capital's leading sixth form colleges. A strong sense of community and an excellent rapport between staff and students are also defining features of the college today.

The imposing sixth form college building located in South Kensington, London, contains a range of classrooms, laboratories and a computer room to meet all the students' needs. A supervised study area is provided along with a fully equipped internet café to enable our students to make enjoyable and profitable use of their time throughout the college day. Within lessons and outside them, our priority is to ensure that the students have every chance to fulfil their potential.

A programme of activities takes place throughout the year. These include subject-related excursions like a psychology field trip to a zoo and a biology field trip to a brewery. Drama students are taken on outings to both West End shows and fringe productions. They are also given a chance to put on their own productions over the course of the year and to perform at a theatre.

Places at Duff Miller are offered on the basis of an interview with the Principal or Vice-Principal. This can be arranged by our admissions team who are always ready to answer any questions you might have about the college. If you are interested in joining Duff Miller please don't hesitate to request more information or come and look around.

Regent College

(Founded 2000)

Sai House, 167 Imperial Drive, Harrow, Middlesex HA2 7HD
Tel: 020 8966 9900   Email: application@regentcollege.uk.com
Fax: 020 8429 5639   Website: www.regentcollege.uk.com

Principal: Mr Selva Pankaj MBA, FCMA
School type: Coeducational Day
Age range of pupils: 11–19
No. of pupils enrolled as at 1.4.10: 151
Boys: 93 Girls: 58
Fees per annum as at 1.4.10: Day: £9000
Average size of class: 12
Teacher/pupil ratio: 1:7

Regent College is an independent, coeducational, non-selective senior school and sixth form college which celebrated its tenth anniversary in 2010. The college has grown immeasurably over the past years, not only in number, but in reputation. We are located in Harrow, a pleasant north-west London suburb. There are excellent public transport links available nearby, the college being just one minute from Rayners Lane Tube Station. The large part of our student body is in the GCSE and A level years but we have also recently expanded to accept students from Year 7 upwards. What makes us exceptional as an educational provider is our close student monitoring system and small class sizes which hold a maximum of 15 students, less than half of the average class size. This allows our teaching staff to devote much more time and attention to each student with the end result that students progress at a faster rate.

Aims and ethos

Here at Regent College, we believe it our duty to ensure we do our best for every one of our students, not only academically, but in a wider social context. Our team consists of qualified, dedicated teachers and each department is overseen by a highly experienced Head. We believe in stretching and challenging our students to ensure that they achieve their full potential and aim to provide them with the best possible opportunities to facilitate this. Our students come from a variety of backgrounds and we celebrate the diversity that this brings to our college. When a student completes their education at Regent, we endeavour to make sure that they are well-rounded, confident young men and women ready to take their place in society, both in higher education and beyond, and we try to cultivate a happy, caring and stimulating environment in which our students can realise this.

Facilities

Regent College is located in a modern, refurbished building offering all the facilities students may need including interactive classrooms, a large hall for exams and quiet study, a recently refurbished student common room, a café, well-equipped science laboratories, modern IT facilities, a light and airy art room, and our most recent developments, a sports court and a stunning new library with a vast array of resources. We also have off-site sports facilities for cricket, football and tennis located at several other local schools including the world-renowned Harrow School.

Programmes of study

At Regent College, we follow the basis of the National Curriculum in the senior school. For our older students, we offer not only traditional two-year GCSE and A level programmes, but also offer unique one-year intensive programmes. These programmes allow students who have already taken their exams, but not done as well as they had hoped, to re-take the course within three terms. We are also offering a

new fifteen-week A level course in September for those students who have gained good grades but would like to improve them further. This flexibility guarantees that all students are enrolled on a course that best suits their needs. We also offer our Middlesex University articulated University Foundation Programme to international students wishing to enter into the British university system and we are registered with the BAC and UK Border Agency. Additionally, we have introduced the Regent Medical School Programme as part of our UCAS guidance for those students looking to enrol on competitive courses. However, though we pride ourselves on academic excellence, we do understand that for a student to flourish, they need to have a good balance between their study and extracurricular activities. This is why we promote such pursuits as house debating and sports tournaments which help develop valuable social skills such as teamwork and organisation and reinforce the community spirit that we seek to attain in the college. In addition to this, we try to instil our students with life-long skills and therefore build classes for PSHE, study and exam techniques and tutorial groups into the timetable.

Performance

Regent College has excellent success rates with all its students. We are non-selective yet always outperform various benchmarks. In August 2009 we had a 100% pass rate at GCSE with a remarkable 83% of grades being at A* to B. Our A level pass rate was 98%. Our most recent Ofsted report highlighted "a good quality of education within a calm and positive learning environment which enables students of all ages to thrive and to make good progress," praised our teaching and assessment as having "a number of outstanding features" and noted that students "comment very positively on the support that they receive both in terms of their academic and personal development." Students from Regent College go on to a variety of prestigious universities including Cambridge, Durham, LSE and UCL and follow disciplines such as dentistry, medicine, IT and banking.

Ray Cochrane Beauty School
An International CIDESCO School

(Founded 1954)

118 Baker Street, London W1U 6TT
Tel: 020 7486 6291   Email: email@raycochrane.co.uk
Fax: 020 7935 3405   Website: www.raycochrane.co.uk

Principal: Miss Baljeet Suri CIDESCO, CIBTAC, FETC, IFA
School type: Private Vocational
Age range of pupils: 16–50
No. of pupils enrolled as at 1.4.10: 40
Fees per annum as at 1.4.10: Day: £2195–£8995
Average size of class: 16-18
Teacher/pupil ratio: 1:16

From the day it was founded in 1954, the Ray Cochrane Beauty School has been run with a passionate desire to equip students with the comprehensive knowledge and cutting edge tools to excel in the beauty profession. Throughout the years, the school has constantly challenged its students to reach a higher level of expertise and has continued to learn and grow alongside its students. Today, the school is not only proud to be recognised as the first CIDESCO school in Great Britain but excited in the knowledge that it has established itself as the most reputable beauty therapy training institution in the world.

The Ray Cochrane Beauty School has been providing impeccable training from beginner to practioner level for over fifty years. Our excellent reputation for training to the highest standards are acknowledged throughout the world.

We are pleased to announce that our principal, Ms Baljeet Suri, has been made an honorary member of CIDESCO International at the 53rd CIDESCO World Congress. This honour has been bestowed on her in recognition of her services and dedication to the cause of this international body. She was chosen from a highly competitive field. This award has great significance for our students in that they have a principal with international stature and it also means that the diploma they will receive at the end of their training, acquires an enhanced status.

Schools & Nursery Schools in Central London

Central London

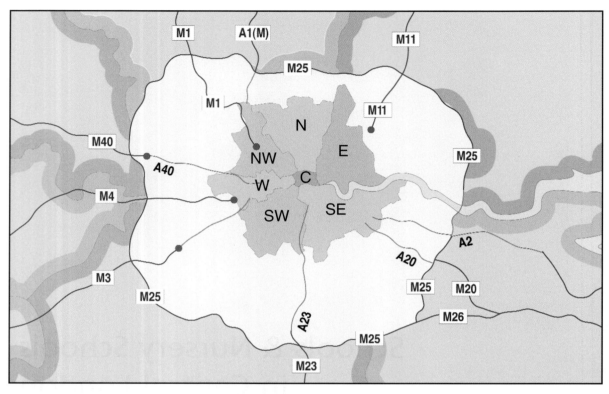

©MAPS IN MINUTES™ 2010
©Crown Copyright, Ordnance Survey 2010

Key to symbols

(♦) Boys' school

(♦) Girls' school

(♦♦) Coeducational school

(♦) International school

16: Tutorial or sixth form college

(A) A levels

(♦) Boarding accommodation

(£) Bursaries

(IB) International Baccalaureate

(♦) Learning support

16: Entrance at 16+

(♦) Vocational qualifications

LONDON

CENTRAL LONDON

Broadgate Day Nursery
21 Curtain Road, Hackney, London EC2A 3LW
Tel: 020 7247 3491
Principal: Jacky Roberts NNEB
Type: Coeducational Day
Age range: 0–5
No. of pupils: 50

CITY OF LONDON SCHOOL
For further details see p. 8
Queen Victoria Street, London EC4V 3AL
Tel: 020 7489 0291
Email: admissions@clsb.org.uk
Website: www.clsb.org.uk
Headmaster: Mr D Levin MA
Type: Boys' Day
Age range: 10–18
No. of pupils: 900 VIth250
Fees: Day £13,050

City of London School for Girls
St Giles' Terrace, Barbican, London EC2Y 8BB
Tel: 020 7847 5500
Headmistress: Miss D Vernon
Type: Girls' Day
Age range: 7–18
No. of pupils: 709
Fees: Day £13,131

Dallington School
8 Dallington Street, Islington, London EC1V 0BQ
Tel: 020 7251 2284
Headteacher: Mrs M C Hercules
Type: Coeducational Day
Age range: 3–11
No. of pupils: 140 B70 G70
Fees: Day £8000–£10,200

Kidsunlimited Nurseries - Mango Tree
62-66 Farringdon Road, London EC1R 3GA
Tel: 08458 500 222
Type: Coeducational Nursery School

Leapfrog Day Nurseries - London City
49 Clifton Street, London EC2A 4EX
Tel: 020 7422 0088
Manager: Jo Collins
Type: Coeducational Nursery School
Age range: 0–5

Leapfrog Day Nurseries - Smithfield
14 West Smithfield, London EC1A 9HY
Tel: 020 7778 0100
Manager: Estelle Cook-Sadeghi
Type: Coeducational Nursery School
Age range: 0–5

St Paul's Cathedral School
2 New Change, London EC4M 9AD
Tel: 020 7248 5156
Headmaster: Mr Neil Chippington MA, FRCO
Type: Coeducational Pre-Prep, Day Prep & Boarding Choir School
Age range: 4–13
No. of pupils: 235
Fees: Day £10,578–£11,388 FB £6588

The Charterhouse Square School
40 Charterhouse Square, London EC1M 6EA
Tel: 020 7600 3805
Head Mistress: Mrs J Malden MA, BEd(Hons)
Type: Coeducational Day
Age range: 4–11
No. of pupils: B90 G80
Fees: Day £8250

The Lyceum
Kayham House, 6 Paul Street, London EC2A 4JH
Tel: 020 7247 1588
Joint Headteachers: Mr Jeremy Rowe & Mrs Lynn Hannay
Type: Coeducational Day
Age range: 4–11
No. of pupils: 97 B51 G46
Fees: Day £9900

The Urdang Academy of Ballet
20-22 Shelton Street, Covent Garden, London WC2H 9JJ
Tel: 0207 713 7710
Principal: Mrs J Crowther BA(Hons)
Type: Coeducational Day
Age range: 10–16
No. of pupils: B3 G20
Fees: Day £6600

EAST LONDON

E1

Al-Mizan School
88 Whitechapel Road, London E1 1JQ
Tel: 020 7377 0234
Head: Mr H S Salekin
Type: Boys' Day
Age range: 7–11
No. of pupils: 36
Fees: Day £1600

Green Gables Montessori Primary School
The Institute, 302 The Highway, Wapping,
London E1W 3DH
Tel: 020 7488 2374
Head: Mrs V Hunt
Type: Coeducational Day
Age range: 0–8
No. of pupils: 45 B25 G20
Fees: Day £740–£10,480

London East Academy
46-80 Whitechapel Road, London E1 1JX
Tel: 020 7650 3070
Type: Boys' Day
Age range: 11–16

Madani Girls School
Myrdle Street, London E1 1HL
Tel: 020 7377 1992
Headteacher: Mrs F Liyawdeen
Type: Girls' Day
Age range: 11–18
No. of pupils: 248 VIth11
Fees: Day £1900

River House Montessori School
3-4 Shadwell Pierhead, Glamis Road, London E1W 3TD
Tel: 020 7538 9886
Headmistress: Miss S Greenwood
Type: Coeducational Day
Age range: 3–12
No. of pupils: B55 G45
Fees: Day £2700–£9000

Spitalfields Nursery
21 Lamb Street, London E1 6EA
Tel: 020 7375 0775
Principal: Angela Dorian
Type: Coeducational Nursery School

E2

Bethnal Green Montessori School
68 Warner Place, Bethnal Green, London E2 7DA
Tel: 020 7739 4343
Head: Sidonie Winter
Type: Coeducational Nursery School
Age range: 2–6
No. of pupils: B22 G23

Gatehouse School
Sewardstone Road, Victoria Park, London E2 9JG
Tel: 020 8980 2978
Headmistress: Mrs Belinda Canham JP, BA(Hons),
PGCE(Froebel)
Type: Coeducational Day
Age range: 3–11
No. of pupils: 300 B148 G152
Fees: Day £6525–£8010

Noah's Ark Nursery
within Mildmay Hospital, Hackney Road, London E2 7NA
Tel: 020 7613 6346
Type: Coeducational Nursery School

The Happy Nest Nursery Ltd
Fellows Court Family Centre, Weymouth Terrace, Hackney,
London E2 8LR
Tel: 020 7739 3193
Type: Coeducational Day

E3

Pillar Box Montessori Nursery & Pre-Prep School
107 Bow Road, London E3 2AN
Tel: 020 8980 0700
Headmistress: Ms Lorraine Redknapp
Type: Coeducational Nursery School
Age range: 0–7
Fees: Day £250–£500

E4

Amhurst Nursery
13, The Avenue, Waltham Forest, London E4
Tel: 020 8527 1614
Officer in Charge: Mrs Mills
Type: Coeducational Day

Billet's Corner Day Nursery
11 Walthamstow Avenue, London E4 8ST
Tel: 020 8523 3823
Principal: B Harmsworth
Type: Coeducational Nursery School

Childsplay Day Nursery
283 Hall Lane, Chingford, London E4 8NU
Tel: 020 8529 6058
Type: Coeducational Nursery School
Age range: 0–5

Chingford Activity Nursery
22 Marlborough Road, Waltham Forest, London E4 9AL
Tel: 020 8347 7000
Head: Mary Farey
Type: Coeducational Day
Age range: 0–5
Fees: Day £5460–£8320

Leapfrog Day Nurseries - Chingford
2 Larkswood Leisure Park, 175 New Road, Chingford, London E4 9EY
Tel: 020 8524 7063
Manager: Catalina Harding
Type: Coeducational Nursery School
Age range: 0–5

Merryfield Montessori Nursery
76 Station Road, Waltham Forest, London E4 7BA
Tel: 020 8524 7697
Type: Coeducational Nursery School
No. of pupils: 45

Normanhurst School
68-74 Station Road, Chingford, London E4 7BA
Tel: 020 8529 4307
Headmistress: Ms H Kacouris MBA, BA(Hons), PGCE, NPQH
Type: Coeducational Day
Age range: 2½–16
No. of pupils: 250 B146 G104
Fees: Day £3105–£9000

E5

Al-Falah Primary School
48 Kenninghall Road, Clapton, London E5 8BY
Tel: 020 8985 1059
Headteacher: Mr Khalil Goddard
Type: Coeducational Day
Age range: 5–11
No. of pupils: 83 B53 G30
Fees: Day £1600

Leaview Community Nursery Ltd
Leaview House, Springfield, London E5 9EJ
Tel: 020 8806 9012
Co-ordinator: Leticia Adu AdvMontDip
Type: Coeducational Nursery School
Age range: 6months–5
No. of pupils: B12 G14
Fees: Day £3000–£6250

Lubavitch House School (Junior Boys)
135 Clapton Common, London E5 9AE
Tel: 020 8800 1044
Head: Rabbi D Golomb
Type: Boys' Day
Age range: 5–11
No. of pupils: 101
Fees: Day £520–£3100

Paragon Christian Academy
233-241 Glyn Road, London E5 0JP
Tel: 020 8985 1119
Headteacher: Mrs J A Lynch
Type: Coeducational Day
Age range: 5–16
No. of pupils: 34 B19 G15

Talmud Torah Machikei Hadass School
96-98 Clapton Common, London E5 9AL
Tel: 020 8800 6070
Headteacher: Rabbi C Silbiger
Type: Boys' Day
Age range: 4–11
No. of pupils: 271

E6

Oliver Thomas Nursery School
Mathews Avenue, East Ham, London E6 6BU
Tel: 020 8552 1177
Head Teacher: Dianne Walls
Type: Coeducational Nursery School
Age range: 3–5
(ﾐ) (✏)

E7

Grangewood Independent School
Chester Road, Forest Gate, London E7 8QT
Tel: 020 8472 3552
Headteacher: Mrs C A Adams
Type: Coeducational Day
Age range: 3–11
No. of pupils: 75
(ﾐ)

Kaye Rowe Nursery School
Osborne Road, London E7 0PH
Tel: 020 8534 4403
Type: Coeducational Nursery School
(ﾐ)

Stepping Stones Day Nursery - Forest Gate
St Bonaventure's School, St Anthony's Road,
London E7 9QB
Tel: 020 8470 6999
Type: Coeducational Nursery School
(ﾐ)

E8

136 Nursery
c/o Ann Taylor Centre, Triangle Road, Hackney, London E8
Tel: 020 7249 9826
Type: Coeducational Day
Fees: Day £10
(ﾐ)

Independent Place Nursery
26/27 Independent Place, Shacklewell Lane, Hackney,
London E8 2HD
Tel: 020 7275 7755
Head: Ms Dawn Pennington
Type: Coeducational Day
Age range: 0–5
No. of pupils: 43
(ﾐ) (✏)

Market Nursery
Wilde Close, Off Pownall Road, Hackney, London E8 4JS
Tel: 020 7241 0978
Head: Ms Hazel Babb
Type: Coeducational Day
No. of pupils: 24 B12 G12
(ﾐ) (✏)

E9

Get Along Gang Playgroup
St Mary of Eton Church Hall, Eastway, Hackney,
London E9 5JA
Tel: 020 8533 0926
Type: Coeducational Day
(ﾐ)

E10

Chesterfield Day Nursery
38 Chesterfield Road, Waltham Forest, London E10 6EW
Tel: 020 8539 5541
Officer in Charge: Karen James
Type: Coeducational Day
(ﾐ)

E11

Forest Glade Nursery
15 Dyson Road, London E11 1NA
Tel: 020 8989 9684
Type: Coeducational Day
Age range: 0–5
No. of pupils: B15 G9
(ﾐ) (✏)

Humpty Dumpty Nursery
24 Fairlop Road, Waltham Forest, London E11 1BL
Tel: 020 8539 3810
Type: Coeducational Day
Age range: 1–5
No. of pupils: B17 G15
(ﾐ)

Little Green Man Nursery
15 Lemna Road, Waltham Forest, London E11 1HX
Tel: 020 8539 7228
Type: Coeducational Day
Age range: 0–5
No. of pupils: 46 B22 G24
(ﾐ)

St Joseph's Convent School For Girls

59 Cambridge Park, Wanstead, London E11 2PR
Tel: 020 8989 4700
Headteacher: Ms C Glover
Type: Girls' Day
Age range: 3–11 G3–11
No. of pupils: 171 B0 G171
Fees: Day £1650

Sunbeams Day Nursery

10 Bushwood, Leytonstone, London E11 3AY
Tel: 020 8530 2784
Principal: Kim Frisby
Type: Coeducational Nursery School

Sunshine Day Nursery

167 Wallward Road, Leytonstone, London E11 1AQ
Tel: 020 8556 6889
Officer in Charge: Ms Nikki Bailey
Type: Coeducational Nursery School

Tree House Nursery & After School

35 Woodbine Place, London E11 2RH
Tel: 020 8532 2535
Type: Coeducational Nursery School

E12

Happy Faces at Wisdom Kids Nursery

524 High Street, London E12 6QN
Tel: 020 8478 2805
Type: Coeducational Nursery School

E13

Alphabet House Nursery School

23 Harold Road, Upton Park, London E13 0SQ
Tel: 020 8548 9466
Principal: Ms Kemi Balogun
Type: Coeducational Day

E14

Smarty Pants Day Nursery

1 Plashet Road, London E13 0PZ
Tel: 020 8471 2620
Principal: Jennifer Lewis & Sylvia Lewis
Type: Coeducational Nursery School
No. of pupils: 46

Bushytails Day Nursery and Nursery School

591 Manchester Road, Docklands, London E14 3NU
Tel: 020 7537 7776
Headmistress: Christine G Bush NNEB
Type: Coeducational Day
Age range: 0–5
No. of pupils: 15

Lanterns Nursery and Pre-school

F4-F6 Lanterns Court, 22 Millharbour, London E14 9TU
Tel: 020 7363 0951
Type: Coeducational Day

Magic Roundabout Nursery - Docklands

Jack Dash House, 2 Lawn House Close, Marsh Wall,
London E14 9YQ
Tel: 020 7364 6028
Type: Coeducational Nursery School

E15

Alphabet House Day (Montessori) Nursery

Methodist Church, Windmill Lane, Stratford,
London E15 1PG
Tel: 020 8519 2023
Principal: Ms Kemi Balogun
Type: Coeducational Day

Stepping Stones Day Nursery - Stratford

Brickfield Congregational Church, Welfare Road,
London E15 4HT
Tel: 020 8534 8777
Type: Coeducational Nursery School

E16

Leapfrog Day Nurseries - London Excel

5 Western Gateway, London E16 1AU
Tel: 020 7474 7487
Manager: Sarah Jordan
Type: Coeducational Nursery School
Age range: 0–5

E17

Forest School

College Place, Snaresbrook, London E17 3PY
Tel: 020 8520 1744
Warden: Mrs S J Kerr-Dineen MA
Type: Coeducational Day
Age range: 4–18
No. of pupils: 1232 B617 G615 VIth250
Fees: Day £8475–£12,894

(**) (A) (£) (/) (16+)

Happy Child Day Nursery

The Old Town Hall, 14B Orford Road, Walthamstow
Village, London E17 9NL
Tel: 020 8520 8880
Head: Mrs Margaret Murphy
Type: Coeducational Day

(**)

Hyland House School

896 Forest Road, Walthamstow, London E17 4AE
Tel: 020 8520 4186
Headmistress: Mrs T Thorpe
Type: Coeducational Day
Age range: 3–11
No. of pupils: B50 G52
Fees: Day £2520

(**)

Low Hall Nursery

Low Hall Lane, London E17 8BE
Tel: 020 8520 1689
Type: Coeducational Day

(**)

Magic Roundabout Nursery - Walthamstow

161 Wadham Road, Centre Way, Walthamstow,
London E17 4HU
Tel: 020 8523 5551
Type: Coeducational Nursery School

(**)

Rascals Day Nursery

34 Verulam Avenue, Walthamstow, London E17 8ER
Tel: 020 8520 2417
Head: Teresa Aguda
Type: Coeducational Nursery School
Age range: 2–5
No. of pupils: B30 G30

(**)

Tinkerbells Nursery

185 Coppermill Lane, Walthamstow, London E17 7HU
Tel: 020 8520 8338
Principal: Sue Walker
Type: Coeducational Nursery School

(**)

Tom Thumb Nursery

1-7 Beulah Road, London E17 9LG
Tel: 020 8520 1329
Type: Coeducational Nursery School
Age range: 2–5
No. of pupils: 32

(**)

E18

Clevelands Day Nursery

71 Cleveland Road, South Woodford, London E18 2AE
Tel: 020 8518 8855
Head: Mrs L Ferdinando
Type: Coeducational Day

(**)

Kids Inc Day Nursery

71 Cleveland Road, South Woodford, London E18 2AE
Tel: 020 8518 8855
Manager: Sarah-Jane Smith NNEB
Type: Coeducational Nursery School
Age range: 3months–5

(**)

Snaresbrook College

75 Woodford Road, South Woodford, London E18 2EA
Tel: 020 8989 2394
Head Mistress: Mrs L J Chiverrell CertEd
Type: Coeducational Day
Age range: 3–11
No. of pupils: 164 B84 G80
Fees: Day £5913–£7909

(**) (/)

Winston House Preparatory School

140 High Road, London E18 2QS
Tel: 020 8505 6565
Head Teacher: Mrs Marian Kemp
Type: Coeducational Day
Age range: 3–11
Fees: Day £5850–£7050

(**)

NORTH LONDON

N1

Floral Place Day Nursery

2 Floral Place, Northampton Grove, London N1 2PL
Tel: 020 7354 9945
Type: Coeducational Day

(**)

MARS Montessori Islington Green Nursery
4 Collins Yard, Islington Green, London N1 2XU
Tel: 020 7704 2805
Head: Angela Euesden
Type: Coeducational Day
Age range: 2–5
No. of pupils: 24
(symbols)

Mustard School
Parish Hall, Nuttall Street, London N1 5LR
Tel: 020 7739 3499
Headteacher: Mr A F Johnson
Type: Coeducational Day
Age range: 3–18
No. of pupils: 47 B32 G15 VIth3
Fees: Day £3060
(symbols)

Rosemary Works Independent School
1 Branch Place, London N1 5PH
Tel: 020 7739 3950
Head: Dorothy Davey
Type: Coeducational Day
Age range: 3–11
No. of pupils: 104 B60 G44
Fees: Day £6195
(symbols)

St Andrew's Montessori
St Andrew's Church, Thornhill Square, London N1 1BQ
Tel: 020 7700 2961
Head: Samantha Rawson MontDip
Type: Coeducational Day
Age range: 2–5
No. of pupils: 40
Fees: Day £4200–£6525
(symbols)

St Paul's Steiner School
1 St Paul's Road, Islington, London N1 2QH
Tel: 020 7226 4454
College of Teachers: College of Teachers
Type: Coeducational Day
Age range: 2–14
No. of pupils: 136 B69 G67
(symbols)

The Children's House School
77 Elmore Street, London N1 3AQ
Tel: 020 7354 2113
Head: Jill Rothwell
Type: Coeducational Nursery School
Age range: 2½–4
No. of pupils: 73 B37 G36
Fees: Day £1550–£1675
(symbols)

The Children's House Upper School
King Henry's Walk, London N1 4PB
Tel: 020 7249 6273
Headteacher: Mrs J Rothwell
Type: Coeducational Day
Age range: 4–7
No. of pupils: 60 B29 G31
Fees: Day £3250
(symbols)

The Grove Nursery
91 Shepperton Raod, Islington, London N1 3DF
Tel: 020 7226 4037
Owners: Ms Rebecca Browne & Ms Elaine Catchpole
Type: Coeducational Nursery School
Age range: 0–5
(symbols)

N2

Annemount School
18 Holne Chase, Hampstead Garden Suburb,
London N2 0QN
Tel: 020 8455 2132
Principal: Mrs G Maidment BA(Hons), MontDip
Type: Coeducational Day
Age range: 2–7
No. of pupils: 100
Fees: Day £1950–£3500
(symbols)

Kerem House
18 Kingsley Way, London N2 0ER
Tel: 020 8455 7524
Headmistress: Mrs D Rose
Type: Coeducational Day
Age range: 2½–5
No. of pupils: 96
Fees: Day £2025–£5160
(symbols)

The Kerem School
Norrice Lea, London N2 0RE
Tel: 020 8455 0909
Headteacher: Mrs R Goulden MEd, BEd(Hons)
Type: Coeducational Day
Age range: 4–11
No. of pupils: B79 G89
Fees: Day £6510–£6675
(symbols)

N3

Finchley & Acton Yochien School
6 Hendon Avenue, Finchley, London N3 1UE
Tel: 020 8343 2191
Headteacher: Mr Katsumasa Kitagaki
Type: Coeducational Day
Age range: 2–6
No. of pupils: 145 B72 G73

Pardes House Grammar School
Hendon Lane, Finchley, London N3 1SA
Tel: 020 8349 4222
Headteacher: Rabbi D Dunner
Type: Boys' Day
Age range: 10–16
No. of pupils: 222

Pentland Day Nursery
224 Squires Lane, Finchley, London N3 2QL
Tel: 020 8970 2441
Principal: Rachele Parker
Type: Coeducational Nursery School

N4

Asquith Nursery - Crouch Hill
33 Crouch Hill, London N4 4AP
Tel: 020 7561 1533
Type: Coeducational Nursery School
Age range: 3 months–5

Asquith Nursery - Finsbury Park
Dulas Street, Finsbury Park, Islington, London N4 3AF
Tel: 020 7263 3090
Type: Coeducational Nursery School
Age range: 3 months–5

Beis Chinuch Lebonos Girls School
Woodberry Down Centre, Woodberry Down,
London N4 2SH
Tel: 020 8807 737
Headmistress: Mrs Bertha Schneck
Type: Girls' Day
Age range: 2–16
No. of pupils: 421

Caribbean Community Centre Nursery
416 Seven Sisters Road, Hackney, London N4 2LX
Tel: 020 8802 0550
Head: Sister J Harding
Type: Coeducational Day
Age range: 1–5

Holly Park Montessori School
The Holly Park Methodist Church Hall, Crouch Hill,
London N4 4BY
Tel: 020 7263 6563
Headmistress: Mrs A Lake AMI Montessori Dip, BEd(Hons)
Type: Coeducational Day
Age range: 2–7
No. of pupils: 60 B30 G30
Fees: Day £1400–£2320

N5

New Park Montessori School
67 Highbury New Park, Islington, London N5 2EU
Tel: 020 7226 1109
Type: Coeducational Nursery School

N6

Avenue Nursery & Pre-Preparatory School
2 Highgate Avenue, London N6 5RX
Tel: 020 8348 6815
Headteacher: Mrs Mary Fysh
Type: Coeducational Day
Age range: 2½–7
No. of pupils: 79 B37 G42

CHANNING SCHOOL
For further details see p. 7
Highgate, London N6 5HF
Tel: 020 8340 2328
Email: info@channing.co.uk
Website: www.channing.co.uk
Head: Mrs B Elliott MA(Cantab)
Type: Girls' Day
Age range: 4–18
No. of pupils: 600 VIth80
Fees: Day £11,430–£12,390

Highgate Junior School

Cholmeley House, 3 Bishopswood Road, London N6 4AY
Tel: 020 8340 9193
Principal: Mr S M James BA
Type: Coeducational Day
Age range: 7–11
No. of pupils: B388 G223
Fees: Day £10,695–£11,955

Highgate Pre-Preparatory School

7 Bishopswood Road, London N6 4PH
Tel: 020 8340 9196
Head: Mrs Sarah Kennedy
Type: Coeducational Day
Age range: 3½–7

HIGHGATE SCHOOL

For further details see p. 22

North Road, Highgate, London N6 4AY
Tel: 020 8340 1524
Email: office@highgateschool.org.uk
Website: www.highgateschool.org.uk
Head Master: Mr A S Pettitt MA
Type: Coeducational Day
Age range: 3–18
No. of pupils: B917 G490 VIth327
Fees: Day £13,095–£15,120

(♯♯) (A) (£) (16+)

The Highgate Activity Nurseries

1 Church Road, Highgate, London N6 4QH
Tel: 020 8348 9248
Head: Helena Prior
Type: Coeducational Nursery School
Age range: 2–5
Fees: Day £5460–£9620

N7

Kidsunlimited Nurseries - Camden

The Mary Seacole Nursery, Tollington Way,
London N7 8QX
Tel: 01625 585222
Type: Coeducational Nursery School

(♯♯)

Pre-School Learning Alliance

The Fitzpatrick Building, 188 York Way, London N7 9AD
Tel: 020 7697 2500
Chief Executive: Steve Alexander
Type: Coeducational Day

(♯♯)

The Gower School

18 North Road, Islington, London N7 9EY
Tel: 020 7700 2445
Principal: Emma Gowers
Type: Coeducational Day
Age range: 3 months–11 years
No. of pupils: 180 B90 G90
Fees: Day £4680–£15,840

The Sam Morris Centre

Parkside Crescent, London N7 7JG
Tel: 020 7609 1735
Type: Coeducational Nursery School

N8

North London Rudolf Steiner School

1-3 The Campsbourne, London N8 7PN
Tel: 020 8341 3770
Type: Coeducational Day
Age range: 2½–7
No. of pupils: 40 B20 G20

Phoenix Academy

85 Bounces Road, Edmonton, London N9 8LD
Tel: 020 8887 6888
Headteacher: Mr A Hawkes
Type: Coeducational Day
Age range: 11–16
No. of pupils: 19 B9 G10

(♯♯)

N10

Montessori House

5 Princes Avenue, Muswell Hill, London N10 3LS
Tel: 020 8444 4399
Head: Mrs Lisa Christoforou
Type: Coeducational Nursery School
Age range: 6 months–7 years
No. of pupils: 100 B50 G50
Fees: Day £4725–£8400

Norfolk House School

10 Muswell Avenue, Muswell Hill, London N10 2EG
Tel: 020 8883 4584
Headmaster: Mr Mark Malley BAHons(Ed)
Type: Coeducational Day
Age range: 4–11
No. of pupils: B65 G65
Fees: Day £8550

The Montessori House
5 Princes Avenue, Muswell Hill, London N10 3LS
Tel: 020 8444 4399
Type: Coeducational Nursery School
(♟)

N11

Teddies Nurseries New Southgate
60 Beaconsfield Road, New Soutgate, London N11 3AE
Tel: 020 8368 7915
Type: Coeducational Day
Age range: 3 months–5 years
(♟)

THE NORTH LONDON INTERNATIONAL SCHOOL
For further details see p. 100
6 Friern Barnet Lane, London N11 3LX
Tel: +44 (0)20 8920 0600
Email: admissions@nlis.org
Website: www.nlis.org
Head of School: Mr David Rose MA(Ed), BA, CertEd
Type: Coeducational International Day
Age range: 2–19
No. of pupils: 400
Fees: Day £3225–£15,480
(♟) (🌐) (£) (IB) (✎) (16)

N12

Busy Bees Nursery
c/o David Lloyd Leisure Club, Leisure Way, High Road, Finchley, London N12 0QZ
Tel: 020 8343 8500
Manager: Toni Difonzo
Type: Coeducational Nursery School
Age range: 3months–5
No. of pupils: 18
(♟)

Laurel Way Playgroup
Nansen Village, 21 Woodside Avenue, London N12 8AQ
Tel: 020 8445 7514
Head: Mrs Susan Farber
Type: Coeducational Nursery School
Age range: 3–5
(♟)

N14

Primary Steps Day Nursery
37 Moss Hall Grove, Finchley, London N12 8PE
Tel: 020 8446 9135
Manager: Ms Carol Kewley NNEB, CPQS, NVQ
Type: Coeducational Nursery School
Age range: 1–5
No. of pupils: 36
(♟)

Asquith Nursery - Salcombe
33 The Green, Southgate, London N14 6EN
Tel: 020 8882 2136
Type: Coeducational Nursery School
(♟)

Salcombe Preparatory School
Green Road, Southgate, London N14 4PL
Tel: 020 8441 5282
Headmaster: Mr B Curzon
Type: Coeducational Day
Age range: 4–11
No. of pupils: 236 B140 G96
Fees: Day £7890
(♟) (£)

Salcombe Pre-School
33 The Green, Southgate, London N14 6EN
Tel: 020 8882 2136
Type: Coeducational Nursery School
(♟)

Tiny Tots Nursery School
Walker Hall, Christchurch Parish Centre, The Green, Waterfall Road, Southgate, London N14 7EG
Tel: 020 8447 9098
Type: Coeducational Nursery School
Age range: 2–5
(♟)

Vita et Pax School
Priory Close, Southgate, London N14 4AT
Tel: 020 8449 8336
Headmistress: Mrs M O'Connor BEd(Hons)
Type: Coeducational Day
Age range: 3–11
No. of pupils: B90 G84
Fees: Day £6150
(♟)

N15

Wisdom Primary & Secondary School
336 Philip Lane, London N15 4AB
Tel: 020 8880 9070
Headteacher: Ramazan G̦veli BA, MSc
Type: Coeducational Day
Age range: 5–16
Fees: Day £4400–£5400
(♟) (A)

N16

Appletree Nursery
59A Osbaldeston Road, Hackney, London N16
Tel: 020 8806 3525
Type: Coeducational Day
(♟)

Beatty Road Nursery
162 Albion Road, Hackney, London N16 9JS
Tel: 020 7249 7404
Principal: Geraldine Sinnolt
Type: Coeducational Day

Beis Aharon School
97-99 Bethune Road, London N16 5ED
Tel: 020 88007 368
Head: Y Pomerantz
Type: Boys' Day
Age range: 2–12
No. of pupils: 177

Beis Malka Girls School
93 Alkham Road, London N16 6XD
Tel: 020 8806 2070
Headmaster: M Dresdner
Type: Girls' Day
Age range: 5–16
No. of pupils: 339

Beis Rochel D'Satmar Girls School
51-57 Amhurst Park, London N16 5DL
Tel: 020 8800 9060
Headmistress: Mrs A Scher
Type: Girls' Day
Age range: 2–17
No. of pupils: 788

Beis Trana Girls' School
21 Northfield Road, London N16 5RL
Tel: 020 8809 7737
Type: Girls' Day
Age range: 2–13

Bnois Jerusalem School
79-81 Amhurst Park, London N16 5DL
Tel: 020 8802 7470
Head: Mrs Sonnenschein
Type: Girls' Day
Age range: 3–16

Coconut Nursery
133 Stoke Newington Church Street, London N16 0UH
Tel: 020 7923 0720
Type: Coeducational Day

Getters Talmud Torah
86 Amhurst Park, London N16 5AR
Tel: 020 8802 2512
Headteacher: Mr David Kahana
Type: Boys' Day
Age range: 4–11
No. of pupils: 171

Hackney Care For Kids
61 Evering Road, Hackney, London N16 7PR
Tel: 020 7923 3471
Type: Coeducational Day

Lubavitch House School (Senior Girls)
107-115 Stamford Hill, Hackney, London N16 5RP
Tel: 020 8800 0022
Headmaster: Rabbi Shmuel Lew FRSA
Type: Girls' Day
Age range: 11–17
No. of pupils: 102
Fees: Day £3900

Lubavitch Orthodox Jewish Nursery - North London
107-115 Stamford Hill, Hackney, London N16 5RP
Tel: 020 8800 0022
Head: Mrs F Sudak
Type: Coeducational Nursery School

Phoenix House Nursery School
27 Stamford Hill, London N16 5TU
Tel: 020 8880 2550
Principal: Noreen Payne
Type: Coeducational Nursery School

Rainbow Nursery
Yorkshire Grove Estate, Nevill Road, London N16 8SP
Tel: 020 7254 7930
Type: Coeducational Nursery School

Sunrise Day Nursery
1 Cazenove Road, Hackney, London N16 6PA
Tel: 020 8806 6279/8885 3354
Principal: Didi Ananda Manika
Type: Coeducational Day
Age range: 2–11
No. of pupils: 50
Fees: Day £3900–£4976

Talmud Torah Bobov Primary School
87 Egerton Road, London N16 6UE
Tel: 020 8809 1025
Headteacher: Rabbi A Just
Type: Boys' Day
Age range: 3–13
No. of pupils: 320 B302 G18

Talmud Torah Chaim Meirim School
26 Lampard Grove, London N16 6XB
Tel: 020 8806 0898
Principal: Rabbi S Hoffman
Type: Boys' Day
Age range: 6–13

Talmud Torah School
122 Bethune Road, London N16 5DU
Tel: 020 8802 2512
Type: Boys' Day
Age range: 3–11
No. of pupils: 60

Talmud Torah Yetev Lev School
111-115 Cazenove Road, London N16 6AX
Tel: 020 8806 3834
Headteacher: Mr J Stauber
Type: Boys' Day
Age range: 2–11
No. of pupils: 567

Tawhid Boys School
21 Cazenove Road, London N16 6PA
Tel: 020 8806 2999
Headteacher: Mr Usman Mapara
Type: Boys' Day
Age range: 10–15
No. of pupils: 115
Fees: Day £2000

Tayyibah Girls School
88 Filey Avenue, Stamford Hill, London N16 6JJ
Tel: 020 8880 0085
Headmistress: Mrs N B Qureishi MSc
Type: Girls' Day
Age range: 5–15
No. of pupils: 270
Fees: Day £1630

TTTYY School
14 Heathland Road, London N16 5NH
Tel: 020 8802 1348
Headmaster: Mr S B Gluck
Type: Boys' Day
Age range: 2–13
No. of pupils: 187

Yesodey Hatorah School
2-4 Amhurst Park, London N16 5AE
Tel: 020 8826 5500
Headteacher: Rabbi Pinter
Type: Coeducational Day
Age range: 3–16
No. of pupils: 920 B249 G671

N17

Parkside Preparatory School
Church Lane, Bruce Grove, Tottenham, London N17 7AA
Tel: 020 8808 1451
Headmistress: Mrs T Sargent
Type: Coeducational Day
Age range: 3–11
No. of pupils: 54 B28 G26
Fees: Day £3240–£3308

Sunrise Primary School
55 Coniston Road, Tottenham, London N17 0EX
Tel: 020 8806 6279 (Office); 020 8885 3354 (School)
Head: Mrs Mary-Anne Lovage MontDipEd, BA
Type: Coeducational Day
Age range: 2–11
No. of pupils: 30 B15 G15
Fees: Day £3900

N18

North London Muslim School
131-133 Fore Street, Edmonton, London N18 2XF
Tel: 020 8345 7008
Headteacher: Mr W Abdulla
Type: Coeducational Day
Age range: 4–10
No. of pupils: 21 B14 G7

N19

Beehive School
Ground Floor, Arkansas House, New Orleans Walk,
London N19 3SZ
Tel: 020 7686 7514
Head: Mr Paul Kelly
Type: Coeducational Day
Age range: 3–11
No. of pupils: 34

N20

Wellgrove School
4 Well Grove, Whetstone, London N20 9EQ
Tel: 020 84468855
Headteacher: Mr W Jones
Type: Coeducational Day
Age range: 11–16
No. of pupils: 75 B32 G43

N21

Grange Park Preparatory School
13 The Chine, Grange Park, Winchmore Hill,
London N21 2EA
Tel: 020 8360 1469
Headmaster: Mr A T Martin
Type: Girls' Day
Age range: 4–11
No. of pupils: 109
Fees: Day £7605

Keble Preparatory School
Wades Hill, London N21 1BG
Tel: 020 8360 3359
Headmaster: Mr G McCarthy
Type: Boys' Day
Age range: 4–13
No. of pupils: 200
Fees: Day £8970–£11,160

Leapfrog Day Nurseries - Enfield
2 Florey Square, Highlands Village, London N21 1UJ
Tel: 020 8360 6610
Manager: Emma Howell
Type: Coeducational Nursery School
Age range: 0–5

Palmers Green High School
Hoppers Road, Winchmore Hill, London N21 3LJ
Tel: 020 8886 1135
Headmistress: Mrs Christine Edmundson BMus(Hons),
MBA, PGCE, LRAM, ARCM
Type: Girls' Day
Age range: 3–16
No. of pupils: 300
Fees: Day £5985–£10,785

Woodberry Day Nursery
63 Church Hill, Winchmore Hill, London N21 1LE
Tel: 020 8882 6917
Manager: Michelle Miller
Type: Coeducational Nursery School
Age range: 6 weeks–5
No. of pupils: 62

N22

3-4-5 Pre-School
Springfield, The Grove, Muswell Hill, London N22 7AY
Tel: 07778 739319
Type: Coeducational Nursery School

Greek Secondary School of London
Avenue Lodge, Bounds Green Road, London N22 7EU
Tel: 020 8881 9320
Type: Coeducational Day
Age range: 13–18
No. of pupils: 200

NORTH-WEST LONDON

NW1

FRANCIS HOLLAND SCHOOL, REGENT'S PARK, NW1
For further details see p. 16
Clarence Gate, Ivor Place, Regent's Park, London NW1 6XR
Tel: 020 7723 0176
Email: registrar@fhs-nw1.org.uk
Website: www.francisholland.org.uk
Head: Mrs Vivienne Durham MA(Oxon)
Type: Independent Girls' Day
Age range: 11–18
No. of pupils: 445 VIth110
Fees: Day £13,890

International Community School
4 York Terrace East, Regent's Park, London NW1 4PT
Tel: 020 7935 1206
Head of School: Mr Philip D M Hurd
Type: Coeducational Day & Boarding
Age range: 3–18
No. of pupils: 360 B190 G170
Fees: Day £10,641–£13,947

Kidsunlimited Nurseries - Regents Place
1 Triton Mall, Regents Place, Longford Street,
London NW1 3FN
Tel: 01625 585222
Type: Coeducational Nursery School

Kidsunlimited Nurseries - St Pancras
The Fig Tree Nursery, St Pancras Hospital, 4 St Pancras Way,
London NW1 0PE
Tel: 01625 585222
Type: Coeducational Nursery School

North Bridge House Prep School
1 Gloucester Avenue, London NW1 7AB
Tel: 020 7267 6266
Head: Mr B Bibby
Type: Coeducational Day
Age range: B8–13 G8–11
No. of pupils: 280
Fees: Day £12,390

North Bridge House School
1 Gloucester Avenue, London NW1 7AB
Tel: 020 7267 6266
Head of Senior School: Miss A Ayre
Type: Coeducational Day
Age range: 2½–16
No. of pupils: 860 B518 G342
Fees: Day £3375–£12,930

North Bridge House Senior School
1 Gloucester Avenue, London NW1 7AB
Tel: 020 7267 6266
Head: Ms A Ayre
Type: Coeducational Day
Age range: 11–16
No. of pupils: 190
Fees: Day £12,390

Ready Steady Go
Primrose Hill Business Centre, 110 Gloucester Avenue,
Primrose Hill, London NW1 8HX
Tel: 020 7586 5862
Headmistress: Jennifer Silverton BA(Hons), PGTC
Type: Coeducational Nursery School
Age range: 2–5
No. of pupils: B11 G15
Fees: Day £1800–£3960

Ready Steady Go Nursery School
123 St Pancras Way, London NW1 0SY
Tel: 020 7267 4241
Principal: Jennifer Silverton
Type: Coeducational Nursery School

St Marks Square Nursery School
St Marks Church, Regents Park Road, Primrose Hill,
London NW1 7TN
Tel: 020 7586 8383
Head: Dr Sheema Parsons BEd
Type: Coeducational Nursery School
Age range: 2–6
No. of pupils: 28 B14 G14
Fees: Day £2400

THE CAVENDISH SCHOOL
For further details see p. 40
31 Inverness Street, Camden Town, London NW1 7HB
Tel: 020 7485 1958
Email: admissions@cavendish-school.co.uk
Website: www.cavendishschool.co.uk
Headmistress: Mrs T Dunbar BSc(Hons), PGCE, NPQH
Type: Girls' Day
Age range: 3–11
No. of pupils: 190
Fees: Day £11,250

Torah Vodaas
41 Dunstan Road, London NW1 8AE
Tel: 020 8458 4003
Headteacher: Mr Stanley Klor
Type: Boys' Day
Age range: 2–10
No. of pupils: 130

NW2

Abbey Nursery School
Cricklewood Baptist Church, Sneyd Road, Cricklewood,
London NW2 6AN
Tel: 020 8208 2202
Head: Mrs Ruby Azam
Type: Coeducational Day
♟

Neasden Montessori School
St Catherine's Church Hall, Dudden Hill Lane,
London NW2 7RX
Tel: 020 8208 1631
Head: Mrs J Sen Gupta BA, MontDip(AMI)
Type: Coeducational Day
Age range: 2–5
♟

The Little Ark Montessori
80 Westbere Road, London NW2 3RU
Tel: 020 7794 6359
Principal: Angela Coyne MontDip
Type: Coeducational Day
Age range: 2–5
No. of pupils: B14 G14
♟

The Mulberry House School
7 Minster Road, West Hampstead, London NW2 3SD
Tel: 020 8452 7340
Headteacher: Ms B Lewis-Powell CertEd
Type: Coeducational Day
Age range: 2–8
No. of pupils: B109 G75
Fees: Day £7050–£9399
♟

NW3

Chalcot Montessori School AMI
9 Chalcot Gardens, London NW3 4YB
Tel: 020 7722 1386
Principal: Ms Joanna Morfey AMI Dip
Type: Coeducational Day
Age range: 2–6
No. of pupils: 24 B12 G12
Fees: Day £2850–£6000
♟

Cherryfields Nursery School
523 Finchley Road, Hampstead, London NW3 7BB
Tel: 020 8905 3350
Head: Mrs Pamela Stewart
Type: Coeducational Day
♟

Church Row Nursery
Crypt Room, Hampstead Parish Church, Church Row,
Hampstead, London NW3 6UU
Tel: 020 7431 2603
Head: Mrs Marianne Wilson
Type: Coeducational Day
♟

DEVONSHIRE HOUSE PREPARATORY SCHOOL
For further details see p. 10
2 Arkwright Road, Hampstead, London NW3 6AE
Tel: 020 7435 1916
Email: enquiries@devonshirehouseprepschool.co.uk
Website: www.devonshirehouseschool.co.uk
Headmistress: Mrs S Alexander BA(Hons)
Type: Preparatory, Pre-preparatory & Nursery Day School
Age range: B2½–13 G2½–11
No. of pupils: 560 B319 G241
Fees: Day £6750–£12,855
♟ £

Eton Nursery Montessori School
45 Buckland Crescent, London NW3 5DJ
Tel: 020 7722 1532
Head: Mrs H Smith
Type: Coeducational Day
♟

Hampstead Hill Pre-Prep & Nursery School
St Stephen's Hall, Pond Street, Hampstead,
London NW3 2PP
Tel: 020 7435 6262
Principal: Mrs Andrea Taylor
Type: Coeducational Day
Age range: B2–8+ G2–7+
No. of pupils: 280 B180 G100
Fees: Day £6710–£11,880
♟ ✎

Heathside Preparatory School
16 New End, Hampstead, London NW3 1JA
Tel: 020 7794 5857
Heads: Ms Melissa Remus MA & Ms Jill White MA
Type: Coeducational Day
Age range: 2½–11
No. of pupils: B85 G80
Fees: Day £6750–£9585
♟

Hereward House School

14 Strathray Gardens, London NW3 4NY
Tel: 020 7794 4820
Headmistress: Mrs L Sampson BA
Type: Boys' Day
Age range: 4–13
No. of pupils: 170
Fees: Day £9885–£11,955

LYNDHURST HOUSE PREP SCHOOL
For further details see p. 29

24 Lyndhurst Gardens, Hampstead, London NW3 5NW
Tel: 020 7435 4936
Email: pmg@lyndhursthouse.co.uk
Website: www.lyndhursthouse.co.uk
Headmaster: Andrew Reid MA(Oxon)
Type: Boys' Day
Age range: 4–13
No. of pupils: 150
Fees: Day £12,660–£14,160

Maria Montessori School - Hampstead

26 Lyndhurst Gardens, London NW3 5NW
Tel: 020 7435 3646
Director of School: Mrs L Lawrence
Type: Coeducational Day
Age range: 2½–11
No. of pupils: 60 B30 G30
Fees: Day £5400

North Bridge House Junior School

8 Netherhall Gardens, London NW3 5RR
Tel: 020 7435 2884
Head: Mrs A Allsopp
Type: Coeducational Day
Age range: 5–8
No. of pupils: 190
Fees: Day £12,390

North Bridge House Nursery

33 Fitzjohns Avenue, London NW3 5JY
Tel: 020 7435 9641
Head: Mrs A Allsopp
Type: Coeducational Day
Age range: 2 years 9 months–5 years
No. of pupils: 229
Fees: Day £3225–£11,865

Octagon Nursery School

St Saviour's Church Hall, Eton Road, London NW3 4SU
Tel: 020 7586 3206
Type: Coeducational Day

Sarum Hall

15 Eton Avenue, London NW3 3EL
Tel: 020 7794 2261
Headmistress: Mrs Christine Smith
Type: Girls' Day
Age range: 3–11
No. of pupils: 170 G170
Fees: Day £6048–£10,065

South Hampstead High School GDST

3 Maresfield Gardens, London NW3 5SS
Tel: 020 7435 2899
Headmistress: Mrs J E Stephen BSc
Type: Girls' Day
Age range: 4–18
No. of pupils: 852 VIth162
Fees: Day £8148–£10,470

Southbank International School - Hampstead

16 Netherhall Gardens, London NW3 5TH
Tel: 020 7243 3803
Principal: Helen O'Donoghue
Type: Coeducational Day
Age range: 3–11
No. of pupils: 216 B108 G108
Fees: Day £11,400–£18,150

St Anthony's School

90 Fitzjohn's Avenue, Hampstead, London NW3 6NP
Tel: 020 7431 1066
Headmaster: Chris McGovern
Type: Boys' Day
Age range: 5–13
No. of pupils: 295 B295
Fees: Day £12,345–£12,690

St Christopher's School

32 Belsize Lane, Hampstead, London NW3 5AE
Tel: 020 7435 1521
Head: Mrs S A West BA(Hons), PGCE, MA
Type: Girls' Day
Age range: G4–11
No. of pupils: 235
Fees: Day £10,950

St Margaret's School
18 Kidderpore Gardens, Hampstead, London NW3 7SR
Tel: 020 7435 2439
Principal: Mr M Webster BSc, PGCE
Type: Girls' Day
Age range: 4–16
No. of pupils: 148
Fees: Day £8778–£10,116

ST MARY'S SCHOOL HAMPSTEAD
For further details see p. 35
47 Fitzjohn's Avenue, Hampstead, London NW3 6PG
Tel: 020 7435 1868
Email: enquiries@stmh.co.uk
Website: www.stmh.co.uk
Head: Miss Angela Rawlinson BA, MA(1st Class Honours), DipTchng, NPQH
Type: Coeducational Day
Age range: 2 years 9 months–11 years
No. of pupils: 287 B27 G260
Fees: Day £5550–£10,920

The Academy School
2 Pilgrim's Place, Rosslyn Hill, London NW3 1NG
Tel: 020 7435 6621
Headteacher: Mr Evans
Type: Coeducational Day
Age range: 6–14

The Hall School
23 Crossfield Road, Hampstead, London NW3 4NU
Tel: 020 7722 1700
Headmaster: P Lough MA
Type: Boys' Day
Age range: 4–13
No. of pupils: 440
Fees: Day £9300–£11,400

The Oak Tree Nursery
2 Arkwright Road, Hampstead, London NW3 6AD
Tel: 020 7435 1916
Head: Mrs S Alexander
Type: Coeducational Day
Age range: 2½–3
No. of pupils: B22 G22
Fees: Day £4650

The Phoenix School
36 College Crescent, London NW3 5LF
Tel: 020 7722 4433
Headmistress: Mrs Lisa Mason-Jones
Type: Coeducational Day
Age range: 3–7
No. of pupils: 130 B70 G60
Fees: Day £2585–£3795

THE ROYAL SCHOOL, HAMPSTEAD
For further details see p. 101
65 Rosslyn Hill, Hampstead, London NW3 5UD
Tel: 020 7794 7708
Email: enquiries@royalschoolhampstead.net
Website: www.royalschoolhampstead.net
Headmistress: Ms J Ebner BEd(Hons)(Cantab), MA(London), PGDipCouns, Cert FT, NPQH
Type: Girls' Day & Boarding
Age range: 3–16
No. of pupils: 210
Fees: Day £8940–£10,500 WB £15,870 FB £20,700

THE VILLAGE SCHOOL
For further details see p. 45
2 Parkhill Road, Belsize Park, London NW3 2YN
Tel: 020 7485 4673
Email: admin@thevillageschool.co.uk
Website: www.thevillageschool.co.uk
Headmistress: Miss C E F Gay BSc(Hons), PGCE
Type: Girls' Preparatory Day
Age range: 3–11
No. of pupils: 135
Fees: Day £11,430

Trevor Roberts School
55-57 Eton Avenue, London NW3 3ET
Tel: 020 7586 1444
Headmaster: Simon Trevor-Roberts BA
Type: Coeducational Day
Age range: 5–13
No. of pupils: 176 B116 G60
Fees: Day £10,026–£12,240

University College School
Frognal, Hampstead, London NW3 6XH
Tel: 020 7435 2215
Headmaster: Mr K J Durham MA
Type: Boys' Day
Age range: 11–18
No. of pupils: 763 B735 G33 VIth253
Fees: Day £12,495

University College School (Junior)
11 Holly Hill, London NW3 6QN
Tel: 020 7435 3068
Headmaster: Mr K J Douglas BA, BSc
Type: Boys' Day
Age range: 7–11
No. of pupils: 240
Fees: Day £4580

NW4

Asquith Nursery - Hendon
46 Allington Road, Hendon, London NW4 3DE
Tel: 020 8203 9020
Type: Coeducational Nursery School
Age range: 3 months–5

Asquith Nursery - Hill Park
5 Sunningfields Road, Hendon, London NW4 4QR
Tel: 020 8201 5816
Type: Coeducational Nursery School
Age range: 3 months–5

Beth Jacob Grammar School for Girls
Stratford Road, Hendon, London NW4 2AT
Tel: 020 8203 4322
Headteacher: Mrs D Steinberg
Type: Girls' Day
Age range: 11–17
No. of pupils: 264

Hendon Montessori School
7 Denehurst Gardens, London NW4 3QS
Tel: 020 8202 8516
Type: Coeducational Nursery School

Hendon Preparatory School
20 Tenterden Grove, Hendon, London NW4 1TD
Tel: 020 8203 7727
Headmaster: Mr David Baldwin
Type: Coeducational Day
Age range: 2–13
No. of pupils: B170 G81
Fees: Day £7650–£9945

Hill Park Pre-School
5 Sunningfields Road, Hendon, London NW4 4QR
Tel: 020 8201 5816
Type: Coeducational Day
Age range: 1–5
No. of pupils: 92

London Jewish Girls' High School
18 Raleigh Close, Hendon, London NW4 2TA
Tel: 020 8203 8618
Headteacher: Mr Joel Rabinowitz
Type: Girls' Day
Age range: 11–16

OYH Primary School
Finchley Lane, Hendon, London NW4 1DJ
Tel: 020 8202 5646
Headteacher: D A David
Type: Coeducational Day
Age range: 3–11
No. of pupils: 180 B89 G91

NW5

Talmud Torah Torat Emet
27 Green Lane, London NW4 2NL
Tel: 020 8201 7770
Headteacher: Rabbi M Nissim
Type: Boys' Day
Age range: 5–9

Bluebells Nursery
Our Lady Help of Christians Church Hall, Lady Margaret
Road, London NW5 2NE
Tel: 020 7284 3952
Principal: Ms Anita Pearson
Type: Coeducational Day
Age range: 2½–5
No. of pupils: 20

Camden Community Nurseries
99 Leighton Road, London NW5 2RB
Tel: 020 7485 2105
Type: Coeducational Day

Chaston Nursery & Pre-preparatory School
Chaston Place, Off Grafton Terrace, London NW5 4JH
Tel: 020 7482 0701
Head: Mrs Sandra Witten DipEd, DMS
Type: Coeducational Day
Age range: 0–5
No. of pupils: 69 B46 G23
Fees: Day £7020–£12,732

Cresswood Nursery

215 Queens Crescent, London NW5 4DP
Tel: 020 7485 1551
Proprietor: Miss L Pennell
Type: Coeducational Day
(♦♦)

Highgate Children's Centre

Highgate Studios, 53-79 Highgate Road, London NW5 1TL
Tel: 020 7485 5252
Principal: Lorraine Thompson
Type: Coeducational Nursery School
(♦♦)

Kentish Town Day Nursery

37 Ryland Road, London NW5 3EH
Tel: 020 7284 3600
Manager: Marie Sista
Type: Coeducational Nursery School
Age range: 3 months–5 years
No. of pupils: 55
(♦♦)

Kentish Town Montessori School

34 Oakford Road, Kentish Town, London NW5 1AH
Tel: 020 7485 1056
Type: Coeducational Nursery School
(♦♦)

L'Ile Aux Enfants

22 Vicar's Road, London NW5 4NL
Tel: 020 7267 7119
Headmistress: Mrs Chailleux
Type: Coeducational Day
Age range: 3–11
No. of pupils: 192
Fees: Day £3270
(♦♦)

Rooftops Nursery

Preistly House, Athlone Street, London NW5 4LN
Tel: 020 7267 7949
Type: Coeducational Nursery School
(♦♦)

York Rise Nursery

St Mary Brookfield Hall, York Rise, London NW5 1SB
Tel: 020 7485 7962
Headmistress: Miss Becca Coles
Type: Coeducational Day
Age range: 2–5
No. of pupils: B10 G10
(♦♦) (✏)

NW6

Al-Sadiq & Al-Zahra Schools

134 Salusbury Road, London NW6 6PF
Tel: 020 7372 7706
Headteacher: Dr M Movahedi
Type: Coeducational Day
Age range: 4–16
No. of pupils: 389 B185 G204
(♦♦)

Asquith Nursery - West Hampstead

11 Woodchurch Road, West Hampstead, London NW6 3PL
Tel: 020 7328 4787
Type: Coeducational Nursery School
Age range: 3 months–5
(♦♦)

Beehive Montessori School

Christchurch Hall, Christchurch Avenue, Brondebury Park, London NW6
Tel: 020 8451 5477
Headmistress: Ms Lucilla Baj
Type: Coeducational Day
Age range: 2–5
No. of pupils: B8 G9
Fees: Day £2550
(♦♦)

Broadhurst School

19 Greencroft Gardens, London NW6 3LP
Tel: 020 7328 4280
Headmistress: Miss D M Berkery CertEd
Type: Coeducational Day
Age range: 2–5
No. of pupils: 145 B72 G73
Fees: Day £6480–£10,950
(♦♦) (✏)

Brondesbury College for Boys

8 Brondesbury Park, London NW6 7BT
Tel: 020 8830 4522
Headteacher: Mr Dan Salahuddin Clifton
Type: Boys' Day
Age range: 11–16
No. of pupils: 93
(♦) (£)

Chaston Nursery School

30 Palmerston Road, London NW6 2JL
Tel: 020 7372 2120
Head: Mr Roger Witten
Type: Coeducational Day
Age range: 0–5
No. of pupils: 48 B26 G22
Fees: Day £6504–£12,216
(♦♦)

Happy Child Day Nursery
2 Victoria Road, Kilburn, London NW6 6QG
Tel: 020 7328 8791
Type: Coeducational Day
Age range: 3 months–5

Happy Child Day Nursery
St Anne's & St Andrew's Church Hall, 125 Salisbury Road,
Queens Park, London NW6 6RG
Tel: 020 7625 1966
Type: Coeducational Nursery School
Age range: 2–5

Islamia Girls' High School
129 Salusbury Road, London NW6 6PE
Tel: 020 7372 3472
Headteacher: Miss Asmat Ali
Type: Girls' Day
Age range: 11–16
No. of pupils: 120
Fees: Day £6100

Maria Montessori Children's House - West Hampstead
St Mary's Community Hall, 134a Abbey Road,
London NW6 4SN
Tel: 020 7624 5917
Type: Coeducational Nursery School

Naima Jewish Preparatory School
21 Andover Place, London NW6 5ED
Tel: 020 7328 2802
Headteacher: Mr Michael Cohen MA, NPQH
Type: Coeducational Day
Age range: 3–11
No. of pupils: B83 G82
Fees: Day £5997–£7470

Rainbow Montessori School
13 Woodchurch Road, Hampstead, London NW6 3PL
Tel: 020 7328 8986
Principal: Linda Madden MontDipAdv
Type: Coeducational Day
Age range: 5–12
No. of pupils: B60 G60
Fees: Day £2950–£2990

Teddies Nurseries West Hampstead
2 West End Lane, London NW6 4NT
Tel: 020 7372 3290
Type: Coeducational Day
Age range: 3 months–5 years

The Beehive on Queen's Park Montessori School
147 Chevening Road, London NW6 6DZ
Tel: 020 8969 2235
Type: Coeducational Nursery School
Age range: 2–5
No. of pupils: B10 G12
Fees: Day £3900–£4300

The Islamia Schools' Trust
129 Salusbury Road, London NW6 6PE
Tel: 020 7372 3472
Type: Girls' Day
Age range: 11–16
No. of pupils: 124
Fees: Day £4200

The School of the Islamic Republic of Iran
100 Carlton Vale, London NW6 5HE
Tel: 020 7372 8051
Headteacher: Mr Farzad Farzan
Type: Coeducational Day
Age range: 6–16
No. of pupils: 53 B22 G31

NW7

Belmont, Mill Hill Preparatory School
The Ridgeway, London NW7 4ED
Tel: 020 8906 7270
Head: Mrs L C Duncan BSc, PGCE
Type: Coeducational Day
Age range: 7–13
No. of pupils: 392 B245 G177
Fees: Day £13,371

Goodwyn School
Hammers Lane, Mill Hill, London NW7 4DB
Tel: 020 8959 3756
Principal: Struan Robertson
Type: Coeducational Day
Age range: 3–11
No. of pupils: 223 B104 G119
Fees: Day £3645–£7673

Grimsdell, Mill Hill Pre-Preparatory School

Winterstoke House, Wills Grove, Mill Hil ,
London NW7 1QR
Tel: 020 8959 6884
Head: Mrs Pauline E R Bennett-Mills CertEd
Type: Coeducational Day
Age range: 3–7
No. of pupils: 182 B105 G77
Fees: Day £1687–£3668

Leapfrog Day Nurseries - Mill Hill

30 Millway, Mill Hill, London NW7 3RB
Tel: 020 8906 9123
Manager: Ellen Pollard
Type: Coeducational Nursery School
Age range: 0–5

Little Cherubs Kindergarten

2 Belgrave Close, Mill Hill, London NW7 3QG
Tel: 020 8959 2420
Head: Mrs Pauline D Mitson
Type: Coeducational Nursery School
No. of pupils: 19

Mill Hill School

The Ridgeway, Mill Hill Village, London NW7 1QS
Tel: 020 8959 1176
Head: Dr Dominic Luckett
Type: Coeducational Boarding & Day
Age range: 13–18
No. of pupils: 689 B492 G197 VIth259
Fees: Day £13,860 FB £21,900

St Martin's School

22 Goodwyn Avenue, Mill Hill, London NW7 3RG
Tel: 020 8959 1965
Head: Mrs Angela Wilson DipEd
Type: Coeducational Day
Age range: 3–11
No. of pupils: 100
Fees: Day £5890

Sunflower Days Nursery

41 Selvage Lane, London NW7 3SS
Tel: 020 8906 1609
Type: Coeducational Day and Nursery
Age range: 6months–8

The Mount School

Milespit Hill, Mill Hill, London NW7 2RX
Tel: 020 8959 3403
Head: Ms Catherine Cozens
Type: Girls' Day
Age range: 4–18
No. of pupils: 307 G307 VIth24
Fees: Day £2912–£3510

NW8

Abercorn School

Infant Department, 28 Abercorn Place, London NW8 9XP
Tel: 020 7286 4785
High Mistress: Mrs Andrea Greystoke BA(Hons)
Type: Coeducational Pre-preparatory & Preparatory Day
Age range: 2½–13½
No. of pupils: 360 B180 G180
Fees: Day £7245–£13,425

Arnold House School

1 Loudoun Road, St John's Wood, London NW8 0LH
Tel: 020 7266 4840
Headmaster: Mr Vivian Thomas
Type: Boys' Day
Age range: 5–13
No. of pupils: 250
Fees: Day £4700

Pre-School Playgroups Association

Barrow Hill Junior School, Barrow Hill Road,
London NW8 7AL
Tel: 020 7586 8879
Type: Coeducational Nursery School

Ready Steady Go Nursery School

St Johns Wood Adventure Playground, St Johns Wood
Terrace, London NW8 6LP
Tel: 020 7722 0007
Type: Coeducational Nursery School

St Christina's R C Preparatory School

25 St Edmunds Terrace, Regent's Park, London NW8 7PY
Tel: 020 7722 8784
Headteacher: Miss N Clyne-Wilson
Type: Preparatory School
Age range: B3–7 G3–11
No. of pupils: 202 B47 G155
Fees: Day £8745

St Johns Wood Pre-Preparatory School

St Johns Hall, Lords Roundabout, Prince Albert Road,
London NW8 7NE
Tel: 020 7722 7149
Headmistress: Mrs H Ellis
Type: Coeducational Day
Age range: 3–7
No. of pupils: 65 B33 G32
Fees: Day £5238–£9600

The American School in London

One Waverley Place, London NW8 0NP
Tel: 020 7449 1221
Head: Mrs Coreen Hester
Type: Coeducational Day
Age range: 4–18
No. of pupils: 1323 B660 G663
Fees: Day £17,780–£21,500

Toddlers Inn Nursery School

Cicely Davies Hall, Cochrane Street, London NW8 7NX
Tel: 020 7586 0520
Principal: Laura McCole
Type: Coeducational Nursery School

NW9

Ayesha Community Education

133 West Hendon, Broadway, London NW9 7DY
Tel: 07782 151554
Headteacher: Mrs Fatima D'oyen
Type: Girls' Day
Age range: 11–16
No. of pupils: 23

Beis Soroh Schneirer

Arbiter House, Wilberforce Road, London NW9 6AT
Tel: 020 8343 1190
Head: Mrs R Weiss
Type: Girls' Day
Age range: 2–11
No. of pupils: 150

Gower House School & Nursery

Blackbird Hill, London NW9 8RR
Tel: 020 8205 2509
Headmaster: Mr M Keane
Type: Coeducational Day
Age range: 2–11
No. of pupils: 200 B110 G90
Fees: Day £5010–£5835

Joel Nursery

214 Colindeep Lane, Colindale, London NW9 6DF
Tel: 020 8200 0189
Type: Coeducational Day
Age range: 2–5
No. of pupils: B24 G18

St Nicholas School

22 Salmon Street, London NW9 8PN
Tel: 020 8205 7153
Headmistress: Mrs Alyce Gregory CertEd
Type: Coeducational Day
Age range: 5–11
No. of pupils: 80 B40 G40
Fees: Day £5760

NW10

Happy Child Day Nursery

59 Longstone Avenue, Harlesden, London NW10 3TY
Tel: 020 8961 3485
Type: Coeducational Day
Age range: 3 months–5

Kindercare Montessori Nursery

Bridge Park Business Centre, Harrow Road,
London NW10 0RG
Tel: 020 8838 1688
Type: Coeducational Day
Age range: 2–5
No. of pupils: B18 G12
Fees: Day £4420

Swaminarayan School

260 Brentfield Road, Neasden, London NW10 8HE
Tel: 020 8965 8381
Headteacher: Mr Mahendra Savjani
Type: Coeducational Day
Age range: 2–18
No. of pupils: 452 B242 G210 VIth36
Fees: Day £5280–£7560

The Childrens Centre

40 Nicoll Road, London NW10 9AB
Tel: 020 8961 6648
Type: Coeducational Nursery School
Age range: 2–5
No. of pupils: 50

The Childrens Centre
Christ Church, St Albans Road, London NW10 8UG
Tel: 020 8961 9250
Head: Denise Lepore
Type: Coeducational Nursery School
Age range: 18 months–5
No. of pupils: 25
(�) (♠)

The Welsh School (Ysgol Gymraeg Llundain)
c/o The Stonebridge School, Shakespeare Avenue,
London NW10 8NG
Tel: 020 8965 3585
Headteacher: Mr Matthew Davies
Type: Coeducational Day and Nursery
Age range: 2½–11
No. of pupils: 30
Fees: Day £1950
(♠)

NW11

Asquith Nursery - Golders Green
212 Golders Green Road, Golders Green,
London NW11 9AT
Tel: 020 8458 7388
Type: Coeducational Day
Age range: 1–5
No. of pupils: 68
(♠)

Beis Hamedrash Elyon
211 Golders Green Road, London NW11 9EY
Tel: 020 8201 8668
Headteacher: Mr C Steinhart
Type: Boys' Day
Age range: 11–14
No. of pupils: 45
(♠)

Bilingual Montessori Nursery of St Michaels
St Michael's Cathedral, The Riding, Golders Green,
London NW11 8HL
Tel: 020 8455 8511
Type: Coeducational Nursery School
(♠)

Golders Hill School
666 Finchley Road, London NW11 7NT
Tel: 020 8455 2589
Headmistress: Mrs A T Eglash BA(Hons)
Type: Coeducational Day
Age range: 2–7
No. of pupils: 180 B100 G80
Fees: Day £831–£6870
(♠)

The King Alfred School
Manor Wood, North End Road, London NW11 7HY
Tel: 020 8457 5200
Head: Mrs Dawn Moore MA(London)
Type: Coeducational Day
Age range: 4–18
No. of pupils: 615 VIth70
Fees: Day £10,743–£12,930
(♠) (A) (£) (♠) (16·)

SOUTH-EAST LONDON

SE1

Bright Horizons at Tabard Square
10-12 Empire Square, Tabard Street, London SE1 4NA
Tel: 020 7407 2068
Type: Coeducational Nursery School
(♠)

Chrysolyte Independent Christian School
Bethel House, Lansdowne Place, London SE1 4XH
Tel: 020 7407 9990/9996
Matron: Mrs R Ikiebe
Type: Coeducational Day
Age range: 2–11
No. of pupils: B50 G53
Fees: Day £3750–£5100
(♠) (£) (♠)

St Patricks Montessori Nursery School
91 Cornwall Road, London SE1 8TH
Tel: 020 7928 5557
Type: Coeducational Day
(♠)

Waterloo Day Nursery
The Chandlery, 50 Westminster Bridge Road,
London SE1 7QY
Tel: 020 7721 7432
Principal: Julie Ellis
Type: Coeducational Day
(♠)

SE3

Blackheath & Bluecoats Day Nursery
Old Dover Road, Blackheath, London SE3
Tel: 020 8858 8221 Ext 147
Principal: Tracy Malyon
Type: Coeducational Day
(♠)

Blackheath Day Nursery
The Rectory Field, Charlton, London SE3
Tel: 020 8305 2526
Headmistress: Mrs Shipley
Type: Coeducational Day
Age range: 0–5
No. of pupils: 61

BLACKHEATH HIGH SCHOOL GDST
For further details see p. 5
Vanbrugh Park, Blackheath, London SE3 7AG
Tel: 020 8853 2929
Email: info@bla.gdst.net
Website: www.blackheathhighschool.gdst.net
Head: Mrs Elizabeth Laws BA(Hons), PGCE
Type: Girls' Day
Age range: 3–18
No. of pupils: 650
Fees: Day £6966–£11,601

Blackheath Montessori Centre
Independents Road, Blackheath, London SE3 9LF
Tel: 020 8852 6765
Headmistress: Mrs Jane Skillen MontDip
Type: Coeducational Nursery School
Age range: 3–5
No. of pupils: 36

Blackheath Nursery & Preparatory School
4 St Germans Place, Blackheath, London SE3 ONJ
Tel: 020 8858 0692
Headmistress: Mrs P J Thompson
Type: Coeducational Day
Age range: 3–11
No. of pupils: 366 B184 G182
Fees: Day £4560–£9315

Greenwich Steiner School
Hollyhedge House, Wat Tyler Road, Blackheath, London SE3 0QZ
Tel: 07528 783 520
Type: Coeducational Day
Age range: 3–14
No. of pupils: 90 B50 G40
Fees: Day £4000–£5600

Heath House Preparatory School
37 Wemyss Road, Blackheath, London SE3 0TG
Tel: 020 8297 1900
Headmaster: Mr Ian Laslett MA, FRGS
Type: Coeducational Day
Age range: 4–11
No. of pupils: 95 B47 G48
Fees: Day £9600–£10,200

Lingfield Day Nursery (Blackheath)
37 Kidbrooke Grove, Kidbrooke, London SE3 0LJ
Tel: 020 8858 1388
Manager: Sophie Campbell
Type: Coeducational Nursery School
Age range: 18 months–5
No. of pupils: 30
Fees: Day £9350

SE4

The Pointer School
19 Stratheden Road, Blackheath, London SE3 7TH
Tel: 020 8293 1331
Headmaster: Mr R J S Higgins MA, BEd, CertEd, FCollP
Type: Coeducational Day
Age range: 3–11
No. of pupils: 300 B150 G150
Fees: Day £1150–£10,182

Hillyfields Day Nursery
41 Harcourt Road, Brockley, London SE4 2AJ
Tel: 020 8694 1069
Head: Ms Lisa Reeves
Type: Coeducational Day

SE5

Mother Goose Nursery
The Pavilion, 65 Greendale Fields, off Wanley Road, London SE5 8JZ
Tel: 020 7738 7700
Type: Coeducational Nursery School
Age range: 0–5

SE6

Broadfields Day Nursery
96 Broadfields Road, Catford, London SE6 1NG
Tel: 020 8697 1488
Head: Elainne Dalton
Type: Coeducational Day
Age range: 4 months–5

Peter Pan Nursery
353 Bromley Road, London SE6 2RP
Tel: 020 8695 0082
Type: Coeducational Nursery School

Springfield Christian School
145 Perry Hill, Catford, London SE6 4LP
Tel: 020 8291 4433
Principal: Mr B Oludimu BSc
Type: Coeducational Primary
Age range: 2½–11
No. of pupils: 85
Fees: Day £2550–£4710

St Dunstan's College
Stanstead Road, London SE6 4TY
Tel: 020 8516 7200
Headmistress: Mrs J D Davies BSc
Type: Academically Selective Coeducational Day
Age range: 3–18
No. of pupils: 870
Fees: Day £6918–£12,174

The Pavilion Nursery
Catford Cricket Club Pavilion, Penerley Road,
London SE6 2LQ
Tel: 020 8698 0878
Head: Mrs Karen Weller
Type: Coeducational Nursery School
Age range: 2–5
No. of pupils: B18 G15

Thornsbeach Day Nursery
10 Thornsbeach Road, London SE6 1DX
Tel: 020 8697 7699
Manager: Mrs M James
Type: Coeducational Nursery School
Age range: 2–5
No. of pupils: B15 G10

SE9

Asquith Nursery - Elizabeth Terrace
18-22 Elizabeth Terrace, Eltham, London SE9 5DR
Tel: 020 8294 0377
Type: Coeducational Nursery School
Age range: 3 months–5

Asquith Nursery - New Eltham
699 Sidcup Road, New Eltham, London SE9 3AQ
Tel: 020 8851 5057
Type: Coeducational Nursery School
Age range: 3 months–5

Eltham College
Grove Park Road, Mottingham, London SE9 4QF
Tel: 020 8857 1455
Headmaster: Mr P J Henderson BA, FRSA
Type: Boys' Day
Age range: B7–18 G16–18
No. of pupils: 830 B770 G60 VIth210
Fees: Day £10,320–£11,970

Eltham Green Day Nursery
Eltham Green School, Queenscroft Road, London SE9 5EQ
Tel: 020 8850 4720
Head: Mrs Walker
Type: Coeducational Day
Age range: 3months–5
No. of pupils: 30

Happy Faces Montessori
35 West Park, London SE9 4RZ
Tel: 020 8857 9990
Type: Coeducational Nursery School
Age range: 18 months–5

Lollipops Child Care Ltd
27 Southwood Road, London SE9 3QE
Tel: 020 8859 5832
Principal: Miss L Thompson
Type: Coeducational Nursery School

St Olave's Preparatory School
106 Southwood Road, New Eltham, London SE9 3QS
Tel: 020 8294 8930
Headmistress: Mrs Fisher
Type: Coeducational Day
Age range: 3–11
No. of pupils: 220 B130 G90
Fees: Day £4680–£7380

Willow Park
19 Glenlyon Road, Eltham, London SE9
Tel: 020 8850 8753
Principal: Mrs McMahon
Type: Coeducational Day

SE10

Teddies Nurseries Greenwich
Chevening Road, Greenwich, London SE10 0LB
Tel: 020 8858 8266
Type: Coeducational Day
Age range: 3 months–5 years
(♣)

SE11

Toad Hall Montessori Nursery School
37 St Mary's Gardens, Kennington, London SE11 4UF
Tel: 020 7735 5087
Principal: Mrs V K Rees NNEB, MontDip
Type: Coeducational Day
Age range: 2–5
No. of pupils: 40
Fees: Day £6300
(♣)

SE12

COLFE'S
For further details see p. 9
Horn Park Lane, Greenwich, London SE12 8AW
Tel: 020 8852 2283
Email: head@colfes.com
Website: www.colfes.com
Head: Mr R F Russell MA(Cantab)
Type: Coeducational
Age range: 3–18
No. of pupils: 1020
(♣) (A) (£) (✐) (16·)

Colfe's Preparatory School
Horn Park Lane, Lee, London SE12 8AW
Tel: 020 8852 2283
Headmaster: Mr John Gallagher
Type: Coeducational Day
Age range: 3–11
No. of pupils: 327
Fees: Day £8478–£9846
(♣) (✐)

Lingfield Day Nursery (Grove Park)
155 Baring Road, London SE12 0LA
Tel: 020 8851 7800
Manager: Samantha Goodwright
Type: Coeducational Nursery School
Age range: 18 months–5
No. of pupils: 30
Fees: Day £8700
(♣)

Riverston School
63-69 Eltham Road, Lee Green, London SE12 8UF
Tel: 020 8318 4327
Headmistress: Mrs Sarah Salathiel
Type: Coeducational Day
Age range: 1–16
No. of pupils: 350 B210 G140
Fees: Day £3708–£4946
(♣) (£) (✐) (❀)

SE13

Mother Goose Nursery (Head Office)
133 Brookbank Road, Lewisham, London SE13 7DA
Tel: 020 8694 8700
Type: Coeducational Nursery School
Age range: 1–5
(♣)

Step by Step Day Nursery
Benden House, Monument Gardens, Campshill Road,
Hither Green, London SE13 6PY
Tel: 020 8297 5070
Co-ordinator: Mrs Irene Langford
Type: Coeducational Nursery School
(♣)

The Village Montessori School
Kingswood Hall, Kingswood Place, London SE13 5BU
Tel: 020 8318 6720
Director: Catherine Westlake MontDip
Type: Coeducational Nursery School
Age range: 3–5
No. of pupils: B15 G15
Fees: Day £1491
(♣)

The Village Nursery
St Mary's Centre, 180 Ladywell Road, Lewisham,
London SE13 7HU
Tel: 020 8690 6766
Principal: Frances Rogers
Type: Coeducational Nursery School
(♣)

Kings Kids Christian School
New Testament Church of God, Bawtree Road, New Cross,
London SE14 6ET
Tel: 020 8691 5813
Headteacher: Mrs M Okenwa
Type: Coeducational Day
Age range: 5–11
No. of pupils: 36 B22 G14
(♣)

Asquith Nursery - Peckham Rye
24 Waveney Avenue, Peckham Rye, London SE15 3 JE
Tel: 020 7635 5501
Type: Coeducational Nursery School
Age range: 4 months–5

SE15

Bellenden Day Nursery
Faith Chapel, 198 Bellenden Road, London SE15
Tel: 020 7639 4896
Manager: Jason Cranston
Type: Coeducational Day

Happy Faces Nursery
161 Sumner Road, Peckham, London SE15 6JL
Tel: 020 7701 3320
Type: Coeducational Nursery School

Mother Goose Nursery
34 Waveney Avenue, Nunhead, London SE15 3 JE
Tel: 020 7277 5951
Type: Coeducational Nursery School
Age range: 1–5

Nell Gwynn Nursery
Meeting House Lane, London SE15 2TT
Tel: 020 7252 8265
Type: Coeducational Nursery School

The Villa Pre-Preparatory School & Nursery
54 Lyndhurst Grove, Peckham, London SE15 5AH
Tel: 020 7703 6216
Head Teacher: Gillian Quinn BPrim Ed(Hons)
Type: Nursery & Pre-prep day school
Age range: 2–7
No. of pupils: 110

SE16

Five Steps Community Nursery
31-32 Alpine Road, London SE16 2RE
Tel: 020 7237 2376
Type: Coeducational Day

Scallywags Day Nursery
St Crispin Hall, Southwark Park Road, London SE16 2HU
Tel: 020 7252 3225
Headmistress: Miss Allison Armstrong NVQ
Type: Coeducational Nursery School
Age range: 3 months–5 years
No. of pupils: 65

Trinity Child Care
Holy Trinity Church Hall, Bryan Road, London SE16 5HF
Tel: 020 7231 5842
Manager: Sharron Williams
Type: Coeducational Nursery School
Age range: 2–5
No. of pupils: 60 B40 G20
Fees: Day £6240

SE17

Magic Roundabout Nursery - Kennington
35 Sutherland House, Sutherland Square,
London SE17 3EE
Tel: 020 7277 3643
Type: Coeducational Nursery School

SE19

Virgo Fidelis Preparatory School
Central Hill, Upper Norwood, London SE19 1RS
Tel: 020 8653 2169
Head Teacher: Mrs Meg Baines
Type: Coeducational Day and Nursery
Age range: 3–11
No. of pupils: B125 G119
Fees: Day £2250–£6285

SE20

Anerley Montessori Nursery
45 Anerley Park, London SE20 8NQ
Tel: 020 8778 2810
Headmistress: Mrs P Bhatia
Type: Coeducational Day
Age range: 3 months–5
No. of pupils: B40 G35
Fees: Day £2750–£4600

SE21

Asquith Nursery - West Dulwich
Chancellor Grove, West Dulwich, London SE21 8EG
Tel: 020 8761 6750
Type: Coeducational Nursery School
Age range: 3 months–5

Clive Hall Day Nursery
rear of 54 Clive Road, London SE21 8BY
Tel: 020 8761 9000
Type: Coeducational Nursery School

Dulwich College
London SE21 7LD
Tel: 020 8299 9263
Master: Dr J Spence
Type: Boys' Day & Boarding
Age range: 7–18
No. of pupils: 1400 VIth420
Fees: Day £14,184 WB £27,441 FB £28,971

Dulwich College Kindergarten & Infants School
Eller Bank, 87 College Road, London SE21 7HH
Tel: 020 8693 1538
Head: Mrs H M Friell
Type: Coeducational Day
Age range: 3 months–7 years
No. of pupils: 240
Fees: Day £2880–£9690

DULWICH COLLEGE PREPARATORY SCHOOL
For further details see p. 12
42 Alleyn Park, Dulwich, London SE21 7AA
Tel: 020 8670 3217
Email: registrar@dcpslondon.org
Website: www.dcpslondon.org
Headmaster: Mr M W Roulston
Type: Independent Preparatory Boys' School
Age range: B3–13 G3–5
No. of pupils: 817 B793 G24
Fees: Day £4350–£13,542 WB £18,213–£19,662

Oakfield Preparatory School
125-128 Thurlow Park Road, Dulwich, London SE21 8HP
Tel: 020 8670 4206
Principal: Mr John Gibson BEd(Hons)
Type: Coeducational Day
Age range: 2–11
No. of pupils: 450 B235 G215
Fees: Day £4600–£7335

Rosemead Preparatory School and Pre Prep
70 Thurlow Park Road, London SE21 8HZ
Tel: 020 8670 5865
Head: Mrs C Brown CertEd, DipEd, RSA DipSpLD
Type: Coeducational Day
Age range: 3–11
No. of pupils: 314 B151 G163
Fees: Day £8310–£8820

SE22

Alleyn's School
Townley Road, Dulwich, London SE22 8SU
Tel: 020 8557 1500
Headmaster: Dr C Diggory BSc, MA, EdD, CMath, FIMA, FRSA (until August 2010), Dr G Savage, MA, PhD (from September 2010).
Type: Independent Coeducational Day
Age range: 4–18
No. of pupils: 1198 B580 G618 VIth278
Fees: Day £11,061–£13,437

Dulwich Nursery
adj Sainsbury's Dulwich Store, 80 Dog Kennel Hill, London SE22 8DB
Tel: 020 7738 4007
Principal: Amanda Shead
Type: Coeducational Nursery School

First Steps Montessori Day Nursery & Pre School
254 Upland Road, East Dulwich, London SE22 0DN
Tel: 020 8299 6897
Principal: Karime Dinkha
Type: Coeducational Nursery School
Age range: 2–5
No. of pupils: 43

James Allen's Girls' School
East Dulwich Grove, Dulwich, London SE22 8TE
Tel: 020 8693 1181
Headmistress: Mrs Marion Gibbs BA(Hons), PGCE, MLitt, FRSA
Type: Girls' Day
Age range: 4–18
No. of pupils: 1077
Fees: Day £10,260–£12,630

Mother Goose Nursery
248 Upland Road, East Dulwich, London SE22 0NU
Tel: 020 8693 9429
Type: Coeducational Nursery School
Age range: 1–5

The Oak Tree Nursery
Tell Grove, Southwark, London SE22 8RH
Tel: 020 8693 0306
Type: Coeducational Nursery School

SE24

Half Moon Montessori Nursery
Methodist Church Hall, 155 Half Moon Lane,
London SE24 9HU
Tel: 020 7326 5300
Type: Coeducational Day
Age range: 2–5
No. of pupils: 65 B29 G36

HERNE HILL SCHOOL
For further details see p. 21
The Old Vicarage, 127 Herne Hill, London SE24 9LY
Tel: 020 7274 6336
Email: enquiries@hernehillschool.co.uk
Website: www.hernehillschool.co.uk
Head: Mrs Jane Beales
Type: Coeducational Day
Age range: 3–7
No. of pupils: 240
Fees: Day £3840–£9570

SE25

Children's Paradise
2-4 Crowther Road, London SE25 5QW
Tel: 020 8654 1737
Type: Coeducational Day

SE26

Little Cherubs Day Nursery
2a Bell Green Lane, London SE26 5TB
Tel: 020 8778 3232
Type: Coeducational Nursery School

Sydenham High School GDST
19 Westwood Hill, London SE26 6BL
Tel: 020 8768 8000
Headteacher: Mrs K Pullen MA
Type: Girls' Day
Age range: 4–18
No. of pupils: 649 VIth70
Fees: Day £4764–£6132

SE27

ABC Childrens Centre
48 Chapel Rd, West Norwood, London SE27 0UR
Tel: 020 8766 0246
Principal: Ms E Carr
Type: Coeducational Day

One World Day Nursery
11 Thurlby Road, London SE27 0RN
Tel: 020 8761 3308
Type: Coeducational Nursery School

Teddies Nurseries West Dulwich
Baptist Church, Gipsy Road, West Norwood,
London SE27 9RB
Tel: 020 8761 8827
Type: Coeducational Day
Age range: 3 months–5 years

SOUTH-WEST LONDON

SW1

Eaton House Belgravia
3-5 Eaton Gate, London SW1W 9BA
Tel: 020 7730 9343
Headmistress: Miss Lucy Watts
Type: Boys' Day
Age range: 4–8
No. of pupils: 220
Fees: Day £11,385

EATON SQUARE SCHOOL
For further details see p. 14
79 Eccleston Square, London SW1V 1PP
Tel: 020 7931 9469
Email: admissions@eatonsquareschool.com
Website: www.eatonsquareschool.com
Headmaster: Mr Sebastian Hepher BEd(Hons)
Type: Coeducational Day
Age range: 2½–13
No. of pupils: 529 B280 G249
Fees: Day £2550–£14,610

Fairley House School

30 Causton Street, London SW1P 4AU
Tel: 020 7976 5456
Principal & Educational Psychologist: Jacqueline Murray
BA(Hons), MEd, MSc, DipPsychol, DipRSA(SpLD)
Type: Coeducational Day
Age range: 5–14
No. of pupils: 140 B105 G35
Fees: Day £24,750

FRANCIS HOLLAND SCHOOL, SLOANE SQUARE, SW1

For further details see p. 17

39 Graham Terrace, London SW1W 8JF
Tel: 020 7730 2971
Email: registrar@fhs-sw1.org.uk
Website: www.francisholland.org.uk
Head: Miss Stephanie Pattenden BSc
Type: Independent Girls' Day
Age range: 4–18
No. of pupils: 450 VIth70
Fees: Day £12,060–£14,205

HILL HOUSE INTERNATIONAL JUNIOR SCHOOL

For further details see p. 23

17 Hans Place, Chelsea, London SW1X 0EP
Tel: 020 7584 1331
Email: info@hillhouseschool.co.uk
Website: www.hillhouseschool.co.uk
Headmaster: Richard Townend FLSM(Chm)
Type: Coeducational Day
Age range: 4–13
No. of pupils: 980 B560 G420
Fees: Day £9000–£12,300

Knightsbridge School

67 Pont Street, Knightsbridge, London SW1X 0BD
Tel: 020 7590 9000
Head: Mr Magoo Giles
Type: Coeducational Day
Age range: 3–13
No. of pupils: 270 B147 G123
Fees: Day £11,550–£13,449

Little Acorns Nursery School

Church of St James The Less, Moreton Street,
London SW1V
Tel: 020 7931 0898
Type: Coeducational Day

Miss Daisy's Nursery School

Fountain Court Club Room, Ebury Square,
London SW1W 9SU
Tel: 020 7730 5797
Head: Daisy Harrison
Type: Coeducational Nursery School
Age range: 2–5
No. of pupils: 30
Fees: Day £1050–£5550

More House School

22-24 Pont Street, London SW1X 0AA
Tel: 020 7235 2855
Head: Mr R M Carlysle
Type: Girls' Day
Age range: 11–18
No. of pupils: 200 VIth45
Fees: Day £13,497

Ringrose Kindergarten - Pimlico

32a Lupus Street, London SW1V 3DZ
Tel: 020 7976 6511
Headmistress: Mrs C Stark SRN, DipMont, RNI
Type: Coeducational Nursery School
Age range: 2–5
No. of pupils: B20 G20
Fees: Day £2250

Small Steps Community Childcare Centre

Bessborough Street, London SW1V 2JD
Tel: 020 7641 5998
Type: Coeducational Nursery School

Sussex House School

68 Cadogan Square, Knightsbridge, London SW1X 0EA
Tel: 020 7584 1741
Headmaster: Mr N P Kaye MA(Cantab), ACP, FRSA
Type: Boys' Day
Age range: 8–13
No. of pupils: 182
Fees: Day £12,855

The Knightsbridge Kindergarten

St Peter's Church, 119 Eaton Square, London SW1W 0HQ
Tel: 020 7235 5305
Headmistress: Mrs P Powell-Harper
Type: Coeducational Day
Age range: 2–5
No. of pupils: B40 G40
Fees: Day £4000

Thomas's Kindergarten - Pimlico
14 Ranelagh Grove, London SW1W 8PD
Tel: 020 7730 3596
Headmistress: Miss Tamara Spierenburg HBO
Type: Coeducational Nursery School

Westminster Abbey Choir School
Dean's Yard, London SW1P 3NY
Tel: 020 7222 6151
Headmaster: Jonathan Milton BEd
Type: Boys' Boarding
Age range: 8–13
No. of pupils: 34
Fees: FB £5607

Westminster Cathedral Choir School
Ambrosden Avenue, London SW1P 1QH
Tel: 020 7798 9081
Headmaster: Mr Neil McLaughlan
Type: Boys' Day & Boarding
Age range: 8–13
No. of pupils: 150
Fees: Day £13,656 FB £6945

Westminster School
17 Dean's Yard, Westminster, London SW1P 3PF
Tel: 020 7963 1003
Headmaster: Dr Stephen Spurr
Type: Boys' Boarding & Day
Age range: B13–18 G16–18
No. of pupils: 750 B615 G135
Fees: Day £19,056–£20,664 FB £27,516

Westminster Under School
Adrian House, 27 Vincent Square, London SW1P 2NN
Tel: 020 7821 5788
Master: Jeremy Edwards BA, MA
Type: Boys' Day
Age range: 7–13
No. of pupils: 265
Fees: Day £12,489

Young England Kindergarten
St Saviour's Hall, St George's Square, London SW1V 3QW
Tel: 020 7834 3171
Principal: Mrs Kay C King MontDip
Type: Coeducational Day
Age range: 2½–5
No. of pupils: B35 G35
Fees: Day £3300–£4950

SW2

Elm Park Nursery School
90 Clarence Avenue, Clapham, London SW2
Tel: 020 8678 1990
Joint Heads: Mr & Mrs Taylor
Type: Coeducational Day
No. of pupils: 113

Happy Nursery Days
Valens House, 132a Uppertulse Hill, London SW2 2RX
Tel: 020 8674 7804
Type: Coeducational Nursery School
Age range: 3 months–5

Mini Stars Day Nursery
St Margarets Church, Barcombe Avenue,
London SW2 3HH
Tel: 020 8678 8600
Type: Coeducational Nursery School
Age range: 6 months–5
No. of pupils: 26

Streatham Montessori Nursery School
66 Blairderry Road, Streatham Hill, London SW2 4SB
Tel: 020 8674 2208
Type: Coeducational Nursery School

SW3

CAMERON HOUSE
For further details see p. 6
4 The Vale, Chelsea, London SW3 6AH
Tel: 020 7352 4040
Email: info@cameronhouseschool.org
Website: www.cameronhouseschool.org
www.gabbitas.co.uk
Headmistress: Mrs Lucie Moore BEd(Hons)
Type: Coeducational Day
Age range: 4–11
No. of pupils: 115 B52 G63
Fees: Day £13,170

Garden House School
Boys' School & Girls' School, Turk's Row, London SW3 4TW
Tel: 020 7730 1652
Headmistresses: Mrs J Webb CertEd, Southampton (Girls'
Upper School)
Type: Girls' Day & Boys' Day
Age range: B3–8 G3–11
No. of pupils: 449
Fees: Day £9300–£15,885

GEMS HAMPSHIRE SCHOOL
For further details see p. 18
15 Manresa Road, Chelsea, London SW3 6NB
Tel: 020 7352 7077
Email: hampshire@indschool.org
Website: www.ths.westminster.sch.uk
Principal: Mr A G Bray MISA, CertEd
Type: Coeducational Day
Age range: 3–13
No. of pupils: B132 G79
Fees: Day £8970–£12,990

Ringrose Kindergarten - Chelsea
St Lukes Church Hall, St Lukes Street, London SW3 3RP
Tel: 020 7352 8784
Type: Coeducational Nursery School

The Rainbow Playgroup
St Luke's Church Hall, St Luke's Street, London SW3 3RR
Tel: 020 7352 8156
Type: Coeducational Nursery School
Age range: 2–5

SW4

Abacus Support Services
Clapham United Church, Grafton Square,
London SW4 0DE
Tel: 020 7720 7290
Headmistress: Mrs Cynthia Clarke
Type: Coeducational Day

Clapham Montessori
St Paul's Community Centre, St Paul's Church, Rectory
Grove, London SW4 0DX
Tel: 020 7498 8324
Head: Mrs R Bowles BSc, IntMontDip
Type: Coeducational Day
Age range: 2–5

Clapham Park Montessori
St James' Church House, 10 West Road, Clapham,
London SW4 7DN
Tel: 020 7627 0352
Head: Mrs R Bowles BSc, IntMontDip
Type: Coeducational Day
Age range: 2–5

Eaton House The Manor Girls School
58 Clapham Common Northside, London SW4 9RU
Tel: 020 7924 6000
Head: Mrs S Lang
Type: Girls' Day
Age range: 4–11
No. of pupils: 90
Fees: Day £11,385

Eaton House The Manor School
58 Clapham Common Northside, London SW4 9RU
Tel: 020 7924 6000
Head: S Hepher BEd(Hons)
Type: Boys' Day
Age range: B2–13 G2–4
No. of pupils: 350 B320 G30
Fees: Day £11,385–£14,085

L'Ecole du Parc
12 Rodenhurst Road, London SW4 8AR
Tel: 020 8671 5287
Headteacher: Mrs E Sicking-Bressler
Type: Coeducational Day
Age range: 1–5
No. of pupils: 55 B25 G30
Fees: Day £4000–£7500

Magic Roundabout Nursery - Stockwell
Surrey Hall, Binfield Road, Stockwell, London SW4 6TB
Tel: 020 7498 1194
Type: Coeducational Nursery School

Montessori School
St Paul's Community Centre, Rectory Grove, Clapham,
London SW4 0DX
Tel: 020 7498 8324
Type: Coeducational Nursery School
Age range: 6 months–6

Oliver House Preparatory School
7 Nightingale Lane, London SW4 9AH
Tel: 020 8772 1911
Headteacher: Mr Robert Teague BSc(Hons)
Type: Coeducational Day
Age range: 2½–13
No. of pupils: 144 B68 G76
Fees: Day £4200–£9300

PARKGATE HOUSE SCHOOL
For further details see p. 31
80 Clapham Common North Side, London SW4 9SD
Tel: 020 7350 2461
Email: admissions@parkgate-school.co.uk
Website: www.parkgate-school.co.uk
Principal: Miss C M Shanley
Type: Coeducational Day
Age range: 2–11 years
No. of pupils: 233
Fees: Day £3960–£10,920

SW5

L'Ecole Bilingue
24 Collingham Road, St Jude's Church, London SW5 0LX
Tel: 020 7835 1144
Headteacher: Ms Veronique Ferreira
Type: Coeducational Day
Age range: 3–11
No. of pupils: 68 B42 G26
Fees: Day £6000–£6600

SW6

Al-Muntada Islamic School
7 Bridges Place, Parsons Green, London SW6 4HW
Tel: 020 7471 8283
Headmaster: Mr Z Chehimi
Type: Coeducational Day
Age range: 4–11
No. of pupils: 165
Fees: Day £2500

Bobby's Playhouse
16 Lettice Street, London SW6 4EH
Tel: 020 7384 1190
Principal: Mrs Emma Hannay
Type: Coeducational Nursery School
Age range: 3 months–5 years
No. of pupils: B68 G56
Fees: Day £11,000

Dawmouse Montessori Nursery School
34 Haldane Road, Fulham, London SW6 7EU
Tel: 020 7381 9385
Principal: Mrs Emma V Woodcock NNEB, MontDip
Type: Coeducational Day
Age range: 2–5
No. of pupils: 72

Eridge House Preparatory School
1 Fulham Park Road, Fulham, London SW6 4LJ
Tel: 020 7471 4816
Headteacher: Mrs Janie Richardson
Type: Coeducational Day
Age range: 3–11
No. of pupils: 180 B90 G90
Fees: Day £3962–£4212

Kensington Prep School GDST
596 Fulham Road, London SW6 5PA
Tel: 020 7731 9300
Head: Mrs P Lynch MA(Hons)
Type: Independent Day School for Girls
Age range: 4–11
No. of pupils: 280
Fees: Day £11,103

Leapfrog Day Nurseries - Fulham
The Hume Centre, Cortayne Road, Fulham,
London SW6 3QA
Tel: 020 7384 0406
Manager: Elaine Stevenson
Type: Coeducational Nursery School
Age range: 0–5

L'ECOLE DES PETITS
For further details see p. 27
2 Hazlebury Road, Fulham, London SW6 2NB
Tel: 020 7371 8350
Email: admin@lecoledespetits.co.uk
Website: www.lecoledespetits.co.uk
Head: Mrs F Brisset
Type: Independent Bilingual Pre-Prep
Age range: 3–6
No. of pupils: 136 B70 G66
Fees: Day £8610–£8910

Little People of Fulham
250a Lillie Road, Fulham, London SW6 7PX
Tel: 020 7386 0006
Owner: Miss Jane Gleasure
Type: Coeducational Nursery School
Age range: 4 months–5

London Study Centre
Munster House, 676 Fulham Road, London SW6 5SA
Tel: 020 7731 3549/736 4990
Principal: Margaret McLeod
Type: Coeducational Day
Age range: 16
No. of pupils: B400 G450

Melrose House Nursery School
55 Finlay Street, London SW6 6HF
Tel: 020 7736 9296
Type: Coeducational Nursery School

Peques Anglo-Spanish School
St John's Church, North End Road, Fulham,
London SW6 1PB
Tel: 020 7385 0055
Type: Coeducational Nursery School
Age range: 3 months–5

Rising Star Montessori School
St Clement Church Hall, 286 Fulham Palace Road,
London SW6 6HP
Tel: 020 7381 3511
Headmistress: Mrs Hortense Casson MontDip
Type: Coeducational Nursery School
Age range: 2–5
No. of pupils: 24
Fees: Day £2700

SINCLAIR HOUSE SCHOOL
For further details see p. 34
159 Munster Road, Fulham, London SW6 6DA
Tel: 020 7736 9182
Email: info@sinclairhouseschool.co.uk
Website: www.sinclairhouseschool.co.uk
Headmistress: Mrs Carlotta T M O'Sullivan
Type: Coeducational Day
Age range: 2–11
No. of pupils: B50 G30
Fees: Day £3105–£8805

STUDIO DAY NURSERY
For further details see p. 39
91-93 Moore Park Road, Fulham, London SW6 2DA
Tel: 020 7736 9256
Head: Miss J M R Williams NNEB, RSH(Norlander)
Type: Coeducational Day
Age range: 2–5

The Moat School
Bishops Avenue, Fulham, London SW6 6ED
Tel: 020 7610 9018
Head: Abigail Gray
Type: Coeducational Day
Age range: 11–16
No. of pupils: B65 G26
Fees: Day £23,145

The Zebedee Nursery School
4 Parsons Green, London SW6 4TN
Tel: 020 7371 9224
Headmistress: Miss Su Gahan NNEB, RSH
Type: Coeducational Nursery School
Age range: 2–5
No. of pupils: 32 B15 G17
Fees: Day £3900

Thomas's Preparatory School - Fulham
Hugon Road, London SW6 3ES
Tel: 020 7751 8200
Head: Miss Annette Dobson BEd(Hons), PGCertDys
Type: Coeducational Day Preparatory
Age range: 4–11

SW7

Twice Times Montessori School
The Cricket Pavilion, South Park, London SW6 3AF
Tel: 020 7731 4929
Heads: Mrs A Welch MontDip & Mrs S Henderson MontDip
Type: Coeducational Nursery School
Age range: 2–5
No. of pupils: 50

Falkner House
19 Brechin Place, South Kensington, London SW7 4QB
Tel: 020 7373 4501
Headmistress: Mrs Anita Griggs BA(Hons), PGCE
Type: Girls' Day School with Coeducational Nursery
Age range: B3–4 G3–11
No. of pupils: 182 B10 G172
Fees: Day £12,600

GLENDOWER SCHOOL
For further details see p. 19

87 Queen's Gate, London SW7 5JX
Tel: 020 7370 1927
Email: office@glendower.kensington.sch.uk
Website: www.glendowerprep.org
Headmistress: Mrs R E Bowman BA, PGCE
Type: Girls' Preparatory Day
Age range: 4–11+
No. of pupils: 190
Fees: Day £12,555

Lycee Francais Charles de Gaulle

35 Cromwell Road, London SW7 2DG
Tel: 020 7584 6322
Proviseur: Mr Bernard Vasseur
Type: Coeducational Day
Age range: 3–18
No. of pupils: 3780 VIth467
Fees: Day £4311–£8472

Pooh Corner Kindergarten

St Stephen's House, 48 Emperors Gate, London SW7 4HJ
Tel: 020 7373 6111
Type: Coeducational Nursery School

Queen's Gate School

133 Queen's Gate, London SW7 5LE
Tel: 020 7589 3587
Principal: Mrs R M Kamaryc BA, MSc, PGCE
Type: Girls' Day
Age range: 4–18
No. of pupils: 400 VIth66
Fees: Day £11,400–£13,950

Ravenstone Preparatory School and Nursery

24 Elvaston Place, South Kensington, London SW7 5NL
Tel: 020 7225 3131
Headmistress: Mrs Elizabeth Heath BA, PGCE
Type: Coeducational Day
Age range: 2³⁄₄–11
No. of pupils: 110 B62 G48
Fees: Day £11,800–£12,020

ST NICHOLAS PREPARATORY SCHOOL
For further details see p. 38

23 Princes Gate, Kensington, London SW7 1PT
Tel: 020 7225 1277
Email: info@stnicholasprep.co.uk
Website: www.stnicholasprep.co.uk
Head: Mr David Wilson MA, BEd, Dip TEFL
Type: Coeducational Pre-preparatory & Preparatory Day
Age range: 2 years 9 months–11+ years
No. of pupils: 280
Fees: Day £11,055–£12,630

St Philip's School

6 Wetherby Place, London SW7 4NE
Tel: 020 7373 3944
Headmaster: H J Biggs-Davison MA(Cantab)
Type: Boys' Preparatory
Age range: 7–13
No. of pupils: 106
Fees: Day £11,160

The Vale School

2 Elvaston Place, London SW7 5QH
Tel: 020 7924 6000
Headmaster: Mr R Greenwood
Type: Coeducational Day
Age range: B3–8 G3–11
No. of pupils: 70 B35 G35
Fees: Day £11,385

SW8

Clapham Day Nursery

3 Peardon Street, London SW8 3BW
Tel: 020 7498 3165
Manager: Nicolette Warnes NNEB, NVQ4
Type: Coeducational Nursery School
Age range: 3 months–5
No. of pupils: 72

NEWTON PREP
For further details see p. 30

149 Battersea Park Road, London SW8 4BX
Tel: 020 7720 4091
Email: admin@newtonprep.co.uk
Website: www.newtonprep.co.uk
Headmaster: Mr Nicholas M Allen BA, PGCE
Type: Coeducational Pre-preparatory & Preparatory Day
Age range: 3–13
No. of pupils: 517 B279 G238
Fees: Day £6420–£12,960

The Oval Montessori Nursery School
within Vauxhall Park, Fentiman Road, London SW8 1LA
Tel: 020 7735 4816
Head: Ms Louise Norwood
Type: Coeducational Nursery School
Age range: 2½–5
No. of pupils: B14 G14
Fees: Day £3000

The Willow Nursery School
c/o Clapham Baptist Church, 823-825 Wandsworth Road,
London SW8 3JX
Tel: 020 7498 0319
Head: Mrs Harriet Baring MontDip
Type: Coeducational Day
Age range: 2–5
No. of pupils: B17 G18
Fees: Day £3000–£3100

SW9

Asquith Nursery - Lambeth
50 Groveway, Stockwell, London SW9 0AR
Tel: 020 7793 9922
Type: Coeducational Day
Age range: 0–5
No. of pupils: 25

Ladybird Nursery School
9 Knowle Close, London SW9 0TQ
Tel: 020 7924 9505
Type: Coeducational Day

New Mind School
Suite 9 Warwick House, Overton Road, Brixton,
London SW9 7JP
Tel: 020 7978 9978
Headteacher: Odartei L Muhammad BSc(Hons), PGCE
Type: Coeducational Day
Age range: 2½–11
No. of pupils: 18 B10 G8

Thomas Francis Academy
297-299 Coldharbour Lane, Brixton, London SW9 8RP
Tel: 020 7737 7900
Headteacher: Ms K Thomas
Type: Coeducational Day
Age range: 5–16
No. of pupils: 20 B12 G8

Wiltshire Nursery
85 Wiltshire Road, Brixton, London SW9 7NZ
Tel: 020 7274 4446
Type: Coeducational Nursery School

SW10

Chelsea Kindergarten
St Andrews Church, Park Walk, Chelsea,
London SW10 0AU
Tel: 020 7352 4856
Headmistress: Miss Lulu Tindall MontDip
Type: Coeducational Day
Age range: 2–5
No. of pupils: B22 G22
Fees: Day £3900–£6120

Paint Pots Montessori School - Chelsea
Chelsea Christian Centre, Edith Grove, London SW10 0LB
Tel: 020 7376 5780
Principal: Miss G Hood MontDip
Type: Coeducational Nursery School
Age range: 2½–5
No. of pupils: 42
Fees: Day £2130–£6360

REDCLIFFE SCHOOL TRUST LTD
For further details see p. 33
47 Redcliffe Gardens, Chelsea, London SW10 9JH
Tel: 020 7352 9247
Email: admissions@redcliffeschool.com
Website: www.redcliffeschool.com
Head: Mrs Susan Bourne BSc, PGCE
Type: Coeducational Day
Age range: B2½–8 G2½–11
No. of pupils: B43 G92
Fees: Day £11,280

The Boltons Nursery School
262b Fulham Road, Chelsea, London SW10 9EL
Tel: 020 7351 6993
Type: Coeducational Day
Age range: 2–5
No. of pupils: 60
Fees: Day £2370–£4200

Alphabet Nursery School
Chatham Hall, Northcote Road, Battersea,
London SW11 6DY
Tel: 020 8871 7473
Principal: Mrs A McKenzie-Lewis
Type: Coeducational Day
No. of pupils: 40
Fees: Day £1500–£1800

Asquith Nursery - Battersea
18/30 Latchmere Road, Battersea, London SW11 2DX
Tel: 020 7228 7008
Type: Coeducational Nursery School
Age range: 3 months–5

Battersea Pre-School & Nursery
18/30 Latchmere Road, Battersea, London SW11 2DX
Tel: 020 7228 4722
Head: Miss Sharon Nelson
Type: Coeducational Day
Age range: 0–5
No. of pupils: 86

Blundells Day Nursery
The Old Court, 194-196 Sheepcote Lane, Battersea,
London SW11 5BW
Tel: 020 7924 4204
Headmistress: Susan Stevens
Type: Coeducational Nursery School
Age range: 18 months–5
No. of pupils: 66
Fees: Day £4655–£8575

Bumble Bee School
Church Hall, Church of the Ascension, Putney,
London SW11 5TU
Tel: 020 7350 2970
Principal: Bella Lyle
Type: Coeducational Day

Centre Academy London
92 St John's Hill, Battersea, London SW11 1SH
Tel: 020 7738 2344
Principal: Duncan Rollo BA, MA, PhD
Type: Independent Coeducational Day
Age range: 9–18
No. of pupils: 60 B45 G15 VIth13
Fees: Day £24,369–£32,400

DOLPHIN SCHOOL
For further details see p. 11
106 Northcote Road, London SW11 6QW
Tel: 020 7924 3472
Email: admissions@dolphinschool.org.uk
Website: www.dolphinschool.org.uk
Principal: Mrs Jo Glen BA(Hons)
Type: Coeducational Day and Nursery
Age range: 2½–11
No. of pupils: 245
Fees: Day £7485–£8070

Emanuel School
Battersea Rise, London SW11 1HS
Tel: 020 8870 4171
Headmaster: Mr Mark Hanley-Browne
Type: Coeducational Day
Age range: 10–18
No. of pupils: 720 B480 G240 VIth160
Fees: Day £14,139

Happy Times Nursery
40 Parkgate Road, London SW11 4NP
Tel: 020 7350 5959
Type: Coeducational Nursery School

L'ECOLE DE BATTERSEA
For further details see p. 26
Trott Street, Battersea, London SW11 3DS
Tel: 020 7371 8350
Email: admin@lecoledespetits.co.uk
Website: www.lecoledespetits.co.uk
Head: Mrs F Brisset
Type: Coeducational International Day
Age range: 3–11
No. of pupils: 230
Fees: Day £8730–£8910

Little Red Hen Nursery School
Church of the Nazarene, 2 Grant Road, Battersea,
London SW11 2NU
Tel: 020 7738 0321
Type: Coeducational Nursery School
Age range: 2–5
No. of pupils: B10 G14
Fees: Day £1470–£1740

Noah's Ark Nursery Schools
Dolphin School Trust, 106 Northcote Road,
London SW11 6QW
Tel: 020 7228 9593
Head: Miss A Miller
Type: Coeducational Nursery School
Age range: 2½–5
No. of pupils: 112
Fees: Day £4089

Northcote Lodge School
26 Bolingbroke Grove, London SW11 6EL
Tel: 020 8682 8888
Headmaster: Mr John Hansford
Type: Boys' Day
Age range: 8–13
No. of pupils: 195
Fees: Day £13,485

Thames Christian College
Wye Street, Battersea, London SW11 2HB
Tel: 020 7228 3933
Executive Head: Stephen Holsgrove PhD
Type: Coeducational Day
Age range: 11–16
No. of pupils: 100 B55 G45
Fees: Day £9240

The Mouse House Nursery School
27 Mallinson Road, London SW11 1BW
Tel: 020 7924 1893
Headmistress: Amanda White-Spunner
Type: Coeducational Day
Age range: 2–5
No. of pupils: B80 G80
Fees: Day £1650–£4125

The Park Kindergarten
St Saviour's Church, 351 Battersea Park Road,
London SW11 4LH
Tel: 020 7627 5125
Principal: Miss Lisa Neilsen MontDip
Type: Coeducational Nursery School
Age range: 2–5
No. of pupils: B14 G16
Fees: Day £2370

Thomas's Kindergarten - Battersea
St Mary's Church, Battersea Church Road,
London SW11 3NA
Tel: 020 7738 0400
Headmistress: Miss Iona Jennings
Type: Coeducational Nursery School
Age range: 2–5
No. of pupils: B25 G25
Fees: Day £1365–£2100

Thomas's Preparatory School - Battersea
28-40 Battersea High Street, London SW11 3JB
Tel: 020 7978 0900
Head: Ben V R Thomas MA
Type: Coeducational Day
Age range: 4–13
No. of pupils: 474 B254 G220
Fees: Day £8292–£11,715

Thomas's Preparatory School - Clapham
Broomwood Road, London SW11 6JZ
Tel: 020 7326 9300
Headmistress: Mrs Carol Evelegh DipCE, DipSpLD
Type: Coeducational Day
Age range: 4–13
No. of pupils: B264 G275
Fees: Day £10,365–£11,730

SW12

ABACUS Early Learning Nursery School
135 Laitwood Road, Balham, London SW12 9QH
Tel: 020 8675 8093
Type: Coeducational Day

Asquith Nursery - Balham
36 Radbourne Road, Balham, London SW12 0EF
Tel: 020 8673 1405
Type: Coeducational Nursery School

Broomwood Hall School
68-74 Nightingale Lane, London SW12 8NR
Tel: 020 8682 8810
Principal: Lady Colquhoun BEd, DipT
Type: Coeducational Day
Age range: B4–8 G4–13
No. of pupils: 607 B183 G424
Fees: Day £10,950–£13,350

Caterpillar 2 Nursery School
14A Boundaries Road, London SW12 8EX
Tel: 020 8265 5224
Head: Mrs Maralyn Hassell CertEd
Type: Coeducational Day
Age range: 2–5
No. of pupils: 46 B22 G24
Fees: Day £1500–£2778

Cresset Kindergarten
The Waldorf School of South West London, 12 Ballam Park Road, London SW12 8DR
Tel: 020 8673 4881
Principal: Pat Hague
Type: Coeducational Day

Gateway House Nursery School
St Judes Church Hall, Heslop Road, London SW12 8EG
Tel: 020 8675 8258
Principal: Miss Elizabeth Marshall
Type: Coeducational Day
Age range: 2–4
No. of pupils: 30 B13 G17
Fees: Day £1010–£1060

HORNSBY HOUSE SCHOOL
For further details see p. 24
Hearnville Road, Balham, London SW12 8RS
Tel: 020 8673 7573
Email: school@hornsby-house.co.uk
Website: www.hornsby-house.co.uk
Head: Mr Jon Gray
Type: Coeducational Day
Age range: 4–11
No. of pupils: B202 G183
Fees: Day £11,130–£11,940

Nightingale Montessori Nursery
St Lukes Community Hall, 194 Ramsden Road, London SW12 8RQ
Tel: 020 8675 8070
Principal: Mrs Tejas Earp
Type: Coeducational Nursery School
Age range: 2–5

Noah's Ark Nursery School
Endlesham Church Hall, 48 Endlesham Road, London SW12 8JL
Tel: 020 7228 9593
Type: Coeducational Nursery School
No. of pupils: 32
Fees: Day £1935

The Crescent Kindergarten Three
70 Thornton Road, London SW12 0LF
Tel: 020 8675 9659
Type: Coeducational Nursery School

The White House Preparatory School & Woodentops Kindergarten
24 Thornton Road, London SW12 0LF
Tel: 020 8674 9514
Head: Ms Mary McCahery
Type: Coeducational Day
Age range: 2–11
No. of pupils: B65 G65
Fees: Day £7785–£8385

SW13

Colet Court (St Paul's Preparatory School)
Colet Court, Lonsdale Road, London SW13 9JT
Tel: 020 8748 3461
Headmaster: Mr T A Meunier MA(Cantab)
Type: Boys' Day
Age range: 7–13
No. of pupils: 434
Fees: Day £14,334

Lowther Nursery Unit
Stillingfleet Road, Barnes, London SW13 9AE
Tel: 020 8563 7769
Type: Coeducational Nursery School
Age range: 3–5

St Michaels Nursery School
St Michaels Church Hall, Elm Bank Gardens, London SW13 0NX
Tel: 020 8878 0116
Principal: Mrs J L Gould
Type: Coeducational Nursery School
Age range: 2–5
No. of pupils: 36

St Paul's School
Lonsdale Road, Barnes, London SW13 9JT
Tel: 020 8748 9162
High Master: Martin Stephen
Type: Boys' Boarding & Day
Age range: 13–18
No. of pupils: 815 VIth320
Fees: Day £11,085 FB £16,485

Swedish School
82 Lonsdale Road, London SW13 9JS
Tel: 020 8741 1751
Headmaster: Mr Jan Dackenberg
Type: Coeducational Day
Age range: 3–18
No. of pupils: 242 B104 G138
Fees: Day £6600

The Harrodian School
Lonsdale Road, London SW13 9QN
Tel: 020 8748 6117
Headmaster: James R Hooke
Type: Coeducational Day
Age range: 5–18
No. of pupils: 890 B460 G430 VIth95
Fees: Day £10,407–£15,219

The Montessori Pavilion - The Kindergarten School
Vine Road, Barnes, London SW13 0NE
Tel: 020 8878 9695
Type: Coeducational Nursery School
Age range: 3–8
No. of pupils: 50
Fees: Day £1950–£3600

SW14

Happy Times Nursery
The Limes, 123 Mortlake High Street, London SW14 8SN
Tel: 0800 652 2424
Type: Coeducational Nursery School

Primary Steps Day Nursery
459b Upper Richmond Road West, East Sheen,
London SW14 7PR
Tel: 020 8876 8144
Manager: Ms Joyce Kledo NNEB
Type: Coeducational Nursery School
Age range: 1–5
No. of pupils: 75

Tower House School
188 Sheen Lane, London SW14 8LF
Tel: 020 8876 3323
Head: Mrs Jackie Compton-Howlett LRAM, ARCM, PGCE, FRSA
Type: Boys' Day
Age range: 4–13
No. of pupils: 175
Fees: Day £9507–£10,764

SW15

Asquith Nursery - Putney
107-109 Norroy Road, Putney, London SW15 1PH
Tel: 020 8246 5611
Type: Coeducational Nursery School
Age range: 3 months–5

Beehive Nursery School
St Margarets Church Hall, Putney Park Lane, London SW15
Tel: 020 8780 5333
Headmistress: Lindsay Deans
Type: Coeducational Day
Age range: 2–5
No. of pupils: 16
Fees: Day £1140

Bees Knees Nursery School
within Brookside Community Hall, 12 Priory Lane,
London SW15 5JL
Tel: 020 8876 8252
Headmistress: Jo Wood
Type: Coeducational Nursery School
Age range: 2–5

Busy Bee Nursery School
106 Felsham Road, Putney, London SW15
Tel: 020 8780 1615
Headmistress: Mrs Lucy Lindsay
Type: Coeducational Day
Age range: 2–5

Busy Bee Nursery School
19 Lytton Grove, Putney, London SW15 2EZ
Tel: 020 8789 0132
Headmistress: Dr Sally Corbett
Type: Coeducational Day
Age range: 2–5

Hurlingham School

122 Putney Bridge Road, Putney, London SW15 2NQ
Tel: 020 8874 7186
Headteacher: Mrs Val Willmott
Type: Coeducational Day
Age range: 4–11
No. of pupils: 310 B130 G180
Fees: Day £10,200–£10,800

Ibstock Place School

Clarence Lane, Roehampton, London SW15 5PY
Tel: 020 8876 9991
Head: Mrs Anna Sylvester-Johnson BA(Hons), PGCE
Type: Coeducational Day
Age range: 3–18
No. of pupils: B450 G420
Fees: Day £5700–£14,500

LION HOUSE SCHOOL
For further details see p. 28

The Old Methodist Hall, Gwendolen Avenue,
London SW15 6EH
Tel: 020 8780 9446
Email: office@lionhouseschool.co.uk
Website: www.lionhouseschool.co.uk
Head: Miss H J Luard MontDip
Type: Coeducational Day
Age range: 2½–7½
No. of pupils: 115

Prospect House School

75 Putney Hill, London SW15 3NT
Tel: 020 8780 0456
Headmistress: Mrs D Barratt
Type: Coeducational Day
Age range: 3–11
No. of pupils: 174 B83 G91
Fees: Day £1600–£3470

Putney High School GDST

35 Putney Hill, London SW15 6BH
Tel: 020 8788 4886
Headmistress: Dr Denise Lodge BSc, MSc, PhD
Type: Girls' Day
Age range: 4–18
No. of pupils: 875 VIth150
Fees: Day £9069–£11,655

Putney Park School

Woodborough Road, London SW15 6PY
Tel: 020 8788 8316
Headmistress: Mrs Ruth Mann BSc(Hons), PGCE,
DPSE(School Management)
Type: Coeducational Day
Age range: B4–8 G4–16
No. of pupils: 247 B44 G203
Fees: Day £9990–£11,415

Square One Nursery School

12 Ravenna Road, Putney, London SW15 6AW
Tel: 020 8788 1546
Type: Coeducational Nursery School

The Merlin School

4 Carlton Drive, Putney Hill, London SW15 2BZ
Tel: 020 8788 2769
Principal: Mrs K Prest
Type: Coeducational Day
Age range: 4–8
No. of pupils: 170

Tiggers Nursery School

87 Putney Bridge Road, London SW15 2PA
Tel: 020 8874 4668
Headmistress: Natasha Green MontDip
Type: Coeducational Nursery School
Age range: 2–5
No. of pupils: B11 G7
Fees: Day £1425–£1725

SW16

ABACUS Early Learning Nursery School

7 Drewstead Road, Streatham, London SW16 1LY
Tel: 020 8677 9117
Principal: Mrs M Taylor BEd & Ms S Petgrave
Type: Coeducational Day
Age range: 12 mths–5 years
No. of pupils: 40

Beechwood School

55 Leigham Court Road, Streatham, London SW16 2NJ
Tel: 020 8677 8778
Headmistress: Mrs M Marshall
Type: Coeducational Day
Age range: 0–11
No. of pupils: 100
Fees: Day £6726–£7875

Carmena Christian Day Nurseries

47 Thrale Road, Streatham, London SW16 1NT
Tel: 020 8677 8231
Head: Mrs S Allen
Type: Coeducational Day

Streatham & Clapham High School GDST

42 Abbotswood Road, London SW16 1AW
Tel: 020 8677 8400
Head: Mrs S Mitchell MA(St Hugh's College)Oxford,
PGCE(Leeds)
Type: Girls' Day
Age range: B3–5 G3–18
No. of pupils: 603 B3 G600 VIth70
Fees: Day £5886–£9810

Teddies Nurseries Streatham

113 Blegborough Road, London SW16 6DL
Tel: 020 8835 9898
Type: Coeducational Day
Age range: 3 months–5 years

Telten Montessori Nursery School

Norbury Park Lawn Tennis Club, Ederline Avenue,
London SW16 4RZ
Tel: 020 8764 2531/07974 249726
Proprietress: Mrs A Oke
Type: Coeducational Nursery School
Age range: 2–5
No. of pupils: B126 G19
Fees: Day £562–£3693

The Waldorf School of South West London

Woodfields, Abbotswood Road, Streatham,
London SW16 1AP
Tel: 020 8769 6587
Type: Coeducational Day
Age range: 4–14
No. of pupils: 80
Fees: Day £3090–£4414

SW17

Balham Preparatory School

145 Upper Tooting Road, London SW17 7TJ
Tel: 020 8767 6057
Headmaster: Mr K Bahauddin
Type: Coeducational Day
Age range: 3–16
No. of pupils: 250 B110 G140

Bertrum House School

290 Balham High Road, London SW17 7AL
Tel: 020 8767 4051
Principal: Mrs Jane Fletcher
Type: Nursery & Pre-preparatory
Age range: 2½–7
No. of pupils: B74 G58
Fees: Day £900–£9450

Eveline Day & Nursery Schools

14 Trinity Crescent, Upper Tooting, London SW17 7AE
Tel: 020 8672 4673
Headmistress: Ms Eveline Drut
Type: Coeducational Day
Age range: 3 months–11 years
No. of pupils: 80

Finton House School

171 Trinity Road, London SW17 7HL
Tel: 020 8682 0921
Head: Adrian Floyd BSc, PGCE
Type: Coeducational Day
Age range: 4–11
No. of pupils: 305 B109 G196
Fees: Day £11,880

Headstart Montessori

St Mary's Church Hall, 46 Wimbledon Road, Tooting,
London SW17 0UQ
Tel: 020 8947 7359
Type: Coeducational Day
Age range: 2–7
No. of pupils: 12 B7 G5

Red Balloon Nursery School

St Mary Magdalene Church Hall, Trinity Road, Tooting,
London SW17 7SD
Tel: 020 8672 4711
Headmistress: Ms T Millington-Drake MontDip
Type: Coeducational Day
Age range: 2–5
No. of pupils: B30 G40
Fees: Day £3270–£3450

Teddies Nurseries Balham

272 Balham High Road, London SW17 7AJ
Tel: 020 8672 4809
Type: Coeducational Day
Age range: 3 months–5 years

The Crescent Kindergarten
10 Trinity Crescent, Tooting, London SW17 7AE
Tel: 020 8767 5882
Principal: Philip Evelegh
Type: Coeducational Nursery School

The Crescent Kindergarten Two
Holy Trinity Church, Trinity Road, London SW17 7RH
Tel: 020 8682 3020
Type: Coeducational Nursery School

The Eveline Day Nursery Schools - Tooting
30 Ritherdon Road, Upper Tooting, London SW17 8QD
Tel: 020 8672 7549
Principal: Mrs T Larche
Type: Coeducational Nursery School

The Eveline Day Nursery Schools Ltd - SW17
Seeley Hall, Chillerton Road, London SW17 9BE
Tel: 020 8672 0501
Type: Coeducational Nursery School

Toots Day Nursery
214 Totterdown Street, Tooting, London SW17 8TD
Tel: 020 8767 7017
Principal: Angela Duffell
Type: Coeducational Nursery School
Age range: 1–5

SW18

345 Nursery School
Fitzhugh Community Clubroom, Fitzhugh Grove, Trinity Road, London SW18 3SA
Tel: 020 8874 8021
Principal: Mrs Annabel Dixon
Type: Coeducational Nursery School
Age range: 3–5
No. of pupils: 42 B21 G21
Fees: Day £3555

Leapfrog Day Nurseries - Wandsworth
Dolphin House, Riverside West, Smugglers Way, Wandsworth, London SW18 1DE
Tel: 020 8877 1135
Manager: Clare Myers-Shaw
Type: Coeducational Nursery School
Age range: 0–5

Melrose House Nursery School
39 Melrose Road, London SW18 1LX
Tel: 020 8874 7769
Type: Coeducational Nursery School
Age range: 2–5
No. of pupils: B13 G12

Teddies Nurseries Southfields
Duntshill Mill, 21 Riverdale Drive, London SW18 4UR
Tel: 020 8870 2009
Type: Coeducational Day
Age range: 3 months–5 years

The Eveline Day Nursery Schools Ltd - SW18
United Reform Church, Geraldine Road, London SW18 2NU
Tel: 020 8870 0966
Type: Coeducational Nursery School

THE ROCHE SCHOOL
For further details see p. 43
11 Frogmore, London SW18 1HW
Tel: 020 8877 0823
Email: office@therocheschool.co.uk
Website: www.therocheschool.co.uk
Principal: J A Roche BSc, PhD
Type: Coeducational Day
Age range: 2–11
No. of pupils: 190 B95 G95
Fees: Day £9450–£10,230

The St Michael Steiner School
5 Merton Road, Wandsworth, London SW18 4TP
Tel: 020 8870 0500
Type: Coeducational Day
Age range: 3–11
No. of pupils: 73
Fees: Day £3000–£4400

Wimbledon Park Montessori School
206 Heythorp Street, Southfields, London SW18 5BU
Tel: 020 8944 8584
Head: Ms Clare Collins
Type: Coeducational Day
Age range: 2–5
No. of pupils: B30 G34
Fees: Day £830–£950

SW19

Cosmopolitan Day Nursery
65-67 High Street, Colliers Wood, London SW19 2JF
Tel: 020 8544 0758
Principal: Ms Wendy S Bignall
Type: Coeducational Day

Crown Kindergartens
Coronation House, Ashcombe Road, Wimbledon,
London SW19 8JP
Tel: 020 8540 8820
Principal: Mrs Acres
Type: Coeducational Day
Age range: 1–5
No. of pupils: 28

Donhead
33 Edge Hill, London SW19 4NP
Tel: 020 8946 7000
Headmaster: Mr G C McGrath BA(Hons), PGCE, MBA(Ed)
Type: Boys' Day
Age range: 4–11
No. of pupils: 280
Fees: Day £7800–£8325

King's College Junior School
Southside, Wimbledon Common, London SW19 4TT
Tel: 020 8255 5335
Headmaster: Dr G A Silverlock
Type: Boys' Day
Age range: 7–13
No. of pupils: 451
Fees: Day £12,345–£13,920

King's College School
Southside, Wimbledon Common, London SW19 4TT
Tel: 020 8255 5352
Head Master: A D Halls MA
Type: Boys' Day
Age range: 13–18
No. of pupils: 762 VIth295
Fees: Day £15,450

Noddy's Nursery School
Trinity Church Hall, Beaumont Road, Wimbledon,
London SW19 6SP
Tel: 020 8785 9191
Principal: Mrs Sarah Edwards NNEB, Mont Dip
Type: Coeducational Nursery School
Age range: 2–5
No. of pupils: B50 G50

Playdays Day Nursery & Nursery School Ltd
58 Queens Road, Wimbledon, London SW19 8LR
Tel: 020 8946 8139
Type: Coeducational Nursery School

The Castle Kindergarten
20 Henfield Road, London SW19 3HU
Tel: 020 8544 0089
Headmistress: Mrs Beverley Davis DipEd
Type: Coeducational Nursery School
Age range: 2–5
No. of pupils: B34 G34

The Eveline Day Nursery Schools Ltd - SW19
87a Quicks Road, London SW19 1EX
Tel: 020 8545 0699
Type: Coeducational Nursery School

The Maria Montessori Children's House
St John's Ambulance Hall, 122-124 Kingston Road,
London SW19 1LY
Tel: 020 8543 6353
Type: Coeducational Nursery School
Age range: 2½–5

The Montessori Childrens House Ltd
St John's Church, 1 Spencer Hill, London SW19 4NZ
Tel: 020 8971 9135
Type: Coeducational Nursery School
Age range: 2–5

The Study Preparatory School
Wilberforce House, Camp Road, Wimbledon Common,
London SW19 4UN
Tel: 020 8947 6969
Headmistress: Mrs J Nicol MA, CertEd
Type: Girls' Day
Age range: 4–11
No. of pupils: 320
Fees: Day £3195

The Wimbledon Village Montessori School
26 Lingfield Road, London SW19 4QD
Tel: 020 8944 0772
Type: Coeducational Nursery School

Willington School
Worcester Road, Wimbledon, London SW19 7QQ
Tel: 020 8944 7020
Head: Graham Hill MA(Oxon)
Type: Boys' Day
Age range: 4–13
No. of pupils: 240
Fees: Day £7950–£9450

Wimbledon Common Preparatory
113 Ridgway, Wimbledon, London SW19 4TA
Tel: 020 8946 1001
Headmaster: Neil J Worsey
Type: Boys' Day
Age range: 4–8
No. of pupils: 160
Fees: Day £6930–£7725

Wimbledon High School GDST
Mansel Road, Wimbledon, London SW19 4AB
Tel: 020 8971 0900
Headmistress: Mrs H Hanbury
Type: Girls' Day
Age range: 4–18
No. of pupils: 900 VIth155
Fees: Day £8637–£11,100

SW20

Asquith Nursery - Raynes Park
c/o David Lloyd Leisure Club, Bushey Road, Raynes Park,
London SW20 8TE
Tel: 020 8543 9005
Type: Coeducational Nursery School
Age range: 3 months–5

Teddies Nurseries Raynes Park
3 Spencer Road, Wimbledon, London SW20 0QN
Tel: 020 8947 2398
Type: Coeducational Day
Age range: 3 months–5 years

The Hall School, Wimbledon
17 The Downs, Wimbledon, London SW20 8HF
Tel: 020 8879 9200
Headmaster: Timothy J Hobbs MA
Type: Coeducational Day
Age range: 4–16
No. of pupils: 550 B320 G230
Fees: Day £8310–£10,989

The Norwegian School
28 Arterberry Road, Wimbledon, London SW20 8AH
Tel: 020 8947 6617
Head: Ms Kirsti H Jacobsen
Type: Coeducational Day
Age range: 3–16
No. of pupils: B52 G52

The Rowans School
19 Drax Avenue, Wimbledon, London SW20 0EG
Tel: 020 8946 8220
Headteacher: Mrs E Tyrrell
Type: Coeducational Day
Age range: 3–8
No. of pupils: B80 G48
Fees: Day £3945–£7725

Ursuline Preparatory School
18 The Downs, London SW20 8HR
Tel: 020 8947 0859
Headmistress: Jeannette Maidment, BA(Hons)
Theology(Durham), PGCE(Dist)
Type: Coeducational Day Preparatory
Age range: B3–7 G3–11
No. of pupils: B65 G140
Fees: Day £3660–£6210

WEST LONDON

W1

Great Beginnings Montessori School
The Welsh Church Hall, 82a Chiltern Street, Marylebone,
London W1M 1PS
Tel: 020 7486 2276
Type: Coeducational Day
Age range: 2–6
No. of pupils: B35 G35
Fees: Day £1095–£1650

Jumbo Montessori Nursery School
22 George Street, London W1H 3QY
Tel: 020 7935 2441
Type: Coeducational Day
Age range: 2–5
No. of pupils: 35 B13 G22
Fees: Day £1785

Portland Place School
56-58 Portland Place, London W1N 1NJ
Tel: 020 7307 8700
Headteacher: Mr R Walker BSc, CChem, MRSC
Type: Coeducational Day
Age range: 11–18
No. of pupils: 300 B200 G100 VIth50
Fees: Day £12,585

QUEEN'S COLLEGE
For further details see p. 32
43-49 Harley Street, London W1G 8BT
Tel: 020 7291 7000
Email: queens@qcl.org.uk
Website: www.qcl.org.uk
Head: Dr F M R Ramsey MA, DPhil(Oxon)
Type: Girls' Day
Age range: 11–18
No. of pupils: 360 VIth90

Southbank International School - Westminster
63-65 Portland Place, London W1B 1QR
Tel: 020 7243 3803
Principal: Terry Hedger
Type: Coeducational Day
Age range: 11–19
No. of pupils: 318 B143 G175 VIth108
Fees: Day £19,380–£21,450

W2

Connaught House School
47 Connaught Square, London W2 2HL
Tel: 020 7262 8830
Principals: Mrs J Hampton & Mr F Hampton MA, RCA
Type: Coeducational Day
Age range: B4–8 G4–11
No. of pupils: 70
Fees: Day £10,500–£12,900

Maria Montessori School - Bayswater
St Matthew's Parish Church, 29 St Petersburgh Place,
London W2 4LA
Tel: 020 7435 3646
Type: Coeducational Nursery School

Paint Pots Montessori School - Bayswater
Bayswater United Reformed Church, Newton Road,
London W2 5LS
Tel: 020 7792 0433
Principal: Miss G Hood MontDip
Type: Coeducational Nursery School
Age range: 2–5
No. of pupils: B12 G12
Fees: Day £1284–£3981

Pembridge Hall School for Girls
18 Pembridge Square, London W2 4EH
Tel: 020 7229 0121
Headteacher: Mrs Elizabeth Marsden
Type: Girls' Day Preparatory
Age range: 4–11
No. of pupils: 385
Fees: Day £13,905

Primary Steps Creche
Harbour Club, 1 Alfred Road, London W2 5EU
Tel: 020 7266 9310
Manager: Nelufa Akanjee CACHE Dip
Type: Coeducational Nursery School

Ravenstone Day Nursery & Nursery School
The Long Garden, St George's Fields, Albion Street,
London W2 2AX
Tel: 020 7262 1190
Headmistress: Mrs Elizabeth Heath BA, PGCE
Type: Day Nursery and Nursery School
Age range: 10 months–5 years
No. of pupils: 79
Fees: Day £10,560

The Minors Nursery School
10 Pembridge Square, London W2 4ED
Tel: 020 7727 7253
Headteacher: Ms Jane Ritchie
Type: Coeducational Nursery School
Age range: 2½–5

Wetherby Pre-Preparatory School
11 Pembridge Square, London W2 4ED
Tel: 020 7727 9581
Headmaster: Mr Mark Snell
Type: Boys' Day Pre-Preparatory
Age range: 4–8
No. of pupils: 245 B245
Fees: Day £14,595

W3

Acton Yochien Nursery School
The Pavilion, Queens Drive Playing Fields, Acton,
London W3 0HT
Tel: 020 8343 2192
Type: Coeducational Nursery School
(👥)

Ealing Montessori School
St Martin's Church Hall, Hale Gardens, London W3 9SQ
Tel: 020 8992 4513
Head: Mrs Soin
Type: Coeducational Nursery School
No. of pupils: 36
(👥)

Greek Primary School of London
3 Pierrepoint Road, Acton, London W3 9JF
Tel: 020 8992 6156
Type: Coeducational Day
Age range: 1–11
(👥)

Happy Child Day Nursery
St Gabriel's Church, Noel Road, Acton, London W3 0JE
Tel: 020 8992 0855
Type: Coeducational Day
Age range: 6 months–5
(👥)

International School of London
139 Gunnersbury Avenue, Acton, London W3 8LG
Tel: +44 (0)20 8992 5823
Head of School: Huw Davies
Type: Coeducational Day
Age range: 3–18
No. of pupils: 350 B190 G160 VIth50
Fees: Day £14,250–£19,750
(👥) (🌍) (IB) (✎) (16+)

King Fahad Academy
Bromyard Avenue, Acton, London W3 7HD
Tel: 020 8743 0131
Director: Dr Sumaya Alyusuf
Type: Coeducational Day
Age range: 3–18
No. of pupils: 446
Fees: Day £3000
(👥) (🌍) (A) (£) (16+)

The Ark Montessori Nursery
All Saints Church, Bollo Bridge Road, Acton,
London W3 8AX
Tel: 020 8993 3540
Type: Coeducational Nursery School
(👥)

The City Mission Neighbourhood Nursery Ltd
St Aidans Community Centre, Old Oak Common Lane, East
Acton, London W3 7DD
Tel: 020 8811 2540
Type: Coeducational Nursery School
Age range: 6 months–5
No. of pupils: 42
(👥)

The Japanese School
87 Creffield Road, Acton, London W3 9PU
Tel: 020 8993 7145
Headteacher: Mrs Kiyoe Tsuruoka
Type: Coeducational Day
Age range: 6–16
No. of pupils: 500 B257 G243
(👥)

W4

Buttercups Day Nursery
38 Grange Road, Chiswick, London W4 4DD
Tel: 020 8995 6750
Type: Coeducational Day
(👥)

Caterpillar Montessori Nursery School
St Albans Church Hall, South Parade, Chiswick,
London W4 3HY
Tel: 020 8747 8531
Head: Mrs Alison Scott
Type: Coeducational Day
Age range: 2–5
No. of pupils: B24 G24
Fees: Day £2700
(👥)

Chiswick & Bedford Park Prep School
Priory House, Priory Avenue, London W4 1TX
Tel: 020 8994 1804
Headmistress: Mrs C A Sunderland
Type: Coeducational Day
Age range: B4–7+ G4–11
No. of pupils: 180
Fees: Day £8850
(👥)

Devonshire Day Nursery
The Vicarage, Bennet Street, Chiswick, London W4 2AH
Tel: 020 8995 9538
Manager: Dawn Freeman
Type: Coeducational Nursery School
Age range: 6 weeks–5
No. of pupils: 70
(👥)

Elmwood Montessori School
St Michaels Centre, Elmwood Road, London W4 3DY
Tel: 020 8994 8177/995 2621
Headmistress: Mrs S Herbert BA
Type: Coeducational Day
Age range: 2–5
No. of pupils: B20 G20
Fees: Day £3480–£4440

Heathfield House School
Turnham Green Church Hall, Heathfield Gardens,
Chiswick, London W4 4JU
Tel: 020 8994 3385
Headteacher: Mrs Goodsman
Type: Coeducational Day
Age range: 4–11
No. of pupils: B50 G50
Fees: Day £6300–£6900

HOUSE SCHOOLS GROUP
For further details see p. 25
42 Hartington Road, London W4 3TX
Tel: 020 8580 9626
Website: www.houseschools.com
Type: Coeducational Day

Leapfrog Day Nurseries - Chiswick
4 Marlborough Road, Chiswick, London W4 4ET
Tel: 020 8742 0011
Manager: Zahira Ghaswala
Type: Coeducational Nursery School
Age range: 0–5

Orchard House School
16 Newton Grove, Bedford Park, London W4 1LB
Tel: 020 8742 8544
Headmistress: Mrs S A B Hobbs BA(Hons)(Exon), PGCE,
AMBDA, MontDip
Type: Coeducational Day
Age range: 3–11
No. of pupils: 234 B90 G144
Fees: Day £6006–£12,390

Primary Steps Day Nursery
Homefield Recreation Ground, Chiswick Lane,
London W4 2QA
Tel: 020 8995 4648
Manager: Ms Maggie Wozniak
Type: Coeducational Nursery School

Teddies Nurseries Chiswick Park
Evershed Walk, London W4 5BW
Tel: 020 8995 4766
Type: Coeducational Day
Age range: 3 months–5 years

The Ark Montessori School
The Scout Hall, Rugby Road, Chiswick, London W4 1AL
Tel: 020 8932 4766
Type: Coeducational Nursery School

The Falcons School for Boys
2 Burnaby Gardens, Chiswick, London W4 3DT
Tel: 020 8747 8393
Acting Head: Mr Henk Weyers
Type: Boys' Pre-Preparatory
Age range: 3–7
No. of pupils: 225
Fees: Day £3875–£11,625

The Meadows Montessori School
Dukes Meadows Community Centre, Alexandra Gardens,
London W4 2TD
Tel: 020 8742 1327/8995 2621
Headmistress: Mrs S Herbert BA
Type: Coeducational Day
Age range: 2–5
No. of pupils: B20 G20
Fees: Day £3030–£3870

W5

Aston House School
1 Aston Road, Ealing, London W5 2RL
Tel: 020 8566 7300
Headmistress: Mrs P Seabrook BA(Hons), MA
Type: Coeducational Day
Age range: 3–11
No. of pupils: 120 B60 G60
Fees: Day £6060–£7545

Buttercups Day Nursery
9 Florence Road, Ealing, London W5 3TU
Tel: 020 8840 4838
Type: Coeducational Day

Buttercups Nursery School
The Dance Centre, 96 Pitshanger Lane, Ealing, London W5
Tel: 020 8998 2774
Principal: Mrs C Whitehouse
Type: Coeducational Day

Clifton Lodge
8 Mattock Lane, Ealing, London W5 5BG
Tel: 020 8579 3662
Head: Mr A Gibson
Type: Boys' Day
Age range: 4–13
No. of pupils: 105
Fees: Day £8994–£9759

Durston House
12-14 Castlebar Road, Ealing, London W5 2DR
Tel: 020 8991 6532
Headmaster: Mr Ian Kendrick MA, BEd(Hons)
Type: Boys' Day
Age range: B4–13
No. of pupils: 390 B383
Fees: Day £9090–£12,090

Happy Child Day Nursery
283-287 Windmill Road, Ealing, London W5 4DP
Tel: 020 8567 2244
Type: Coeducational Day
Age range: 3 months–5

Happy Child Day Nursery
2A The Grove, Ealing, London W5 5LH
Tel: 020 8566 1546
Type: Coeducational Day
Age range: 1–5

Happy Child Day Nursery
Woodgrange Avenue, Ealing Common, London W5 3NY
Tel: 020 8992 0209
Type: Coeducational Day
Age range: 3 months–5

Harvington School
20 Castlebar Road, Ealing, London W5 2DS
Tel: 020 8997 1583
Headmistress: Mrs Anna Evans
Type: Girls' Day
Age range: B3–4 G3–16
No. of pupils: 210 B10 G200
Fees: Day £7560–£9840

St Augustine's Priory
Hillcrest Road, Ealing, London W5 2JL
Tel: 020 8997 2022
Headmistress: Mrs F J Gumley-Mason MA(Cantab)
Type: Independent Catholic Day School for Girls
Age range: 4–18
No. of pupils: 492
Fees: Day £7095–£9900

ST BENEDICT'S SCHOOL
For further details see p. 36
54 Eaton Rise, Ealing, London W5 2ES
Tel: 020 8862 2000
Email: enquiries@stbenedicts.org.uk
Website: www.stbenedicts.org.uk
Headmaster: Mr C J Cleugh BSc, MSc
Type: Coeducational Day
Age range: 3–18
No. of pupils: 987 B786 G201 VIth180
Fees: Day £10,320–£11,760

St Matthews Montessori School
North Common Road, Ealing, London W5 2QA
Tel: 020 8579 2304
Principal: Mrs Y Abdulrahman
Type: Coeducational Day

The Falcons School for Girls
15 Gunnersbury Avenue, Ealing, London W5 3XD
Tel: 020 8992 5189
Principal: Miss Joan McGillewie
Type: Girls' Preparatory
Age range: 4–11
No. of pupils: 120
Fees: Day £7500

The Maria Montessori School
Church of the Ascension Hall, Beaufort Road, Ealing, London W5 3EB
Tel: 020 8997 6979
Type: Coeducational Nursery School

World of Children Nursery
Ninth Ealing Scouts Hall, 255 Northfields Avenue, London W5 4UA
Tel: 020 8566 5962
Type: Coeducational Nursery School

W6

Bayonne Nursery School
50 Paynes Walk, London W6 9PF
Tel: 020 7385 5366
Type: Coeducational Day
Age range: 3–5
No. of pupils: 80

Bute House Preparatory School for Girls
Bute House, Luxemburg Gardens, London W6 7EA
Tel: 020 7603 7381
Head: Mrs S Salvidant BEd(Hons)
Type: Girls' Day
Age range: 4–11
No. of pupils: 307
Fees: Day £11,505

Ecole Francaise Jacques Prevert
59 Brook Green, London W6 7BE
Tel: 020 7602 6871
Principal: C Gachet
Type: Coeducational Day
Age range: 4–11
No. of pupils: B108 G141
Fees: Day £3850

Latymer Prep School
36 Upper Mall, Hammersmith, London W6 9TA
Tel: 0845 638 5700
Principal: Mr Stuart Dorrian BA(Hons), PGCE
Type: Coeducational Day
Age range: 7–11
No. of pupils: 165
Fees: Day £12,705

Latymer Upper School
King Street, Hammersmith, London W6 9LR
Tel: 0845 638 580
Head: Mr P Winter MA(Oxon)
Type: Coeducational Day
Age range: 11–18
No. of pupils: 1123 VIth354
Fees: Day £13,800

Le Herisson
River Court Methodist Church, Rover Court Road,
Hammersmith, London W6 9JT
Tel: 020 8563 7664
Head: B Rios
Type: Coeducational Day
Age range: 2–6
No. of pupils: 64
Fees: Day £3060–£4260

Leapfrog Day Nurseries - Hammersmith, Bute Gardens
Bute Hall, 3a Bute Gardens, Hammersmith,
London W6 7DR
Tel: 020 8741 9445
Manager: Nadine Primus
Type: Coeducational Nursery School
Age range: 0–5
No. of pupils: B36 G87

Leapfrog Day Nurseries - Hammersmith, Centre West
Broadway Shopping Centre, Hammersmith Broadway,
London W6 9YD
Tel: 020 8563 7982
Deputy Manager: Suzanne Jn-Pierre
Type: Coeducational Nursery School
Age range: 0–5

One World Montessori Nursery & Pre-Prep
69-71 Brock Green, Hammersmith, London W6 7BE
Tel: 020 7603 6065
Headteacher: Ms N Greer
Type: Coeducational Day
Age range: 2–8
No. of pupils: 21 B14 G7

Ravenscourt Park Preparatory School
16 Ravenscourt Avenue, London W6 0SL
Tel: 020 8846 9153
Headmaster: Mr Robert Relton
Type: Coeducational Day
Age range: 4–11
No. of pupils: 252 B120 G132
Fees: Day £10,650

Ravenscourt Theatre School
8-30 Galena Road, Hammersmith, London W6 0LT
Tel: 020 8741 0707
Head: Judy Swinney
Type: Coeducational Day
Age range: 7–16
No. of pupils: B45 G48
Fees: Day £4350

Richford Street Day Nursery
50 Richford Gate, 61-69 Richford Street, London W6 7HZ
Tel: 020 8746 1015
Manager: Marion Bones NVQ
Type: Coeducational Nursery School
Age range: 3 months–5 years
No. of pupils: 70

St Paul's Girls' School
Brook Green, London W6 7BS
Tel: 020 7603 2288
High Mistress: Ms Clarissa Farr BA, MA, PGCE
Type: Girls' Day
Age range: 11–18
No. of pupils: 710 G710 VIth200
Fees: Day £13,623

The Godolphin and Latymer School
Iffley Road, Hammersmith, London W6 0PG
Tel: +44 (0)20 8741 1936
Head Mistress: Mrs R Mercer BA
Type: Girls' Day
Age range: 11–18
No. of pupils: 700
Fees: Day £13,470

The Jordans Nursery School
Holy Innocents Church, Paddenswick Road,
London W6 0UB
Tel: 020 8741 3230
Headmistresses: Victoria Turrell & Sara Green
Type: Coeducational Day
Age range: 2–5
No. of pupils: B41 G45
Fees: Day £1356–£3270

W7

Buttons Day Nursery School
99 Oaklands Road, London W7 2DT
Tel: 020 8840 3355
Head: Julie Parhar BSc, NVQ3
Type: Coeducational Day
Age range: 3 months–5
No. of pupils: 62 B35 G27

Playhouse Day Nursery
Leighton Hall, Elthorne Park Road, London W7 2JD
Tel: 020 8840 2851
Type: Coeducational Nursery School
Age range: 2–5

W8

Ashbourne Middle School
17 Old Court Place, Kensington, London W8 4PL
Tel: 020 7937 3858
Principal: M J Kirby MSc, BApSc
Type: Coeducational Day
Age range: 13–16
No. of pupils: B80 G90 VIth150
Fees: Day £14,725 FB £21,500

HAWKESDOWN HOUSE SCHOOL KENSINGTON
For further details see p. 20
27 Edge Street, Kensington, London W8 7PN
Tel: 020 7727 9090
Email: admin@hawkesdown.co.uk
Website: www.hawkesdown.co.uk
Head: Mrs C Bourne MA(Cantab)
Type: Boys' Independent Pre-prep Day
Age range: 3–8
No. of pupils: 130
Fees: Day £11,325–£12,975

Little Cherubs Nursery School
Our Lady of Victories Church Hall, 16 Abingdon Road,
Kensington, London W8 6AF
Tel: 020 7376 4460/07810 712241
Principal: Mrs M Colvin MontDip
Type: Coeducational Nursery School
Age range: 2–5
No. of pupils: 42 B20 G22
Fees: Day £5970–£10,170

Thomas's Preparatory School - Kensington
17-19 Cottesmore Gardens, London W8 5PR
Tel: 020 7361 6500
Headmistress: Mrs Diana Maine MA, BEd(Hons), NPQH
Type: Coeducational Day
Age range: 4–11
No. of pupils: B166 G185
Fees: Day £14,505–£15,795

W9

Little Sweethearts Montessori
St Saviours Church Hall, Warwick Avenue, London W9 2PT
Tel: 020 7266 1616
Type: Coeducational Nursery School

Windmill Montessori Nursery School
62 Shirland Road, London W9 2EH
Tel: 020 7289 3410
Principal: Miss M H Leoni & Miss J Davidson
Type: Coeducational Nursery School
No. of pupils: 48
Fees: Day £3600

W10

Bassett House School
60 Bassett Road, London W10 6JP
Tel: 020 8969 0313
Headmistress: Mrs Andrea Harris BEd(Lond), MontCert,
CEPLF(CAEN)
Type: Coeducational Day
Age range: 3–11
No. of pupils: 161 B65 G96
Fees: Day £6006–£12,390

Colegio Espanol Vicente Canada Blanch
317 Portobello Road, London W10 5SZ
Tel: 020 8969 2664
Principal: Mr A Vitria
Type: Coeducational Day
Age range: 4–19
No. of pupils: 405

La Petite Ecole Francais
90 Oxford Gardens, London W10 5UW
Tel: 020 8960 1278
Principal: Ms A Stones
Type: Coeducational Day
Age range: 2–6

THE LLOYD WILLIAMSON SCHOOL
For further details see p. 41
12 Telford Road, London W10 5SH
Tel: 020 8962 0345
Email: lloydwilliamsonschools@yahoo.co.uk
Website: www.lloydwilliamsonschools.co.uk
Co-Principals: Lucy Meyer & Aaron Williams
Type: Coeducational Day
Age range: 6 months–14 years
Fees: Day £9705

W11

Acorn Nursery School
2 Lansdowne Crescent, London W11 2NH
Tel: 020 7727 2122
Principal: Mrs Jane Cameron BEd(Hons)
Type: Coeducational Nursery School
Age range: 2–5
No. of pupils: B50 G50
Fees: Day £2400

Holland Park Nursery School
St Johns Church, Lansdowne Crescent, London W11 2NN
Tel: 020 7221 2194
Type: Coeducational Day
Age range: 3–5
No. of pupils: B12 G12
Fees: Day £3900

Kidsunlimited Nurseries - Ladbroke Grove
34 Ladbroke Grove, London W11 3BQ
Tel: 0845 850 0222
Type: Coeducational Nursery School

Ladbroke Square Montessori School
43 Ladbroke Square, London W11 3ND
Tel: 020 7229 0125
Principal: Mrs Sophia Russell-Cobb MontDip
Type: Coeducational Day
Age range: 3–5
No. of pupils: B50 G50
Fees: Day £850–£1350

Maria Montessori Children's House - Notting Hill
28 Powis Gardens, London W11 1JG
Tel: 020 7221 4141
Head: Mrs L Lawrence
Type: Coeducational Day
Age range: 2–6
No. of pupils: 20
Fees: Day £4500

Norland Place School
162-166 Holland Park Avenue, London W11 4UH
Tel: 020 7603 9103
Headmaster: Mr Patrick Mattar MA
Type: Coeducational Day
Age range: B4–8 G4–11
No. of pupils: 240
Fees: Day £9654–£12,186

Notting Hill Preparatory School
95 Lancaster Road, London W11 1QQ
Tel: 020 7221 0727
Headmistress: Mrs Jane Cameron
Type: Coeducational Day
Age range: 5–13
No. of pupils: 240 B125 G115
Fees: Day £4135

Rolfe's Nursery School
206-208 Kensington Park Road, London W11 1NR
Tel: 020 7727 8300
Head: Mr Greg McDonald
Type: Coeducational Day
Age range: 2½–5
No. of pupils: B50 G50
Fees: Day £4950–£8595

Southbank International School - Kensington
36-38 Kensington Park Road, London W11 3BU
Tel: 020 7243 3803
Principal: Judith Kingsbury
Type: Coeducational Day
Age range: 3–11
No. of pupils: 202 B98 G104
Fees: Day £11,400–£18,150

St Peters Nursery School
59a Portobello Road, London W11 3DB
Tel: 020 7243 2617
Headmistress: Beverley Gibbs
Type: Coeducational Nursery School

Tabernacle School
32 St Anns Villas, Holland Park, London W11 4RS
Tel: 020 7602 6232
Headteacher: Mrs P Wilson
Type: Coeducational Day
Age range: 3–16
Fees: Day £4500

The Square Montessori School
18 Holland Park Avenue, London W11 3QU
Tel: 020 7221 6004
Principal: Mrs V Lawson-Tancred
Type: Coeducational Nursery School
No. of pupils: 20
Fees: Day £2220

W12

Little People of Shepherds Bush
61 Hadyn Park Road, Shepherds Bush, London W12 9AQ
Tel: 020 8749 5080
Owner: Miss Jane Gleasure
Type: Coeducational Nursery School
Age range: 4 months–5

Little People of Willow Vale
9 Willow Vale, London W12 0PA
Tel: 020 8749 2877
Head: Miss Jane Gleasure
Type: Coeducational Nursery School
Age range: 4 months–5

W13

Avenue House School
70 The Avenue, Ealing, London W13 8LS
Tel: 020 8998 9981
Headteacher: Mrs Carolyn Self CertEd(Bristol University)
Type: Coeducational Day
Age range: 3–11
No. of pupils: 120
Fees: Day £4920–£8250

Buttercups Day Nursery
St Lukes, Drayton Grove, Ealing, London W13 0LA
Tel: 020 8997 8965
Type: Coeducational Day

Ealing College Upper School
83 The Avenue, Ealing, London W13 8JS
Tel: 020 8248 2312
Headmaster: Mr Christopher Morris
Type: Coeducational Day
Age range: 11–18
No. of pupils: 82 B70 G12 VIth28
Fees: Day £8200

Happy Child Day Nursery
Green Man Passage, Ealing, London W13 0TG
Tel: 020 8566 5515
Type: Coeducational Day
Age range: 3 months–5

Jigsaw Nursery & Montessori School
1 Courtfield Gardens, London W13 0EY
Tel: 020 8997 8330
Type: Coeducational Day

Notting Hill & Ealing High School GDST

2 Cleveland Road, West Ealing, London W13 8AX
Tel: 020 8991 2165
Headmistress: Ms Lucinda Hunt
Type: Girls' Day
Age range– 4–18
No. of pupils: 870 VIth130
Fees: Day £9069–£11,655

W14

Bright Sparks Montessori School

25 Minford Gardens, London W14 0AP
Tel: 020 7371 4697
Headmistress: Matilda D'Angelo
Type: Coeducational Day
Age range: 2–5
No. of pupils: 16

Busy Bee Nursery School

Addison Boys Club, Redan Street, London W14
Tel: 020 7602 8905
Type: Coeducational Day

Fulham Prep School

200 Greyhound Road, London W14 9SD
Tel: 020 7386 2448
Head: Mrs J Emmett
Type: Coeducational Day
Age range: 4½–13
No. of pupils: 559 B349 G210
Fees: Day £12,225–£13,575

Holland Park Pre Prep School and Day Nursery

5 & 9 Holland Road, Kensington, London W14 8HJ
Tel: 020 7602 9066/020 7602 9266
Principal: Mrs Kitty Mason
Type: Coeducational day school and day nursery
Age range: 3 months–8 years
No. of pupils: 128 B68 G60
Fees: Day £4650–£10,935

James Lee Nursery School

Gliddon Road, London W14 9BH
Tel: 020 8741 8877
Type: Coeducational Day

Montessori Neighbourhood Nursery School

St Andrew's Church, Star Road, London W14 9QE
Tel: 020 7386 5818
Head: Anita Grebot
Type: Coeducational Nursery School
Age range: 18 mths–5 yrs

St James Junior Schools

Earsby Street, London W14 8SH
Tel: 020 7348 1777
Head Teacher: Mr P Moss CertEd
Type: Girls' Day & Boys' Day
Age range: 4–10½
No. of pupils: B113 G146
Fees: Day £8070–£8550

St James Senior Girls' School

Earsby Street, London W14 8SH
Tel: 020 7348 1777
Headmistress: Mrs Laura Hyde CertEd
Type: Girls' Day
Age range: 10–18
No. of pupils: 264 VIth41
Fees: Day £11,100

The Sinclair Montessori Nursery School

The Garden Flat, 142 Sinclair Road, London W14 0NL
Tel: 020 7602 3745
Headmistress: Miss C Burnaby-Atkins MontDipEd, SENDip, NVQ
Type: Coeducational Nursery School
Age range: 2½–5
No. of pupils: 24

Wetherby Preparatory School

48 Bryanston Square, London W1H 2EA
Tel: 020 7535 3520
Headteacher: Mr Nick Baker
Type: Boys' Preparatory
Age range: 8–13
No. of pupils: 192
Fees: Day £4665

Schools in Greater London

Greater London

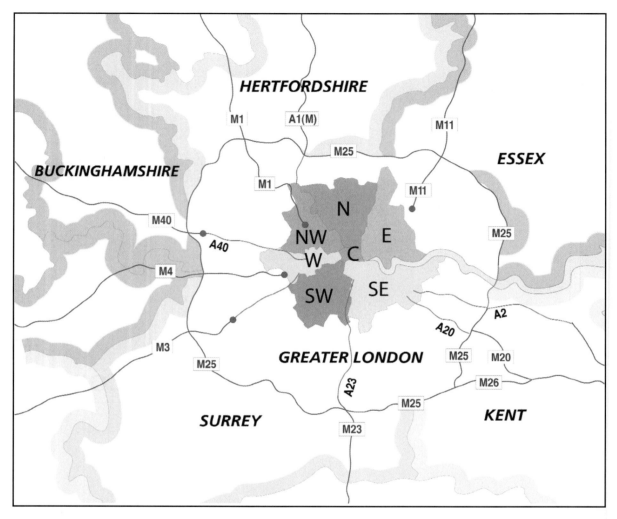

Key to symbols

- 🚹 Boys' school
- 🚺 Girls' school
- 🚼 Coeducational school
- 🌐 International school
- 🏠 Tutorial or sixth form college
- Ⓐ A levels

- 🏫 Boarding accommodation
- £ Bursaries
- Ⓘ𝐁 International Baccalaureate
- ✎ Learning support
- 16+ Entrance at 16+
- Vocational qualifications

ACS HILLINGDON INTERNATIONAL SCHOOL
For further details see p. 90
Hillingdon Court, 108 Vine Lane, Hillingdon, Uxbridge, Middlesex UB10 0BE
Tel: 01895 259 771
Email: hillingdonadmissions@acs-england.co.uk
Website: www.acs-england.co.uk
Head of School: Ginger Apple
Type: Coeducational Day
Age range: 4–18
No. of pupils: 539 B280 G259
Fees: Day £8820–£18,560

Al-Khair School
109-117 Cherry Orchard Road, Croydon, Surrey CR0 6BE
Tel: 020 8662 8664
Headteacher: Mr Usman Qureshi
Type: Coeducational Day
Age range: 5–16
No. of pupils: 126 B86 G40

Al-Noor Primary School
619-625 Green Lane, Goodmayes, Ilford, Essex IG3 9RP
Tel: 020 8597 7576
Head: Mrs Someera Butt
Type: Coeducational Day
Age range: 4–10
No. of pupils: 175
Fees: Day £2550–£2750

Alpha Preparatory School
21 Hindes Road, Harrow, Middlesex HA1 1SH
Tel: 020 8427 1471
Head: P J Wylie BA(Hons), CertEd
Type: Coeducational Day
Age range: 2–11
No. of pupils: 150 B80 G70
Fees: Day £5100–£7410

Ashgrove School
116 Widmore Road, Bromley, Kent BR1 3BE
Tel: 020 8460 4143
Principal: Patricia Ash CertEd, BSc(Hons), PhD, CMath, FIMA
Type: Coeducational Day
Age range: 3–11
No. of pupils: B57 G59
Fees: Day £7065

Ashton House School
50-52 Eversley Crescent, Isleworth, Middlesex TW7 4LW
Tel: 020 8560 3902
Headteacher: Mrs M Grundberg MA PGCE
Type: Coeducational Day
Age range: 3–11
No. of pupils: B70 G60
Fees: Day £6000–£8349

Athelstan House School
36 Percy Road, Hampton, Middlesex TW12 2LA
Tel: 020 8979 1045
Headmistress: Elsa Woolf
Type: Coeducational Day
Age range: 3–7
No. of pupils: 65

Avon House
490-492 High Road, Woodford Green, Essex IG8 0PN
Tel: 020 8504 1749
Principal: Mrs S Ferrari
Type: Coeducational Day
Age range: 3–11
No. of pupils: B100 G80
Fees: Day £5910–£7080

Babington House School
Grange Drive, Chislehurst, Kent BR7 5ES
Tel: 020 8467 5537
Headteacher: Miss D Odysseas-Bailey
Type: Coeducational Day
Age range: B3–7 G3–16
No. of pupils: 256 B60 G196
Fees: Day £1090–£3670

Bancroft's School
Woodford Green, Essex IG8 0RF
Tel: 020 8505 4821
Head: Mrs M E Ireland
Type: Coeducational Day
Age range: 7–18
No. of pupils: 1005 B539 G466 VIth250
Fees: Day £9075–£11,955

Beehive Preparatory School
233 Beehive Lane, Redbridge, Ilford, Essex IG4 5ED
Tel: 020 8550 3224
Headmaster: Mr C J Beasant BEd
Type: Coeducational Day
Age range: 4–11
No. of pupils: 90 B45 G45
Fees: Day £3450

Bickley Park School
24 Page Heath Lane, Bickley, Bromley, Kent BR1 2DS
Tel: 020 8467 2195
Headmaster: Mr Paul Ashley
Type: Boys' Day
Age range: B3–13 G3–4
No. of pupils: 370 B350 G20
Fees: Day £6525–£11,925

Bishop Challoner School
228 Bromley Road, Shortlands, Bromley, Kent BR2 0BS
Tel: 020 8460 3546
Headteacher: Karen Barry
Type: Coeducational Day
Age range: 3–18
No. of pupils: B260 G118 VIth29
Fees: Day £5850–£8235

Breaside Preparatory School
41-43 Orchard Road, Bromley, Kent BR1 2PR
Tel: 020 8460 0916
Headmistress: Mrs Karen Nicholson BEd, NPQH, Diploma in Early Years
Type: Coeducational Day
Age range: 2½–11
No. of pupils: B140 G110
Fees: Day £7650–£8925

BROMLEY HIGH SCHOOL GDST
For further details see p. 49
Blackbrook Lane, Bickley, Bromley, Kent BR1 2TW
Tel: 020 8468 7000
Email: bhs@bro.gdst.net
Website: www.bromleyhigh.gdst.net
Head: Mrs Louise Simpson BSc(UCW)
Type: Independent Selective Day School for Girls
Age range: 4–18
No. of pupils: 894 VIth125
Fees: Day £9027–£11,601

Buckingham College Preparatory School
458 Rayners Lane, Pinner, Middlesex HA5 5DT
Tel: 020 8866 2737
Headmaster: Mr L S Smith BA(Hons), MSc, LCP, PGDE, CertEd
Type: Boys' Day
Age range: 4–11
No. of pupils: 104 B104
Fees: Day £6660–£8712

Buckingham College School
Hindes Road, Harrow, Middlesex HA1 1SH
Tel: 020 8427 1220
Headmaster: Mr S Larter BA(Hons), PGCE
Type: Boys' Day
Age range: B11–18 G16–18
No. of pupils: 150 VIth27
Fees: Day £5010–£5895

Buxlow Preparatory School
5/6 Castleton Gardens, Wembley, Middlesex HA9 7QJ
Tel: 020 8904 3615
Headmistress: Mrs Ann Baines
Type: Coeducational Day
Age range: 4–11
No. of pupils: B46 G42
Fees: Day £6585

Canbury School
Kingston Hill, Kingston upon Thames, Surrey KT2 7LN
Tel: 020 8549 8622
Headmaster: R F Metters BEd
Type: Coeducational Day
Age range: 11–16
No. of pupils: 65 B50 G15
Fees: Day £12,855

Clarks Preparatory School
81/85 York Road, Ilford, Essex IG1 3AF
Tel: 020 8478 6510
Headmistress: Ms N C Woodman
Type: Coeducational Day
Age range: 0–7
No. of pupils: 90 B49 G41
Fees: Day £5200

Collingwood School
3 Springfield Road, Wallington, Surrey SM6 0BD
Tel: 020 8647 4607
Headmaster: Mr Chris Fenwick
Type: Coeducational Day
Age range: 2–11
No. of pupils: 150
Fees: Day £640–£6120

Cranbrook College
Mansfield Road, Ilford, Essex IG1 3BD
Tel: 020 8554 1757
Head: Mr A Moss
Type: Boys' Day
Age range: 4–16
No. of pupils: 200
Fees: Day £6405–£8235

Croydon High School GDST
Old Farleigh Road, Selsdon, South Croydon,
Surrey CR2 8YB
Tel: 020 8260 7508
Headmistress: Mrs Zelma Braganza MSc, CB ol, MIBiol
Type: Girls' Day
Age range: 3–18
No. of pupils: 735 VIth142
Fees: Day £6966–£11,601

Cumnor House School
168 Pampisford Road, South Croydon, Surrey CR2 6DA
Tel: 020 8660 3445
Head: Mr P J Clare-Hunt MA, CertEd
Type: Boys' Day
Age range: B2–13 G2–4
No. of pupils: 414 B409 G5
Fees: Day £7185–£9300

Darul Uloom London
Foxbury Avenue, Perry Street, Chislehurst, Kent BR7 6SD
Tel: 020 8295 0637
Principal: Mufti Mustafa
Type: Boys' Boarding
Age range: 11–18
No. of pupils: 160
Fees: FB £2400

Denmead School
41-43 Wensleydale Road, Hampton, Middlesex TW12 2 P
Tel: 020 8979 1844
Headmaster: Mr M T McKaughan BEd
Type: Coeducational Day
Age range: 3–11
No. of pupils: B162 G18
Fees: Day £4050–£9345

Eastcourt Independent School
1 Eastwood Road, Goodmayes, Ilford, Essex IG3 8UW
Tel: 020 8590 5472
Headmistress: Mrs Christine Redgrave
BSc(Hons),DipEd,MEd
Type: Coeducational Day
Age range: 3–11
No. of pupils: B165 G166
Fees: Day £5070

Educare Small School
12 Cowleaze Road, Kingston upon Thames,
Surrey KT2 6DZ
Tel: 020 8547 0144
Head: Mrs E Steinthal
Type: Coeducational Day
Age range: 3–11
No. of pupils: 34
Fees: Day £3900

Elmhurst School
44-48 South Park Hill Rd, South Croydon, Surrey CR2 7DW
Tel: 020 8688 0661
Headmaster: Mr M J Apsley BA(Hons), PGCE
Type: Boys' Day
Age range: 4–11
No. of pupils: 207
Fees: Day £6300–£7545

Farringtons School
Perry Street, Chislehurst, Kent BR7 6LR
Tel: 020 8467 0256
Headmistress: Mrs C E James MA
Type: Coeducational Day & Boarding
Age range: 3–19
No. of pupils: 480 VIth60
Fees: Day £8220–£11,220 WB £20,010 FB £21,300

Folly's End Christian School
Folly's End Church, 5-9 Surrey Street, Croydon,
Surrey CR0 1RG
Tel: 020 8649 9121
Senior Leaders: Dave & Ze Markee
Type: Coeducational Day
Age range: 3–11
No. of pupils: B27 G26
Fees: Day £4740

Gidea Park College
2 Balgores Lane, Gidea Park, Romford, Essex RM2 5JR
Tel: 01708 740381
Headmistress: Mrs V S Lee BA
Type: Coeducational Day
Age range: 2–11
No. of pupils: 177 B88 G89
Fees: Day £1140–£2320

Glenarm College
20 Coventry Road, Ilford, Essex IG1 4QR
Tel: 020 8554 1760
Principal: Mrs V Mullooly
Type: Coeducational Day
Age range: 3–11
No. of pupils: B53 G80
Fees: Day £4755–£5055

Goodrington School
17 Walden Road, Hornchurch, Essex RM11 2JT
Tel: 01708 448349
Head: Mrs J R Ellenby
Type: Coeducational Day
Age range: 3–11
No. of pupils: 73 B38 G35
Fees: Day £3900

Halliford School
Russell Road, Shepperton, Middlesex TW17 9HX
Tel: 01932 223593
Head: Mr Philip V Cottam MA(Oxon), FRGS
Type: Independent Day School for Boys Coeducational
Sixth Form
Age range: B11–18 G16–18
No. of pupils: B400 G11
Fees: Day £10,659

Hampton School
Hanworth Road, Hampton, Middlesex TW12 3HD
Tel: 020 8979 5526
Headmaster: Mr B R Martin MA(Cantab), MBA, FCMI,
FRSA
Type: Boys' Day
Age range: 11–18
No. of pupils: 1130 VIth330
Fees: Day £12,870

Harenc Preparatory School for Boys
Church House, 167 Rectory Lane, Foots Cray, Sidcup,
Kent DA14 5BU
Tel: 020 8309 0619
Headmistress: Miss S J Woodward BA, FRSA
Type: Boys' Day
Age range: 3–11
No. of pupils: 126
Fees: Day £5868–£7692

Harrow School
5 High Street, Harrow on the Hill, Middlesex HA1 3HT
Tel: 020 8872 8007
Head Master: Mr Barnaby J Lenon MA
Type: Boys' Boarding
Age range: 13–18
No. of pupils: 800 VIth320
Fees: FB £28,545

HEATHFIELD SCHOOL GDST
For further details see p. 52
Beaulieu Drive, Pinner, Middlesex HA5 1NB
Tel: 020 8868 2346
Email: enquiries@hea.gdst.net
Website: www.heathfield.gdst.net
Head: Christine Juett BSc(Hons), PGCE, (Member of ASCL)
Type: Girls' Day
Age range: 3–18
No. of pupils: 533 VIth85
Fees: Day £6966–£11,601

Holland House School
1 Broadhurst Avenue, Edgware, Middlesex HA8 8TP
Tel: 020 8958 6979
Headmistress: Mrs Irinia Tyk BA(Hons)
Type: Coeducational Day
Age range: 4–11
No. of pupils: B70 G70
Fees: Day £3120

Holy Cross Preparatory School
George Road, Kingston upon Thames, Surrey KT2 7NU
Tel: 020 8942 0729
Head: Mrs M K Hayes MA
Type: Girls' Preparatory Day
Age range: 4–11
No. of pupils: 250
Fees: Day £10,785

Homefield School
Western Road, Sutton, Surrey SM1 2TE
Tel: 020 8642 0965
Headteacher: Mr P R Mowbray MA(Cantab)
Type: Boys' Day
Age range: 2½–13
No. of pupils: 430
Fees: Day £3960–£9240

Ilford Grammar School
785 High Road, Seven Kings, Ilford, Essex IG3 8RV
Tel: 020 8599 8822
Headmistress: B P M Wiggs BSc(Hons), PGCE
Type: Coeducational Day
Age range: 3–16
No. of pupils: B114 G80
Fees: Day £5250–£7200

Ilford Ursuline R C Preparatory School
2 Coventry Road, Ilford, Essex IG1 4QR
Tel: 020 8518 4050
Headmistress: Mrs C Spinner
Type: Girls' Day
Age range: 3–11
No. of pupils: 159
Fees: Day £5697

Immanuel School
Havering Grange Centre, Havering Road North, Romford, Essex RM1 4HR
Tel: 01708 764449
Principal: Miss Norcross
Type: Coeducational Day
Age range: 3–16
No. of pupils: B71 G57

Jack and Jill School
30 Nightingale Road, Hampton, Middlesex TW12 3HX
Tel: 020 8979 3195
Principal: Miss K Papirnik BEd(Hons)
Type: Girls' Day School with Coeducational Nursery
Age range: B2–5 G2–7
No. of pupils: 131 B21 G110
Fees: Day £4080–£8460

Kew College
24-26 Cumberland Road, Kew, Surrey TW9 3HQ
Tel: 020 8940 2039
Headmistress: Mrs Anne Dobell MA(Oxon), PGCE
Type: Coeducational Day
Age range: 3–11
No. of pupils: B123 G137
Fees: Day £3975–£7485

King's House School
68 King's Road, Richmond, Surrey TW10 6ES
Tel: 020 8940 1878
Head: Mrs S Piper BA
Type: Boys' Day
Age range: 4–13
No. of pupils: 385
Fees: Day £4800–£6495

Laleham Lea Preparatory School
29 Peaks Hill, Purley, Surrey CR8 3JJ
Tel: 020 8660 3351
Headteacher: Mr J Power
Type: Coeducational Day
Age range: 3–11
No. of pupils: B78 G61
Fees: Day £4950

Linley House
6 Berrylands Road, Surbiton, Surrey KT5 8RA
Tel: 020 8399 4979
Principal: Mrs S M Mallin CertEd(Bristol)
Type: Coeducational Day
Age range: 3–7
No. of pupils: 32 B18 G14
Fees: Day £3528–£7149

Little Eden & Eden High SDA School
Fortescue House, Park Road, Hanworth,
Middlesex TW13 6PN
Tel: 020 8751 1844
Headteacher: Mrs L Osei BEd MA
Type: Coeducational Day
Age range: 5–18
No. of pupils: 60 B35 G25

Lodge School
11 Woodcote Lane, Purley, Surrey CR8 3HB
Tel: 020 8660 3179
Principal: Miss Pamela Maynard BEd(Hons), MA
Type: Coeducational Day
Age range: B2–11 G2–18
No. of pupils: 271 B80 G191 VIth19
Fees: Day £6300–£11,100

LYONSDOWN SCHOOL TRUST
For further details see p. 53
3 Richmond Road, New Barnet, Barnet,
Hertfordshire EN5 1SA
Tel: 020 8449 0225
Email: enquiries@lyonsdownschool.co.uk
Website: www.lyonsdownschool.co.uk
Head: Mrs L Maggs-Wellings BEd
Type: Independent Coeducational Day
Age range: B3–7 G3–11
No. of pupils: 210 B43 G167
Fees: Day £2835–£7206

Marymount International School London
George Road, Kingston upon Thames, Surrey KT2 7PE
Tel: +44 (0)20 8949 0571
Headmistress: Sister Michaeline O'Dwyer RSHM
Type: Girls' Day & Boarding
Age range: G11–18
No. of pupils: 246 VIth110
Fees: Day £15,340–£17,530 WB £25,990–£28,180
FB £27,240–£29,430

Maytime Preparatory School
87 York Road, Ilford, Essex IG1 3AF
Tel: 020 8553 1524
Headteacher: Mrs M O'Mahoney
Type: Coeducational Day
Age range: 0–6

Menorah Grammar School
Abbots Road, Edgware, Middlesex HA8 0QS
Tel: 020 8906 9756
Headteacher: Rabbi A M Goldblatt
Type: Boys' Day
Age range: 11–17
No. of pupils: 203

Merchant Taylors' School
Sandy Lodge, Northwood, Middlesex HA6 2HT
Tel: 01923 820644
Head Master: Mr S N Wright MA(Cantab)
Type: Boys' Day
Age range: 11–18
No. of pupils: 850 VIth291
Fees: Day £14,680

Merton Court Preparatory School
38 Knoll Road, Sidcup, Kent DA14 4QU
Tel: 020 8300 2112
Headmaster: Mr Dominic Price BEd, MBA
Type: Coeducational Day
Age range: 3–11
No. of pupils: B141 G127
Fees: Day £8115–£8910

New Life Christian Primary School
Cairo New Road, Croydon, Surrey CR0 1XP
Tel: 020 8680 7671 ext 327
Headteacher: Mrs S Kehinde
Type: Coeducational Day
Age range: 4–11
No. of pupils: B63 G45
Fees: Day £4032

Newland House School
32-34 Waldegrave Park, Twickenham, Middlesex TW1 4TQ
Tel: 020 8892 7479
Headmaster: D J Ott BSc, UED(Rhodes)
Type: Coeducational Day
Age range: B4–13 G4–11
No. of pupils: B274 G149
Fees: Day £8100–£9090

Norfolk Lodge Montessori Nursery & Pre-Prep School
Dancers Hill Road, Barnet, Hertfordshire EN5 4RP
Tel: 020 8447 1565
Head Teacher: Mrs Mary Wales
Type: Coeducational Day
Age range: 6 months–7 years
No. of pupils: 140
Fees: Day £2200–£2400

North London Collegiate School
Canons, Canons Drive, Edgware, Middlesex HA8 7RJ
Tel: +44 (0)20 8952 0912
Headmistress: Mrs Bernice McCabe
Type: Girls' Day
Age range: 4–18
No. of pupils: 1060
Fees: Day £10,926–£12,924

NORTHWOOD COLLEGE
For further details see p. 54
Maxwell Road, Northwood, Middlesex HA6 2YE
Tel: 01923 825446
Email: admissions@northwoodcollege.co.uk
Website: www.northwoodcollege.co.uk
Head: Miss Jacqualyn Pain MA, MA, MBA
Type: Girls' Day
Age range: 3–18
No. of pupils: 820 VIth125
Fees: Day £7650–£12,600

Oak Heights
3 Red Lion Court, Alexandra Road, Hounslow,
Middlesex TW3 1JS
Tel: 020 8577 1827
Head: Mr S Dhillon
Type: Coeducational Day
Age range: 11–16
No. of pupils: 48
Fees: Day £6000

Oakfields Montessori School
Harwood Hall, Harwood Hall Lane, Corbets Tey,
Essex RM14 2YG
Tel: 01708 220117
Headmistress: Mrs K Malandreniotis
Type: Coeducational Day
Age range: 2½–11
Fees: Day £2508–£4260

Oakwood Independent School
Godstone Road, Purley, Surrey CR8 2AN
Tel: 020 8668 8080
Headmaster: Mr Ciro Candia BA(Hons), PGCE
Type: Coeducational Day
Age range: 2–11
No. of pupils: 143 B78 G65
Fees: Day £3690–£5670

Old Palace of John Whitgift School
Old Palace Road, Croydon, Surrey CR0 1AX
Tel: 020 8688 2027
Head: Dr J Harris
Type: Girls' Day
Age range: B3 months–4 years G3 months–19 years
No. of pupils: 850 VIth160
Fees: Day £6846–£9159

Old Vicarage School
48 Richmond Hill, Richmond, Surrey TW10 6QX
Tel: 020 8940 0922
Headmistress: Mrs J R Harrison
Type: Girls' Day
Age range: 4–11
No. of pupils: 170
Fees: Day £6030–£6690

Orley Farm School
South Hill Avenue, Harrow, Middlesex HA1 3NU
Tel: 020 8869 7600
Headmaster: Mark Dunning
Type: Coeducational Day
Age range: 4–13
No. of pupils: 496 B337 G159
Fees: Day £3315–£3875

Park Hill School
8 Queens Road, Kingston upon Thames, Surrey KT2 7SH
Tel: 020 8546 5496
Principal: Mrs Marie Christie
Type: Preparatory School & Nursery
Age range: B3–8 G3–11
No. of pupils: 100 B40 G60
Fees: Day £6735–£7380

Park School for Girls

20 Park Avenue, Ilford, Essex IG1 4RS
Tel: 020 8554 2466
Headmistress: Mrs N O'Brien BA
Type: Girls' Day
Age range: 7–18
No. of pupils: 230 VIth19
Fees: Day £4755–£6285

Peterborough & St Margaret's School

Common Road, Stanmore, Middlesex HA7 3JB
Tel: 020 8950 3600
Headmistress: Mrs Susan Watts
Type: Girls' Day
Age range: 4–16
No. of pupils: 170
Fees: Day £5847–£8691

Pinner Day Nursery

485 Rayners Lane, Pinner, Middlesex HA5 5DT
Tel: 020 8868 1260
Manager: Toni Ward BTEC, GNVQ
Type: Coeducational Nursery School
Age range: 0–4
No. of pupils: 27

Quainton Hall School & Nursery

91 Hindes Road, Harrow, Middlesex HA1 1RX
Tel: 020 8427 1304
Headmaster: D P Banister BA, AKC
Type: Coeducational Day and Nursery
Age range: B2½–13 G2½–7
No. of pupils: 200
Fees: Day £7800–£8730

Raphael Independent School

Park Lane, Hornchurch, Essex RM11 1XY
Tel: 01708 744735
Headmistress: Mrs J Lawrence BEd(Hons)
Type: Coeducational Day
Age range: 4–16
No. of pupils: 135 B75 G60
Fees: Day £4020–£7200

Reddiford School

36-38 Cecil Park, Pinner, Middlesex HA5 5HH
Tel: 020 8866 0660
Headteacher: Mrs J Batt CertEd, NPQH
Type: Coeducational Day
Age range: 3–11
No. of pupils: 320 B194 G126
Fees: Day £3480–£8340

Reedham Park School

71A Old Lodge Lane, Purley, Surrey CR8 4DN
Tel: 020 8660 6357
Headteacher: Ms L Shaw BA(Hons), DipEurHum
Type: Coeducational Day
Age range: 4–11
No. of pupils: 105 B55 G50
Fees: Day £2460–£2850

Rokeby

George Road, Kingston upon Thames, Surrey KT2 7PB
Tel: 020 8942 2247
Head: J R Peck
Type: Boys' Preparatory
Age range: 4–13
No. of pupils: 370
Fees: Day £8004–£11,634

Roxeth Mead School

Buckholt House, 25 Middle Road, Harrow,
Middlesex HA2 0HW
Tel: 020 8422 2092
Headmistress: Mrs A Isaacs
Type: Coeducational Day
Age range: 3–7
No. of pupils: 57 B28 G29
Fees: Day £6970

Royal Russell School

Coombe Lane, Croydon, Surrey CR9 5BX
Tel: 020 8657 3669
Head: Dr John R Jennings
Type: Coeducational Day & Boarding
Age range: 11–18
No. of pupils: 590 B310 G280 VIth180
Fees: Day £13,290 FB £19,455–£26,310

Seaton House School

67 Banstead Road South, Sutton, Surrey SM2 5LH
Tel: 020 8642 2332
Headmistress: Mrs V Rickus MA, BEd
Type: Girls' Day
Age range: B3–5 G3–11
No. of pupils: 155 B3 G152
Fees: Day £2553–£7230

Shrewsbury House School

107 Ditton Road, Surbiton, Surrey KT6 6RL
Tel: 020 8399 3066
Headmaster: Mr C M Ross BA, HDipEd, TCD
Type: Boys' Day
Age range: 7–13
No. of pupils: 290
Fees: Day £12,885

St Aubyn's School

Bunces Lane, Woodford Green, Essex IG8 9DU
Tel: 020 8504 1577
Head: Gordon James MA(Oxon)
Type: Coeducational Day
Age range: 3–13
No. of pupils: 500 B290 G210
Fees: Day £3831–£9597

ST CATHERINE'S SCHOOL
For further details see p. 56

Cross Deep, Twickenham, Middlesex TW1 4QJ
Tel: 020 8891 2898
Email: admissions@stcatherineschool.co.uk
Website: www.stcatherineschool.co.uk
Headmistress: Sister Paula Thomas BEd(Hons), MA
Type: Girls' Day
Age range: 3–18
No. of pupils: 386
Fees: Day £7605–£10,515

St Christopher's School

71 Wembley Park Drive, Wembley, Middlesex HA9 8HE
Tel: 020 8902 5069
Headmaster: Mr Jeremy Edwards
Type: Coeducational Day
Age range: 4–11
No. of pupils: 108 B52 G56
Fees: Day £6360–£6660

St Christopher's School

49 Bromley Road, Beckenham, Kent BR3 2PA
Tel: 020 8650 2200
Headmaster: Mr A Velasco MEd, BH(Hons), PGCE
Type: Coeducational Day
Age range: 3–11
No. of pupils: 305 B160 G145
Fees: Day £2250–£6630

St David's College

Beckenham Road, West Wickham, Kent BR4 0QS
Tel: 020 8777 5852
Principal: Mrs A Wagstaff BA(Hons)
Type: Coeducational Day
Age range: 4–11
No. of pupils: 155 B93 G62
Fees: Day £5760–£5910

St David's School

23/25 Woodcote Valley Road, Purley, Surrey CR8 3AL
Tel: 020 8660 0723
Headmistress: Mrs Lindsay Nash BEd(Hons)
Type: Coeducational Day
Age range: 3–11
No. of pupils: 167 B84 G83
Fees: Day £2985–£5940

St Helen's College

Parkway, Hillingdon, Uxbridge, Middlesex UB10 9JX
Tel: 01895 234371
Joint Headteachers: Mr D A Crehan ARCS, BA, BSc, MSc, CPhys & Mrs G R Crehan BA, MA, PGCE
Type: Coeducational Day
Age range: 3–11
No. of pupils: 341 B170 G171
Fees: Day £4035–£6720

ST HELEN'S SCHOOL
For further details see p. 98

Eastbury Road, Northwood, Middlesex HA6 3AS
Tel: +44 (0)1923 843210
Email: enquiries@sthn.co.uk
Website: www.sthn.co.uk
Head: Mrs Mary Morris BA
Type: Girls' Day
Age range: G3–18
No. of pupils: 1122 VIth160
Fees: Day £8343–£12,171

St James Senior Boys School

Pope's Villa, 19 Cross Deep, Twickenham,
Middlesex TW1 4QG
Tel: 020 8892 2002
Headmaster: Mr David Boddy
Type: Boys' Day & Weekly Boarding
Age range: B11–18
No. of pupils: 310 VIth65
Fees: Day £11,100 WB £4350

St John's School

Potter Street Hill, Northwood, Middlesex HA6 3QY
Tel: 020 8866 0067
Headmaster: C R Kelly BA
Type: Boys' Day
Age range: 3–13
No. of pupils: 408
Fees: Day £7300–£10,880

St John's Senior School

North Lodge, The Ridgeway, Enfield, Middlesex EN2 8BE
Tel: 020 8366 0035
Headmaster: Mr A Tardios LLB(Hons), BA(Hons), CertEd
Type: Coeducational Day
Age range: 11–18
No. of pupils: B141 G115 VIth27
Fees: Day £8200

St Martha's Senior School

Camlet Way, Hadley, Barnet, Hertfordshire EN4 0NJ
Tel: 020 8449 6889
Head: Mr James Sheridan
Type: Girls' Day
Age range: 11–18
No. of pupils: 320 VIth35
Fees: Day £6000

St Martin's School

40 Moor Park Road, Northwood, Middlesex HA6 2DJ
Tel: 01923 825740
Headmaster: Mr D T Tidmarsh BSc(Wales)
Type: Boys' Day
Age range: 3–13
No. of pupils: 376
Fees: Day £3750–£11,280

St Mary's Hare Park School & Nursery

South Drive, Gidea Park, Romford, Essex RM2 6HH
Tel: 01708 761220
Head Teacher: Mrs K Karwacinski
Type: Coeducational Day
Age range: 2½–11
No. of pupils: 180 B80 G100
Fees: Day £4485

Staines Preparatory School Trust

3 Gresham Road, Knowle Park, Staines,
Middlesex TW18 2BT
Tel: 01784 450909
Headmaster: Peter Roberts BSc
Type: Coeducational Day
Age range: 2½–11
No. of pupils: 326 B201 G125
Fees: Day £4785–£8010

Surbiton High School

13-15 Surbiton Crescent, Kingston upon Thames,
Surrey KT1 2JT
Tel: 020 8546 5245
Principal: Ann Haydon BSc(Hons)
Type: Girls' Day
Age range: 4–18
No. of pupils: 1210 B135 G1075 VIth186
Fees: Day £6390–£10,857

Susi Earnshaw Theatre School

68 High Street, Barnet, Hertfordshire EN5 5SJ
Tel: 020 8441 5010
Headteacher: Mr David Earnshaw
Type: Coeducational Day
Age range: 10–16
No. of pupils: 59 B19 G40
Fees: Day £6000–£6600

Sutton High School GDST

55 Cheam Road, Sutton, Surrey SM1 2AX
Tel: 020 8642 0594
Headteacher: Mr Stephen Callaghan
Type: Girls' Day
Age range: 3–18
No. of pupils: 766 G766 VIth106
Fees: Day £6285–£10,470

Tashbar of Edgware

Yeshurun Federation Synagogue, Fernhurst Gardens, Edgware, Middlesex HA8 7PH
Tel: 020 8951 0239
Headteacher: Mr N Jaffe
Type: Coeducational Day
Age range: 3–11
No. of pupils: 8

(♦♦)

TCS Tutorial College

55 Palmerston Road, Wealdstone, Middlesex HA3 7RR
Tel: 0208 863 0330
Principal: Dr R Antione MBE
Type: Coeducational Day
Age range: 11–19
No. of pupils: 64 B22 G42

(♦♦)

The Falcons Preparatory School for Boys

41 Few Foot Road, Richmond, Middlesex TW9 2SS
Tel: 0844 225 2211
Principal: Mr A P Shawyer
Type: Boys' Day
Age range: 7–13
No. of pupils: 54
Fees: Day £11,085–£11,310

(♦)(✐)

The Hall Pre-Preparatory School

The Grange, Rickmansworth Road, Northwood, Middlesex HA6 2RB
Tel: 01923 822807
Headmistress: Mrs D E Wesson
Type: Coeducational Day
Age range: 2–7
No. of pupils: B35 G23
Fees: Day £1950–£5850

(♦♦)(✐)

The John Lyon School

Middle Road, Harrow, Middlesex HA2 0HN
Tel: 020 8872 8400
Headmaster: Miss Katherine Haynes BA, MEd
Type: Boys' Day
Age range: 11–18
No. of pupils: 575 VIth150
Fees: Day £13,095

(♦)(A)(£)(✐)(16+)

THE LADY ELEANOR HOLLES SCHOOL

For further details see p. 57
Hanworth Road, Hampton, Middlesex TW12 3HF
Tel: 020 8979 1601
Email: office@lehs.org.uk
Website: www.lehs.org.uk
Head: Mrs Gillian Low MA(Oxon)
Type: Girls' Day
Age range: 7–18
No. of pupils: 875 VIth177
Fees: Day £9960–£13,200

(♦)(A)(£)(✐)(16+)

The Mall School

185 Hampton Road, Twickenham, Middlesex TW2 5NQ
Tel: 020 8977 2523
Headmaster: Dr J G Jeanes
Type: Boys' Day
Age range: 4–13
No. of pupils: 300
Fees: Day £8565–£9900

(♦)(£)(✐)

The Noam Primary School

8-10 Forty Avenue, Wembley, Middlesex HA9 8JW
Tel: 020 8908 9491
Headteacher: Mrs S Simmonds
Type: Coeducational Day
Age range: 3–11
No. of pupils: 154

(♦♦)

The Royal Ballet School

White Lodge, Richmond, Surrey TW10 5HR
Tel: 020 7836 8899
Director: Ms Gailene Stock AM
Type: Coeducational Day & Boarding
Age range: 11–19
No. of pupils: B54 G68 VIth80
Fees: Day £14,394–£18,946 FB £17,709–£25,588

(♦♦)(A)(🏠)(£)(✐)(16+)

The Study School

57 Thetford Road, New Malden, Surrey KT3 5DP
Tel: 020 8942 0754
Head Teacher: Mrs Anne Farnish BA, PGCE
Type: Coeducational Day
Age range: 3–11
No. of pupils: 134 B78 G56
Fees: Day £1114–£2599

(♦♦)

Trinity School
Shirley Park, Croydon, Surrey CR9 7AT
Tel: 020 8656 9541
Headmaster: M J Bishop MA, MBA
Type: Boys' Day
Age range: 10–18
No. of pupils: 890 VIth220
Fees: Day £10,446

TWICKENHAM PREPARATORY SCHOOL
For further details see p. 60
Beveree, 43 High Street, Hampton, Middlesex TW12 2SA
Tel: 020 8979 6216
Email: office@twickenhamprep.co.uk
Website: www.twickenhamprep.co.uk
Head: D Malam BA(Hons)(Southampton), PGCE(Winchester)
Type: Coeducational Day
Age range: B4–13 G4–11
No. of pupils: 265 B144 G121
Fees: Day £8250–£8910

Unicorn School
238 Kew Road, Richmond, Surrey TW9 3JX
Tel: 020 8948 3926
Headmistress: Mrs Roberta Linehan
Type: Coeducational Day
Age range: 3–11
No. of pupils: 169 B83 G86
Fees: Day £5130–£9405

West Dene School
167 Brighton Road, Purley, Surrey CR8 4HE
Tel: 020 8660 2404
Head: Mr Peter Kelly
Type: Coeducational Day
Age range: 2–11
No. of pupils: 116 B57 G59
Fees: Day £842–£1840

West Lodge School
36 Station Road, Sidcup, Kent DA15 7DU
Tel: 020 8300 2489
Head Teacher: Mrs Susan Webb
Type: Coeducational Day
Age range: 3–11
No. of pupils: 160 B40 G120
Fees: Day £4395–£7335

Westbury House
80 Westbury Road, New Malden, Surrey KT3 5AS
Tel: 020 8942 5885
Principal: Mrs M T Morton CertEd
Type: Coeducational Day
Age range: 3–11
No. of pupils: B80 G75
Fees: Day £1045–£2507

Whitgift School
Haling Park, South Croydon, Surrey CR2 6YT
Tel: +44 (0)20 8688 9222
Headmaster: Dr Christopher Barnett
Type: Boys' Day
Age range: 10–18
No. of pupils: 1279
Fees: Day £13,266

Wick School
25A Hardman Road, Kingston upon Thames, Surrey KT2 6RH
Tel: 020 8123 4815
Headmistress: Mrs H Hardy
Type: Coeducational Day
Age range: 5–18
No. of pupils: 320

Wickham Court School
Schiller International, Layhams Road, West Wickham, Kent BR4 9HW
Tel: 020 8777 2942
Head: Mrs Barbara Hunter
Type: Coeducational Day
Age range: 2–16
No. of pupils: 121 B50 G71
Fees: Day £4481–£6900

Woodford Green Preparatory School
Glengall Road, Snakes Lane, Woodford Green, Essex IG8 0BZ
Tel: 020 8504 5045
Headmaster: Mr A J Blackhurst BA(Hons), AdvDipEd
Type: Coeducational Day
Age range: 3–11
No. of pupils: 384 B196 G188
Fees: Day £3735–£6210

Schools in the South-East

South-East England

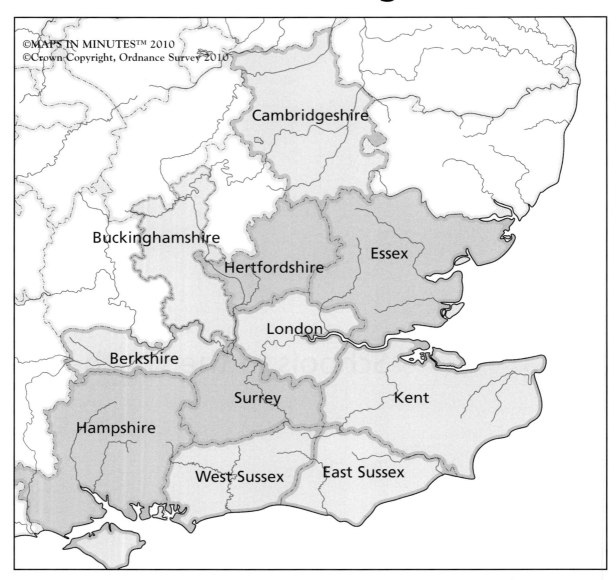

Cambridgeshire

Buckinghamshire

Hertfordshire

Essex

London

Berkshire

Surrey

Kent

Hampshire

West Sussex

East Sussex

Key to symbols

- Boys' school
- Girls' school
- Coeducational school
- International school
- Tutorial or sixth form college
- Ⓐ A levels

- Boarding accommodation
- £ Bursaries
- IB International Baccalaureate
- Learning support
- 16 Entrance at 16+
- Vocational qualifications

BRACKNELL FOREST

Eagle House School
Sandhurst, Bracknell Forest GU47 8PH
Tel: 01344 772134
Headmaster: Mr A P N Barnard BA(Hons), PGCE
Type: Coeducational Day & Boarding
Age range: 3–13
No. of pupils: 326 B205 G121
Fees: Day £7995–£13,290 FB £17,850

(ᛏᛏ) (ᛒ) (£) (✐)

Lambrook School
Winkfield Row, Bracknell, Bracknell Forest RG42 6LU
Tel: 01344 882717
Headmaster: Mr James Barnes
Type: Coeducational Boarding & Day
Age range: 3–13
No. of pupils: 461 B292 G169
Fees: Day £8490–£14,199 FB £17,270–£19,299

(ᛏᛏ) (ᛒ) (£) (✐)

Meadowbrook Montessori School
Malt Hill Road, Warfield, Bracknell,
Bracknell Forest RG12 6JQ
Tel: 01344 890869
Head of School: Mrs S Gunn
Type: Coeducational Day
Age range: 2½–12
No. of pupils: B60 G60
Fees: Day £670–£2215

(ᛏᛏ) (£) (✐)

Newbold School
Popeswood Road, Binfield, Bracknell,
Bracknell Forest RG42 4AH
Tel: 01344 421088
Headteacher: Mrs P Eastwood
Type: Coeducational Day
Age range: 3–11
No. of pupils: B40 G40
Fees: Day £2500–£3000

(ᛏᛏ)

Wellington College
Duke's Ride, Crowthorne, Bracknell Forest RG45 7PU
Tel: +44 (0)1344 444 000
Master: Dr Anthony Seldon
Type: Coeducational Boarding & Day
Age range: 13–18
No. of pupils: 940 B630 G310 VIth400
Fees: Day £20,760–£23,535 FB £27,705

(ᛏᛏ) (🌐) (A) (ᛒ) (£) (IB) (✐) (16+)

BRIGHTON & HOVE

Brighton & Hove High School GDST
Montpelier Road, Brighton, Brighton & Hove BN1 3AT
Tel: 01273 734112
Head: Mrs Lorna Duggleby
Type: Girls' Day
Age range: 3–18
No. of pupils: 680 VIth70
Fees: Day £5028–£8898

(👧) (A) (£) (✐) (16+)

Brighton & Hove Montessori School
67 Stanford Avenue, Brighton, Brighton & Hove BN1 6FB
Tel: 01273 702485
Headteacher: Mrs Daisy Cockburn AMI, MontDip
Type: Coeducational Day
Age range: 2–11
No. of pupils: B33 G27
Fees: Day £1400–£5900

(ᛏᛏ) (✐)

BRIGHTON COLLEGE
For further details see p. 94
Eastern Road, Brighton, Brighton & Hove BN2 0AL
Tel: 01273 704200
Email: registrar@brightoncollege.net
Website: www.brightoncollege.org.uk
Headmaster: Richard Cairns MA
Type: Coeducational Pre-Prep, Prep and Senior
Age range: 3–18
No. of pupils: 730 VIth300
Fees: Day £3747–£15,534 FB £21,150–£24,078

(ᛏᛏ) (🌐) (A) (ᛒ) (£) (✐) (16+)

Brighton Steiner School
John Howard House, Roedean Road, Brighton,
Brighton & Hove BN2 5RA
Tel: 01273 386300
Chair of the College of Teachers: Maddy Pettit
Type: Coeducational Day
Age range: 3–16
No. of pupils: B88 G102
Fees: Day £5967

(ᛏᛏ) (£) (✐)

DEEPDENE SCHOOL
For further details see p. 73
195 New Church Road, Hove, Brighton & Hove BN3 4ED
Tel: 01273 418984
Email: info@deepdeneschool.com
Website: www.deepdeneschool.com
Heads: Mrs L V Clark-Darby BEd(Hons), CertFS & Mrs N K Gane NNEB
Type: Coeducational Day
Age range: 1–11
No. of pupils: B114 G106
Fees: Day £1800–£5760

Dharma School
The White House, Ladies Mile Road, Patcham, Brighton, Brighton & Hove BN1 8TB
Tel: 01273 502055
Headmaster: Kevin Fossey BEd
Type: Coeducational Day
Age range: 3–11
No. of pupils: B33 G31
Fees: Day £3000

K-BIS Theatre School
Clermont Hall, Cumberland Road, Brighton, Brighton & Hove BN1 6SL
Tel: 01273 566739
Principal: Mrs Marcia King LGSM
Type: Coeducational Day
Age range: 5–18
No. of pupils: B11 G33 VIth7
Fees: Day £5790

Lancing College Preparatory School at Mowden
The Droveway, Hove, Brighton & Hove BN3 6LU
Tel: 01273 503452
Headmaster: A P Laurent
Type: Coeducational Day
Age range: 3–13
No. of pupils: 181 B136 G45
Fees: Day £2550–£10,155

Roedean School
Roedean Way, Brighton, Brighton & Hove BN2 5RQ
Tel: 01273 667500
Headmistress: Mrs Frances King MA(Oxon), MA(London), MBA(Hull)
Type: Girls' Boarding & Day
Age range: B3–11 G3–18
No. of pupils: VIth168
Fees: Day £4860–£5600 FB £8700–£9675

St Aubyns
76 High Street, Rottingdean, Brighton, Brighton & Hove BN2 7JN
Tel: 01273 302170
Headmaster: Mr Simon Hitchings
Type: Coeducational Day, Weekly & Flexi Boarding
Age range: 3–13
No. of pupils: B117 G67
Fees: Day £4992–£13,350 WB £12,000–£15,900

St Christopher's School
33 New Church Road, Hove, Brighton & Hove BN3 4AD
Tel: 01273 735404
Headmaster: Mr I McIntyre
Type: Coeducational Day
Age range: 4–13
No. of pupils: B177 G65
Fees: Day £6570–£8688

The Drive Prep School
101 The Drive, Hove, Brighton & Hove BN3 3JE
Tel: 01273 738444
Head Teacher: Mrs S Parkinson CertEd, CertPerfArts
Type: Coeducational Pre-preparatory & Preparatory Day
Age range: 3–16
No. of pupils: B57 G41
Fees: Day £2685–£5850

The Fold School
201 New Church Road, Hove, Brighton & Hove BN3 4ED
Tel: 01273 410901
Principal: Dr Carolyn Drake
Type: Coeducational Day
Age range: 3–11
No. of pupils: B37 G37
Fees: Day £3540–£4200

Torah Academy
31 New Church Road, Hove, Brighton & Hove BN3 4AD
Tel: 01273 683 390
Principal: P Efune
Type: Coeducational Day
Age range: 4–11
No. of pupils: B24 G28

Windlesham School
190 Dyke Road, Brighton, Brighton & Hove BN1 5AA
Tel: 01273 553645
Headmistress: Mrs Aoife Bennett-Odlum
Type: Coeducational Day and Nursery
Age range: 3–11
No. of pupils: 233 B118 G115
Fees: Day £2775–£5700

BUCKINGHAMSHIRE

Akeley Wood School
Akeley Wood, Buckingham, Buckinghamshire MK18 5AE
Tel: 01280 812000
Headmaster: Dr Jerry Grundy BA, PhD
Type: Coeducational Day
Age range: 3–18
No. of pupils: 856 B493 G363
Fees: Day £6345–£9435

Ashfold School
Dorton House, Dorton, Aylesbury,
Buckinghamshire HP18 9NG
Tel: 01844 238237
Headmaster: Mr M O M Chitty BSc
Type: Coeducational Day & Weekly Boarding
Age range: 3–13
No. of pupils: B179 G109 VIth30
Fees: Day £7155–£12,615 WB £14,745

Caldicott
Crown Lane, Farnham Royal, Buckinghamshire SL2 3SL
Tel: 01753 649301
Headmaster: Mr S J G Doggart BA(Cantab)
Type: Boys' Boarding & Day
Age range: 7–13
No. of pupils: 256
Fees: Day £12,822–£13,869 FB £18,849

Chesham Preparatory School
Two Dells Lane, Chesham, Buckinghamshire HP5 3QF
Tel: 01494 782619
Headmaster: Mr J D B Marjoribanks
Type: Coeducational Day
Age range: 4–13
No. of pupils: B199 G168
Fees: Day £7965–£10,620

Crown House School
19 London Road, High Wycombe,
Buckinghamshire HP11 1BJ
Tel: 01494 529927
Headmaster: Ali Khan BSc(Hons), MBA
Type: Coeducational Day
Age range: 4–11
No. of pupils: 120 B71 G40
Fees: Day £5985–£6570

Dair House School
Bishops Blake, Beaconsfield Road, Farnham Royal,
Buckinghamshire SL2 3BY
Tel: 01753 643964
Headmaster: Mr Terry Wintle BEd(Hons)
Type: Coeducational Day
Age range: 3–11
No. of pupils: 104 B64 G40
Fees: Day £2907–£8526

Davenies School
Station Road, Beaconsfield, Buckinghamshire HP9 1AA
Tel: 01494 685400
Headmaster: C Watson MA, BEd(Hons)
Type: Boys' Day
Age range: 4–13
No. of pupils: 325
Fees: Day £10,035–£11,955

Gateway School
1 High Street, Great Missenden,
Buckinghamshire HP16 9AA
Tel: 01494 862407
Headteacher: Mr S J Y Wade MA, PGCE
Type: Coeducational Day
Age range: 2–12
No. of pupils: 333 B190 G143
Fees: Day £8412

Gayhurst School
Bull Lane, Gerrards Cross, Buckinghamshire SL9 8RJ
Tel: 01753 882690
Headmaster: A J Sims MA(Cantab)
Type: Boys' Day
Age range: 4–13
No. of pupils: 265
Fees: Day £7089–£9009

Godstowe Preparatory School
Shrubbery Road, High Wycombe,
Buckinghamshire HP13 6PR
Tel: 01494 529273
Headmaster: Mr David Gainer
Type: Boys' & Girls' Day
Age range: B3–7 G3–13
No. of pupils: B29 G351
Fees: Day £8175–£12,735 WB £18,705 FB £18,705

Heatherton House School
Copperkins Lane, Chesham Bois, Amersham,
Buckinghamshire HP6 5QB
Tel: 01494 726433
Headmaster: Mr Peter Rushforth
Type: Girls' Day
Age range: G2½–11
No. of pupils: 165
Fees: Day £1185–£9450

High March School
23 Ledborough Lane, Beaconsfield,
Buckinghamshire HP9 2PZ
Tel: 01494 675186
Headmistress: Mrs S J Clifford
Type: Girls' Day
Age range: 3–11
No. of pupils: 254 B4 G250
Fees: Day £510–£10,575

Holy Cross Convent School
The Grange, Chalfont St Peter, Gerrards Cross,
Buckinghamshire SL9 9DW
Tel: 01753 895600
Headmistress: Mrs Margaret Shinkwin BA, MA(Ed), NPQH
Type: Girls' Day
Age range: 3–18
No. of pupils: 255
Fees: Day £752–£6186 FB £9000

Kingscote Pre-Preparatory School
Oval Way, Gerrards Cross, Buckinghamshire SL9 8PZ
Tel: 01753 885535
Headmistress: Mrs S A Tunstall CertEd
Type: Boys' Day
Age range: B3–7
No. of pupils: 100
Fees: Day £3900–£8145

Ladymede School
Little Kimble, Aylesbury, Buckinghamshire HP17 0XP
Tel: 01844 346154
Headmistress: Carole Hawkins
Type: Coeducational Day
Age range: 3–11
No. of pupils: 100 B45 G55
Fees: Day £2592–£8040

Maltman's Green School
Maltman's Lane, Gerrards Cross, Buckinghamshire SL9 8RR
Tel: 01753 883022
Headmistress: Mrs Joanna Pardon MA, BSc(Hons), PGCE
Type: Girls' Day Preparatory
Age range: 3–11
No. of pupils: 400
Fees: Day £6090–£9570

Pipers Corner School
Pipers Lane, Great Kingshill, High Wycombe,
Buckinghamshire HP15 6LP
Tel: 01494 718 255
Headmistress: Mrs H J Ness-Gifford BA (Hons), PGCE
Type: Girls' Boarding & Day
Age range: 3–18
No. of pupils: 480 VIth62
Fees: Day £6300–£12,210 WB £16,350–£19,890
FB £16,590–£20,130

Sefton Park School
School Lane, Stoke Poges, Buckinghamshire SL2 4QA
Tel: 01753 662167
Headteacher: Mr Timothy Thorpe
Type: Coeducational Day
Age range: 11–16
No. of pupils: 120 B72 G48

St Mary's School
94 Packhorse Road, Gerrards Cross,
Buckinghamshire SL9 8JQ
Tel: 01753 883370
Headmistress: Mrs F A Balcombe BA(Hons), PGCE
Type: Girls' Day
Age range: 3–18
No. of pupils: 325 VIth40
Fees: Day £3300–£11,670

St Teresa's School
Aylesbury Road, Princes Risborough,
Buckinghamshire HP27 0JW
Tel: 01844 345005
Headmaster: Mr Robert Duigan
Type: Coeducational Day
Age range: 3–11
No. of pupils: 132
Fees: Day £1245–£4980

Stowe School
Buckingham, Buckinghamshire MK18 5EH
Tel: 01280 818000
Headmaster: Dr Anthony Wallersteiner
Type: Coeducational Boarding & Day
Age range: 13–18
No. of pupils: 740 B500 G230 VIth350
Fees: Day £19,860 FB £26,850

The Beacon School
Chesham Bois, Amersham, Buckinghamshire HP6 5PF
Tel: 01494 433654
Headmaster: P Brewster BSc(Hons), PGCE
Type: Boys' Preparatory
Age range: 3–13
No. of pupils: 430 B430
Fees: Day £4350–£11,700

Thorpe House School
Oval Way, Gerrards Cross, Buckinghamshire SL9 8QA
Tel: 01753 882474
Headmaster: Mr Anthony Lock MA(Oxon), PGCE
Type: Boys' Day
Age range: 7–16
No. of pupils: 216
Fees: Day £10,020–£12,000

Wycombe Abbey School
High Wycombe, Buckinghamshire HP11 1PE
Tel: 01494 520381
Headmistress: Mrs Cynthia Hall MA(Oxon)
Type: Girls' Day & Boarding
Age range: 11–18
No. of pupils: 562 VIth161
Fees: Day £21,150 FB £28,200

CAMBRIDGESHIRE

Beechwood School
Cherry Hinton Road, Shelford Bottom, Cambridge,
Cambridgeshire CB22 3BF
Tel: 01223 400190
Headteacher: Mr M T Drake
Type: Coeducational Day
Age range: 11–16
No. of pupils: 29 B17 G12

Cambridge Centre for English Studies
Guildhall Chambers, Guildhall Place, Cambridge,
Cambridgeshire CB2 3QQ
Tel: 01223 357190
Principal: Dr W Ramuz-Nienhuis
Type: Language School

Cambridge International School
Cherry Hinton Hall, Cherry Hinton Road, Cambridge,
Cambridgeshire CB1 8DW
Tel: 01223 416938
Principal: Dr Harriet Sturdy
Type: Coeducational Day
Age range: 4–16
Fees: Day £8115–£9645

Cambridge Steiner School
Hinton Road, Fulbourn, Cambridge,
Cambridgeshire CB21 5DZ
Tel: 01223 882727
Chair of Faculty: Faculty of Teachers
Type: Coeducational Day
Age range: 2½–11
No. of pupils: 100
Fees: Day £1500–£5500

Kimbolton School
Kimbolton, Huntingdon, Cambridgeshire PE28 0EA
Tel: 01480 860505
Headmaster: Jonathan Belbin BA
Type: Coeducational Day & Boarding
Age range: 4–18
No. of pupils: B486 G439 VIth170
Fees: Day £6945–£10,830 FB £17,940

King's Acremont, The King's School Ely Nursery & Pre-Prep
Egremont Street, Ely, Cambridgeshire CB6 1AE
Tel: 01353 662978
Head: Mrs F A Blake BA, PGCE
Type: Coeducational Day
Age range: 2–6
No. of pupils: B79 G75
Fees: Day £5835–£6300

King's College School
West Road, Cambridge, Cambridgeshire CB3 9DN
Tel: 01223 365814
Headmaster: Mr Nicholas Robinson BA, PGCE
Type: Coeducational Day & Boarding
Age range: 4–13
No. of pupils: 385 B195 G155
Fees: Day £8925–£11,505 WB £17,160 FB £17,835

Madingley Pre-Preparatory School
Cambridge Road, Madingley, Cambridge,
Cambridgeshire CB23 8AH
Tel: 01954 210309
Headteacher: Mrs Penelope Evans CertEd, AdvDip
Type: Coeducational Day
Age range: 3–8
No. of pupils: 60 B30 G30
Fees: Day £8550

Sancton Wood School
2 St Paul's Road, Cambridge, Cambridgeshire CB1 2EZ
Tel: 01223 471703
Headmaster: The Reverend Dr Jack McDonald
Type: Coeducational Day
Age range: 3–16
No. of pupils: 193 B103 G90
Fees: Day £5220–£6510

St Faith's
Trumpington Road, Cambridge, Cambridgeshire CB2 2AG
Tel: 01223 352073
Headmaster: Mr C S S Drew
Type: Coeducational Day
Age range: 4–13
No. of pupils: 519 B317 G202
Fees: Day £8955–£11,280

St John's College School
73 Grange Road, Cambridge, Cambridgeshire CB3 9AB
Tel: 01223 353532
Headmaster: Mr K L Jones MA(Cantab)
Type: Coeducational Day & Boarding
Age range: 4–13
No. of pupils: 457 B253 G204
Fees: Day £9000–£11,874 FB £18,753

St Mary's School
Bateman Street, Cambridge, Cambridgeshire CB2 1LY
Tel: 01223 353253
Headmistress: Miss Charlotte Avery
Type: Girls' Day & Boarding
Age range: 4–18
No. of pupils: 633 G633 VIth85
Fees: Day £12,120 WB £22,470 FB £25,584

The King's School Ely
Ely, Cambridgeshire CB7 4DB
Tel: 01353 660700
Head: Mrs Susan Freestone MEd, GRSM, LRAM, ARCM,
FRSA
Type: Coeducational Boarding & Day
Age range: 13–18
No. of pupils: 471 B283 G188 VIth168
Fees: Day £15,570 WB £22,530 FB £22,530

The King's School Ely Junior School
Ely, Cambridgeshire CB7 4DB
Tel: 01353 660732
Head: Mr R J Whymark
Type: Coeducational Day & Boarding
Age range: 7–13
No. of pupils: 343 B204 G139
Fees: Day £9855–£14,865 FB £15,720–£21,510

The Leys School
Cambridge, Cambridgeshire CB2 2AD
Tel: 01223 508900
Headmaster: Mark Slater
Type: Coeducational Boarding & Day
Age range: 11–18
No. of pupils: B330 G210 VIth200

The Perse Girls Junior School
St Eligius Street, Cambridge, Cambridgeshire CE2 1HX
Tel: 01223 346 140
Head: Miss K Milne
Type: Girls' Day
Age range: 7–11
No. of pupils: 150
Fees: Day £10,800
(symbols)

The Perse Girls Senior School
Union Road, Cambridge, Cambridgeshire CB2 1HF
Tel: 01223 454700
Headmistress: Miss P M Kelleher MA(Oxon), MA (Sussex)
Type: Girls' Day
Age range: 11–18
No. of pupils: 585 VIth115
Fees: Day £13,155
(symbols)

The Perse Pelican Nursery and Pre-Preparatory School
Northwold House, 92 Glebe Road, Cambridge,
Cambridgeshire CB1 7TD
Tel: 01223 403940
Headmistress: Mrs P M Oates BEd(Cantab)
Type: Coeducational Day
Age range: 3–7
No. of pupils: 140 B82 G58
Fees: Day £9645
(symbols)

The Perse Preparatory School
Trumpington Road, Cambridge, Cambridgeshire CB2 9EX
Tel: 01223 403920
Head: Gareth Jones BMus, PGCE
Type: Coeducational Day
Age range: 7–11
No. of pupils: 254
Fees: Day £11,403
(symbols)

The Perse School
Hills Road, Cambridge, Cambridgeshire CB2 8QF
Tel: 01223 403800
Head: Mr E C Elliott
Type: Boys' Day
Age range: 11–18
No. of pupils: 750 VIth250
Fees: Day £12,858
(symbols)

Whitehall School
117 High Street, Somersham, Cambridgeshire PE17 3EH
Tel: 01487 840966
Headteacher: Mr Sean Peace
Type: Coeducational Day
Age range: 3–11
No. of pupils: 109 B53 G56
Fees: Day £1510–£1953
(symbols)

Wisbech Grammar School
North Brink, Wisbech, Cambridgeshire PE13 1JX
Tel: 01945 583631
Headmaster: Mr N J G Hammond
Type: Coeducational Day
Age range: 4–18
No. of pupils: 662 B313 G349 VIth120
Fees: Day £6870–£9990
(symbols)

EAST SUSSEX

Ashdown House School
Forest Row, East Sussex RH18 5JY
Tel: 01342 822574
Headmaster: Dominic Floyd
Type: Coeducational Boarding
Age range: 7–13
No. of pupils: 141 B71 G70
Fees: FB £20,640
(symbols)

Battle Abbey School
Battle, East Sussex TN33 0AD
Tel: 01424 772385
Headmaster: Mr R C Clark BA(Hons), MA(Ed)
Type: Coeducational Day & Boarding
Age range: 2–18
No. of pupils: 286 B140 G146 VIth48
Fees: Day £6225–£13,200 FB £22,350
(symbols)

Bodiam Manor School
Bodiam, Robertsbridge, East Sussex TN32 5UJ
Tel: 01580 830225
Headmaster: Mr G Owton
Type: Coeducational Day
Age range: 3–13
No. of pupils: 130
Fees: Day £5625–£10,347
(symbols)

Bricklehurst Manor Preparatory

Bardown Road, Stonegate, Wadhurst, East Sussex TN5 7EL
Tel: 01580 200448
Headteacher: Mrs C Flowers
Type: Coeducational Day
Age range: 3–11
No. of pupils: 133 B56 G77
Fees: Day £3985–£8550

(♟)(£)(✏)

Buckswood School

Broomham Hall, Rye Road, Guestling, Hastings,
East Sussex TN35 4LT
Tel: 01424 813813
Headmaster: Mr Tim Fish BA
Type: Coeducational Day & Boarding
Age range: 10–19
No. of pupils: 280
Fees: Day £9270 WB £14,970 FB £15,660–£19,800

(♟)(🌐)(A)(🏛)(£)(✏)(16·)

Charters Ancaster College

Woodsgate Place, Gunters Lane, Bexhill-on-Sea,
East Sussex TN39 4EB
Tel: 01424 216670
Headmistress: Mrs Miriam Black
Type: Coeducational Day
Age range: 2½–13
No. of pupils: 125 B62 G63
Fees: Day £5325–£6750

(♟)(£)(✏)

Claremont Preparatory & Nursery School

Ebdens Hill, Baldslow, St Leonards-on-Sea,
East Sussex TN37 7PW
Tel: 01424 751555
Headmaster: Mr R Keeble
Type: Coeducational Day
Age range: 1–14
No. of pupils: B200 G200
Fees: Day £5025–£8550

(♟)(£)(✏)

Darvell School

Darvell Bruderhof, Robertsbridge, East Sussex TN32 5DR
Tel: 01580 883300
Headteacher: Mr Arnold Meier
Type: Coeducational Day
Age range: 4–16
No. of pupils: 121 B56 G65

(♟)(✏)

Eastbourne College

Old Wish Road, Eastbourne, East Sussex BN21 4JX
Tel: 01323 452323
Headmaster: Mr S P Davies MA
Type: Coeducational Boarding & Day
Age range: 13–18
No. of pupils: 630 B382 G248 VIth277
Fees: Day £16,305 FB £24,630

(♟)(🌐)(A)(🏛)(£)(✏)(16·)

Greenfields School

Priory Road, Forest Row, East Sussex RH18 5JD
Tel: 01342 822189
Headteacher: Mrs V Tupholme
Type: Coeducational Boarding & Day
Age range: 2–18
No. of pupils: 152 B89 G63 VIth5
Fees: Day £2580–£9960 WB £12,777–£16,410
FB £12,777–£16,410

(♟)(🌐)(A)(🏛)(16·)

Lewes New School

Talbot Terrace, Lewes, East Sussex BN7 2DS
Tel: 01273 477074
Head Teacher: Lizzie Overton
Type: Coeducational Day
Age range: 3–11
No. of pupils: 76
Fees: Day £3300–£3600

(♟)(£)(✏)

Lewes Old Grammar School

High Street, Lewes, East Sussex BN7 1XS
Tel: 01273 472634
Headmaster: Mr Robert Blewitt
Type: Coeducational Day
Age range: 3–18
No. of pupils: 463 B284 G179 VIth50
Fees: Day £5550–£10,815

(♟)(A)(£)(✏)(16·)

Michael Hall School

Kidbrooke Park, Forest Row, East Sussex RH18 5JB
Tel: 01342 822275
Head: Chair of the College of Teachers
Type: Coeducational Day & Boarding
Age range: 3–19
No. of pupils: B233 G281 VIth35
Fees: Day £4600–£10,100 WB £1450–£1850
FB £1750–£2150

(♟)(🌐)(A)(🏛)(✏)(16·)

Moira House Girls School
Upper Carlisle Road, Eastbourne, East Sussex BN20 7TD
Tel: 01323 644144
Principal: Mrs Lesley Watson MA(Ed)
Type: Girls' Boarding & Day
Age range: 2–18
No. of pupils: 360 VIth80
Fees: Day £5835–£13,560 WB £17,115–£21,390
FB £18,420–£23,610

Newlands School
Eastbourne Road, Seaford, East Sussex BN25 4NP
Tel: 01323 490000
Headmaster: Mr C Bridgman BEd(Hons)
Type: Coeducational Day & Boarding
Age range: 2–18
No. of pupils: 360 VIth80
Fees: Day £5400–£10,800 WB £12,450–£17,850
FB £12,600–£18,000

Sacred Heart School
Mayfield Lane, Durgates, Wadhurst, East Sussex TN5 6DQ
Tel: 01892 783414
Headteacher: Mrs H Blake BA(Hons), PGCE
Type: Coeducational Independent Primary School
Age range: 3–11
No. of pupils: B63 G43
Fees: Day £1910

Skippers Hill Manor Prep School
Five Ashes, Mayfield, East Sussex TN20 6HF
Tel: 01825 830234
Headmaster: T W Lewis BA(Exon), PGCE(London)
Type: Coeducational Day
Age range: 4–13
No. of pupils: B59 G38
Fees: Day £4856–£11,880

St Andrew's Preparatory School
Meads, Eastbourne, East Sussex BN20 7RP
Tel: 01323 733203
Headmaster: Jeremy Griffith BA, PGCE
Type: Coeducational Day & Boarding
Age range: 2–13
No. of pupils: B252 G143
Fees: Day £7842–£13,020 WB £16,431 FB £18,495

St Bede's Preparatory School
Duke's Drive, Eastbourne, East Sussex BN20 7XL
Tel: 01323 734222
Head: Mr Nicholas Bevington
Type: Coeducational Day & Boarding
Age range: 3 months–13 years
No. of pupils: 395 B235 G160

St Bede's School
The Dicker, Hailsham, East Sussex BN27 3QH
Tel: 01323 843252
Head: Mr S Cole BA
Type: Coeducational Day & Boarding
Age range: 12½–18+
No. of pupils: 800 B485 G315 VIth295
Fees: Day £13,665 FB £22,230

St Leonards-Mayfield School
The Old Palace, Mayfield, East Sussex TN20 6PH
Tel: 01435 874600
Head: Miss Antonia Beary MA, Mphil (Cantab), PGCE
Type: Girls' Boarding & Day
Age range: 11–18
No. of pupils: 420 G420 VIth100
Fees: Day £15,285 WB £23,010 FB £23,010

Vinehall School
Robertsbridge, East Sussex TN32 5JL
Tel: 01580 880413
Head: Mrs Julie Robinson BA(Hons)
Type: Coeducational Day & Boarding
Age range: 2–13
No. of pupils: 301 B156 G145
Fees: Day £7155–£13,500 FB £17,640

Walsh Manor School
Walshes Road, Crowborough, East Sussex TN6 3RB
Tel: 01892 610823
Headteacher: Miss Kimberley Bradford
Type: Coeducational Day
Age range: 10–16
No. of pupils: 22 B8 G14

ESSEX

Braeside School for Girls
130 High Road, Buckhurst Hill, Essex IG9 5SD
Tel: 020 8504 1133
Head Teacher: Mrs G Haddon BA(Hons), PGCE
Type: Girls' Day
Age range: 3–16
No. of pupils: 203
Fees: Day £3825–£9450

Brentwood Preparatory School
Middleton Hall Lane, Brentwood, Essex CM15 8EQ
Tel: 01277 243333
Headmaster: Mr N L Helliwell MA, BEd(Hons)
Type: Coeducational Day
Age range: 7–11
No. of pupils: 242 B137 G105
Fees: Day £9687

Brentwood Pre-Preparatory School
Shenfield Road, Brentwood, Essex CM15 8BD
Tel: 01277 243239
Headmistress: Mrs S E Wilson BEd, CertEd
Type: Coeducational Day
Age range: 3–7
No. of pupils: B76 G67
Fees: Day £4374–£8742

Brentwood School
Ingrave Road, Brentwood, Essex CM15 8AS
Tel: 01277 243243
Headmaster: Mr D I Davies
Type: Coeducational Day & Boarding
Age range: 11–18
No. of pupils: 1099 B681 G418 VIth334
Fees: Day £12,144 FB £21,426

Chigwell School
High Road, Chigwell, Essex IG7 6QF
Tel: 020 8501 5700
Headmaster: Mr M E Punt MA, MSc
Type: Coeducational Day & Sixth Form Boarding
Age range: 7–18
No. of pupils: 740 VIth273
Fees: Day £8391–£12,903 WB £17,493–£18,567 FB £19,611

Colchester High School
Wellesley Road, Colchester, Essex CO3 3HD
Tel: 01206 573389
Principal: David E Wood MA, CertEd
Type: Coeducational Day
Age range: B3–16 G3–16
No. of pupils: 429 B362 G67
Fees: Day £5184–£8106

Coopersale Hall School
Flux's Lane, off Stewards Green Road, Epping,
Essex CM16 7PE
Tel: 01992 577133
Headmaster: Mr Ray Probyn BA
Type: Coeducational Day
Age range: 2½–11
No. of pupils: 275 B135 G140
Fees: Day £3645–£7275

DAME BRADBURY'S SCHOOL
For further details see p. 69
Ashdon Road, Saffron Walden, Essex CB10 2AL
Tel: 01799 522348
Email: info@damebradburys.com
Website: www.damebradburys.com
Headmistress: Mrs J Crouch
Type: Coeducational Day
Age range: 3–11
No. of pupils: 265
Fees: Day £1638–£8490

Elm Green Preparatory School
Parsonage Lane, Little Baddow, Chelmsford,
Essex CM3 4SU
Tel: 01245 225230
Principal: Ms Ann Milner
Type: Coeducational Day
Age range: 4–11
No. of pupils: 220 B118 G102
Fees: Day £6996

Felsted Preparatory School
Felsted, Great Dunmow, Essex CM6 3JL
Tel: 01371 822610
Headmistress: Mrs Jenny Burrett BA(Dunelm),
MEd(Cantab), PGCE
Type: Coeducational Boarding & Day
Age range: 4–13
No. of pupils: 401 B244 G163
Fees: Day £6195–£13,557 FB £17,328

Felsted School

Felsted, Great Dunmow, Essex CM6 3LL
Tel: +44 (0) 1371 822605
Headmaster: Dr Michael Walker
Type: Coeducational Day & Boarding
Age range: 13–18
No. of pupils: 516
Fees: Day £17,949 FB £23,979

FKS Schools

Edwards House, Braintree Road, Felsted, Essex CM6 3DS
Tel: 01371 820638
Headmistress: Mrs A Woods
Type: Coeducational Day
Age range: 4–11
No. of pupils: 161
Fees: Day £6219–£6864

Friends' School

Mount Pleasant Road, Saffron Walden, Essex CB11 3EB
Tel: 01799 525351
Head: Graham Wigley BA, MA
Type: Coeducational Day & Boarding
Age range: 3–18
No. of pupils: B230 G170 VIth50
Fees: Day £2060–£2830 WB £5345–£6495 FB £5575–£7095

Gosfield School

Cut Hedge Park, Halstead Road, Gosfield, Halstead, Essex CO9 1PF
Tel: 01787 474040
Principal: Claire Goodchild BSc(Hons), CertEd
Type: Coeducational Day & Boarding
Age range: 4–18
No. of pupils: B122 G66 VIth12
Fees: Day £5160–£9150 WB £10,860–£12,720

Great Warley School

Warley Street, Great Warley, Brentwood, Essex CM13 3LA
Tel: 01277 233288
Head: Mrs B Harding
Type: Coeducational Day
Age range: 3–11
No. of pupils: B70 G56
Fees: Day £2250–£3500

Guru Gobind Singh Khalsa College

Roding Lane, Chigwell, Essex IG7 6BQ
Tel: 020 8559 9160
Principal: Mr Amarjit Singh Toor BSc(Hons), BSc, BT
Type: Coeducational Day
Age range: 3–17
No. of pupils: B88 G122
Fees: Day £3900

Heathcote School

Eves Corner, Danbury, Chelmsford, Essex CM3 4QB
Tel: 01245 223131
Head Teacher: Mr K Gladwyn BEd
Type: Coeducational Day
Age range: 2–11
No. of pupils: B98 G87
Fees: Day £344–£5175

Herington House School

1 Mount Avenue, Hutton, Brentwood, Essex CM13 2NS
Tel: 01277 211595
Principal: Mr R Dudley-Cooke
Type: Coeducational Day
Age range: 3–11
No. of pupils: 129
Fees: Day £4365–£8670

Holmwood House

Lexden, Colchester, Essex CO3 9ST
Tel: 01206 574305
Headmaster: Alexander Mitchell
Type: Coeducational Day & Boarding
Age range: 4–13
No. of pupils: 387 B254 G133
Fees: Day £7224–£12,870 WB £16,644

Hutton Manor School

428 Rayleigh Road, Hutton, Brentwood, Essex CM13 1SD
Tel: 01277 245585
Head: Mr P Pryke
Type: Coeducational Day
Age range: 3–11
No. of pupils: B73 G73
Fees: Day £2975–£3995

Littlegarth School
Horkesley Park, Nayland, Colchester, Essex CO6 4JR
Tel: 01206 262332
Headmaster: Mr Peter Jones
Type: Coeducational Day
Age range: 2–11
No. of pupils: 318 B167 G151
Fees: Day £6000–£7890

Loyola Preparatory School
103 Palmerston Road, Buckhurst Hill, Essex IG9 5NH
Tel: 020 8504 7372
Headmaster: Mr P G M Nicholson CertEd, BEd(Hons)
Type: Boys' Day
Age range: 3–11
No. of pupils: 182
Fees: Day £4482–£7470

Maldon Court Preparatory School
Silver Street, Maldon, Essex CM9 4QE
Tel: 01621 853529
Headteacher: Mrs L Guest
Type: Coeducational Day
Age range: 3–11
No. of pupils: 124 B62 G62
Fees: Day £6579

New Hall School
Boreham, Chelmsford, Essex CM3 3HT
Tel: 01245 467588
Headmistress: Mrs Katherine Jeffrey MA, BA, PGCE,
MA(Ed Mg), NPQH
Type: Coeducational Day & Boarding
Age range: B3–11 G3–18
No. of pupils: B94 G593 VIth108
Fees: Day £5820–£11,910 FB £14,250–£17,910

Oaklands School
8 Albion Hill, Loughton, Essex IG10 4RA
Tel: 020 8508 3517
Headmistress: Mrs Pam Simmonds MA(Oxon), BSc
Type: Coeducational Day
Age range: B2½–7 G2½–11
No. of pupils: 243 B62 G181
Fees: Day £3795–£7650

Oxford House School
2-4 Lexden Road, Colchester, Essex CO3 3NE
Tel: 01206 576686
Principal: Mr D Wood
Type: Coeducational Day
Age range: 2½–11
No. of pupils: 130 B65 G65
Fees: Day £1140–£2270

Peniel Academy
Brizes Park, Ongar Road, Kelvedon Hatch, Brentwood,
Essex CM15 0DG
Tel: 01277 374123
Headmaster: Reverend M S B Reid BD
Type: Coeducational Day
Age range: 4–18

St Anne's Preparatory School
New London Road, Chelmsford, Essex CM2 0AW
Tel: 01245 353488
Headmistress: Mrs Fiona Pirrie BEd(Hons)
Type: Coeducational Day
Age range: 3–11
No. of pupils: 160 B70 G90
Fees: Day £550–£5850

St Cedd's School Educational Trust
Maltese Road, Chelmsford, Essex CM1 2PB
Tel: 01245 354380
Head Teacher: Mrs B A Windley
Type: Coeducational Day
Age range: 4–11
No. of pupils: B157 G169
Fees: Day £2225–£2385

St John's School
Stock Road, Billericay, Essex CM12 0AR
Tel: 01277 623070
Head Teacher: Mrs F Armour BEd(Hons)
Type: Coeducational Day
Age range: 3–16
No. of pupils: 445 B246 G199
Fees: Day £4863–£9195

St Margaret's School
Gosfield Hall Park, Gosfield, Halstead, Essex CO9 1SE
Tel: 01787 472134
Principal: Mrs B Y Boyton
Type: Coeducational Day
Age range: 2–11
No. of pupils: 248 B123 G125
Fees: Day £292–£2402

St Mary's School
Lexden Road, Colchester, Essex CO3 3RB
Tel: 01206 572544
Principal: Mrs H K Vipond MEd, BSc(Hons), NPQH
Type: Girls' Day
Age range: 4–16
No. of pupils: 424
Fees: Day £6180–£8610

St Nicholas School
Hillingdon House, Hobbs Cross Road, Harlow,
Essex CM17 0NJ
Tel: 01279 429910
Headmaster: R Cusworth BSc(Hons), PGCE, MBA
Type: Coeducational Day
Age range: 4–16
No. of pupils: 380 B190 G190
Fees: Day £5805–£7680

St Philomena's Preparatory School
Hadleigh Road, Frinton-on-Sea, Essex CO13 9HQ
Tel: 01255 674492
Headmistress: Mrs Bernadette Buck CertEd
Type: Coeducational Day
Age range: 3–11
No. of pupils: B67 G73
Fees: Day £4320–£5100

The Daiglen School
68 Palmerston Road, Buckhurst Hill, Essex IG9 5LG
Tel: 020 8504 7108
Headteacher: Mrs M Bradfield
Type: Coeducational Day
Age range: 3–11
No. of pupils: 130 B100 G30
Fees: Day £6360

Ursuline Preparatory School
Old Great Ropers, Great Ropers Lane, Warley, Brentwood,
Essex CM13 3HR
Tel: 01277 227152
Headmistress: Mrs Pauline Wilson MSc
Type: Coeducational Day
Age range: 3–11
No. of pupils: B79 G86
Fees: Day £2610–£4950

Widford Lodge School
Widford Road, Chelmsford, Essex CM2 9AN
Tel: 01245 352581
Headmaster: Mr Simon Trowell
Type: Coeducational Day
Age range: 2–11
No. of pupils: B99 G72
Fees: Day £5400–£7050

HAMPSHIRE

Allbrook School
The Old School, Pitmore Road, Allbrook, Eastleigh,
Hampshire SO50 4LW
Tel: 023 8061 6316
Head of Studies: Mrs Hilary Laider
Type: Coeducational Day
Age range: 11–16
No. of pupils: 79 B51 G28

Alton Convent School
Anstey Lane, Alton, Hampshire GU34 2NG
Tel: 01420 82070/83878
Headmistress: Mrs S Kirkham BA(Hons), MA
Type: Coeducational Day
Age range: B2–11 G2–18
No. of pupils: B64 G351 VIth35
Fees: Day £7905–£9465

Ballard School
Fernhill Lane, New Milton, Hampshire BH25 5SU
Tel: 01425 611153
Headmaster: Mr Alastair Reid
Type: Coeducational Day
Age range: 1½–16
No. of pupils: 500
Fees: Day £540–£10,758

Bedales School

Church Road, Steep, Petersfield, Hampshire GU32 2DG
Tel: 01730 711569
Head: Keith Budge MA
Type: Coeducational Boarding & Day
Age range: 13–18
No. of pupils: 451 B217 G234 VIth166
Fees: Day £20,976 FB £26,664

Boundary Oak School

Roche Court, Fareham, Hampshire PO17 5BL
Tel: 01329 280955/820373
Headmaster: Mr Stephen Symonds BAEd(Hons)
Type: Coeducational Day & Boarding
Age range: 2¾–13
No. of pupils: 140
Fees: Day £3240–£10,800 WB £11,310–£15,390
FB £14,970–£17,295

Brockwood Park & Inwoods School

Bramdean, Hampshire SO24 0LQ
Tel: 01962 771 744
Co-Principles: Bill Taylor & Adrian Sydenham
Type: Coeducational Boarding
Age range: 4–19
No. of pupils: 92 B46 G46
Fees: Day £3150 FB £14,200

Brookham School

Highfield Lane, Liphook, Hampshire GU30 7LQ
Tel: 01428 722005
Headmistress: Mrs D Gardiner
Type: Coeducational Day
Age range: 3–8
No. of pupils: 141 B76 G65
Fees: Day £2190–£7875

Churcher's College

Petersfield, Hampshire GU31 4AS
Tel: 01730 263033
Headmaster: Mr Simon Williams MA, BSc
Type: Coeducational Day
Age range: 4–18
No. of pupils: B562 G422 VIth168
Fees: Day £6840–£10,740

Daneshill School

Stratfield Turgis, Basingstoke, Hampshire RG27 0AR
Tel: 01256 882707
Headmaster: S V Spencer CertEd, DipPhysEd
Type: Coeducational Day
Age range: 3–13
No. of pupils: B147 G150
Fees: Day £3900–£9150

Ditcham Park School

Ditcham Park, Petersfield, Hampshire GU31 5RN
Tel: 01730 825659
Headteacher: K Morton BEd, CertEd, DipEd
Type: Coeducational Day
Age range: 4–16
No. of pupils: 348 B192 G156
Fees: Day £6471–£10,803

Dunhurst (Bedales Junior School)

Petersfield, Hampshire GU32 2DP
Tel: 01730 300200
Head: Penny Watkins
Type: Coeducational Boarding & Day
Age range: 8–13
No. of pupils: B103 G87
Fees: Day £13,695 FB £17,622

Durlston Court

Becton Lane, Barton-on-Sea, New Milton,
Hampshire BH25 7AQ
Tel: 01425 610010
Headmaster: David Wansey
Type: Coeducational Day
Age range: 2–13
No. of pupils: 286 B159 G127
Fees: Day £3540–£12,255

Farleigh School

Red Rice, Andover, Hampshire SP11 7PW
Tel: 01264 710766
Headmaster: Father Simon Everson
Type: Coeducational Day & Boarding
Age range: 3–13
No. of pupils: B230 G188
Fees: Day £3870–£14,085 FB £16,515–£18,345

Farnborough Hill

Farnborough Road, Farnborough, Hampshire GU14 8AT
Tel: 01252 545197
Headmistress: Mrs S Buckle BSc, MA, PGCE, NPQH
Type: Girls' Day
Age range: 11–18
No. of pupils: 504 VIth60
Fees: Day £10,320

Forres Sandle Manor

Fordingbridge, Hampshire SP6 1NS
Tel: 01425 653181
Headmaster: Mr R P J Moore BA, PGCE
Type: Coeducational Day & Boarding
Age range: 3–13
No. of pupils: 284
Fees: Day £2985–£13,485 FB £18,300

Glenhurst School

16 Beechworth Road, Havant, Hampshire PO9 1AX
Tel: 023 9248 4054
Principal: Mrs E M Haines
Type: Coeducational Day
Age range: 3 months–8 years
No. of pupils: B50 G50
Fees: Day £4500

Hampshire Collegiate Junior School

Embley Park, Romsey, Hampshire SO51 6ZE
Tel: 01794 515737
Headteacher: Mrs Elaine Hooton BA, PGCE, FRGS
Type: Coeducational Day
Age range: 3–11
No. of pupils: 300 B60 G240
Fees: Day £6747–£7539

Hampshire Collegiate School

Embley Park, Romsey, Hampshire SO51 6ZE
Tel: 01794 512206
Principal: Hector McDonald
Type: Coeducational Day & Boarding
Age range: 11–18
No. of pupils: 850 B375 G475 VIth100
Fees: Day £10,800 WB £19,800 FB £19,800

Highfield School

Liphook, Hampshire GU30 7LQ
Tel: 01428 728000
Headmaster: Mr Philip Evitt MA
Type: Coeducational Boarding & Day
Age range: 8–13
No. of pupils: B114 G105
Fees: Day £10,800–£14,100 FB £14,100–£16,050

Hill Head Preparatory School

51 Crofton Lane, Hill Head, Fareham,
Hampshire PO14 3LW
Tel: 01329 662666
Headmistress: Mrs B M A Barber BEd(Hons), CertEd
Type: Coeducational Day
Age range: 2–8
No. of pupils: 55 B24 G31
Fees: Day £2400–£2700

Hordle Walhampton School

Walhampton, Lymington, Hampshire SO41 5ZG
Tel: 01590 672013
Headmaster: R H C Phillips BA(Hons), CertEd, LGSM
Type: Coeducational Day & Boarding
Age range: 2–13
No. of pupils: B177 G159
Fees: Day £5970–£11,940 FB £15,720

Kings School Senior

Lakesmere House, Allington Lane, Fair Oak, Eastleigh,
Hampshire SO50 7DB
Tel: 023 8060 0956
Head Teacher: Mrs Ruth Pierson
Type: Coeducational Day
Age range: 11–16
No. of pupils: 112 B67 G45
Fees: Day £4200

Kingscourt School

Catherington Lane, Catherington, Hampshire PO8 9NJ
Tel: 023 9259 3251
Headmistress: Mrs J L Easton
Type: Coeducational Day
Age range: 2¾–11
No. of pupils: B80 G80
Fees: Day £5430

Lord Wandsworth College
Long Sutton, Hook, Hampshire RG29 1TB
Tel: 01256 862201
Headmaster: Mr Fergus Livingstone MA(Oxon)
Type: Coeducational Boarding & Day
Age range: 11–18
No. of pupils: 530 VIth160
Fees: Day £16,623–£17,511 WB £22,263–£23,496
FB £22,263–£24,681
(👫) (🌍) (Ⓐ) (🏛) (✏) (16+)

Marycourt School
27 Crescent Road, Alverstoke, Gosport,
Hampshire PO12 2DJ
Tel: 023 9258 1766
Headteacher: Mrs Jane Norman BEd
Type: Coeducational Day
Age range: 3–11
No. of pupils: B40 G42
Fees: Day £2550–£4658
(👫)

Meoncross School
Burnt House Lane, Stubbington, Fareham,
Hampshire PO14 2EF
Tel: 01329 662182
Headmaster: Mr Adrian Steele
Type: Coeducational Day
Age range: 2¾–16
No. of pupils: 405
Fees: Day £5940–£8835
(👫) (£) (✏)

Moyles Court School
Moyles Court, Ringwood, Hampshire BH24 3NF
Tel: 01425 472856
Headmaster: Mr Dean
Type: Coeducational Day & Boarding
Age range: 3–16
No. of pupils: B83 G63
Fees: Day £3285–£4650 FB £6690–£7740
(👫) (🌍) (🏛)

Nethercliffe School
Hatherley Road, Winchester, Hampshire SO22 6RS
Tel: 01962 854570
Headmaster: Mr R F G Whitfield TCert
Type: Coeducational Day
Age range: 3–11
No. of pupils: 145 B84 G61
Fees: Day £2301–£4731
(👫) (✏)

Prince's Mead School
Worthy Park House, Kings Worthy, Winchester,
Hampshire SO21 1AN
Tel: 01962 888000
Headmistress: Miss P S Kirk
Type: Coeducational Day
Age range: 3–11
No. of pupils: 235 B85 G150
Fees: Day £8700–£10,500
(👫) (£) (✏)

Ringwood Waldorf School
Folly Farm Lane, Ashley, Ringwood, Hampshire BH24 2NN
Tel: 01425 472664
Type: Coeducational Day
Age range: 3–16
No. of pupils: B125 G100
Fees: Day £1500–£6000
(👫) (£) (✏)

Rookesbury Park School
Wickham, Hampshire PO17 6HT
Tel: 01329 833108
Head: Mrs P Harris-Burland
Type: Coeducational Day & Boarding
Age range: 3–13
No. of pupils: 90 B45 G45
Fees: Day £3000–£10,500 FB £18,000
(👫) (🏛) (£) (✏)

Rookwood School
Weyhill Road, Andover, Hampshire SP10 3AL
Tel: 01264 325900
Headmistress: Mrs M P Langley BSc(Hons)
Type: Coeducational Day & Boarding
Age range: 3–16
No. of pupils: B120 G189
Fees: Day £6885–£11,340 FB £17,340–£20,295
(👫) (🌍) (🏛) (£) (✏)

Salesian College
Reading Road, Farnborough, Hampshire GU14 6PA
Tel: 01252 893000
Headmaster: Mr P A Wilson BA(Hons), MA, CertEd
Type: Boys' Day
Age range: 16–18 B11–18
No. of pupils: 600 B590 G10 VIth100
Fees: Day £8300
(👨) (Ⓐ) (£) (✏) (16+)

Sherborne House School

Lakewood Road, Chandlers Ford, Eastleigh,
Hampshire SO53 1EU
Tel: 023 8025 2440
Headmistress: Mrs Heather Hopson-Hill
Type: Coeducational Day
Age range: 2 3/4–11
No. of pupils: 257 B120 G137
Fees: Day £1761–£6885

Sherfield

Sherfield-on-Loddon, Hook, Hampshire RG27 0HT
Tel: 01256 884 800
Executive Principal: Professor Pat Preedy
Type: Coeducational Day
Age range: 3 months–18 years
No. of pupils: 517 B277 G247 VIth16
Fees: Day £6570–£11,724

St Neot's School

St Neot's Road, Eversley, Hook, Hampshire RG27 0PN
Tel: 0118 973 2118
Headmaster: Mr R J Thorp BA(Dunelm), PGCE(Cantab)
Type: Coeducational Day & Boarding
Age range: 3 months–13 years
No. of pupils: B150 G100
Fees: Day £5040–£11,250 WB £13,905

St Nicholas School

Redfields House, Redfields Lane, Church Crookham, Fleet,
Hampshire GU13 0RE
Tel: 01252 850121
Headmistress: Mrs A V Whatmough BA, CertEd
Type: Girls' Day
Age range: B3–7 G3–16
No. of pupils: 415 B16 G399
Fees: Day £3843–£10,440

St Swithun's Junior School

Alresford Road, Winchester, Hampshire SO21 1HA
Tel: 01962 835750
Headmistress: Mrs P Grimes BA(Hons)
Type: Coeducational Day
Age range: B3–7 G3–11
No. of pupils: 186 B22 G164
Fees: Day £3510–£9000

St Swithun's School

Alresford Road, Winchester, Hampshire SO21 1HA
Tel: 01962 835700
Headmistress: Dr H L Harvey BSc, PhD(London)
Type: Girls' Boarding & Day
Age range: 11–18
No. of pupils: 482 VIth120
Fees: Day £14,400 FB £23,745

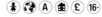

Stanbridge Earls School

Stanbridge Lane, Romsey, Hampshire SO51 0ZS
Tel: 01794 529400
Head: Mr G Link CertEd, MEd
Type: Coeducational Boarding & Day
Age range: 10–19
No. of pupils: 176 B144 G32 VIth46
Fees: Day £14,232–£15,489 FB £19,095–£20,895

Stockton House School

Stockton Avenue, Fleet, Hampshire GU13 8NS
Tel: 01252 616323
Early Years Manager: Mrs Sally Forrest
Type: Coeducational Day
Age range: 2–6
No. of pupils: B35 G35
Fees: Day £1020–£3720

The Grey House School

Mount Pleasant, Hartley Wintney, Hampshire RG27 8PW
Tel: 01252 842353
Head: Mrs C E Allen BEd(Cantab)
Type: Coeducational Day
Age range: 4–11+
No. of pupils: B93 G50
Fees: Day £6450–£8094

The King's School

Basingstoke Community Church, Sarum Hill, Basingstoke,
Hampshire RG21 8SR
Tel: 01256 467092
Headteacher: Mr David Robotham
Type: Coeducational Day
Age range: 7–16
No. of pupils: 172 B99 G73

The Pilgrims' School

3 The Close, Winchester, Hampshire SO23 9LT
Tel: 01962 854189
Headmaster: Rev Dr Brian Rees BA, BD, DipMin, PhD
Type: Boys' Boarding & Day
Age range: 4–13
No. of pupils: 204
Fees: Day £14,205 FB £17,970

The Stroud School

Highwood House, Highwood Lane, Romsey,
Hampshire SO51 9ZH
Tel: 01794 513231
Headmaster: Mr Alastair J L Dodds MA(Cantab)
Type: Coeducational Day
Age range: 3–13
No. of pupils: B170 G135
Fees: Day £3323–£11,985

Twyford School

Twyford, Winchester, Hampshire SO21 1NW
Tel: 01962 712269
Headmaster: Dr D Livingstone BSc, PhD
Type: Coeducational Day & Boarding
Age range: 3–13
No. of pupils: 361 B215 G146
Fees: Day £3960–14,085 WB £18,195

West Hill Park Preparatory School

Titchfield, Fareham, Hampshire PO14 4BS
Tel: 01329 842356
Headmaster: E P K Hudson CertEd
Type: Coeducational Boarding & Day
Age range: 2½–13
No. of pupils: B180 G108
Fees: Day £7935–£13,410 FB £17,598

Winchester Christian School

86 Stanmore Lane, Winchester, Hampshire SO22 4BT
Tel: 077 66 111 496
Type: Coeducational Day
Age range: 4–11
No. of pupils: 28 B11 G17
Fees: Day £2340

Winchester College

College Street, Winchester, Hampshire SO23 9NA
Tel: 01962 621247
Headmaster: R D Townsend MA, DPhil
Type: Boys' Boarding & Day
Age range: 13–18
No. of pupils: 680 VIth280
Fees: Day £27,405 FB £28,845

Wykeham House School

East Street, Fareham, Hampshire PO16 0BW
Tel: 01329 280178
Headmistress: Mrs L Clarke BSc(Hons), PGCE, PGDip
Type: Girls' Day
Age range: 2¾–16
No. of pupils: 250
Fees: Day £9000

Yateley Manor School

51 Reading Road, Yateley, Hampshire GU46 7UQ
Tel: 01252 405500
Headmaster: Mr R J Williams MA(Hons)Edinburgh, PGCE
Bedford
Type: Coeducational Day
Age range: 3–13
No. of pupils: 453 B287 G166
Fees: Day £3900–£10,752

HERTFORDSHIRE

Abbot's Hill School

Bunkers Lane, Hemel Hempstead, Hertfordshire HP3 8RP
Tel: 01442 240333
Headmistress: Mrs K Lewis MA(Cantab), BSc(Open), PGCE,
FRSA, MIMgt
Type: Girls' Day
Age range: B3–5 G3–16
No. of pupils: 472
Fees: Day £1734–£13,320

Aldenham School

Elstree, Hertfordshire WD6 3AJ
Tel: 01923 858122
Headmaster: J C Fowler MA
Type: Coeducational Boarding & Day
Age range: 3–18
No. of pupils: 700 B550 G150 VIth160
Fees: Day £11,874–£17,085 FB £17,784–£24,837

Aldwickbury School

Wheathampstead Road, Harpenden,
Hertfordshire AL5 1AD
Tel: 01582 713022
Headmaster: Mr V W Hales
Type: Boys' Day & Boarding
Age range: 4–13
No. of pupils: 310
Fees: Day £2002–£3012 WB £3800–£3884

Beechwood Park

Markyate, St Albans, Hertfordshire AL3 8AW
Tel: 01582 840333
Headmaster: Mr P C E Atkinson BSc(Hons), MIBiol, PGCE
Type: Coeducational Day & Boarding
Age range: 2½–13
No. of pupils: 495 B294 G201
Fees: Day £8844–£12,096 WB £15,375

Berkhamsted School

133 High Street, Berkhamsted, Hertfordshire HP4 2DJ
Tel: 01442 358000
Principal: Mr Mark Steed MA(Cantab), MA
Type: Coeducational Boarding & Day
Age range: 3–18
No. of pupils: 1518 B846 G672
Fees: Day £6900–£15,582 FB £22,461–£24,792

Bhaktivedanta Manor School

Hilfield Lane, Aldenham, Watford,
Hertfordshire WD25 8EZ
Tel: 01923 851000 Ext241
Administrator: Mrs Wendy Harrison
Type: Coeducational Day
Age range: 4½–12
No. of pupils: 30 B15 G15
Fees: Day £1200

Bishop's Stortford College

10 Maze Green Road, Bishop's Stortford,
Hertfordshire CM23 2PJ
Tel: 01279 838575
Headmaster: Mr John Trotman
Type: Coeducational Day & Boarding
Age range: 13–18
No. of pupils: B297 G213 VIth213
Fees: Day £13,950 WB £19,392 FB £19,587–£19,776

Bishop's Stortford College Junior School

Maze Green Road, Bishop's Stortford,
Hertfordshire CM23 2PH
Tel: 01279 838607
Head of Junior School: J A Greathead BEd
Type: Coeducational Day & Boarding
Age range: 4–13
No. of pupils: B300 G246
Fees: Day £6522–£11,160 WB £13,512–£14,697
FB £13,647–£14,991

C K H R Immanuel College

87/91 Elstree Road, Bushey, Hertfordshire WD23 4BE
Tel: 020 8950 0604
Headmaster: Mr Philip Skelker MA
Type: Coeducational Day
Age range: 11–18
No. of pupils: 520 B263 G257 VIth127
Fees: Day £10,995

Duncombe School

4 Warren Park Road, Bengeo, Hertford,
Hertfordshire SG14 3JA
Tel: 01992 414100
Headmistress: Mrs Verity White BEd
Type: Coeducational Day
Age range: 2–11
No. of pupils: 322 B166 G156
Fees: Day £2916–£10,125

Edge Grove School

Aldenham Village, Hertfordshire WD2 8BL
Tel: 01923 855724
Headmaster: Mr Michael Davies
Type: Coeducational Boarding & Day
Age range: 3–13
No. of pupils: 384 B253 G131
Fees: Day £4245–£12,555 FB £14,025–£17,115

Egerton Rothesay School

Durrants Lane, Berkhamsted, Hertfordshire HP4 3UJ
Tel: 01442 877060
Headteacher: Mrs N I Boddam-Whetham BA(Hons), PGTC
Type: Coeducational Day
Age range: 5–16
No. of pupils: 200
Fees: Day £10,725–£22,170

Francis House Preparatory School
Aylesbury Road, Tring, Hertfordshire HP23 4DL
Tel: 01442 822315
Head: Mrs Janice Hiley
Type: Coeducational Day
Age range: 2–11
No. of pupils: 113 B55 G58
Fees: Day £630–£2365

Haberdashers' Aske's School
Butterfly Lane, Elstree, Borehamwood,
Hertfordshire WD6 3AF
Tel: 020 8266 1700
Headmaster: Mr P B Hamilton MA
Type: Boys' Day
Age range: 5–18
No. of pupils: 1402 VIth310
Fees: Day £9675–£12,885

Haberdashers' Aske's School for Girls
Aldenham Road, Elstree, Borehamwood,
Hertfordshire WD6 3BT
Tel: 020 8266 2300
Headmistress: Mrs E J Radice MA(Oxon)
Type: Girls' Day
Age range: 4–18
No. of pupils: 1141
Fees: Day £8802–£10,686

Haileybury
Haileybury, Hertford, Hertfordshire SG13 7NU
Tel: +44 (0)1992 706200
The Master: J S Davies MA(Cantab)
Type: Coeducational Boarding & Day
Age range: 11–18
No. of pupils: 759
Fees: Day £12,852–£19,338 FB £16,332–£25,749

Haresfoot School
Chesham Road, Berkhamsted, Hertfordshire HP4 2SZ
Tel: 01442 872742
Principal: Mrs Carole Hawkins BA, PGCE
Type: Coeducational Day
Age range: 0–11
No. of pupils: B98 G90
Fees: Day £1845–£7770

Heath Mount School
Woodhall Park, Watton-at-Stone, Hertford,
Hertfordshire SG14 3NG
Tel: 01920 830230
Headmaster: Rev H J Matthews MA, BSc, PGCE
Type: Coeducational Day & Boarding
Age range: 3–13
No. of pupils: B207 G153
Fees: Day £2715–£9315 WB £12,630–£12,960

Howe Green House School
Great Hallingbury, Bishops Stortford,
Hertfordshire CM22 7UF
Tel: 01279 657706
Headmaster: Mr Graham R Gorton BA(Hons), PGCE
Type: Coeducational Day
Age range: 2–11
No. of pupils: B82 G72
Fees: Day £5427–£8622

Kingshott
St Ippolyts, Hitchin, Hertfordshire SG4 7JX
Tel: 01462 432009
Headmaster: Mr Iain Gilmont
Type: Coeducational Day
Age range: 4–13
No. of pupils: B237 G100
Fees: Day £7725–£9345

Little Acorns Montessori School
Lincolnsfield Centre, Bushey Hall Drive, Bushey,
Hertfordshire WD23 2ER
Tel: 01923 230705
Head of School: Lola Davies BPA, AMIDip
Type: Coeducational Day
Age range: 2½–6
No. of pupils: 28
Fees: Day £2120

Lochinver House School
Heath Road, Little Heath, Potters Bar,
Hertfordshire EN6 1LW
Tel: 01707 653064
Headmaster: Jeremy Gear BEd(Hons)
Type: Boys' Day
Age range: 4–13
No. of pupils: 344
Fees: Day £8301–£10,875

Lockers Park School
Lockers Park Lane, Hemel Hempstead,
Hertfordshire HP1 1TL
Tel: 01442 251712
Headmaster: Mr H J Wickham
Type: Boys' Boarding & Day
Age range: 5–13+
No. of pupils: 142
Fees: Day £7500–£13,890 FB £17,190

Longwood School
Bushey Hall Drive, Bushey, Hertfordshire WD23 2QG
Tel: 01923 253715
Head Teacher: Mrs Muriel Garman
Type: Coeducational Day
Age range: 3–11
No. of pupils: B56 G44
Fees: Day £4590–£5790

Manor Lodge School
Rectory Lane, Ridge Hill, Shenley, Hertfordshire WD7 9BG
Tel: 01707 642424
Headmistress: Mrs Judith Smart CertEd, BA(Open)
Type: Coeducational Day
Age range: 3–11
No. of pupils: 382 B215 G205
Fees: Day £7560–£8820

Northwood Preparatory School
Moor Farm, Sandy Lodge Road, Rickmansworth,
Hertfordshire WD3 1LW
Tel: 01923 825648
Headmaster: Dr T D Lee BEd(Hons)
Type: Boys' Day
Age range: 4–13 G3+ only
No. of pupils: 300
Fees: Day £2613–£9414

Princess Helena College
Preston, Hitchin, Hertfordshire SG4 7RT
Tel: 01462 432100
Headmistress: Mrs Jo-Anne Duncan
Type: Girls' Boarding & Day
Age range: 11–18
No. of pupils: 158 VIth40
Fees: Day £12,540–£15,840 FB £17,910–£22 875

Queenswood
Shepherd's Way, Brookmans Park, Hatfield,
Hertfordshire AL9 6NS
Tel: 01707 602500
Principal: Mrs P C Edgar BA(Hons) London, PGCE
Type: Girls' Boarding & Day
Age range: 11–18
No. of pupils: 410 VIth109
Fees: Day £18,015–£19,680 FB £23,370–£25,485

Radlett Preparatory School
Kendal Hall, Watling Street, Radlett,
Hertfordshire WD7 7LY
Tel: 01923 856812
Principal: Mr W N Warren BEd(Hons), FCollP
Type: Coeducational Day
Age range: 4–11
No. of pupils: B240 G225
Fees: Day £6540–£6840

Redemption Academy
PO Box 352, Stevenage, Hertfordshire SG1 9AG
Tel: 01438 727370
Headteacher: Mrs S J Neale
Type: Coeducational Day
Age range: 2–16
No. of pupils: 41 B16 G25
Fees: Day £2400–£2880

Rickmansworth PNEU School
88 The Drive, Rickmansworth, Hertfordshire WD3 4DU
Tel: 01923 772101
Headmistress: Mrs S J Hayes BA(Hons)
Type: Girls' Day
Age range: 3–11
No. of pupils: 150
Fees: Day £2610–£9000

Rudolf Steiner School
Langley Hill, Kings Langley, Hertfordshire WD4 9HG
Tel: 01923 262505
Type: Coeducational Day
Age range: 3–19
No. of pupils: 405
Fees: Day £2985–£7800

Sherrardswood School

Lockleys, Welwyn, Hertfordshire AL6 0BJ
Tel: 01438 714282
Headmistress: Mrs L Corry
Type: Coeducational Day
Age range: 2–18
No. of pupils: 357 B220 G175
Fees: Day £6720–£12,750

St Albans High School for Girls

Townsend Avenue, St Albans, Hertfordshire AL1 3SJ
Tel: 01727 853800
Headmistress: Mrs Rosemary Martin MEd, NPQH, FRSA
Type: Girls' Day
Age range: 4–18
No. of pupils: 940 VIth170
Fees: Day £9015–£11,460

St Albans School

Abbey Gateway, St Albans, Hertfordshire AL3 4HB
Tel: 01727 855521
Headmaster: Mr A R Grant MA(Cantab), FRSA
Type: Boys' Day
Age range: B11–18 G16–18
No. of pupils: 774 B740 G34 VIth272
Fees: Day £12,690

St Andrew's Montessori Prep School

Garston Manor, High Elms Lane, Watford,
Hertfordshire WD25 0JX
Tel: 01923 681103
Headmistress: Mrs Sheila O'Neill MontDipDist, TCert, BA,
AMI Dip
Type: Coeducational Day
Age range: 6 months–11 years
No. of pupils: 90 B45 G45
Fees: Day £380–£8000

St Christopher School

Barrington Road, Letchworth, Hertfordshire SG6 3JZ
Tel: 01462 650 850
Head: Richard Palmer
Type: Coeducational Day & Boarding
Age range: 2½–18 B3–18 G3–18
No. of pupils: B307 G196 VIth78
Fees: Day £3270–£14,040 FB £19,050–£24,645

St Columba's College

King Harry Lane, St Albans, Hertfordshire AL3 4AW
Tel: 01727 855185
Head Master: David R Buxton
Type: Boys' Day
Age range: B4–18
No. of pupils: 850 B850 VIth150
Fees: Day £8235–£10,416

St Columba's College Prep School

King Harry Lane, St Albans, Hertfordshire AL3 4AW
Tel: 01727 862616
Head of Prep: Mrs Ruth Loveman
Type: Boys' Day
Age range: 4–11
No. of pupils: 230
Fees: Day £8235–£9294

St Edmund's College

Old Hall Green, Nr Ware, Hertfordshire SG11 1DS
Tel: 01920 821504
Headmaster: Mr Chris Long BA
Type: Coeducational Day & Boarding
Age range: 3–18
No. of pupils: 814 B514 G300 VIth158
Fees: Day £8550–£13,680 WB £17,625–£20,070
FB £19,425–£22,215

St Francis' College

The Broadway, Letchworth, Hertfordshire SG6 3PJ
Tel: 01462 670511
Headmistress: Miss M Hegarty BA, HDipEd, DHS
Type: Girls' Day & Boarding
Age range: 3–18+
No. of pupils: 500 VIth62
Fees: Day £4920–£9585 WB £13,245–£15,855
FB £16,275–£18,855

St Hilda's School

28 Douglas Road, Harpenden, Hertfordshire AL5 2ES
Tel: 01582 712307
Headmistress: Mrs C Godlee
Type: Girls' Day
Age range: 3–11
No. of pupils: 163
Fees: Day £1320–£7872

St Hilda's School
High Street, Bushey, Hertfordshire WD23 3DA
Tel: 020 8950 1751
Headmistress: Mrs Loraine Cavanagh
Type: Girls' Day
Age range: B3–5 G3–11
No. of pupils: 142 B6 G136
Fees: Day £4635–£8685

St Hugh's School
Old Hall Green, Ware, Hertfordshire SG11 1DS
Tel: 01920 824239
Head: Mr L J Blom BEd(Hons), BA, NPQH, HDE PhysEd
Type: Coeducational Day
Age range: 3–11
No. of pupils: 187 B117 G71
Fees: Day £2480–£3715

St John's Preparatory School
The Ridgeway, Potters Bar, Hertfordshire EN6 5QT
Tel: 01707 657294
Headmistress: Mrs C Tardios BA(Hons)
Type: Coeducational Day
Age range: 4–11
No. of pupils: B112 G91
Fees: Day £7140–£7680

St Joseph's In The Park
St Mary's Lane, Hertingfordbury, Hertford, Hertfordshire SG14 2LX
Tel: 01992 581378
Headmaster: Mr Neil Jones
Type: Coeducational Day
Age range: 3–11 B3–11 G3–11
No. of pupils: B94 G84
Fees: Day £4971–£13,629

Stanborough School
Stanborough Park, Garston, Watford, Hertfordshire WD25 9JT
Tel: 01923 673268
Head: Mr Roger Murphy
Type: Coeducational Day & Boarding
Age range: 3–19
No. of pupils: 300 B128 G172 VIth20
Fees: Day £3660–£5500 WB £12,834–£15,846

Stormont
The Causeway, Potters Bar, Hertfordshire EN6 5HA
Tel: 01707 654037
Headmistress: Mrs M E Johnston BA(Hons), PGCE
Type: Girls' Day
Age range: 4–11
No. of pupils: 168 G168
Fees: Day £9030–£9495

The Christian School (Takeley)
Dunmow Road, Brewers End, Takeley, Bishop's Stortford, Hertfordshire CM22 6QH
Tel: 01279 871182
Headmaster: M E Humphries
Type: Coeducational Day
Age range: 5–16
No. of pupils: B23 G22
Fees: Day £3720

The King's School
Elmfield, Ambrose Lane, Harpenden, Hertfordshire AL5 4DU
Tel: 01582 767566
Principal: Mr Clive John Case BA, HDE
Type: Coeducational Day
Age range: 5–16
No. of pupils: B101 G94
Fees: Day £4380

The Purcell School, London
Aldenham Road, Bushey, Hertfordshire WD2 3TS
Tel: 01923 331100
Headmaster: Mr Peter Crook MA, BMus, ARAM, ARCO
Type: Coeducational Day & Boarding
Age range: 8–18
No. of pupils: 167 B57 G110 VIth70
Fees: WB £22,452 FB £28,716

The Royal Masonic School for Girls
Rickmansworth Park, Rickmansworth, Hertfordshire WD3 4HF
Tel: 01923 773168
Headmistress: Mrs Diana Rose MA(Cantab)
Type: Girls' Day & Boarding
Age range: 4–18
No. of pupils: 810
Fees: Day £7170–£13,380 WB £12,510–£20,865
FB £12,720–£21,390

Tring Park School for the Performing Arts

Tring Park, Tring, Hertfordshire HP23 5LX
Tel: 01442 824255
Principal: Mr Stefan Anderson MA, ARCM, ARCT
Type: Coeducational Boarding & Day
Age range: 8–19
No. of pupils: 294 B72 G222 VIth107
Fees: Day £12,600–£19,710 FB £19,485–£27,525

Westbrook Hay Prep School

London Road, Hemel Hempstead, Hertfordshire HP1 2RF
Tel: 01442 256143
Headmaster: Keith D Young BEd(Hons)
Type: Coeducational Day & Weekly Boarding
Age range: 3–13
No. of pupils: 285 B190 G95
Fees: Day £6735–£11,445

York House School

Redheath, Sarratt Road, Croxley Green, Rickmansworth, Hertfordshire WD3 4LW
Tel: 01923 772395
Headmaster: Peter MacDougall BEd(Hons)
Type: Boys' Day
Age range: 2½–13
No. of pupils: 280
Fees: Day £10,020

KENT

ASHFORD SCHOOL
For further details see p. 85

East Hill, Ashford, Kent TN24 8PB
Tel: 01233 739030
Email: registrar@ashfordschool.co.uk
Website: www.ashfordschool.co.uk
Head: Mr M R Buchanan BSc(Hons), CertEd, NPQH, CPhys
Type: Coeducational Day & Boarding
Age range: 3 months–18 years
No. of pupils: 724
Fees: Day £5850–£13,530 FB £21,810–£24,615

Beech Grove School

Beech Grove Bruderhof, Sandwich Road, Nonington, Dover, Kent CT15 4HH
Tel: 01304 842980
Head: Mr Benjamin Shirky
Type: Coeducational Day
Age range: 4–14
No. of pupils: 63 B33 G30

Beechwood Sacred Heart

12 Pembury Road, Tunbridge Wells, Kent TN2 3QD
Tel: 01892 532747
Headmaster: Mr Nicholas Beesley MA(Oxon)
Type: Coeducational Day & Boarding School
Age range: 3–18
No. of pupils: B141 G272 VIth55
Fees: Day £6855–£14,100 WB £16,740–£20,745
FB £19,425–£23,400

Bell Bedgebury International School

Bedgebury Park, Goudhurst, Cranbrook, Kent TN17 2SH
Tel: 01580 879100
Head: Eric Squires
Type: Coeducational Boarding
Age range: 12–19
Fees: FB £24,900

Benenden School

Cranbrook, Kent TN17 4AA
Tel: 01580 240592
Headmistress: Mrs C M Oulton MA(Oxon)
Type: Girls' Boarding
Age range: 11–18
No. of pupils: 520 VIth186
Fees: FB £26,100

Bethany School

Goudhurst, Cranbrook, Kent TN17 1LB
Tel: 01580 211273
Headmaster: Mr N D B Dorey MA(Cantab)
Type: Coeducational Boarding & Day
Age range: 11–18
No. of pupils: B293 G136 VIth128
Fees: Day £14,184 WB £21,504 FB £22,143

Bronte School

Mayfield, 7 Pelham Road, Gravesend, Kent DA11 0HN
Tel: 01474 533805
Headmaster: Mr R Dyson
Type: Coeducational Day
Age range: 3–11
No. of pupils: 120 B70 G50
Fees: Day £3930–£6210

Bryony School
Marshall Road, Rainham, Gillingham, Kent ME3 OAJ
Tel: 01634 231511
Joint Heads: D E and Mrs M P Edmunds
Type: Coeducational Day
Age range: 2–11
No. of pupils: 210 B108 G102
Fees: Day £3979–£4422

Canterbury Steiner School
Garlinge Green, Chartham, Canterbury, Kent CT4 5=U
Tel: 01227 738285
Type: Coeducational Day
Age range: 3–18
No. of pupils: B112 G121
Fees: Day £3246–£4406

Chartfield School
45 Minster Road, Westgate on Sea, Kent CT8 8DA
Tel: 01843 831716
Head & Proprietor: Miss L P Shipley
Type: Coeducational Day
Age range: 4–11
No. of pupils: 50 B25 G25
Fees: Day £2580–£3000

Cobham Hall School
Cobham, Gravesend, Kent DA12 3BL
Tel: 01474 823371
Headmaster: Mr Paul Mitchell BSc
Type: Girls' Boarding & Day
Age range: 11–18
No. of pupils: 200 VIth60
Fees: Day £13,500–£16,950 FB £20,250–£25,500

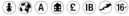

Combe Bank School
Sundridge, Sevenoaks, Kent TN14 6AE
Tel: 01959 563720
Head: Mrs J Abbotts MEd, NPQH
Type: Girls' Day School with Coeducational Nursery
Age range: B3–5 G3–18
No. of pupils: 418 B18 G400 VIth50
Fees: Day £7170–£12,840

Derwent Lodge School for Girls
Somerhill, Tonbridge, Kent TN11 0NJ
Tel: 01732 352124
Headmistress: Mrs S Michau MA(Oxon), PGCE
Type: Girls' Day
Age range: 7–11
No. of pupils: 144
Fees: Day £11,115

Dover College
Effingham Crescent, Dover, Kent CT17 9RH
Tel: 01304 205969 Ext 201
Headmaster: Stephen Jones
Type: Coeducational Boarding & Day
Age range: 3–18
No. of pupils: 340 B170 G170 VIth100
Fees: Day £5940–£12,585 WB £17,304–£20,622
FB £14,493–£25,437

Dulwich Preparatory School
Coursehorn, Cranbrook, Kent TN17 3NP
Tel: 01580 712179
Acting Headmaster: Roger Kidney BA(Hons), PGCE
Type: Coeducational Preparatory
Age range: 3–13
No. of pupils: B289 G234
Fees: Day £4404–£12,915

Elliott Park School
18-20 Marina Drive, Minster, Sheerness, Kent ME12 2DP
Tel: 01795 873372
Head: Mr R Barson
Type: Coeducational Day
Age range: 4–11
No. of pupils: 60
Fees: Day £3897

FOSSE BANK SCHOOL
For further details see p. 75
Mountains, Noble Tree Road, Hildenborough, Tonbridge,
Kent TN11 8ND
Tel: 01732 834212
Email: office@fossebankschool.co.uk
Website: www.fossebankschool.co.uk
Headmistress: Mrs Lovatt-Young
Type: Coeducational Day
Age range: 3–11
No. of pupils: 124 B74 G50
Fees: Day £6300–£8655

Haddon Dene School

57 Gladstone Road, Broadstairs, Kent CT10 2HY
Tel: 01843 861176
Head: Mr Alexander
Type: Coeducational Day
Age range: 3–11
No. of pupils: 200 B105 G95
Fees: Day £4950–£6135

Hilden Grange School

62 Dry Hill Park Road, Tonbridge, Kent TN10 3BX
Tel: 01732 352706
Headmaster: Mr J Withers BA(Hons)
Type: Coeducational Day
Age range: 3–13
No. of pupils: B200 G100
Fees: Day £3600–£9900

Hilden Oaks School

38 Dry Hill Park Road, Tonbridge, Kent TN10 3BU
Tel: 01732 353941
Headmistress: Mrs S A Sunderland
Type: Coeducational Day
Age range: B0–7 G0–11
No. of pupils: B24 G129
Fees: Day £6315–£8805

Holmewood House School

Langton Green, Tunbridge Wells, Kent TN3 0EB
Tel: 01892 860000
Headmaster: Mr A S R Corbett MA
Type: Coeducational Day & Weekly Boarding
Age range: 3–13 B3–13 G3–13
No. of pupils: 440 B260 G180
Fees: Day £5165–£15,165

Junior King's School

Milner Court, Sturry, Canterbury, Kent CT2 0AY
Tel: 01227 714000
Headmaster: Mr P M Wells BEd
Type: Coeducational Boarding & Day
Age range: 3–13
No. of pupils: 401 B221 G180
Fees: Day £5490–£13,230 WB £17,880 FB £17,880

Kent College

Whitstable Road, Canterbury, Kent CT2 9DT
Tel: 01227 763231
Head Master: Dr D J Lamper
Type: Coeducational Day & Boarding
Age range: 11–18
No. of pupils: 465 B270 G195 VIth157
Fees: Day £14,000–£14,541 WB £23,000–£23,340
FB £24,690–£25,026

Kent College Infant & Junior School

Vernon Holme, Harbledown, Canterbury, Kent CT2 9AQ
Tel: 01227 762436
Headmaster: Mr A J Carter
Type: Coeducational Day & Boarding
Age range: 3–11
No. of pupils: 190 B101 G89
Fees: Day £6465–£9615 WB £14,196 FB £14,196

KENT COLLEGE PEMBURY
For further details see p. 93

Old Church Road, Pembury, Tunbridge Wells,
Kent TN2 4AX
Tel: 01892 822006
Email: admissions@kentcollege.kent.sch.uk
Website: www.kent-college.co.uk
Headmistress: Mrs Sally-Anne Huang MA(Oxon), PGCE
Type: Girls' Day & Boarding
Age range: 3–18
No. of pupils: 524 VIth88
Fees: Day £7047–£15,474 FB £19,182–£24,945

Linton Park School

3 Eccleston Road, Tovil, Maidstone, Kent ME17 4HT
Tel: 01622 740820
Headteacher: Mr C Allen
Type: Coeducational Day
Age range: 7–18
No. of pupils: 134 B80 G54

Lorenden Preparatory School

Painter's Forstal, Faversham, Kent ME13 0EN
Tel: 01795 590030
Headmistress: Mrs P Tebbit CertEd, DipPrimEng(Adu)
Type: Coeducational Day
Age range: 3–11
No. of pupils: 100 B50 G50
Fees: Day £3060–£8142

Marlborough House School
High Street, Hawkhurst, Kent TN18 4PY
Tel: 01580 753555
Headmaster: Mr David N Hopkins MA(Oxon), PGCE
Type: Coeducational Day & Weekly Boarding
Age range: 3–13
No. of pupils: B193 G135
Fees: Day £3540–£12,285

Meredale Independent Primary School
Solomon Road, Rainham, Gillingham, Kent ME8 8EE
Tel: 01634 231405
Headteacher: Miss Michelle Ingledew
Type: Coeducational Day
Age range: 3–11
No. of pupils: 50 B34 G16
Fees: Day £4800

Northbourne Park School
Betteshanger, Deal, Kent CT14 0NW
Tel: 01304 611215/218
Headmaster: Mr Edward Balfour
Type: Coeducational Day & Boarding
Age range: 3–13
No. of pupils: 185 B95 G90
Fees: Day £7200–£12,750 WB £15,210–£17.340
FB £16,260–£20,400

Oakwood School
Bowles Well Gardens, Folkestone, Kent CT19 6PQ
Tel: 01303 240033
Headteacher: Mrs P Triffitt
Type: Coeducational Day
Age range: 3–18
No. of pupils: 57 B26 G31

Rose Hill School
Coniston Avenue, Tunbridge Wells, Kent TN4 9SY
Tel: 01892 525591
Headmaster: Mr D Westcombe BA, PGCE
Type: Coeducational Day
Age range: 3–13
No. of pupils: 310 B170 G140
Fees: Day £4200–£11,355

Russell House School
Station Road, Otford, Sevenoaks, Kent TN14 5QU
Tel: 01959 522352
Headmistress: Mrs Alison Cooke
Type: Coeducational Day
Age range: 2–11
No. of pupils: B96 G97
Fees: Day £4050–£8400

Sackville School
Tonbridge Rd, Hildenborough, Tonbridge, Kent TN11 9HN
Tel: 01732 838888
Headteacher: Mrs M Sinclair MA
Type: Coeducational Day
Age range: 11–18
No. of pupils: B171 G38 VIth18
Fees: Day £8250–£9825

Saint Ronan's School
Water Lane, Hawkhurst, Kent TN18 5DJ
Tel: 01580 752271
Headmaster: William Trelawny-Vernon BSc(Hons)
Type: Coeducational Day & Boarding Preparatory School
Age range: 2½–13+
No. of pupils: 300 B170 G130
Fees: Day £6951–£11,892 WB £5048

Sevenoaks Preparatory School
Fawke Cottage, Godden Green, Sevenoaks, Kent TN15 0JU
Tel: 01732 762336
Headmaster: Mr P J Oldroyd
Type: Coeducational Day
Age range: 2–13
No. of pupils: 388 B224 G164
Fees: Day £2320–£3280

Sevenoaks School
Sevenoaks, Kent TN13 1HU
Tel: +44 (0)1732 455133
Head: Mrs Katy Ricks MA
Type: Coeducational Boarding & Day
Age range: 11–18
No. of pupils: 1000 VIth435
Fees: Day £16,413–£18,645 FB £26,322–£28,554

Shernold School
Hill Place, Queens Avenue, Maidstone, Kent ME16 0ER
Tel: 01622 752868
Headmistress: Mrs L Dack
Type: Coeducational Day
Age range: 3–11
No. of pupils: 142 B50 G92
Fees: Day £3525–£4200

Solefield School
Solefield Road, Sevenoaks, Kent TN13 1PH
Tel: 01732 452142
Headmaster: Mr D A Philps BSc(Hons)
Type: Boys' Day
Age range: B4–13
No. of pupils: 160 B160
Fees: Day £2730–£3360

Somerhill Pre-Prep
Somerhill, Five Oak Green Road, Tonbridge,
Kent TN11 0NJ
Tel: 01732 352124
Headmistress: Mrs J Ruth Sorensen BEd(Hons), CertEd
Type: Coeducational Day
Age range: 3–7
No. of pupils: 245 B141 G104
Fees: Day £7380–£8550

Spring Grove School
Harville Road, Wye, Ashford, Kent TN25 5EZ
Tel: 01233 812337
Headmaster: Mr C Gibbs
Type: Coeducational Day
Age range: 2–13
No. of pupils: 194
Fees: Day £1767–£2783

St Christopher's School
New Dover Road, Canterbury, Kent CT1 3DT
Tel: 01227 462960
The Master: Mr D Evans
Type: Coeducational Day
Age range: 3–11
No. of pupils: B70 G70
Fees: Day £7600

St Edmund's Junior School
St Thomas Hill, Canterbury, Kent CT2 8HU
Tel: 01227 475600
Master: R G Bacon BA(Hons)(Durham)
Type: Coeducational Day & Boarding
Age range: 3–13
No. of pupils: 230 B140 G90
Fees: Day £5100–£14,724 WB £14,526 FB £15,942–£22,803

St Edmund's School
St Thomas' Hill, Canterbury, Kent CT2 8HU
Tel: 01227 475600
Headmaster: Mr J M Gladwin BSc(Hons)
Type: Coeducational Day & Boarding
Age range: 13–18
No. of pupils: 310 B170 G140 VIth120
Fees: Day £15,999 FB £24,900

St Faiths at Ash School
5 The Street, Ash, Canterbury, Kent CT3 2HH
Tel: 01304 813409
Headmaster: Mr S G I Kerruish MA(Cantab),
CertEd(London)
Type: Coeducational Day
Age range: 3–11
No. of pupils: 220 B110 G110
Fees: Day £2950–£6036

St Joseph's Convent Prep School
46 Old Road East, Gravesend, Kent DA12 1NR
Tel: 01474 533012
Headteacher: Mrs Carola Timney
Type: Coeducational Day
Age range: 3–11
No. of pupils: 198 B101 G97
Fees: Day £4500

St Lawrence College
Ramsgate, Kent CT11 7AE
Tel: 01843 572931
Headmaster: Reverend Mark Aitken
Type: Coeducational Boarding & Day
Age range: 3–18
No. of pupils: 528 B314 G214 VIth117
Fees: Day £5568–£14,049 WB £18,327–£24,387
FB £18,327–£24,387

St Michael's School
Otford Court, Otford, Sevenoaks, Kent TN14 5SA
Tel: 01959 522137
Headmaster: Mr K Crombie
Type: Coeducational Day
Age range: 2–13
No. of pupils: 460 B264 G196
Fees: Day £1710–£11,085

Steephill School
Off Castle Hill, Fawkham, Longfield, Kent DA3 7BG
Tel: 01474 702107
Head: Mrs C Birtwell BSc, MBA, PGCE
Type: Coeducational Day
Age range: 3–11
No. of pupils: 131 B66 G65
Fees: Day £6860

Sutton Valence Preparatory School
Underhill, Chart Sutton, Maidstone, Kent ME17 3RF
Tel: 01622 842117
Head: Mr C Gibbs BA(Hons), HDE(1st Class)
Type: Coeducational Day
Age range: 3–11
No. of pupils: 375 B200 G175
Fees: Day £1630–£9135

Sutton Valence School
Sutton Valence, Maidstone, Kent ME17 3HL
Tel: 01622 845200
Headmaster: Mr B C W Grindlay MA(Cantab, MusB, FRCO, CHM
Type: Coeducational Day & Boarding
Age range: 11–18
No. of pupils: 520 B358 G162
Fees: Day £12,840–£16,800 WB £20,190–£25,620
FB £20,190–£25,620

The Cedars School
70 Maidstone Road, Rochester, Kent ME1 3DE
Tel: 01634 847163
Headteacher: Mrs B M V Gross
Type: Coeducational Day
Age range: 2–16
No. of pupils: 21 B12 G9

The Granville School
2 Bradbourne Park Road, Sevenoaks, Kent TN13 3LJ
Tel: 01732 453039
Headmistress: Mrs J D Evans CertEd(Cantab)
Type: Girls' Day
Age range: B3–4 G3–11
No. of pupils: 190
Fees: Day £3270–£8550

The King's School, Canterbury
Canterbury, Kent CT1 2ES
Tel: 01227 595501
Head: Nicholas Clements MA, BSc, RMCS Shrivenham
Type: Coeducational Boarding & Day
Age range: 13–18
No. of pupils: 790 B438 G352 VIth359
Fees: Day £18,330 FB £24,690

The Mead School
16 Frant Road, Tunbridge Wells, Kent TN2 5SN
Tel: 01892 525837
Headmistress: Mrs A Culley CertEd(Oxon)
Type: Coeducational Day
Age range: 3–11
No. of pupils: B97 G91
Fees: Day £2628–£8951

The New Beacon School
Brittains Lane, Sevenoaks, Kent TN13 2PB
Tel: 01732 452131
Headmaster: Mr M Piercy BA(Hons)
Type: Boys' Day
Age range: 4–13
No. of pupils: 400
Fees: Day £7500–£9675

TONBRIDGE SCHOOL
For further details see p. 102
Tonbridge, Kent TN9 1JP
Tel: 01732 365555
Email: hmsec@tonbridge-school.org
Website: www.tonbridge-school.co.uk
Headmaster: T H P Haynes
Type: Boys' Day & Boarding
Age range: 13–18
No. of pupils: 750 VIth330
Fees: Day £20,910 FB £28,140

Walthamstow Hall Pre-Prep and Junior School
Sevenoaks, Kent TN13 3LD
Tel: 01732 451334
Headmistress: Mrs Jill Milner MA(Oxford)
Type: Girls' Day
Age range: 2½–11
No. of pupils: 218
Fees: Day £1230–£9990

Walthamstow Hall School
Sevenoaks, Kent TN13 3UL
Tel: 01732 451334
Headmistress: Mrs J Milner MA(Oxford)
Type: Girls' Day
Age range: 2½–18
No. of pupils: 500 VIth80
Fees: Day £8070–£13,710

WELLESLEY HOUSE
For further details see p. 80
114 Ramsgate Road, Broadstairs, Kent CT10 2DG
Tel: 01843 862991
Email: hmsec@wellesleyhouse.net
Website: www.wellesleyhouse.org
Headmaster: Mr S T P O'Malley MA(Hons), PGCE
Type: Coeducational Boarding & Day
Age range: 7–13
No. of pupils: 143 B87 G56
Fees: Day £15,300 FB £19,080

Yardley Court
Somerhill, Five Oak Green Road, Tonbridge, Kent TN11 0NJ
Tel: 01732 352124
Headmaster: J T Coakley MA, BA(Hons), PGCE
Type: Boys' Day
Age range: 7–13
No. of pupils: 236
Fees: Day £11,370

MEDWAY

Gad's Hill School
Higham, Rochester, Medway ME3 7PA
Tel: 01474 822366
Headmaster: Mr D G Craggs BSc, MA, NPQH, FCollP, FRSA
Type: Coeducational Day
Age range: 3–16
No. of pupils: 370 B185 G185
Fees: Day £6000–£7600

King's Preparatory School, Rochester
King Edward Road, Rochester, Medway ME1 1UB
Tel: 01634 888577
Headmaster: Mr R P Overend BA, FTCL, ARCM, FRSA
Type: Coeducational Day & Boarding
Age range: 4–13
No. of pupils: 228 B168 G60
Fees: Day £7125–£10,380 FB £16,005

King's School, Rochester
Satis House, Boley Hill, Rochester, Medway ME1 1TE
Tel: 01634 888555
Headmaster: Dr I R Walker BA, PhD, LTh, ABIA, FCollP, FRSA
Type: Coeducational Day & Boarding
Age range: 13–18
No. of pupils: 688 B482 G206 VIth113
Fees: Day £7655–£14,400 FB £17,145–£24,210

St Andrew's School
24-28 Watts Avenue, Rochester, Medway ME1 1SA
Tel: 01634 843479
Principal: Mrs J Jabbour BSc
Type: Coeducational Day
Age range: 3–11
No. of pupils: 378 B193 G185
Fees: Day £4956–£5244

MILTON KEYNES

Broughton Manor Preparatory School
Newport Road, Broughton, Milton Keynes MK10 9AA
Tel: 01908 665234
Headmaster: Mr Ross Urquhart
Type: Coeducational Day
Age range: 2 months–11 years
No. of pupils: B125 G125
Fees: Day £9290

Bury Lawn School
Soskin Drive, Stantonbury Fields, Milton Keynes MK14 6DP
Tel: 01908 574740
Headmaster: Mr John Moreland
Type: Coeducational Day
Age range: 18 months–18 years
No. of pupils: 300 B177 G123 VIth15
Fees: Day £3108–£9171

Fernwood School
Church Road, Aspley Heath, Milton Keynes MK17 8TJ
Tel: 01908 583541
Head: Mrs M E Denyer
Type: Coeducational Day
Age range: 1–9

Filgrave School
Filgrave Village, Newport Pagnell,
Milton Keynes MK16 9ET
Tel: 01234 711534
Headteacher: Mrs H Schofield BA(Hons), MA, PGCE
Type: Coeducational Day
Age range: 2–7
No. of pupils: 27
Fees: Day £5160

Milton Keynes Preparatory School
Tattenhoe Lane, Milton Keynes MK3 7EG
Tel: 01908 642111
Headmistress: Mrs Hilary Pauley BEd
Type: Coeducational Day
Age range: 0–11
No. of pupils: 500 B250 G250
Fees: Day £9975

Swanbourne House School
Swanbourne, Milton Keynes MK17 0HZ
Tel: 01296 720264
Joint Heads: S D Goodhart BEd(Hons) & Mrs J S Goodhart BEd
Type: Coeducational Boarding & Day
Age range: 3–13
No. of pupils: B243 G197
Fees: Day £7770–£13,620 FB £17,460

The Grove Independent School
Redland Drive, Loughton, Milton Keynes MK5 8HD
Tel: 01908 690590
Principal: Mrs Deborah Berkin
Type: Coeducational Day
Age range: 3 months–13 years
No. of pupils: 250 B125 G125
Fees: Day £10,608

Thornton College
Thornton, Milton Keynes MK17 0HJ
Tel: 01280 812610
Headmistress: Miss Agnes T Williams
Type: Girls' Day & Boarding
Age range: B2½–4+ G2½–16
No. of pupils: 370 G370
Fees: Day £6300–£10,095 WB £10,500–£13,305
FB £13,305–£16,545

Walton Pre-Preparatory School & Nursery
The Old Rectory, Walton Drive, Milton Keynes MK7 6BB
Tel: 01908 678403
Headmistress: Mrs M Ramsbotham CertEd
Type: Coeducational Day
Age range: 2 months–7 years
No. of pupils: 120 B60 G60
Fees: Day £8316

PETERBOROUGH

Kirkstone House School
Main Street, Baston, Peterborough PE6 9PA
Tel: 01778 560350
Head: Mrs C Jones BSocSc
Type: Coeducational Day
Age range: 4–16
No. of pupils: 234 B150 G84
Fees: Day £4233–£7539

Peterborough High School
Thorpe Road, Peterborough PE3 6JF
Tel: 01733 343357
Headmaster: Mr A M Meadows BSc(Hons)
Type: Girls' Day & Boarding
Age range: B6 weeks–18 years G6 weeks–18 years
No. of pupils: 360 B90 G270 VIth52
Fees: Day £8131–£11,499 WB £17,412–£18,477
FB £19,788–£21,405

PORTSMOUTH

Mayville High School
35/37 St Simon's Road, Southsea, Portsmouth PO5 2PE
Tel: 023 9273 4847
Headteacher: Mr M Castle BA, PGCE
Type: Coeducational Day
Age range: 6 months–16 years
No. of pupils: 502 B252 G250
Fees: Day £5310–£7800

Portsmouth High School GDST

Kent Road, Southsea, Portsmouth PO5 3EQ
Tel: 023 9282 6714
Headmistress: Mrs Jenny Clough
Type: Girls' Day
Age range: 3–18
No. of pupils: 600 VIth59
Fees: Day £5820–£9720

St John's College

Grove Road South, Southsea, Portsmouth PO5 3QW
Tel: 023 9281 5118
Headmaster: Mr N W Thorne
Type: Coeducational Day & Boarding
Age range: 2–18
No. of pupils: 650 B435 G215 VIth105
Fees: Day £6750–£8895 FB £19,350–£20,700

The Portsmouth Grammar School

High Street, Portsmouth PO1 2LN
Tel: 023 9236 0036
Headmaster: J E Priory MA
Type: Coeducational Day
Age range: 2½–18
No. of pupils: 1603 B1007 G596 VIth289
Fees: Day £6729–£10,491

READING

Alder Bridge School

Bridge House, Mill Lane, Padworth, Reading RG7 4JU
Tel: 0118 971 4471
Type: Coeducational Day and Nursery
Age range: 1–11
No. of pupils: 58 B33 G25
Fees: Day £3420–£4470

BRADFIELD COLLEGE

For further details see p. 92

Bradfield, Reading RG7 6AU
Tel: 0118 964 4510
Email: headmaster@bradfieldcollege.org.uk
Website: www.bradfieldcollege.org.uk
Headmaster: Mr Peter Roberts
Type: Coeducational Boarding
Age range: 13–18
No. of pupils: 724 B484 G240 VIth306
Fees: Day £21,900 FB £27,375

Caversham School

16 Peppard Road, Caversham, Reading RG4 8JZ
Tel: 01189 478 684
Head: Mrs Jacqueline Lawson
Type: Coeducational Day
Age range: 4–11
No. of pupils: 60
Fees: Day £6750

Crosfields School

Shinfield, Reading RG2 9BL
Tel: 0118 987 1810
Headmaster: Mr J P Wansey
Type: Coeducational Day
Age range: 3–13
No. of pupils: 478 B396 G82
Fees: Day £6600–£10,710

Dolphin School

Waltham Road, Hurst, Reading RG10 0FR
Tel: 0118 934 1277
Head: Veronica Gibbs BSc, PGCE
Type: Coeducational Day
Age range: 3–13
No. of pupils: B139 G115
Fees: Day £7545–£10,350

Elstree School

Woolhampton, Reading RG7 5TD
Tel: 0118 971 3302
Headmaster: Mr M J Sayer
Type: Boys' Boarding & Day
Age range: B3–13 G3–7
No. of pupils: 248 B229 G19
Fees: Day £8700–£15,300 FB £19,200

Hemdean House School

Hemdean Road, Caversham, Reading RG4 7SD
Tel: 0118 947 2590
Headmistress: Mrs J Harris BSc
Type: Coeducational Day
Age range: B3–11 G3–16
No. of pupils: B55 G125
Fees: Day £4680–£6540

Leighton Park School

Shinfield Road, Reading RG2 7ED
Tel: 0118 987 9608
Head: John H Dunston MA, AIL, FRSA
Type: Coeducational Day & Boarding
Age range: 11–18
No. of pupils: 490
Fees: Day £14,160–£16,680 WB £19,020–£22,350
FB £21,630–£25,440

Padworth College

Padworth, Reading RG7 4NR
Tel: 0118 983 2644
Principal: Mrs Linde Melhuish
Type: Coeducational Boarding & Day
Age range: 13–19
No. of pupils: 106 B46 G60 VIth50
Fees: Day £9000 WB £15,900 FB £20,850

Pangbourne College

Pangbourne, Reading RG8 8LA
Tel: 0118 984 2101
Headmaster: Thomas J C Garnier
Type: Coeducational Boarding & Day
Age range: 11–18
No. of pupils: 387 B301 G86 VIth117
Fees: Day £7500–£10,335 FB £10,710–£14,745

QUEEN ANNE'S SCHOOL

For further details see p. 97

6 Henley Road, Caversham, Reading RG4 6DX
Tel: 0118 918 7333
Email: admissions@qas.org.uk
Website: www.qas.org.uk
Headmistress: Mrs Julia Harrington BA(Hons), PGCE,
NPQH
Type: Girls' Boarding & Day
Age range: 11–18
No. of pupils: 336 VIth100
Fees: Day £5695 WB £7545–£7975 FB £8395

Reading Blue Coat School

Holme Park, Sonning Lane, Sonning, Reading RG4 6SU
Tel: 0118 944 1005
Headmaster: M J Windsor
Type: Boys' Day
Age range: B11–18 G16–18
No. of pupils: 680 B612 G68 VIth230
Fees: Day £11,340

St Andrew's School

Buckhold, Pangbourne, Reading RG8 8QA
Tel: 0118 974 4276
Headmaster: Mr J M Snow BA, CertEd
Type: Coeducational Day & Weekly Boarding
Age range: 3–13
No. of pupils: B168 G126
Fees: Day £3450–£12,450 WB £14,850

St Edward's School

64 Tilehurst Road, Reading RG30 2JH
Tel: 0118 957 4342
Principal: G W Mottram
Type: Boys' Day
Age range: 4–13 B4–13
No. of pupils: 151 B150
Fees: Day £6660–£8550

St Joseph's Convent School

Upper Redlands Road, Reading RG1 5JT
Tel: 0118 966 1000
Headmistress: Mrs Maureen Sheridan BA(Hons), CertEd,
MA(Ed), NPQH
Type: Coeducational Day
Age range: 3–18
No. of pupils: B11 G320 VIth40
Fees: Day £4965–£8500

The Abbey School

Kendrick Road, Reading RG1 5DZ
Tel: 0118 987 2256
Headmistress: Mrs Barbara Stanley BA(Hons), PGCE, FRGS
Type: Girls' Day
Age range: 3–18
No. of pupils: 1040 VIth163
Fees: Day £2380–£3840

The Highlands School

Wardle Avenue, Tilehurst, Reading RG31 6JR
Tel: 0118 942 7186
Prinicpal: Mr G W Mottram
Type: Coeducational Day
Age range: B2–7 G2–11
No. of pupils: 96 B28 G68
Fees: Day £875–£4275

The Oratory Preparatory School
Great Oaks, Goring Heath, Reading RG8 7SF
Tel: 0118 984 4511
Headmaster: Dr R J Hillier MA, PhD, PGCE
Type: Coeducational Day & Boarding
Age range: 3–13 B3–13 G3–13
No. of pupils: 400 B250 G150
Fees: Day £3330–£11,145 WB £14,145 FB £15,360

The Oratory School
Woodcote, Reading RG8 0PJ
Tel: 01491 683500
Head Master: Mr C I Dytor MC, MA
Type: Boys' Boarding & Day
Age range: 11–18
No. of pupils: 390 VIth120
Fees: Day £11,970–£16,308 FB £16,140–£22,575

The Vine Christian School
SORCF Christian Centre, Basingstoke Road, Three Mile Cross, Reading RG7 1AT
Tel: 01189 886464
Head: Mrs Joan Muirhead
Type: Coeducational Day
Age range: 5–13
No. of pupils: 9

SLOUGH

Eton End PNEU School
35 Eton Road, Datchet, Slough SL3 9AX
Tel: 01753 541075
Headmistress: Mrs V M Pilgerstorfer BA(Hons), PGCE
Type: Girls' Day
Age range: B3–7 G3–11
No. of pupils: 245 B72 G173
Fees: Day £5850–£6900

Langley Manor School
St Mary's Road, Langley, Slough SL3 6BZ
Tel: 01753 825368
Head: Mr N Owlett
Type: Coeducational Day
Age range: 2–11
No. of pupils: 284 B164 G120
Fees: Day £5355–£5595

Long Close School
Upton Court Road, Upton, Slough SL3 7LU
Tel: 01753 520095
Head: Mr David Brazier
Type: Coeducational Day
Age range: 2–16
No. of pupils: 283
Fees: Day £5715–£10,080

St Bernard's Preparatory School
Hawtrey Close, Slough SL1 1TB
Tel: 01753 521821
Head Teacher: Mrs M B Smith CertEd, NPQH
Type: Coeducational Day
Age range: 2½–11
No. of pupils: B149 G97

Teikyo School UK
Framewood Road, Wexham, Slough SL2 4QS
Tel: 01753 663711
Headmaster: A Watanabe BA
Type: Coeducational Day & Boarding
Age range: 16–18
No. of pupils: B58 G42

SOUTHAMPTON

King Edward VI School
Wilton Road, Southampton SO15 5UQ
Tel: 023 8070 4561
Head Master: Mr A J Thould MA(Oxon)
Type: Coeducational Day
Age range: 11–18
No. of pupils: 978 B600 G378 VIth246
Fees: Day £10,875

St Mary's College
57 Midanbury Lane, Bitterne Park, Southampton SO18 4DJ
Tel: 023 8067 1267
Headmaster: J Davis
Type: Coeducational Day
Age range: 3–16
No. of pupils: 470 B350 G120
Fees: Day £1750–£2350

St Winifred's School

17-19 Winn Road, Southampton SO17 1EJ
Tel: 023 8055 7352
Head: Mrs Carole A Pearcey BEd
Type: Coeducational Day
Age range: 2–11
No. of pupils: B63 G53
Fees: Day £6150

The Gregg School

Townhill Park House, Cutbush Lane,
Southampton SO18 2GF
Tel: 023 8047 2133
Headmaster: R D Hart BEd
Type: Coeducational Day
Age range: 11–16
No. of pupils: 305 B168 G137
Fees: Day £9030

The King's School

Lakesmere House, Allington Lane, Fair Oak, Eastleigh,
Southampton SO50 7DB
Tel: 023 8060 0986
Headmaster: Mr Paul Johnson
Type: Coeducational Day
Age range: 3–16
No. of pupils: 256 B126 G130
Fees: Day £3095–£5495

Woodhill Preparatory School

Brook Lane, Botley, Southampton SO30 2ER
Tel: 01489 781112
Principal: Mrs M Dacombe
Type: Coeducational Day
Age range: 3–11
No. of pupils: B70 G70
Fees: Day £1965–£3840

SOUTHEND-ON-SEA

Alleyn Court Preparatory School

Wakering Road, Southend-on-Sea SS3 0PW
Tel: 01702 582553
Headmaster: Mr Gareth Davies BA(Hons), PGCE
Type: Coeducational Day
Age range: 2½–11
No. of pupils: B173 G127
Fees: Day £2088–£8910

Crowstone Preparatory School

121-123 Crowstone Road, Westcliff-on-Sea, Southend-on-Sea SS0 8LH
Tel: 01702 346758
Headmaster: J P Thayer
Type: Coeducational Day
Age range: 3–11
No. of pupils: 133
Fees: Day £2655

Saint Pierre School

16 Leigh Road, Leigh-on-Sea, Southend-on-Sea SS9 1LE
Tel: 01702 474164
Headmaster: Kurt Davies
Type: Coeducational Day
Age range: 2½–11+
No. of pupils: B59 G36
Fees: Day £2062–£6186

St Hilda's School

15 Imperial Avenue, Westcliff-on-Sea, Southend-on-Sea SS0 8NE
Tel: 01702 344542
Headmistress: Mrs Susan O'Riordan BA(Hons), PGCE
Type: Girls' Day
Age range: B3–11 G3–16
No. of pupils: 150
Fees: Day £7200–£8985

St Michael's School

198 Hadleigh Road, Leigh-on-Sea, Southend-on-Sea SS9 2LP
Tel: 01702 478719
Head: Steve Tompkins BSc(Hons), PGCE, MA
Type: Coeducational Day
Age range: 3–11
No. of pupils: 274 B147 G127
Fees: Day £3405–£6795

Thorpe Hall School

Wakering Road, Southend-on-Sea SS1 3RD
Tel: 01702 582340
Headmaster: Mr Andrew Hampton
Type: Coeducational Day
Age range: 2–16
No. of pupils: B210 G140
Fees: Day £3339–£4821

SURREY

Aberdour School
Brighton Road, Burgh Heath, Tadworth, Surrey KT20 6AJ
Tel: 01737 354119
Headmaster: Mr Simon Collins
Type: Coeducational Day
Age range: 2–13
No. of pupils: 255 B150 G105
Fees: Day £3990–£10,605

Abinger Hammer Village School
Hackhurst Lane, Abinger Hammer, Dorking,
Surrey RH5 6SE
Tel: 01306 730343
Headteacher: Mrs Patricia Hammond BA, CertEd
Type: Coeducational Day
Age range: 2½–11
No. of pupils: 19 B11 G8

ACS COBHAM INTERNATIONAL SCHOOL
For further details see p. 86
Heywood, Portsmouth Road, Cobham, Surrey KT11 1BL
Tel: 01932 867251
Email: cobhamadmissions@acs-england.co.uk
Website: www.acs-england.co.uk
Head of School: Mr T Lehman
Type: Coeducational Day & Boarding
Age range: 2–18
No. of pupils: 1352 B755 G597 VIth471
Fees: Day £8840–£19,730 FB £29,100–£32,960

ACS EGHAM INTERNATIONAL SCHOOL
For further details see p. 88
Woodlee, London Road, Egham, Surrey TW20 0HS
Tel: 01784 430 800
Email: eghamadmissions@acs-england.co.uk
Website: www.acs-england.co.uk
Head of School: Jeremy Lewis
Type: Coeducational Day
Age range: 2–18
No. of pupils: 583 B304 G279
Fees: Day £8900–£19,240

Aldro School
Shackleford, Godalming, Surrey GU8 6AS
Tel: 01483 409020
Headmaster: Mr D W N Aston BA(Hons), PGCE
Type: Boys' Boarding & Day
Age range: 7–13
No. of pupils: 220
Fees: Day £14,610 FB £18,795

Amesbury
Hazel Grove, Hindhead, Surrey GU26 6BL
Tel: 01428 604322
Headmaster: Mr Nigel Taylor MA
Type: Coeducational Day
Age range: 2–13
No. of pupils: 325 B203 G122
Fees: Day £7485–£11,475

Barfield School
Runfold, Farnham, Surrey GU10 1PB
Tel: 01252 782271
Head: Robin Davies
Type: Coeducational Day
Age range: 2–13
No. of pupils: 250 B160 G90
Fees: Day £2610–£11,220

Barrow Hills School
Roke Lane, Witley, Godalming, Surrey GU8 5NY
Tel: 01428 683639/682634
Headmaster: Mr M Unsworth BEng, PGCE
Type: Coeducational Day
Age range: 3–13
No. of pupils: 283 B176 G107
Fees: Day £7020–£11,145

Belmont Preparatory School
Feldemore, Holmbury St Mary, Dorking, Surrey RH5 6LQ
Tel: 01306 730852
Headmistress: Mrs Helen Skrine BA, PGCE, NPQH, FRSA
Type: Coeducational Day & Boarding
Age range: 2–13
No. of pupils: 227 B159 G68
Fees: Day £6120–£10,428 WB £15,345

Bishopsgate School
Bishopsgate Road, Englefield Green, Egham,
Surrey TW20 0YJ
Tel: 01784 432109
Headmaster: Mr Andrew Cowell BEd, CPSE
Type: Coeducational Day & Weekly Boarding
Age range: 2½–13
No. of pupils: 336 B216 G120
Fees: Day £3795–£11,400 WB £14,100

Box Hill School

Mickleham, Dorking, Surrey RH5 6EA
Tel: 01372 373382
Headmaster: Mr Mark Eagers MA(Cantab)
Type: Coeducational Boarding & Day
Age range: 11–18
No. of pupils: 425 B280 G145 VIth96
Fees: Day £12,600–£15,000 WB £19,500–£21,000
FB £22,800–£24,600

Bramley School

Chequers Lane, Walton-on-the-Hill, Tadworth,
Surrey KT20 7ST
Tel: 01737 812004
Headmistress: Mrs P Burgess
Type: Girls' Day
Age range: 3–11
No. of pupils: 110
Fees: Day £3858–£8418

Caterham School

Harestone Valley, Caterham, Surrey CR3 6YA
Tel: 01883 343028
Head: Mr J P Thomas BSc(Hons), MBA, FRSA
Type: Coeducational Day & Boarding
Age range: 3–18
No. of pupils: 1063 B631 G432 VIth273
Fees: Day £4137–£13,260 FB £23,469–£24,741

Charterhouse

Godalming, Surrey GU7 2DX
Tel: Admissions: 01483 291501 General Enquiries: 01483
291500
Headmaster: Rev John Witheridge MA
Type: Boys' Boarding & Day
Age range: B13–18 G16–18
No. of pupils: 733 B634 G105 VIth361
Fees: Day £23,505 FB £28,440

Chinthurst School

Tadworth Street, Tadworth, Surrey KT20 5QZ
Tel: 01737 812011
Headmaster: I D Thorpe MA(Ed), BA(Ed)
Type: Boys' Day
Age range: 3–13
No. of pupils: 165
Fees: Day £3375–£9570

City of London Freemen's School

Ashtead Park, Ashtead, Surrey KT21 1ET
Tel: 01372 277933
Headmaster: Mr Philip MacDonald MA(Oxon)
Type: Coeducational Day & Boarding
Age range: 7–18
No. of pupils: 850 VIth223
Fees: Day £10,295–£13,959 FB £22,212

Claremont Fan Court School

Claremont Drive, Esher, Surrey KT10 9LY
Tel: 01372 467841
Principal: Mrs Alice Stanley
Type: Coeducational Day
Age range: 3–18
No. of pupils: 660 B370 G290 VIth60
Fees: Day £3795–£12,693

Cornerstone School

22 West Hill, Epsom, Surrey KT19 8JD
Tel: 01372 742940
Headmaster: Mr G R Davies BEd
Type: Coeducational Day
Age range: 5–16
No. of pupils: B25 G27

Coworth-Flexlands School

Valley End, Chobham, Woking, Surrey GU24 8TE
Tel: 01276 855707
Headmistress: Mrs Sandy Stephen
Type: Coeducational Day
Age range: B3–7 G3–11
No. of pupils: 170 B12 G158
Fees: Day £3825–£9675

Cranleigh Preparatory School

Horseshoe Lane, Cranleigh, Surrey GU6 8QH
Tel: 01483 274199
Headmaster: Mr M T Wilson BSc
Type: Coeducational Day & Boarding
Age range: 7–13
No. of pupils: 290
Fees: Day £11,385 FB £14,025

Cranleigh School

Horseshoe Lane, Cranleigh, Surrey GU6 8QQ
Tel: 01483 273666
Head: Mr G de W Waller MA, MSc, FRSA(Worcester College, Oxford)
Type: Coeducational Boarding & Day
Age range: 13–18
No. of pupils: 606 B401 G205 VIth237
Fees: Day £21,225 FB £26,040

Cranmore School

Epsom Road, West Horsley, Leatherhead, Surrey KT24 6AT
Tel: 01483 280340
Headmaster: Mr M Connolly BSc, BA, MA, MEd
Type: Boys' Day
Age range: 4–13
No. of pupils: 480
Fees: Day £3750–£10,650

DANES HILL SCHOOL

For further details see p. 72

Leatherhead Road, Oxshott, Surrey KT22 0JG
Tel: 01372 842509
Email: registrar@daneshillschool.co.uk
Website: www.daneshillschool.co.uk
Headmaster: Mr W Murdock BA
Type: Coeducational Pre-preparatory & Preparatory Day
Age range: 3–13
No. of pupils: 872 B493 G379
Fees: Day £1589–£4405

Danesfield Manor School

Rydens Avenue, Walton-on-Thames, Surrey KT12 3JB
Tel: 01932 220930
Head: Mrs Lisa Fidler BEd(Hons)
Type: Coeducational Day
Age range: 3 months–11 years
No. of pupils: 175
Fees: Day £5721–£6210

Downsend School

1 Leatherhead Road, Leatherhead, Surrey KT22 8TJ
Tel: 01372 372197
Headmaster: Floyd Steadman
Type: Coeducational Day
Age range: 6–13
No. of pupils: 580 B320 G260
Fees: Day £10,995

Downsend School

Ashtead Lodge, 22 Oakfield Road, Ashtead, Surrey KT21 2RE
Tel: 01372 385439
Head Teacher: Mrs K Barrett
Type: Coeducational Day
Age range: 2–6
No. of pupils: 66 B35 G31
Fees: Day £2190–£8250

Downsend School

Epsom Lodge, 6 Norman Avenue, Epsom, Surrey KT17 3AB
Tel: 01372 721824
Head Teacher: Mrs S Matthews
Type: Coeducational Day
Age range: 2½–6
No. of pupils: 120 B60 G60
Fees: Day £6780–£8250

Downsend School

Leatherhead Lodge, Epsom Road, Leatherhead, Surrey KT22 8ST
Tel: 01372 372123
Headteacher: Mrs Gill Brooks
Type: Coeducational Day
Age range: 2½–6
No. of pupils: B65 G73
Fees: Day £6780–£8250

Drayton House School

35 Austen Road, Guildford, Surrey GU1 3NP
Tel: 01483 504707
Headmistress: Mrs J Tyson-Jones FroÎbelCertEd (LondonUni)
Type: Coeducational Day
Age range: 3 months–7 years
No. of pupils: B45 G45
Fees: Day £4420–£12,500

Duke of Kent School

Peaslake Road, Ewhurst, Cranleigh, Surrey GU6 7NS
Tel: 01483 277313
Headmaster: Dr A D Cameron
Type: Coeducational Boarding & Day
Age range: 3–16
No. of pupils: 194 B126 G68
Fees: Day £4410–£12,855 WB £12,135–£15,270 FB £15,735–£18,855

Dunottar School

High Trees Road, Reigate, Surrey RH2 7EL
Tel: 01737 761945
Headmistress: Mrs Jane Hellier MA, BA(Hons), PGCE
Type: Girls' Day
Age range: G2½–18
No. of pupils: 370
Fees: Day £3045–£11,250

(符) (A) (£) (16+)

Edgeborough

Frensham, Farnham, Surrey GU10 3AH
Tel: 01252 792495
Head Teachers: Mr R A Jackson MA(Cantab), PGCE & Mrs
M A Jackson BEd
Type: Coeducational Boarding & Day
Age range: 2–13
No. of pupils: 291 B185 G106
Fees: Day £8235–£13,425 WB £15,990–£17,280

(符) (符) (£) (✐)

EMBERHURST SCHOOL

For further details see p. 74
94 Ember Lane, Esher, Surrey KT10 8EN
Tel: 020 8398 2933
Email: info@emberhurst-school.com
Website: www.emberhurst-school.com
Headmistress: Mrs P Chadwick BEd
Type: Coeducational Day
Age range: 2½+–7+
No. of pupils: 70 B40 G30
Fees: Day £2265–£6495

(符)

Epsom College

Epsom, Surrey KT17 4JQ
Tel: 01372 821234
Headmaster: Stephen R Borthwick BSc, CPhys, FRSA
Type: Coeducational Boarding & Day
Age range: 13–18
No. of pupils: 720 B474 G246 VIth324
Fees: Day £18,720 WB £25,005 FB £27,405

(符) (符) (A) (符) (£) (✐) (16+)

Essendene Lodge School

Essendene Road, Caterham, Surrey CR3 5PB
Tel: 01883 348349
Head Teacher: Mr S J Haydock
Type: Coeducational Day
Age range: 2–11
No. of pupils: 153 B66 G87
Fees: Day £1860–£4710

(符) (£) (✐)

Ewell Castle School

Church Street, Ewell, Epsom, Surrey KT17 2AW
Tel: 020 8393 1413
Principal: Andrew Tibble
Type: Coeducational Day
Age range: B3–18 G3–11
No. of pupils: 515 B451 G64 VIth60
Fees: Day £5820–£11,100

(符) (A) (£) (✐) (16+)

Feltonfleet School

Cobham, Surrey KT11 1DR
Tel: 01932 862264
Headmaster: P C Ward
Type: Coeducational Day & Weekly Boarding
Age range: 3–13
No. of pupils: 356 B236 G120
Fees: Day £7680–£11,250 WB £15,750

(符) (符) (£) (✐)

Frensham Heights

Rowledge, Farnham, Surrey GU10 4EA
Tel: 01252 792561
Headmaster: Mr Andrew Fisher BA, MEd, FRSA
Type: Coeducational Boarding & Day
Age range: 3–18
No. of pupils: 497 B267 G230 VIth105
Fees: Day £5205–£15,300 FB £19,485–£22,680

(符) (符) (A) (符) (£) (✐) (16+)

Glenesk School

Ockham Road North, East Horsley, Surrey KT24 6NS
Tel: 01483 282329
Headmistress: Mrs S Christie-Hall
Type: Coeducational Day
Age range: 2–7
No. of pupils: B77 G73
Fees: Day £1350–£8112

(符) (£) (✐)

Greenacre School for Girls

Sutton Lane, Banstead, Surrey SM7 3RA
Tel: 01737 352114
Headmistress: Mrs L E Redding
Type: Girls' Day
Age range: 3–18 G3–18
No. of pupils: 400 G370 VIth47
Fees: Day £6810–£11,640

(符) (A) (£) (16+)

Greenfield

Brooklyn Road, Woking, Surrey GU22 7TP
Tel: 01483 772525
Headteacher: Janis Radcliffe BSc, PGCE
Type: Coeducational Day
Age range: 3–11
No. of pupils: B92 G87
Fees: Day £4284–£9450

Guildford High School

London Road, Guildford, Surrey GU1 1SJ
Tel: 01483 561440
Headmistress: Mrs F J Boulton BSc, MA
Type: Girls' Day
Age range: 4–18
No. of pupils: 930 VIth160
Fees: Day £7131–£12,024

Hall Grove School

London Road, Bagshot, Surrey GU19 5HZ
Tel: 01276 473059
Headmaster: Mr A R Graham BSc, PGCE
Type: Coeducational Day, Weekly & Flexi Boarding
Age range: 4–13
No. of pupils: 310
Fees: Day £7110–£9825

Halstead Preparatory School

Woodham Rise, Woking, Surrey GU21 4EE
Tel: 01483 772682
Headmistress: Mrs S G Fellows BA(Hons)
Type: Girls' Preparatory
Age range: 3–11
No. of pupils: 200
Fees: Day £2160–£9924

Hampton Court House

Hampton Court Road, East Molesey, Surrey KT8 9BS
Tel: 020 8943 0889
Headmistress: Lady Houstoun-Boswall
Type: Coeducational Day
Age range: 3–16
No. of pupils: B74 G74 VIth8
Fees: Day £7842–£10,017

Haslemere Preparatory School

The Heights, Hill Road, Haslemere, Surrey GU27 2JP
Tel: 01428 642350
Head: Mr K J Merrick BA(Hons), PGCE
Type: Boys' Day Prep with Coeducational Nursery
Age range: 2–13
No. of pupils: 191
Fees: Day £2199–£3145

Hawley Place School

Fernhill Road, Blackwater, Camberley, Surrey GU17 9HU
Tel: 01276 32028
Co-Principals: Mr T G Pipe BA(CombHons), MA & Mrs M L Pipe LÈs Lettres
Type: Coeducational Day
Age range: B2–11 G2–16
No. of pupils: 370 B105 G265
Fees: Day £7560–£9450

Hazelwood School

Wolf's Hill, Limpsfield, Oxted, Surrey RH8 0QU
Tel: 01883 712194
Head: R McDuff BEd, MA
Type: Coeducational Day
Age range: 2½–13
No. of pupils: 399 B246 G153
Fees: Day £3585–£11,100

Hoe Bridge School

Hoe Place, Old Woking Road, Woking, Surrey GU22 8JE
Tel: 01483 760018 & 01483 772194
Head: Mr N Arkell BSc
Type: Coeducational Day
Age range: 2½–14
No. of pupils: B339 G143
Fees: Day £1620–£11,640

International School of London in Surrey

Old Woking Road, Woking, Surrey GU22 8HY
Tel: 01483 750409
Headmaster: Marco Damhuis
Type: Coeducational Day
Age range: 3–11
No. of pupils: 105 B52 G53
Fees: Day £8580–£14,490

King Edward's School Witley
Petworth Road, Wormley, Godalming, Surrey GU8 5SG
Tel: +44 (0)1428 686735
Head: John F Attwater MA
Type: Coeducational Boarding & Day
Age range: 11–18
No. of pupils: 420
Fees: Day £16,725 FB £23,280

Kingswood House School
56 West Hill, Epsom, Surrey KT19 8LG
Tel: 01372 723590
Headmaster: Mr Peter R Brooks MA, BEd(Hons)
Type: Boys' Day Prep with Coeducational Nursery
Age range: B3–13 G3–7
No. of pupils: 210
Fees: Day £7440–£9825

Lanesborough
Maori Road, Guildford, Surrey GU1 2EL
Tel: 01483 880650
Head: Mrs Clare Turnbull BA(Hons)
Type: Boys' Day
Age range: 3–13
No. of pupils: 350
Fees: Day £7185–£9687

Lingfield Notre Dame School
Lingfield, Surrey RH7 6PH
Tel: 01342 833176
Principal: Mrs N E Shepley BA
Type: Coeducational Day
Age range: 2½–18
No. of pupils: 792 B396 G396 VIth86
Fees: Day £3300–£9360

Longacre School
Shamley Green, Guildford, Surrey GU5 0NQ
Tel: 01483 893225
Headmaster: Mr Mark Beach BA(Hons), AdDipAd, MAAd
Type: Coeducational Day
Age range: 2–11
No. of pupils: 237 B117 G120
Fees: Day £4635–£6540

Lyndhurst School
36 The Avenue, Camberley, Surrey GU15 3NE
Tel: 01276 22895
Headmaster: Mr S G Yeo BMus, LTCL (MusEd), NPQH
Type: Coeducational Day
Age range: 2–11
No. of pupils: 177 B102 G75
Fees: Day £6600–£8040

Manor House School
Manor House Lane, Little Bookham, Leatherhead,
Surrey KT23 4EN
Tel: 01372 458538
Headmistress: Miss Zara Axton
Type: Girls' Day
Age range: 2–16
No. of pupils: 360
Fees: Day £750–£4070

Maple House School
23 Parchmore Road, Thornton Heath, Surrey CR7 8LY
Tel: 020 8653 1827
Headteacher: Mrs Pauline Khoo
Type: Coeducational Day
Age range: 5–10
No. of pupils: 97

Micklefield School
10/12 Somers Road, Reigate, Surrey RH2 9DU
Tel: 01737 242615
Headmistress: Mrs L Rose BEd(Hons), CertEd, Dip PC
Type: Coeducational Day
Age range: 3–11
No. of pupils: 272 B130 G142
Fees: Day £2565–£9030

Milbourne Lodge School
Arbrook Lane, Esher, Surrey KT10 9EG
Tel: 01372 462737
Head: Mrs Wendy Holland
Type: Coeducational Day
Age range: 8–13
No. of pupils: 200 B168 G32
Fees: Day £7450–£8100

Notre Dame Preparatory School

Burwood House, Cobham, Surrey KT11 1HA
Tel: 01932 869991
Headmaster: Mr D S Plummer BEd(Hons), DipHE, FRSA
Type: Girls' Day
Age range: B2–5 G2–11
No. of pupils: 320 B5 G315
Fees: Day £1090–£2850

Notre Dame Senior School

Burwood House, Cobham, Surrey KT11 1HA
Tel: 01932 869990
Headmistress: Mrs Bridget Williams MA, NPQH, BEd(Oxon)
Type: Girls' Day
Age range: 11–18
No. of pupils: 382 VIth57
Fees: Day £11,130

Oakfield School

Coldharbour Road, Pyrford, Woking, Surrey GU22 8SJ
Tel: 01932 342465
Principal: Mrs S H Goddard BA(Joint Hons)
Type: Independent Day School
Age range: B3–7 G3–16
No. of pupils: 170 B20 G150
Fees: Day £7500–£12,600

Oakhyrst Grange School

160 Stanstead Road, Caterham, Surrey CR3 6AF
Tel: 01883 343344
Headmaster: Mr A Gear
Type: Coeducational Day
Age range: 4–11
No. of pupils: 114 B65 G49
Fees: Day £988–£2186

Parkside School

The Manor, Stoke d'Abernon, Cobham, Surrey KT11 3PX
Tel: 01932 862749
Headmaster: Mr David Aylward BEd(Hons), MA
Type: Boys' Day
Age range: B2½–13 G2½–4
No. of pupils: 382 B353 G29

Peaslake School

Colmans Hill, Peaslake, Guildford, Surrey GU5 9ST
Tel: 01306 730411
Headteacher: Mrs J George
Type: Coeducational Day
Age range: 3–7
No. of pupils: 44 B19 G25

Prior's Field School

Priorsfield Road, Godalming, Surrey GU7 2RH
Tel: 01483 810551
Head: Mrs J Roseblade MA
Type: Girls' Boarding & Day
Age range: G11–18
No. of pupils: 380 VIth63
Fees: Day £4555 WB £7365 FB £7365

Priory Preparatory School

Bolters Lane, Banstead, Surrey SM7 2AJ
Tel: 01737 366920
Headmaster: Graham D Malcom MA, BEd, FRSA
Type: Boys' Day
Age range: B2–13
No. of pupils: 175 B175
Fees: Day £3750–£9105

Redehall Preparatory School

Redehall Road, Smallfield, Horley, Surrey RH6 9QL
Tel: 01342 842987
Headmistress: Mrs Gail Foster
Type: Coeducational Day
Age range: 4–11
No. of pupils: B60 G60
Fees: Day £1250

Reed's School

Sandy Lane, Cobham, Surrey KT11 2ES
Tel: 01932 869001
Headmaster: Mr D W Jarrett MA
Type: Boys' Boarding & Day
Age range: B11–18 G16–18
No. of pupils: 575 B530 G45 VIth180
Fees: Day £13,992–£17,499 FB £18,657–£23,151

Reigate Grammar School

Reigate Road, Reigate, Surrey RH2 0QS
Tel: 01737 222231
Headmaster: Mr D Thomas MA
Type: Coeducational Day
Age range: 11–18
No. of pupils: 862 B538 G324 VIth217
Fees: Day £12,072

Reigate St Mary's Prep & Choir School
Chart Lane, Reigate, Surrey RH2 7RN
Tel: 01737 244880
Headmaster: Marcus Culverwell MA
Type: Coeducational Day
Age range: 3–11
No. of pupils: 277 B198 G79

Ripley Court School
Rose Lane, Ripley, Surrey GU23 6NE
Tel: 01483 225217
Headmaster: Mr A J Gough
Type: Coeducational Day
Age range: 3–13
No. of pupils: 262 B181 G81
Fees: Day £6900–£9840

Rowan Preparatory School
6 Fitzalan Road, Claygate, Esher, Surrey KT10 0LX
Tel: 01372 462627
Headteacher: Mrs Kathy Kershaw CertEd
Type: Girls' Day
Age range: 2–11
No. of pupils: 280
Fees: Day £3450–£10,791

Royal Grammar School
High Street, Guildford, Surrey GU1 3BB
Tel: 01483 880600
Headmaster: Mr J M Cox BSc PhD
Type: Boys' Day
Age range: B11–18
No. of pupils: 900
Fees: Day £13,023–£13,305

Royal School Haslemere
Farnham Lane, Haslemere, Surrey GU27 1HQ
Tel: 01428 605805
Headmistress: Mrs Lynne Taylor-Gooby BEd, MA
Type: Girls' Day & Boarding
Age range: 3–18
No. of pupils: 319 VIth50
Fees: Day £5850–£11,868 WB £15,672–£19,191
FB £15,672–£19,191

Rydes Hill Preparatory School
Rydes Hill House, Aldershot Road, Guildford,
Surrey GU2 6BP
Tel: 01483 563160
Headmistress: Mrs Stephanie Bell MA(Oxon)
Type: Girls' Day
Age range: B3–7 G3–11
No. of pupils: 160 B20 G140
Fees: Day £870–£2960

Shrewsbury Lodge School
22 Milbourne Lane, Esher, Surrey KT10 9EA
Tel: 01372 462781
Head: Mrs Gill Hope
Type: Coeducational Day
Age range: 3–7
No. of pupils: B100 G20
Fees: Day £2130–£3370

Sir William Perkins's School
Guildford Road, Chertsey, Surrey KT16 9BN
Tel: 01932 574900
Head: Mrs S D Cooke
Type: Girls' Day
Age range: 11–18
No. of pupils: 573 G573 VIth130
Fees: Day £3923

St Andrew's School
Church Hill House, Horsell, Woking, Surrey GU21 4QW
Tel: 01483 760943
Headmaster: Mr A Perks
Type: Coeducational Day Preparatory
Age range: 3–13
No. of pupils: 310 B228 G82
Fees: Day £2880–£11,895

St Catherine's School
Bramley, Guildford, Surrey GU5 0DF
Tel: 01483 893363
Headmistress: Mrs A M Phillips MA(Cantab)
Type: Girls' Day & Boarding
Age range: 4–18
No. of pupils: 780 VIth140
Fees: Day £5790–£11,760 WB £18,315 FB £18,315

St Christopher's School

6 Downs Road, Epsom, Surrey KT18 5HE
Tel: 01372 721807
Headteacher: Mrs M V Evans CertEd, DipEd
Type: Coeducational Day
Age range: 3–7
No. of pupils: 140 B69 G71
Fees: Day £1185–£2320

St Edmund's School

Portsmouth Road, Hindhead, Surrey GU26 6BH
Tel: 01428 604808
Headmaster: Mr A J Walliker MA(Cantab), MBA, PGCE
Type: Coeducational Day & Boarding
Age range: 2–13
No. of pupils: B195 G35
Fees: Day £2160–£13,842 WB £13,680–£16,692

St George's College

Weybridge Road, Addlestone, Weybridge,
Surrey KT15 2QS
Tel: 01932 839300
Headmaster: Mr Joseph A Peake MA(Oxon), PGCE
Type: Coeducational Day
Age range: 11–18
No. of pupils: 850
Fees: Day £10,470–£12,045

St George's College Junior School

Thames Street, Weybridge, Surrey KT13 8NL
Tel: 01932 839400
Headmaster: Antony Hudson
Type: Coeducational Day
Age range: 3–11
No. of pupils: 620 B334 G286
Fees: Day £3675–£9435

St Hilary's School

Holloway Hill, Godalming, Surrey GU7 1RZ
Tel: 01483 416551
Headmistress: Mrs S Bailes BA(Hons), MA, PGCE
Type: Coeducational Day
Age range: B2½–7 G2½–11
No. of pupils: 270 B83 G187
Fees: Day £7335–£10,575

St Ives School

Three Gates Lane, Haslemere, Surrey GU27 2ES
Tel: 01428 643734
Headteacher: Mrs S E Cattaneo CertEd
Type: Girls' Day
Age range: B3–4 G3–11
No. of pupils: 149
Fees: Day £6600–£9225

St John's School

Epsom Road, Leatherhead, Surrey KT22 8SP
Tel: 01372 373000
Headmaster: N J R Haddock MBE, MA(Oxon)
Type: Boys' Boarding & Day
Age range: 13–18
No. of pupils: 499 B429 G70 VIth236
Fees: Day £18,495 WB £23,430 FB £25,425

St Teresa's Preparatory School

Beech Avenue, Effingham Hill, Dorking, Surrey RH5 6ST
Tel: 01372 453456
Headmistress: Mrs Ann Marie Stewart MA, PGCE
Type: Girls' Day & Boarding
Age range: 2–11
No. of pupils: 115
Fees: Day £660–£9630 WB £16,230–£17,025
FB £17,865–£18,660

St Teresa's School

Effingham Hill, Dorking, Surrey RH5 6ST
Tel: 01372 452037
Head: Mrs L Falconer BSc(Hons)
Type: Girls' Boarding & Day
Age range: 2–18
No. of pupils: 395 VIth90
Fees: Day £12,690–£13,440 WB £20,415–£21,165
FB £22,125–£22,875

Surbiton Preparatory School

3 Avenue Elmers, Surbiton, Surrey KT6 4SP
Tel: 020 8390 6640
Head of Surbiton High, Junior Girls' & Bo: Ms C Bufton
BA(Hons)
Type: Boys' Day
Age range: 4–11
No. of pupils: 135
Fees: Day £6783–£9246

TASIS The American School in England
Coldharbour Lane, Thorpe, Surrey TW20 8TE
Tel: +44 (0)1932 565252
Head: Mr Lyle Rigg
Type: Coeducational Boarding & Day
Age range: 3–18
No. of pupils: 700 B350 G350
Fees: Day £5600–£18,100 FB £29,150

The Hawthorns School
Pendell Court, Bletchingley, Redhill, Surrey RH1 4QJ
Tel: 01883 743048
Headmaster: Mr T R Johns BA, PGCE, FRGS
Type: Coeducational Day
Age range: 2–13
No. of pupils: B309 G221
Fees: Day £1560–£10,500

Tormead School
27 Cranley Road, Guildford, Surrey GU1 2JD
Tel: 01483 575101
Headmistress: Mrs Susan Marks
Type: Girls' Day
Age range: 4–18
No. of pupils: 760 VIth120
Fees: Day £5520–£11,565

Warlingham Park School
Chelsham Common, Warlingham, Surrey CR6 9PB
Tel: 01883 626844
Headmaster: Mr M R Donald BSc
Type: Coeducational Day
Age range: 3–11
No. of pupils: 108 B52 G56
Fees: Day £3390–£6465

Weston Green School
Weston Green Road, Thames Ditton, Surrey KT7 0JN
Tel: 020 8398 2778
Head: Mrs Lucia Harvey CertEd
Type: Coeducational Day
Age range: 3–8
No. of pupils: B70 G70
Fees: Day £2400–£5400

Westward Preparatory School
47 Hersham Road, Walton-on-Thames, Surrey KT12 1LE
Tel: 01932 220911
Headmistress: Mrs P Robertson CertEd
Type: Coeducational Day and Nursery
Age range: 3–12
No. of pupils: 140 B80 G60
Fees: Day £4560–£5655

Woldingham School
Marden Park, Woldingham, Surrey CR3 7YA
Tel: 01883 349431
Headmistress: Mrs Jayne Triffitt MA(Oxon)
Type: Girls' Boarding & Day
Age range: 11–18
No. of pupils: 520 VIth150
Fees: Day £15,405 FB £25,305

Woodcote House School
Snows Ride, Windlesham, Surrey GU20 6PF
Tel: 01276 472115
Headmaster: Mr N H K Paterson BA(Hons), PGCE
Type: Boys' Boarding & Day
Age range: 7–13
No. of pupils: 100
Fees: Day £10,425 FB £14,550

Yehudi Menuhin School
Stoke Road, Stoke d'Abernon, Cobham, Surrey KT11 3QQ
Tel: 01932 864739
Headmaster: Mr P N Chisholm MA
Type: Coeducational Boarding
Age range: 8–18
No. of pupils: B29 G39 VIth21

WEST BERKSHIRE

Brockhurst & Marlston House Schools
Hermitage, Thatcham, West Berkshire RG18 9UL
Tel: 01635 200293
Heads: David Fleming MA(Oxon), MSc & Mrs C E Riley MA, BEd, CertEd(Southampton)
Type: Boys' and Girls' Day and Weekly/Flexi Boarding
Age range: 3–13
No. of pupils: 275
Fees: Day £7410–£12,450 WB £16,530 FB £16,530

Cedars School

Church Road, Aldermaston, West Berkshire RG7 4LR
Tel: 0118 971 4251
Headteacher: Mrs P J O'Halloran
Type: Coeducational Day
Age range: 4–11
No. of pupils: 40 B20 G20
Fees: Day £6080

Cheam School

Headley, Newbury, West Berkshire RG19 8LD
Tel: 01635 268381
Headmaster: Mr Mark Robin Johnson BEd
Type: Coeducational Day & Boarding Preparatory
Age range: 3–13
No. of pupils: 384 B218 G166
Fees: Day £8250–£14,415 FB £19,470

Downe House School

Cold Ash, Thatcham, West Berkshire RG18 9JJ
Tel: 01635 200286
Headmistress: Mrs E McKendrick BA(Liverpool)
Type: Girls' Boarding & Day
Age range: 11–18
No. of pupils: 565 VIth174
Fees: Day £20,250 FB £27,975

Horris Hill

Newtown, Newbury, West Berkshire RG20 9DJ
Tel: 01635 40594
Headmaster: J H L Phillips BEd
Type: Boys' Day & Boarding
Age range: 8–13
No. of pupils: 120
Fees: Day £14,250 FB £19,680

Marlston House Preparatory School

Hermitage, Newbury, West Berkshire RG18 9UL
Tel: 01635 200293
Headmistress: Mrs Caroline Riley MA, BEd
Type: Girls' Day & Boarding
Age range: 3–13
No. of pupils: 110
Fees: Day £7410–£12,450 WB £16,530

St Gabriel's School

Sandleford Priory, Newbury, West Berkshire RG20 9BD
Tel: 01635 555680
Principal: Alun S Jones LTCL, LWCMD
Type: Girls' Day
Age range: B3–7 G3–18
No. of pupils: 550 VIth30
Fees: Day £8610–£12,300

St Michaels School

Harts Lane, Burghclere, Newbury,
West Berkshire RG20 9JW
Tel: 01635 278137
Headmaster: Rev Joseph M Dreher
Type: Coeducational Day & Boarding
Age range: 7–18
No. of pupils: B40 G40 VIth10
Fees: Day £2250 WB £4500–£7000 FB £4500–£7500

Thorngrove School

The Mount, Highclere, Newbury, West Berkshire RG20 9PS
Tel: 01635 253172
Joint Heads: Mr N J Broughton BSc & Mrs C B Broughton BA(Hons)
Type: Coeducational Day
Age range: 2½–13
No. of pupils: B135 G97
Fees: Day £8475–£11,130

WEST SUSSEX

Ardingly College

College Road, Ardingly, Haywards Heath,
West Sussex RH17 6SQ
Tel: +44 (0)1444 893000
Headmaster: Mr Peter Green
Type: Coeducational Boarding & Day
Age range: 13–18
No. of pupils: 488 B280 G184 VIth201
Fees: Day £18,450–£18,915 FB £24,600–£25,215

Ardingly College Preparatory School

Haywards Heath, West Sussex RH17 6SQ
Tel: 01444 893200
Headmaster: Mr Chris Calvey BEd
Type: Coeducational Day & Flexi-boarding
Age range: 2½–13
No. of pupils: B146 G91
Fees: Day £4050–£12,300

Ashton Park School
Brinsbury Campus East, Stane Street, North Heath,
Pulborough, West Sussex RH20 1DJ
Tel: 01798 875836
Head: Mr G Holding
Type: Coeducational Day
Age range: 11–16
No. of pupils: 66

Brambletye
Brambletye, East Grinstead, West Sussex RH19 3PD
Tel: 01342 321004
Headmaster: Mr H Cocke BA, CertEd
Type: Coeducational Day & Boarding
Age range: 2½–13
No. of pupils: 260 B150 G110
Fees: Day £17,790 FB £19,350

Broadwater Manor School
Broadwater Road, Worthing, West Sussex BN14 8HU
Tel: 01903 201123
Headteacher: Mrs E K Woodley BA(Hons), CertEd
Type: Coeducational Day
Age range: 2–13
No. of pupils: 289
Fees: Day £660–£7680

Burgess Hill School for Girls
Keymer Road, Burgess Hill, West Sussex RH15 0EG
Tel: 01444 241050
Headmistress: Mrs Ann Aughwane BSc, CertEd, NPQH
Type: Girls' Day & Boarding
Age range: B2½–4 G2½–18
No. of pupils: 680
Fees: Day £5940–£12,450 FB £21,630

Christ's Hospital
Horsham, West Sussex RH13 0YP
Tel: 01403 211293
Headmaster: John R Franklin BA, MEd(Admin)
Type: Coeducational Boarding
Age range: 11–18
No. of pupils: 816 B414 G402 VIth255
Fees: FB £24,000

Conifers School
Easebourne, Midhurst, West Sussex GU29 9BG
Tel: 01730 813243
Headmistress: Mrs Jennie Peel
Type: Coeducational Day
Age range: 2–11
No. of pupils: 107
Fees: Day £6030–£8400

Copthorne Prep School
Effingham Lane, Copthorne, Crawley,
West Sussex RH10 3HR
Tel: 01342 712311
Headmaster: Mr C Jones
Type: Coeducational Day & Boarding
Age range: 3–13
No. of pupils: 245 B140 G105
Fees: Day £5220–£9390 WB £10,800

Cottesmore School
Buchan Hill, Pease Pottage, West Sussex RH11 9AU
Tel: 01293 520648
Head: T F Rogerson
Type: Coeducational Day & Boarding
Age range: 4–13
No. of pupils: 150 B100 G50
Fees: Day £4800–£12,600 WB £16,875 FB £18,750

Cumnor House School
Danehill, Haywards Heath, West Sussex RH17 7HT
Tel: 01825 790347
Headmaster: C St J Heinrich BA
Type: Coeducational Day & Boarding
Age range: 4–13
No. of pupils: 368 B186 G182
Fees: Day £7890–£17,715 FB £17,715

Dorset House School
The Manor, Church Lane, Bury, Pulborough,
West Sussex RH20 1PB
Tel: 01798 831456
Headmaster: R C M Brown MA, PGCE
Type: Coeducational Day & Boarding
Age range: 3–13
No. of pupils: 123
Fees: Day £6780–£13,674 WB £14,700–£16,521

Farlington School
Strood Park, Horsham, West Sussex RH12 3PN
Tel: 01403 254967
Headmistress: Mrs Jonnie Goyer MA
Type: Girls' Day & Boarding
Age range: 3–18
No. of pupils: 420
Fees: Day £6090–£12,966 WB £18,066–£20,202
FB £18,483–£20,619

Fonthill Lodge
Coombe Hill Road, East Grinstead, West Sussex RH9 4LY
Tel: 01342 321635
Headmaster: Dr S G Willcocks
Type: Coeducational Day
Age range: 2–11
No. of pupils: 132 B68 G64
Fees: Day £1260–£3757

Great Ballard School
Eartham, Chichester, West Sussex PO18 0LR
Tel: 01243 814236
Head: Mr Richard E T Jennings CertEd
Type: Coeducational Day & Weekly Boarding
Age range: 2½–13
No. of pupils: 192 B103 G89
Fees: Day £3000–£10,800 WB £12,975

Great Walstead School
East Mascalls Lane, Lindfield, Haywards Heath,
West Sussex RH16 2QL
Tel: 01444 483528
Headmaster: Mr J Sykes MA(Cantab), MA(Oxon)
Type: Boys' and Girls' Day and Weekly/Flexi Boarding
Age range: 2½–13
No. of pupils: 400 B235 G165
Fees: Day £5730–£11,325

Handcross Park School
Handcross, Haywards Heath, West Sussex RH17 6HF
Tel: 01444 400526
Headmaster: Mr W J Hilton BA, CertEd
Type: Coeducational Day & Weekly Boarding
Age range: 2–13
No. of pupils: 276 B156 G120
Fees: Day £1590–£13,551 WB £15,879

Hurstpierpoint College
Hassocks, West Sussex BN6 9JS
Tel: 01273 833636
Headmaster: Mr T J Manly BA, MSc
Type: Coeducational Boarding & Day
Age range: 13–18
No. of pupils: 566 B333 G233 VIth246
Fees: Day £17,235 WB £21,930 FB £23,175

Hurstpierpoint College Prep School
Hurstpierpoint, Hassocks, West Sussex BN6 9JS
Tel: 01273 834975
Head: Mrs H Beeby BH, MA
Type: Coeducational Day & Boarding
Age range: 4–13
No. of pupils: B150 G90
Fees: Day £3580–£4120 WB £4740

LANCING COLLEGE
For further details see p. 96
Lancing, West Sussex BN15 0RW
Tel: 01273 452213
Email: admissions@lancing.org.uk
Website: www.lancingcollege.co.uk
Headmaster: Mr Jonathan W J Gillespie MA
Type: Coeducational Boarding & Day
Age range: 13–18
No. of pupils: 523 VIth241
Fees: Day £18,705 FB £26,775

Lavant House
West Lavant, Chichester, West Sussex PO18 9AB
Tel: 01243 527211
Headmistress: Mrs K Bartholomew MA(London)
Type: Girls' Day & Boarding
Age range: 3–18
No. of pupils: 160 VIth15
Fees: Day £6210–£12,585 FB £16,500–£19,800

Oakwood School
Chichester, West Sussex PO18 9AN
Tel: 01243 575209
Headmaster: Mr Johnnie Kittermaster
Type: Coeducational Day
Age range: 2½–11
No. of pupils: 280
Fees: Day £2760–£8880

Our Lady of Sion School
Gratwicke Road, Worthing, West Sussex BN11 4BL
Tel: 01903 204063
Headmaster: Mr M Scullion MA, BEd
Type: Coeducational Day
Age range: 2½–18
No. of pupils: 528 B255 G273 VIth55
Fees: Day £5715–£9150

Pennthorpe School
Church Street, Rudgwick, Horsham, West Sussex RH12 3HJ
Tel: 01403 822391
Headmaster: Mr Simon Moll BEd(Hons)
Type: Coeducational Day
Age range: 2–13
No. of pupils: 355 B235 G120
Fees: Day £1356–£12,315

Rikkyo School in England
Guildford Road, Rudgwick, Horsham,
West Sussex RH12 3BE
Tel: 01403 822107
Headmaster: Mr Makio Higashi
Type: Coeducational Boarding
Age range: 10–18
No. of pupils: 130 B80 G50
Fees: FB £12,000–£17,100

Seaford College
Lavington Park, Petworth, West Sussex GU28 0NB
Tel: 01798 867392
Headmaster: T J Mullins MBA, BA
Type: Coeducational Boarding & Day
Age range: 7–18
No. of pupils: 603 B398 G205 VIth128
Fees: Day £2286–£5200 WB £5300–£6800 FB £6010–£8025

Shoreham College
St Julians Lane, Shoreham-by-Sea, West Sussex BN43 6YW
Tel: 01273 592681
Headmaster: Mr J S Stearns MA, BSc, PGCE, NPQH
Type: Coeducational Day
Age range: 3–16
No. of pupils: B301 G124
Fees: Day £6825–£11,100

Slindon College
Slindon House, Slindon, Arundel, West Sussex BN18 0RH
Tel: 01243 814320
Headmaster: Mr I P Graham BEd, MA
Type: Boys' Boarding & Day
Age range: B9–16
No. of pupils: 100

Sompting Abbotts Preparatory School for Boys and Girls
Church Lane, Sompting, West Sussex BN15 0AZ
Tel: 01903 235960
Principal: Mrs P M Sinclair
Type: Coeducational Day & Weekly Boarding
Age range: 3–13
No. of pupils: 185 B135 G50
Fees: Day £7050–£9030 WB £10,965

St Peter's School
Cambrian House, Upper St John's Road, Burgess Hill,
West Sussex RH15 8HB
Tel: 01444 235880
Headmaster: Mr H G Stevens BSc
Type: Coeducational Day
Age range: 2½–13
No. of pupils: B105 G76
Fees: Day £615–£2358

Tavistock & Summerhill School
Summerhill Lane, Haywards Heath, West Sussex RH16 1RP
Tel: 01444 450256
Headmaster: Mr M Barber BEd, FRGS
Type: Coeducational Day
Age range: 3–13
No. of pupils: 170 B100 G70
Fees: Day £3000–£5400

The Prebendal School
54 West Street, Chichester, West Sussex PO19 1RT
Tel: 01243 782 026
Head Master: Mr T R Cannell
Type: Coeducational Day & Boarding
Age range: 3–13
No. of pupils: 219 B126 G93
Fees: Day £3000–£11,352 WB £14,706 FB £15,351

The Towers Convent School
Convent of the Blessed Sacrement, Henfield Road, Upper
Beeding, Steyning, West Sussex BN44 3TF
Tel: 01903 812185
Headmistress: Mrs Carole A Baker MA, BEd
Type: Girls' Day & Boarding
Age range: B3–8 G3–16
No. of pupils: 313 B6 G307
Fees: Day £5760–£7740 WB £11,070–£12,000
FB £11,910–£13,020

Westbourne House School
Shopwyke, Chichester, West Sussex PO20 2BH
Tel: 01243 782739
Headmaster: Mr Law
Type: Coeducational Day & Boarding
Age range: 2½–13
No. of pupils: 439 B244 G195
Fees: Day £7035–£12,855 FB £15,765

Windlesham House School
Washington, Pulborough, West Sussex RH20 4AY
Tel: 01903 874700
Headmaster: Mr Richard Foster BEd(Hons)
Type: Coeducational Boarding & Day
Age range: 4–13
No. of pupils: 302 B174 G116
Fees: Day £7080 FB £19,500

WORTH SCHOOL
For further details see p. 103
Paddockhurst Road, Turners Hill, Crawley,
West Sussex RH10 4SD
Tel: 01342 710200
Email: registry@worth.org.uk
Website: www.worthschool.co.uk
Headmaster: Mr Gino Carminati MA, FRSA
Type: Catholic coeducational 11-18 boarding & day
Age range: 11–18
No. of pupils: 506 VIth229
Fees: Day £16,026–£18,339 FB £21,627–£24,756

WINDSOR & MAIDENHEAD

Brigidine School Windsor
Queensmead, King's Road, Windsor,
Windsor & Maidenhead SL4 2AX
Tel: 01753 863779
Headmistress: Mrs Elizabeth Robinson
Type: Independent Day School
Age range: B2–7 G3–18
No. of pupils: 300
Fees: Day £3945–£11,865

Claires Court School
Ray Mill Road East, Maidenhead,
Windsor & Maidenhead SL6 8TE
Tel: 01628 411470
Headmaster: Mr J T Wilding BSc, FRSA
Type: Boys' Day
Age range: 11–16
No. of pupils: 300 VIth140
Fees: Day £9360–£10,935

Claires Court Schools, Ridgeway
Maidenhead Thicket, Maidenhead,
Windsor & Maidenhead SL6 3QE
Tel: 01628 411490
Head: K M Rogg BEd
Type: Boys' Day
Age range: 4–11
No. of pupils: 232
Fees: Day £6435–£9585

Claires Court Schools, The College
1 College Avenue, Maidenhead,
Windsor & Maidenhead SL6 6AW
Tel: 01628 411480
Head: Mrs L Green CPhys, MInstP, BSc, PGCE
Type: Girls' Day
Age range: B16–18 G3–18
No. of pupils: B42 G310 VIth140
Fees: Day £6435–£10,980

Eton College
Windsor, Windsor & Maidenhead SL4 6DW
Tel: 01753 671249
Head Master: A R M Little MA
Type: Boys' Boarding
Age range: 13–18
No. of pupils: 1300 VIth515
Fees: FB £24,990

Heathfield St Mary's School
London Road, Ascot, Windsor & Maidenhead SL5 8BQ
Tel: 01344 898 343
Headmistress: Mrs Frances King MA(Oxon), MA(London), MBA(Hull), PGCE(London)
Type: Girls' Boarding
Age range: 11–18
No. of pupils: 225 VIth78
Fees: FB £22,890

Herries School
Dean Lane, Cookham Dean,
Windsor & Maidenhead SL6 9BD
Tel: 01628 483350
Headmistress: Mrs Bradberry
Type: Coeducational Day
Age range: 3–11
No. of pupils: B33 G59
Fees: Day £5925–£8025

Highfield School
2 West Road, Maidenhead,
Windsor & Maidenhead SL6 1PD
Tel: 01628 624918
Headteacher: Mr H J Matthews MA, BSc, PGCE
Type: Girls' Day
Age range: B2½–5 G2½–11
No. of pupils: 170 B6 G164
Fees: Day £1278–£7560

Hurst Lodge
Bagshot Road, Ascot, Windsor & Maidenhead SL5 9JU
Tel: 01344 622154
Principal: Miss V Smit
Type: Girls' Day & Weekly Boarding
Age range: B3–11 G3–18
No. of pupils: 182 B21 G161 VIth18
Fees: Day £4005–£12,540 WB £20,430

Licensed Victuallers' School
London Road, Ascot, Windsor & Maidenhead SL5 8DF
Tel: 01344 882770
Principal: Mr I Mullins BEd(Hons), MSc, MCMI
Type: Coeducational Day & Boarding
Age range: 4–18
No. of pupils: 906 B516 G390 VIth152
Fees: Day £7500–£14,115 FB £19,200–£22,755

Papplewick School
Windsor Road, Ascot, Windsor & Maidenhead SL5 7LH
Tel: 01344 621488
Head: Mr T W Bunbury BA, PGCE
Type: Boys' Day, Weekly, Full Boarding
Age range: 6–13
No. of pupils: 195

St George's School
Wells Lane, Ascot, Windsor & Maidenhead SL5 7DZ
Tel: 01344 629900
Headmistress: Mrs Caroline Jordan MA(Oxon), PGCE
Type: Girls' Boarding & Day
Age range: 11–18
No. of pupils: 280 VIth85
Fees: Day £16,440 FB £25,350

St George's School
Windsor Castle, Windsor, Windsor & Maidenhead SL4 1QF
Tel: 01753 865553
Headmaster: J R Jones BEd(Oxon)
Type: Coeducational Day & Boarding
Age range: 3–13
No. of pupils: B245 G162
Fees: Day £7656–12,699 WB £16,866 FB £17,316

St John's Beaumont Preparatory School
Old Windsor, Windsor & Maidenhead SL4 2JN
Tel: 01784 432428
Headmaster: Mr G E F Delaney BA(Hons), PGCE
Type: Boys' Day & Boarding
Age range: 3½–13
No. of pupils: 310
Fees: Day £7140–£13,320 WB £17,520 FB £20,250

St Mary's School Ascot
St Mary's Road, Ascot, Windsor & Maidenhead SL5 9JF
Tel: 01344 293614
Headmistress: Mrs Mary Breen BSc, MSc
Type: Girls' Boarding & Day
Age range: 11–18
No. of pupils: 370 G370 VIth104
Fees: Day £18,930 FB £26,610

St Piran's Preparatory School
Gringer Hill, Maidenhead, Windsor & Maidenhead SL6 7LZ
Tel: 01628 594300
Headmaster: Mr J A Carroll BA(Hons), BPhilEd, PGCE, NPQH
Type: Coeducational Day
Age range: 2½–13
No. of pupils: B192 G184
Fees: Day £2850–£10,560

Sunningdale School
Sunningdale, Windsor & Maidenhead SL5 9PY
Tel: 01344 620159
Headmaster: T A C N Dawson MA, PGCE
Type: Boys' Boarding
Age range: 8–13
No. of pupils: 100
Fees: Day £12,960 FB £15,690

The Marist Convent Preparatory School
King's Road, Sunninghill, Ascot,
Windsor & Maidenhead SL5 7PS
Tel: 01344 626137
Headteacher: Mrs J A Peachey BEd, MA
Type: Girls' Day
Age range: 3–11
No. of pupils: 242
Fees: Day £6780

The Marist Schools
King's Road, Sunninghill, Ascot,
Windsor & Maidenhead SL5 7PS
Tel: 01344 624291
Headteachers: Mr K McCloskey (Senior School)
Type: Girls' Day
Age range: 2½–18
No. of pupils: 550 VIth65
Fees: Day £7230–£9900

Upton House School
115 St Leonard's Road, Windsor,
Windsor & Maidenhead SL4 3DF
Tel: 01753 862610
Headmistress: Mrs Madeleine Collins BA(Hons), PGCE(Oxford)
Type: Girls' Day
Age range: B2–7 G2–11
No. of pupils: 250 B80 G170
Fees: Day £3900–£10,425

Winbury School
Hibbert Road, Bray, Maidenhead,
Windsor & Maidenhead SL6 1UU
Tel: 01628 627412
Headmistress: Mrs P Prewett CertEd
Type: Coeducational Day
Age range: 2–8
No. of pupils: 60 B35 G25
Fees: Day £1144–£1980

WOKINGHAM

Bearwood College
Bearwood, Wokingham RG41 5BG
Tel: 0118 974 8300
Headmaster: Mr S G G Aiano MA(Cantab)
Type: Coeducational Boarding & Day
Age range: 0–18
No. of pupils: 426 VIth77
Fees: Day £12,846–£15,132 WB £22,527–£25,965
FB £22,527–£25,965

Holme Grange School
Heathlands Road, Wokingham RG40 3AL
Tel: 0118 978 1566
Headteacher: Mrs C Robinson
Type: Coeducational Day
Age range: 3–13
No. of pupils: 257 B153 G104
Fees: Day £4350–£10,236

Luckley-Oakfield School
Luckley Road, Wokingham RG40 3EU
Tel: 0118 978 4175
Headmistress: Miss V A Davis BSc(London), ARCS
Type: Girls' Boarding & Day
Age range: 11–18
No. of pupils: 300 VIth50
Fees: Day £12,735 WB £20,109 FB £21,699

Ludgrove
Wokingham RG40 3AB
Tel: 0118 978 9881
Heads: S W T Barber & A C T Inglis
Type: Boys' Boarding
Age range: 8–13
No. of pupils: 180
Fees: FB £20,250

Our Lady's Preparatory School
The Avenue, Crowthorne, Wokingham RG45 6PB
Tel: 01344 773394
Headmistress: Mrs Helene Robinson
Type: Coeducational Day
Age range: 3 months–11 years
No. of pupils: 100 B50 G50
Fees: Day £5328–£10,464

Waverley School
Waverley Way, Finchampstead, Wokingham RG40 4YD
Tel: 0118 973 1121
Principal: Mrs Jane Sculpher
Type: Coeducational Day
Age range: 3–11
No. of pupils: B78 G60
Fees: Day £3300–£7362

White House Preparatory School
Finchampstead Road, Wokingham RG40 3HD
Tel: 0118 978 5151
Headmistress: Mrs Sarah Gilliam
Type: Girls' Day
Age range: B2–4 G2–11
No. of pupils: 120
Fees: Day £2271–£8175

International Schools

Key to symbols

(🧍) Boys' school

(🧍) Girls' school

(🧍🧍) Coeducational school

(🌍) International school

(16) Tutorial or sixth form college

(A) A levels

(🛏) Boarding accommodation

(£) Bursaries

(IB) International Baccalaureate

(✏) Learning support

(16) Entrance at 16+

(🎞) Vocational qualifications

LONDON

NORTH LONDON

THE NORTH LONDON INTERNATIONAL SCHOOL
For further details see p. 100

6 Friern Barnet Lane, London N11 3LX
Tel: +44 (0)20 8920 0600
Email: admissions@nlis.org
Website: www.nlis.org
Head of School: Mr David Rose MA(Ed), BA, CertEd
Type: Coeducational International Day
Age range: 2–19
No. of pupils: 400
Fees: Day £3225–£15,480

NORTH-WEST LONDON

International Community School

4 York Terrace East, Regent's Park, London NW1 4PT
Tel: 020 7935 1206
Head of School: Mr Philip D M Hurd
Type: Coeducational Day & Boarding
Age range: 3–18
No. of pupils: 360 B190 G170
Fees: Day £10,641–£13,947

Mill Hill School

The Ridgeway, Mill Hill Village, London NW7 1QS
Tel: 020 8959 1176
Head: Dr Dominic Luckett
Type: Coeducational Boarding & Day
Age range: 13–18
No. of pupils: 689 B492 G197 VIth259
Fees: Day £13,860 FB £21,900

Southbank International School - Hampstead

16 Netherhall Gardens, London NW3 5TH
Tel: 020 7243 3803
Principal: Helen O'Donoghue
Type: Coeducational Day
Age range: 3–11
No. of pupils: 216 B108 G108
Fees: Day £11,400–£18,150

The American School in London

One Waverley Place, London NW8 0NP
Tel: 020 7449 1221
Head: Mrs Coreen Hester
Type: Coeducational Day
Age range: 4–18
No. of pupils: 1323 B660 G663
Fees: Day £17,780–£21,500

THE ROYAL SCHOOL, HAMPSTEAD
For further details see p. 101

65 Rosslyn Hill, Hampstead, London NW3 5UD
Tel: 020 7794 7708
Email: enquiries@royalschoolhampstead.net
Website: www.royalschoolhampstead.net
Headmistress: Ms J Ebner BEd(Hons)(Cantab),
MA(London), PGDipCouns, Cert FT, NPQH
Type: Girls' Day & Boarding
Age range: 3–16
No. of pupils: 210
Fees: Day £8940–£10,500 WB £15,870 FB £20,700

SOUTH-EAST LONDON

Dulwich College

London SE21 7LD
Tel: 020 8299 9263
Master: Dr J Spence
Type: Boys' Day & Boarding
Age range: 7–18
No. of pupils: 1400 VIth420
Fees: Day £14,184 WB £27,441 FB £28,971

St Dunstan's College

Stanstead Road, London SE6 4TY
Tel: 020 8516 7200
Headmistress: Mrs J D Davies BSc
Type: Academically Selective Coeducational Day
Age range: 3–18
No. of pupils: 870
Fees: Day £6918–£12,174

SOUTH-WEST LONDON

Centre Academy London

92 St John's Hill, Battersea, London SW11 1SH
Tel: 020 7738 2344
Principal: Duncan Rollo BA, MA, PhD
Type: Independent Coeducational Day
Age range: 9–18
No. of pupils: 60 B45 G15 VIth13
Fees: Day £24,369–£32,400

King's College School

Southside, Wimbledon Common, London SW19 4TT
Tel: 020 8255 5352
Head Master: A D Halls MA
Type: Boys' Day
Age range: 13–18
No. of pupils: 762 VIth295
Fees: Day £15,450

St Paul's School
Lonsdale Road, Barnes, London SW13 9JT
Tel: 020 8748 9162
High Master: Martin Stephen
Type: Boys' Boarding & Day
Age range: 13–18
No. of pupils: 815 VIth320
Fees: Day £11,085 FB £16,485

Westminster School
17 Dean's Yard, Westminster, London SW1P 3PF
Tel: 020 7963 1003
Headmaster: Dr Stephen Spurr
Type: Boys' Boarding & Day
Age range: B13–18 G16–18
No. of pupils: 750 B615 G135
Fees: Day £19,056–£20,664 FB £27,516

WEST LONDON

International School of London
139 Gunnersbury Avenue, Acton, London W3 8LG
Tel: +44 (0)20 8992 5823
Head of School: Huw Davies
Type: Coeducational Day
Age range: 3–18
No. of pupils: 350 B190 G160 VIth50
Fees: Day £14,250–£19,750

King Fahad Academy
Bromyard Avenue, Acton, London W3 7HD
Tel: 020 8743 0131
Director: Dr Sumaya Alyusuf
Type: Coeducational Day
Age range: 3–18
No. of pupils: 446
Fees: Day £3000

Southbank International School - Kensington
36-38 Kensington Park Road, London W11 3BU
Tel: 020 7243 3803
Principal: Judith Kingsbury
Type: Coeducational Day
Age range: 3–11
No. of pupils: 202 B98 G104
Fees: Day £11,400–£18,150

Southbank International School - Westminster
63-65 Portland Place, London W1B 1QR
Tel: 020 7243 3803
Principal: Terry Hedger
Type: Coeducational Day
Age range: 11–19
No. of pupils: 318 B143 G175 VIth108
Fees: Day £19,380–£21,450

The Godolphin and Latymer School
Iffley Road, Hammersmith, London W6 0PG
Tel: +44 (0)20 8741 1936
Head Mistress: Mrs R Mercer BA
Type: Girls' Day
Age range: 11–18
No. of pupils: 700
Fees: Day £13,470

GREATER LONDON

ACS HILLINGDON INTERNATIONAL SCHOOL
For further details see p. 90
Hillingdon Court, 108 Vine Lane, Hillingdon, Uxbridge, Middlesex UB10 0BE
Tel: 01895 259 771
Email: hillingdonadmissions@acs-england.co.uk
Website: www.acs-england.co.uk
Head of School: Ginger Apple
Type: Coeducational Day
Age range: 4–18
No. of pupils: 539 B280 G259
Fees: Day £8820–£18,560

Farringtons School
Perry Street, Chislehurst, Kent BR7 6LR
Tel: 020 8467 0256
Headmistress: Mrs C E James MA
Type: Coeducational Day & Boarding
Age range: 3–19
No. of pupils: 480 VIth60
Fees: Day £8220–£11,220 WB £20,010 FB £21,300

Harrow School
5 High Street, Harrow on the Hill, Middlesex HA1 3HT
Tel: 020 8872 8007
Head Master: Mr Barnaby J Lenon MA
Type: Boys' Boarding
Age range: 13–18
No. of pupils: 800 VIth320
Fees: FB £28,545

Marymount International School London
George Road, Kingston upon Thames, Surrey KT2 7PE
Tel: +44 (0)20 8949 0571
Headmistress: Sister Michaeline O'Dwyer RSHM
Type: Girls' Day & Boarding
Age range: G11–18
No. of pupils: 246 VIth110
Fees: Day £15,340–£17,530 WB £25,990–£28,180
FB £27,240–£29,430

North London Collegiate School
Canons, Canons Drive, Edgware, Middlesex HA8 7RJ
Tel: +44 (0)20 8952 0912
Headmistress: Mrs Bernice McCabe
Type: Girls' Day
Age range: 4–18
No. of pupils: 1060
Fees: Day £10,926–£12,924

Royal Russell School
Coombe Lane, Croydon, Surrey CR9 5BX
Tel: 020 8657 3669
Head: Dr John R Jennings
Type: Coeducational Day & Boarding
Age range: 11–18
No. of pupils: 590 B310 G280 VIth180
Fees: Day £13,290 FB £19,455–£26,310

ST HELEN'S SCHOOL
For further details see p. 98
Eastbury Road, Northwood, Middlesex HA6 3AS
Tel: +44 (0)1923 843210
Email: enquiries@sthn.co.uk
Website: www.sthn.co.uk
Head: Mrs Mary Morris BA
Type: Girls' Day
Age range: G3–18
No. of pupils: 1122 VIth160
Fees: Day £8343–£12,171

St James Senior Boys School
Pope's Villa, 19 Cross Deep, Twickenham,
Middlesex TW1 4QG
Tel: 020 8892 2002
Headmaster: Mr David Boddy
Type: Boys' Day & Weekly Boarding
Age range: B11–18
No. of pupils: 310 VIth65
Fees: Day £11,100 WB £4350

Whitgift School
Haling Park, South Croydon, Surrey CR2 6YT
Tel: +44 (0)20 8688 9222
Headmaster: Dr Christopher Barnett
Type: Boys' Day
Age range: 10–18
No. of pupils: 1279
Fees: Day £13,266

SOUTH EAST

BRACKNELL FOREST

Wellington College
Duke's Ride, Crowthorne, Bracknell Forest RG45 7PU
Tel: +44 (0)1344 444 000
Master: Dr Anthony Seldon
Type: Coeducational Boarding & Day
Age range: 13–18
No. of pupils: 940 B630 G310 VIth400
Fees: Day £20,760–£23,535 FB £27,705

BRIGHTON & HOVE

BRIGHTON COLLEGE
For further details see p. 94
Eastern Road, Brighton, Brighton & Hove BN2 0AL
Tel: 01273 704200
Email: registrar@brightoncollege.net
Website: www.brightoncollege.org.uk
Headmaster: Richard Cairns MA
Type: Coeducational Pre-Prep, Prep and Senior
Age range: 3–18
No. of pupils: 730 VIth300
Fees: Day £3747–£15,534 FB £21,150–£24,078

Roedean School
Roedean Way, Brighton, Brighton & Hove BN2 5RQ
Tel: 01273 667500
Headmistress: Mrs Frances King MA(Oxon), MA(London),
MBA(Hull)
Type: Girls' Boarding & Day
Age range: B3–11 G3–18
No. of pupils: VIth168
Fees: Day £4860–£5600 FB £8700–£9675

BUCKINGHAMSHIRE

Pipers Corner School
Pipers Lane, Great Kingshill, High Wycombe,
Buckinghamshire HP15 6LP
Tel: 01494 718 255
Headmistress: Mrs H J Ness-Gifford BA (Hons), PGCE
Type: Girls' Boarding & Day
Age range: 3–18
No. of pupils: 480 VIth62
Fees: Day £6300–£12,210 WB £16,350–£19,890
FB £16,590–£20,130

Stowe School
Buckingham, Buckinghamshire MK18 5EH
Tel: 01280 818000
Headmaster: Dr Anthony Wallersteiner
Type: Coeducational Boarding & Day
Age range: 13–18
No. of pupils: 740 B500 G230 VIth350
Fees: Day £19,860 FB £26,850

Wycombe Abbey School
High Wycombe, Buckinghamshire HP11 1PE
Tel: 01494 520381
Headmistress: Mrs Cynthia Hall MA(Oxon)
Type: Girls' Day & Boarding
Age range: 11–18
No. of pupils: 562 VIth161
Fees: Day £21,150 FB £28,200

CAMBRIDGESHIRE

Kimbolton School
Kimbolton, Huntingdon, Cambridgeshire PE28 0EA
Tel: 01480 860505
Headmaster: Jonathan Belbin BA
Type: Coeducational Day & Boarding
Age range: 4–18
No. of pupils: B486 G439 VIth170
Fees: Day £6945–£10,830 FB £17,940

St Mary's School
Bateman Street, Cambridge, Cambridgeshire CB2 1LY
Tel: 01223 353253
Headmistress: Miss Charlotte Avery
Type: Girls' Day & Boarding
Age range: 4–18
No. of pupils: 633 G633 VIth85
Fees: Day £12,120 WB £22,470 FB £25,584

The King's School Ely
Ely, Cambridgeshire CB7 4DB
Tel: 01353 660700
Head: Mrs Susan Freestone MEd, GRSM, LRAM, ARCM,
FRSA
Type: Coeducational Boarding & Day
Age range: 13–18
No. of pupils: 471 B283 G188 VIth168
Fees: Day £15,570 WB £22,530 FB £22,530

The Leys School
Cambridge, Cambridgeshire CB2 2AD
Tel: 01223 508900
Headmaster: Mark Slater
Type: Coeducational Boarding & Day
Age range: 11–18
No. of pupils: B330 G210 VIth200

EAST SUSSEX

Battle Abbey School
Battle, East Sussex TN33 0AD
Tel: 01424 772385
Headmaster: Mr R C Clark BA(Hons), MA(Ed)
Type: Coeducational Day & Boarding
Age range: 2–18
No. of pupils: 286 B140 G146 VIth48
Fees: Day £6225–£13,200 FB £22,350

Buckswood School
Broomham Hall, Rye Road, Guestling, Hastings,
East Sussex TN35 4LT
Tel: 01424 813813
Headmaster: Mr Tim Fish BA
Type: Coeducational Day & Boarding
Age range: 10–19
No. of pupils: 280
Fees: Day £9270 WB £14,970 FB £15,660–£19,800

Eastbourne College
Old Wish Road, Eastbourne, East Sussex BN21 4JX
Tel: 01323 452323
Headmaster: Mr S P Davies MA
Type: Coeducational Boarding & Day
Age range: 13–18
No. of pupils: 630 B382 G248 VIth277
Fees: Day £16,305 FB £24,630

Greenfields School
Priory Road, Forest Row, East Sussex RH18 5JD
Tel: 01342 822189
Headteacher: Mrs V Tupholme
Type: Coeducational Boarding & Day
Age range: 2–18
No. of pupils: 152 B89 G63 VIth5
Fees: Day £2580–£9960 WB £12,777–£16,410
FB £12,777–£16,410

(figures)

Michael Hall School
Kidbrooke Park, Forest Row, East Sussex RH18 5JB
Tel: 01342 822275
Head: Chair of the College of Teachers
Type: Coeducational Day & Boarding
Age range: 3–19
No. of pupils: B233 G281 VIth35
Fees: Day £4600–£10,100 WB £1450–£1850
FB £1750–£2150

(figures)

Moira House Girls School
Upper Carlisle Road, Eastbourne, East Sussex BN20 7TD
Tel: 01323 644144
Principal: Mrs Lesley Watson MA(Ed)
Type: Girls' Boarding & Day
Age range: 2–18
No. of pupils: 360 VIth80
Fees: Day £5835–£13,560 WB £17,115–£21,390
FB £18,420–£23,610

(figures)

Newlands School
Eastbourne Road, Seaford, East Sussex BN25 4NP
Tel: 01323 490000
Headmaster: Mr C Bridgman BEd(Hons)
Type: Coeducational Day & Boarding
Age range: 2–18
Fees: Day £5400–£10,800 WB £12,450–£17,850
FB £12,600–£18,000

(figures)

St Bede's School
The Dicker, Hailsham, East Sussex BN27 3QH
Tel: 01323 843252
Head: Mr S Cole BA
Type: Coeducational Day & Boarding
Age range: 12½–18+
No. of pupils: 800 B485 G315 VIth295
Fees: Day £13,665 FB £22,230

(figures)

St Leonards-Mayfield School
The Old Palace, Mayfield, East Sussex TN20 6PH
Tel: 01435 874600
Head: Miss Antonia Beary MA, Mphil (Cantab), PGCE
Type: Girls' Boarding & Day
Age range: 11–18
No. of pupils: 420 G420 VIth100
Fees: Day £15,285 WB £23,010 FB £23,010

(figures)

ESSEX

Brentwood School
Ingrave Road, Brentwood, Essex CM15 8AS
Tel: 01277 243243
Headmaster: Mr D I Davies
Type: Coeducational Day & Boarding
Age range: 11–18
No. of pupils: 1099 B681 G418 VIth334
Fees: Day £12,144 FB £21,426

(figures)

Chigwell School
High Road, Chigwell, Essex IG7 6QF
Tel: 020 8501 5700
Headmaster: Mr M E Punt MA, MSc
Type: Coeducational Day & Sixth Form Boarding
Age range: 7–18
No. of pupils: 740 VIth273
Fees: Day £8391–£12,903 WB £17,493–£18,567 FB £19,611

(figures)

Felsted School
Felsted, Great Dunmow, Essex CM6 3LL
Tel: +44 (0) 1371 822605
Headmaster: Dr Michael Walker
Type: Coeducational Day & Boarding
Age range: 13–18
No. of pupils: 516
Fees: Day £17,949 FB £23,979

(figures)

Friends' School
Mount Pleasant Road, Saffron Walden, Essex CB11 3EB
Tel: 01799 525351
Head: Graham Wigley BA, MA
Type: Coeducational Day & Boarding
Age range: 3–18
No. of pupils: B230 G170 VIth50
Fees: Day £2060–£2830 WB £5345–£6495 FB £5575–£7035

(figures)

Gosfield School

Cut Hedge Park, Halstead Road, Gosfield, Halstead,
Essex CO9 1PF
Tel: 01787 474040
Principal: Claire Goodchild BSc(Hons), CertEd
Type: Coeducational Day & Boarding
Age range: 4–18
No. of pupils: B122 G66 VIth12
Fees: Day £5160–£9150 WB £10,860–£12,720

(⭑⭑) (🌐) (A) (🏛) (£) (✎) (16·)

New Hall School

Boreham, Chelmsford, Essex CM3 3HT
Tel: 01245 467588
Headmistress: Mrs Katherine Jeffrey MA, BA, PGCE,
MA(Ed Mg), NPQH
Type: Coeducational Day & Boarding
Age range: B3–11 G3–18
No. of pupils: B94 G593 VIth108
Fees: Day £5820–£11,910 FB £14,250–£17,910

(⭑⭑) (🌐) (A) (🏛) (£) (✎) (16·)

HAMPSHIRE

Bedales School

Church Road, Steep, Petersfield, Hampshire GU32 2DG
Tel: 01730 711569
Head: Keith Budge MA
Type: Coeducational Boarding & Day
Age range: 13–18
No. of pupils: 451 B217 G234 VIth166
Fees: Day £20,976 FB £26,664

(⭑⭑) (🌐) (A) (🏛) (£) (✎) (16·)

Brockwood Park & Inwoods School

Bramdean, Hampshire SO24 0LQ
Tel: 01962 771 744
Co-Principles: Bill Taylor & Adrian Sydenham
Type: Coeducational Boarding
Age range: 4–19
No. of pupils: 92 B46 G46
Fees: Day £3150 FB £14,200

(⭑⭑) (🌐) (A) (🏛) (✎) (16·)

Hampshire Collegiate School

Embley Park, Romsey, Hampshire SO51 6ZE
Tel: 01794 512206
Principal: Hector McDonald
Type: Coeducational Day & Boarding
Age range: 11–18
No. of pupils: 850 B375 G475 VIth100
Fees: Day £10,800 WB £19,800 FB £19,800

(⭑⭑) (🌐) (A) (🏛) (£) (✎) (16·)

Lord Wandsworth College

Long Sutton, Hook, Hampshire RG29 1TB
Tel: 01256 862201
Headmaster: Mr Fergus Livingstone MA(Oxon)
Type: Coeducational Boarding & Day
Age range: 11–18
No. of pupils: 530 VIth160
Fees: Day £16,623–£17,511 WB £22,263–£23,496
FB £22,263–£24,681

(⭑⭑) (🌐) (A) (🏛) (✎) (16·)

Moyles Court School

Moyles Court, Ringwood, Hampshire BH24 3NF
Tel: 01425 472856
Headmaster: Mr Dean
Type: Coeducational Day & Boarding
Age range: 3–16
No. of pupils: B83 G63
Fees: Day £3285–£4650 FB £6690–£7740

(⭑⭑) (🌐) (🏛)

Rookwood School

Weyhill Road, Andover, Hampshire SP10 3AL
Tel: 01264 325900
Headmistress: Mrs M P Langley BSc(Hons)
Type: Coeducational Day & Boarding
Age range: 3–16
No. of pupils: B120 G189
Fees: Day £6885–£11,340 FB £17,340–£20,295

(⭑⭑) (🌐) (🏛) (£) (✎)

St Swithun's School

Alresford Road, Winchester, Hampshire SO21 1HA
Tel: 01962 835700
Headmistress: Dr H L Harvey BSc, PhD(London)
Type: Girls' Boarding & Day
Age range: 11–18
No. of pupils: 482 VIth120
Fees: Day £14,400 FB £23,745

(⭑) (🌐) (A) (🏛) (£) (16·)

Stanbridge Earls School

Stanbridge Lane, Romsey, Hampshire SO51 0ZS
Tel: 01794 529400
Head: Mr G Link CertEd, MEd
Type: Coeducational Boarding & Day
Age range: 10–19
No. of pupils: 176 B144 G32 VIth46
Fees: Day £14,232–£15,489 FB £19,095–£20,895

(⭑⭑) (🌐) (A) (🏛) (£) (✎) (16·) (🐾)

Winchester College
College Street, Winchester, Hampshire SO23 9NA
Tel: 01962 621247
Headmaster: R D Townsend MA, DPhil
Type: Boys' Boarding & Day
Age range: 13–18
No. of pupils: 680 VIth280
Fees: Day £27,405 FB £28,845

HERTFORDSHIRE

Aldenham School
Elstree, Hertfordshire WD6 3AJ
Tel: 01923 858122
Headmaster: J C Fowler MA
Type: Coeducational Boarding & Day
Age range: 3–18
No. of pupils: 700 B550 G150 VIth160
Fees: Day £11,874–£17,085 FB £17,784–£24,837

Berkhamsted School
133 High Street, Berkhamsted, Hertfordshire HP4 2DJ
Tel: 01442 358000
Principal: Mr Mark Steed MA(Cantab), MA
Type: Coeducational Boarding & Day
Age range: 3–18
No. of pupils: 1518 B846 G672
Fees: Day £6900–£15,582 FB £22,461–£24,792

Bishop's Stortford College
10 Maze Green Road, Bishop's Stortford,
Hertfordshire CM23 2PJ
Tel: 01279 838575
Headmaster: Mr John Trotman
Type: Coeducational Day & Boarding
Age range: 13–18
No. of pupils: B297 G213 VIth213
Fees: Day £13,950 WB £19,392 FB £19,587–£19,776

Haileybury
Haileybury, Hertford, Hertfordshire SG13 7NU
Tel: +44 (0)1992 706200
The Master: J S Davies MA(Cantab)
Type: Coeducational Boarding & Day
Age range: 11–18
No. of pupils: 759
Fees: Day £12,852–£19,338 FB £16,332–£25,749

Princess Helena College
Preston, Hitchin, Hertfordshire SG4 7RT
Tel: 01462 432100
Headmistress: Mrs Jo-Anne Duncan
Type: Girls' Boarding & Day
Age range: 11–18
No. of pupils: 158 VIth40
Fees: Day £12,540–£15,840 FB £17,910–£22,875

Queenswood
Shepherd's Way, Brookmans Park, Hatfield,
Hertfordshire AL9 6NS
Tel: 01707 602500
Principal: Mrs P C Edgar BA(Hons) London, PGCE
Type: Girls' Boarding & Day
Age range: 11–18
No. of pupils: 410 VIth109
Fees: Day £18,015–£19,680 FB £23,370–£25,485

St Christopher School
Barrington Road, Letchworth, Hertfordshire SG6 3JZ
Tel: 01462 650 850
Head: Richard Palmer
Type: Coeducational Day & Boarding
Age range: 2½–18 B3–18 G3–18
No. of pupils: B307 G196 VIth78
Fees: Day £3270–£14,040 FB £19,050–£24,645

St Edmund's College
Old Hall Green, Nr Ware, Hertfordshire SG11 1DS
Tel: 01920 821504
Headmaster: Mr Chris Long BA
Type: Coeducational Day & Boarding
Age range: 3–18
No. of pupils: 814 B514 G300 VIth158
Fees: Day £8550–£13,680 WB £17,625–£20,070
FB £19,425–£22,215

St Francis' College
The Broadway, Letchworth, Hertfordshire SG6 3PJ
Tel: 01462 670511
Headmistress: Miss M Hegarty BA, HDipEd, DHS
Type: Girls' Day & Boarding
Age range: 3–18+
No. of pupils: 500 VIth62
Fees: Day £4920–£9585 WB £13,245–£15,855
FB £16,275–£18,855

Stanborough School
Stanborough Park, Garston, Watford,
Hertfordshire WD25 9JT
Tel: 01923 673268
Head: Mr Roger Murphy
Type: Coeducational Day & Boarding
Age range: 3–19
No. of pupils: 300 B128 G172 VIth20
Fees: Day £3660–£5500 WB £12,834–£15,846

(🏃🏃) (🌐) (🏫) (IB) (16·)

The Purcell School, London
Aldenham Road, Bushey, Hertfordshire WD2 3TS
Tel: 01923 331100
Headmaster: Mr Peter Crook MA, BMus, ARAM, ARCO
Type: Coeducational Day & Boarding
Age range: 8–18
No. of pupils: 167 B57 G110 VIth70
Fees: WB £22,452 FB £28,716

(🏃🏃) (🌐) (A) (🏫) (£) (✏) (16·)

The Royal Masonic School for Girls
Rickmansworth Park, Rickmansworth,
Hertfordshire WD3 4HF
Tel: 01923 773168
Headmistress: Mrs Diana Rose MA(Cantab)
Type: Girls' Day & Boarding
Age range: 4–18
No. of pupils: 810
Fees: Day £7170–£13,380 WB £12,510–£20,865
FB £12,720–£21,390

(🏃) (🌐) (A) (🏫) (£) (16·) (🎾)

Tring Park School for the Performing Arts
Tring Park, Tring, Hertfordshire HP23 5LX
Tel: 01442 824255
Principal: Mr Stefan Anderson MA, ARCM, ARCT
Type: Coeducational Boarding & Day
Age range: 8–19
No. of pupils: 294 B72 G222 VIth107
Fees: Day £12,600–£19,710 FB £19,485–£27,525

(🏃🏃) (🌐) (A) (🏫) (✏) (16·) (🎾)

KENT

ASHFORD SCHOOL
For further details see p. 85
East Hill, Ashford, Kent TN24 8PB
Tel: 01233 739030
Email: registrar@ashfordschool.co.uk
Website: www.ashfordschool.co.uk
Head: Mr M R Buchanan BSc(Hons), CertEd, NPQH, CPhys
Type: Coeducational Day & Boarding
Age range: 3 months–18 years
No. of pupils: 724
Fees: Day £5850–£13,530 FB £21,810–£24,615

(🏃🏃) (🌐) (A) (🏫) (£) (✏) (16·)

Beechwood Sacred Heart
12 Pembury Road, Tunbridge Wells, Kent TN2 3QD
Tel: 01892 532747
Headmaster: Mr Nicholas Beesley MA(Oxon)
Type: Coeducational Day & Boarding School
Age range: 3–18
No. of pupils: B141 G272 VIth55
Fees: Day £6855–£14,100 WB £16,740–£20,745
FB £19,425–£23,400

(🏃) (🏃🏃) (🌐) (A) (🏫) (£) (✏) (16·)

Bell Bedgebury International School
Bedgebury Park, Goudhurst, Cranbrook, Kent TN17 2SH
Tel: 01580 879100
Head: Eric Squires
Type: Coeducational Boarding
Age range: 12–19
Fees: FB £24,900

(🏃) (🏃🏃) (🌐) (A) (🏫) (£) (✏) (16·)

Benenden School
Cranbrook, Kent TN17 4AA
Tel: 01580 240592
Headmistress: Mrs C M Oulton MA(Oxon)
Type: Girls' Boarding
Age range: 11–18
No. of pupils: 520 VIth186
Fees: FB £26,100

(🏃) (🌐) (A) (🏫) (£) (✏) (16·)

Bethany School
Goudhurst, Cranbrook, Kent TN17 1LB
Tel: 01580 211273
Headmaster: Mr N D B Dorey MA(Cantab)
Type: Coeducational Boarding & Day
Age range: 11–18
No. of pupils: B293 G136 VIth128
Fees: Day £14,184 WB £21,504 FB £22,143

(🏃🏃) (🌐) (A) (🏫) (£) (✏) (16·)

Cobham Hall School
Cobham, Gravesend, Kent DA12 3BL
Tel: 01474 823371
Headmaster: Mr Paul Mitchell BSc
Type: Girls' Boarding & Day
Age range: 11–18
No. of pupils: 200 VIth60
Fees: Day £13,500–£16,950 FB £20,250–£25,500

(🏃) (🌐) (A) (🏫) (£) (IB) (✏) (16·)

Dover College
Effingham Crescent, Dover, Kent CT17 9RH
Tel: 01304 205969 Ext 201
Headmaster: Stephen Jones
Type: Coeducational Boarding & Day
Age range: 3–18
No. of pupils: 340 B170 G170 VIth100
Fees: Day £5940–£12,585 WB £17,304–£20,622
FB £14,493–£25,437

Kent College
Whitstable Road, Canterbury, Kent CT2 9DT
Tel: 01227 763231
Head Master: Dr D J Lamper
Type: Coeducational Day & Boarding
Age range: 11–18
No. of pupils: 465 B270 G195 VIth157
Fees: Day £14,000–£14,541 WB £23,000–£23,340
FB £24,690–£25,026

KENT COLLEGE PEMBURY
For further details see p. 93
Old Church Road, Pembury, Tunbridge Wells,
Kent TN2 4AX
Tel: 01892 822006
Email: admissions@kentcollege.kent.sch.uk
Website: www.kent-college.co.uk
Headmistress: Mrs Sally-Anne Huang MA(Oxcn), PGCE
Type: Girls' Day & Boarding
Age range: 3–18
No. of pupils: 524 VIth88
Fees: Day £7047–£15,474 FB £19,182–£24,945

Sevenoaks School
Sevenoaks, Kent TN13 1HU
Tel: +44 (0)1732 455133
Head: Mrs Katy Ricks MA
Type: Coeducational Boarding & Day
Age range: 11–18
No. of pupils: 1000 VIth435
Fees: Day £16,413–£18,645 FB £26,322–£28,554

St Edmund's School
St Thomas' Hill, Canterbury, Kent CT2 8HU
Tel: 01227 475600
Headmaster: Mr J M Gladwin BSc(Hons)
Type: Coeducational Day & Boarding
Age range: 13–18
No. of pupils: 310 B170 G140 VIth120
Fees: Day £15,999 FB £24,900

St Lawrence College
Ramsgate, Kent CT11 7AE
Tel: 01843 572931
Headmaster: Reverend Mark Aitken
Type: Coeducational Boarding & Day
Age range: 3–18
No. of pupils: 528 B314 G214 VIth117
Fees: Day £5568–£14,049 WB £18,327–£24,387
FB £18,327–£24,387

Sutton Valence School
Sutton Valence, Maidstone, Kent ME17 3HL
Tel: 01622 845200
Headmaster: Mr B C W Grindlay MA(Cantab), MusB, FRCO,
CHM
Type: Coeducational Day & Boarding
Age range: 11–18
No. of pupils: 520 B358 G162
Fees: Day £12,840–£16,800 WB £20,190–£25,620
FB £20,190–£25,620

The King's School, Canterbury
Canterbury, Kent CT1 2ES
Tel: 01227 595501
Head: Nicholas Clements MA, BSc, RMCS Shrivenham
Type: Coeducational Boarding & Day
Age range: 13–18
No. of pupils: 790 B438 G352 VIth359
Fees: Day £18,330 FB £24,690

TONBRIDGE SCHOOL
For further details see p. 102
Tonbridge, Kent TN9 1JP
Tel: 01732 365555
Email: hmsec@tonbridge-school.org
Website: www.tonbridge-school.co.uk
Headmaster: T H P Haynes
Type: Boys' Day & Boarding
Age range: 13–18
No. of pupils: 750 VIth330
Fees: Day £20,910 FB £28,140

MEDWAY

King's School, Rochester
Satis House, Boley Hill, Rochester, Medway ME1 1TE
Tel: 01634 888555
Headmaster: Dr I R Walker BA, PhD, LTh, ABIA, FCollP, FRSA
Type: Coeducational Day & Boarding
Age range: 13–18
No. of pupils: 688 B482 G206 VIth113
Fees: Day £7655–£14,400 FB £17,145–£24,210

MILTON KEYNES

Thornton College
Thornton, Milton Keynes MK17 0HJ
Tel: 01280 812610
Headmistress: Miss Agnes T Williams
Type: Girls' Day & Boarding
Age range: B2½–4+ G2½–16
No. of pupils: 370 G370
Fees: Day £6300–£10,095 WB £10,500–£13,305
FB £13,305–£16,545

PETERBOROUGH

Peterborough High School
Thorpe Road, Peterborough PE3 6JF
Tel: 01733 343357
Headmaster: Mr A M Meadows BSc(Hons)
Type: Girls' Day & Boarding
Age range: B6 weeks–18 years G6 weeks–18 years
No. of pupils: 360 B90 G270 VIth52
Fees: Day £8131–£11,499 WB £17,412–£18,477
FB £19,788–£21,405

PORTSMOUTH

St John's College
Grove Road South, Southsea, Portsmouth PO5 3QW
Tel: 023 9281 5118
Headmaster: Mr N W Thorne
Type: Coeducational Day & Boarding
Age range: 2–18
No. of pupils: 650 B435 G215 VIth105
Fees: Day £6750–£8895 FB £19,350–£20,700

The Portsmouth Grammar School
High Street, Portsmouth PO1 2LN
Tel: 023 9236 0036
Headmaster: J E Priory MA
Type: Coeducational Day
Age range: 2½–18
No. of pupils: 1603 B1007 G596 VIth289
Fees: Day £6729–£10,491

READING

BRADFIELD COLLEGE
For further details see p. 92
Bradfield, Reading RG7 6AU
Tel: 0118 964 4510
Email: headmaster@bradfieldcollege.org.uk
Website: www.bradfieldcollege.org.uk
Headmaster: Mr Peter Roberts
Type: Coeducational Boarding
Age range: 13–18
No. of pupils: 724 B484 G240 VIth306
Fees: Day £21,900 FB £27,375

Leighton Park School
Shinfield Road, Reading RG2 7ED
Tel: 0118 987 9608
Head: John H Dunston MA, AIL, FRSA
Type: Coeducational Day & Boarding
Age range: 11–18
No. of pupils: 490
Fees: Day £14,160–£16,680 WB £19,020–£22,350
FB £21,630–£25,440

Padworth College
Padworth, Reading RG7 4NR
Tel: 0118 983 2644
Principal: Mrs Linde Melhuish
Type: Coeducational Boarding & Day
Age range: 13–19
No. of pupils: 106 B46 G60 VIth50
Fees: Day £9000 WB £15,900 FB £20,850

Pangbourne College
Pangbourne, Reading RG8 8LA
Tel: 0118 984 2101
Headmaster: Thomas J C Garnier
Type: Coeducational Boarding & Day
Age range: 11–18
No. of pupils: 387 B301 G86 VIth117
Fees: Day £7500–£10,335 FB £10,710–£14,745

QUEEN ANNE'S SCHOOL
For further details see p. 97
6 Henley Road, Caversham, Reading RG4 6DX
Tel: 0118 918 7333
Email: admissions@qas.org.uk
Website: www.qas.org.uk
Headmistress: Mrs Julia Harrington BA(Hons), PGCE, NPQH
Type: Girls' Boarding & Day
Age range: 11–18
No. of pupils: 336 VIth100
Fees: Day £5695 WB £7545–£7975 FB £8395

The Abbey School
Kendrick Road, Reading RG1 5DZ
Tel: 0118 987 2256
Headmistress: Mrs Barbara Stanley BA(Hons), PGCE FRGS
Type: Girls' Day
Age range: 3–18
No. of pupils: 1040 VIth163
Fees: Day £2380–£3840

The Oratory School
Woodcote, Reading RG8 OPJ
Tel: 01491 683500
Head Master: Mr C I Dytor MC, MA
Type: Boys' Boarding & Day
Age range: 11–18
No. of pupils: 390 VIth120
Fees: Day £11,970–£16,308 FB £16,140–£22,575

SURREY

ACS COBHAM INTERNATIONAL SCHOOL
For further details see p. 86
Heywood, Portsmouth Road, Cobham, Surrey KT11 1BL
Tel: 01932 867251
Email: cobhamadmissions@acs-england.co.uk
Website: www.acs-england.co.uk
Head of School: Mr T Lehman
Type: Coeducational Day & Boarding
Age range: 2–18
No. of pupils: 1352 B755 G597 VIth471
Fees: Day £8840–£19,730 FB £29,100–£32,960

ACS EGHAM INTERNATIONAL SCHOOL
For further details see p. 88
Woodlee, London Road, Egham, Surrey TW20 0HS
Tel: 01784 430 800
Email: eghamadmissions@acs-england.co.uk
Website: www.acs-england.co.uk
Head of School: Jeremy Lewis
Type: Coeducational Day
Age range: 2–18
No. of pupils: 583 B304 G279
Fees: Day £8900–£19,240

Box Hill School
Mickleham, Dorking, Surrey RH5 6EA
Tel: 01372 373382
Headmaster: Mr Mark Eagers MA(Cantab)
Type: Coeducational Boarding & Day
Age range: 11–18
No. of pupils: 425 B280 G145 VIth96
Fees: Day £12,600–£15,000 WB £19,500–£21,000 FB £22,800–£24,600

Caterham School
Harestone Valley, Caterham, Surrey CR3 6YA
Tel: 01883 343028
Head: Mr J P Thomas BSc(Hons), MBA, FRSA
Type: Coeducational Day & Boarding
Age range: 3–18
No. of pupils: 1063 B631 G432 VIth273
Fees: Day £4137–£13,260 FB £23,469–£24,741

Charterhouse
Godalming, Surrey GU7 2DX
Tel: Admissions: 01483 291501 General Enquiries: 01483 291500
Headmaster: Rev John Witheridge MA
Type: Boys' Boarding & Day
Age range: B13–18 G16–18
No. of pupils: 733 B634 G105 VIth361
Fees: Day £23,505 FB £28,440

City of London Freemen's School
Ashtead Park, Ashtead, Surrey KT21 1ET
Tel: 01372 277933
Headmaster: Mr Philip MacDonald MA(Oxon)
Type: Coeducational Day & Boarding
Age range: 7–18
No. of pupils: 850 VIth223
Fees: Day £10,295–£13,959 FB £22,212

Cranleigh School

Horseshoe Lane, Cranleigh, Surrey GU6 8QQ
Tel: 01483 273666
Head: Mr G de W Waller MA, MSc, FRSA(Worcester College, Oxford)
Type: Coeducational Boarding & Day
Age range: 13–18
No. of pupils: 606 B401 G205 VIth237
Fees: Day £21,225 FB £26,040

Duke of Kent School

Peaslake Road, Ewhurst, Cranleigh, Surrey GU6 7NS
Tel: 01483 277313
Headmaster: Dr A D Cameron
Type: Coeducational Boarding & Day
Age range: 3–16
No. of pupils: 194 B126 G68
Fees: Day £4410–£12,855 WB £12,135–£15,270 FB £15,735–£18,855

Epsom College

Epsom, Surrey KT17 4JQ
Tel: 01372 821234
Headmaster: Stephen R Borthwick BSc, CPhys, FRSA
Type: Coeducational Boarding & Day
Age range: 13–18
No. of pupils: 720 B474 G246 VIth324
Fees: Day £18,720 WB £25,005 FB £27,405

Frensham Heights

Rowledge, Farnham, Surrey GU10 4EA
Tel: 01252 792561
Headmaster: Mr Andrew Fisher BA, MEd, FRSA
Type: Coeducational Boarding & Day
Age range: 3–18
No. of pupils: 497 B267 G230 VIth105
Fees: Day £5205–£15,300 FB £19,485–£22,680

International School of London in Surrey

Old Woking Road, Woking, Surrey GU22 8HY
Tel: 01483 750409
Headmaster: Marco Damhuis
Type: Coeducational Day
Age range: 3–11
No. of pupils: 105 B52 G53
Fees: Day £8580–£14,490

King Edward's School Witley

Petworth Road, Wormley, Godalming, Surrey GU8 5SG
Tel: +44 (0)1428 686735
Head: John F Attwater MA
Type: Coeducational Boarding & Day
Age range: 11–18
No. of pupils: 420
Fees: Day £16,725 FB £23,280

Prior's Field School

Priorsfield Road, Godalming, Surrey GU7 2RH
Tel: 01483 810551
Head: Mrs J Roseblade MA
Type: Girls' Boarding & Day
Age range: G11–18
No. of pupils: 380 VIth63
Fees: Day £4555 WB £7365 FB £7365

Reed's School

Sandy Lane, Cobham, Surrey KT11 2ES
Tel: 01932 869001
Headmaster: Mr D W Jarrett MA
Type: Boys' Boarding & Day
Age range: B11–18 G16–18
No. of pupils: 575 B530 G45 VIth180
Fees: Day £13,992–£17,499 FB £18,657–£23,151

Royal School Haslemere

Farnham Lane, Haslemere, Surrey GU27 1HQ
Tel: 01428 605805
Headmistress: Mrs Lynne Taylor-Gooby BEd, MA
Type: Girls' Day & Boarding
Age range: 3–18
No. of pupils: 319 VIth50
Fees: Day £5850–£11,868 WB £15,672–£19,191 FB £15,672–£19,191

St Catherine's School

Bramley, Guildford, Surrey GU5 0DF
Tel: 01483 893363
Headmistress: Mrs A M Phillips MA(Cantab)
Type: Girls' Day & Boarding
Age range: 4–18
No. of pupils: 780 VIth140
Fees: Day £5790–£11,760 WB £18,315 FB £18,315

St John's School

Epsom Road, Leatherhead, Surrey KT22 8SP

Tel: 01372 373000

Headmaster: N J R Haddock MBE, MA(Oxon)

Type: Boys' Boarding & Day

Age range: 13–18

No. of pupils: 499 B429 G70 VIth236

Fees: Day £18,495 WB £23,430 FB £25,425

St Teresa's School

Effingham Hill, Dorking, Surrey RH5 6ST

Tel: 01372 452037

Head: Mrs L Falconer BSc(Hons)

Type: Girls' Boarding & Day

Age range: 2–18

No. of pupils: 395 VIth90

Fees: Day £12,690–£13,440 WB £20,415–£21,165
FB £22,125–£22,875

TASIS The American School in England

Coldharbour Lane, Thorpe, Surrey TW20 8TE

Tel: +44 (0)1932 565252

Head: Mr Lyle Rigg

Type: Coeducational Boarding & Day

Age range: 3–18

No. of pupils: 700 B350 G350

Fees: Day £5600–£18,100 FB £29,150

Woldingham School

Marden Park, Woldingham, Surrey CR3 7YA

Tel: 01883 349431

Headmistress: Mrs Jayne Triffitt MA(Oxon)

Type: Girls' Boarding & Day

Age range: 11–18

No. of pupils: 520 VIth150

Fees: Day £15,405 FB £25,305

Yehudi Menuhin School

Stoke Road, Stoke d'Abernon, Cobham, Surrey KT11 3QQ

Tel: 01932 864739

Headmaster: Mr P N Chisholm MA

Type: Coeducational Boarding

Age range: 8–18

No. of pupils: B29 G39 VIth21

WEST BERKSHIRE

Downe House School

Cold Ash, Thatcham, West Berkshire RG18 9JJ

Tel: 01635 200286

Headmistress: Mrs E McKendrick BA(Liverpool)

Type: Girls' Boarding & Day

Age range: 11–18

No. of pupils: 565 VIth174

Fees: Day £20,250 FB £27,975

WEST SUSSEX

Ardingly College

College Road, Ardingly, Haywards Heath,
West Sussex RH17 6SQ

Tel: +44 (0)1444 893000

Headmaster: Mr Peter Green

Type: Coeducational Boarding & Day

Age range: 13–18

No. of pupils: 488 B280 G184 VIth201

Fees: Day £18,450–£18,915 FB £24,600–£25,215

Burgess Hill School for Girls

Keymer Road, Burgess Hill, West Sussex RH15 0EG

Tel: 01444 241050

Headmistress: Mrs Ann Aughwane BSc, CertEd, NPQH

Type: Girls' Day & Boarding

Age range: B2½–4 G2½–18

No. of pupils: 680

Fees: Day £5940–£12,450 FB £21,630

Christ's Hospital

Horsham, West Sussex RH13 0YP

Tel: 01403 211293

Headmaster: John R Franklin BA, MEd(Admin)

Type: Coeducational Boarding

Age range: 11–18

No. of pupils: 816 B414 G402 VIth255

Fees: FB £24,000

Farlington School

Strood Park, Horsham, West Sussex RH12 3PN

Tel: 01403 254967

Headmistress: Mrs Jonnie Goyer MA

Type: Girls' Day & Boarding

Age range: 3–18

No. of pupils: 420

Fees: Day £6090–£12,966 WB £18,066–£20,202
FB £18,483–£20,619

Hurstpierpoint College
Hassocks, West Sussex BN6 9JS
Tel: 01273 833636
Headmaster: Mr T J Manly BA, MSc
Type: Coeducational Boarding & Day
Age range: 13–18
No. of pupils: 566 B333 G233 VIth246
Fees: Day £17,235 WB £21,930 FB £23,175

(🏃)(🌍)(A)(🏛)(£)(16·)

LANCING COLLEGE
For further details see p. 96
Lancing, West Sussex BN15 0RW
Tel: 01273 452213
Email: admissions@lancing.org.uk
Website: www.lancingcollege.co.uk
Headmaster: Mr Jonathan W J Gillespie MA
Type: Coeducational Boarding & Day
Age range: 13–18
No. of pupils: 523 VIth241
Fees: Day £18,705 FB £26,775

(🏃)(🌍)(A)(🏛)(£)(✏)(16·)

Lavant House
West Lavant, Chichester, West Sussex PO18 9AB
Tel: 01243 527211
Headmistress: Mrs K Bartholomew MA(London)
Type: Girls' Day & Boarding
Age range: 3–18
No. of pupils: 160 VIth15
Fees: Day £6210–£12,585 FB £16,500–£19,800

(🏃)(🌍)(A)(🏛)(£)(✏)(16·)

Seaford College
Lavington Park, Petworth, West Sussex GU28 0NB
Tel: 01798 867392
Headmaster: T J Mullins MBA, BA
Type: Coeducational Boarding & Day
Age range: 7–18
No. of pupils: 603 B398 G205 VIth128
Fees: Day £2286–£5200 WB £5300–£6800 FB £6010–£8025

(🏃)(🌍)(A)(🏛)(£)(✏)(16·)

Slindon College
Slindon House, Slindon, Arundel, West Sussex BN18 0RH
Tel: 01243 814320
Headmaster: Mr I P Graham BEd, MA
Type: Boys' Boarding & Day
Age range: B9–16
No. of pupils: 100

(🏃)(🌍)(🏛)(£)(✏)

The Towers Convent School
Convent of the Blessed Sacrement, Henfield Road, Upper
Beeding, Steyning, West Sussex BN44 3TF
Tel: 01903 812185
Headmistress: Mrs Carole A Baker MA, BEd
Type: Girls' Day & Boarding
Age range: B3–8 G3–16
No. of pupils: 313 B6 G307
Fees: Day £5760–£7740 WB £11,070–£12,000
FB £11,910–£13,020

(🏃)(🌍)(🏛)(£)(✏)

WORTH SCHOOL
For further details see p. 103
Paddockhurst Road, Turners Hill, Crawley,
West Sussex RH10 4SD
Tel: 01342 710200
Email: registry@worth.org.uk
Website: www.worthschool.co.uk
Headmaster: Mr Gino Carminati MA, FRSA
Type: Catholic coeducational 11-18 boarding & day
Age range: 11–18
No. of pupils: 506 VIth229
Fees: Day £16,026–£18,339 FB £21,627–£24,756

(🏃)(🌍)(A)(🏛)(£)(IB)(✏)(16·)

WINDSOR & MAIDENHEAD

Eton College
Windsor, Windsor & Maidenhead SL4 6DW
Tel: 01753 671249
Head Master: A R M Little MA
Type: Boys' Boarding
Age range: 13–18
No. of pupils: 1300 VIth515
Fees: FB £24,990

(🏃)(🌍)(A)(🏛)(£)(✏)(16·)

Heathfield St Mary's School
London Road, Ascot, Windsor & Maidenhead SL5 8BQ
Tel: 01344 898 343
Headmistress: Mrs Frances King MA(Oxon), MA(London),
MBA(Hull), PGCE(London)
Type: Girls' Boarding
Age range: 11–18
No. of pupils: 225 VIth78
Fees: FB £22,890

(🏃)(🌍)(A)(🏛)(£)(✏)(16·)

Hurst Lodge

Bagshot Road, Ascot, Windsor & Maidenhead SL5 9JU
Tel: 01344 622154
Principal: Miss V Smit
Type: Girls' Day & Weekly Boarding
Age range: B3–11 G3–18
No. of pupils: 182 B21 G161 VIth18
Fees: Day £4005–£12,540 WB £20,430

Licensed Victuallers' School

London Road, Ascot, Windsor & Maidenhead SL5 8DR
Tel: 01344 882770
Principal: Mr I Mullins BEd(Hons), MSc, MCMI
Type: Coeducational Day & Boarding
Age range: 4–18
No. of pupils: 906 B516 G390 VIth152
Fees: Day £7500–£14,115 FB £19,200–£22,755

St George's School

Wells Lane, Ascot, Windsor & Maidenhead SL5 7DZ
Tel: 01344 629900
Headmistress: Mrs Caroline Jordan MA(Oxon), PGCE
Type: Girls' Boarding & Day
Age range: 11–18
No. of pupils: 280 VIth85
Fees: Day £16,440 FB £25,350

St Mary's School Ascot

St Mary's Road, Ascot, Windsor & Maidenhead SL5 9JF
Tel: 01344 293614
Headmistress: Mrs Mary Breen BSc, MSc
Type: Girls' Boarding & Day
Age range: 11–18
No. of pupils: 370 G370 VIth104
Fees: Day £18,930 FB £26,610

WOKINGHAM

Bearwood College

Bearwood, Wokingham RG41 5BG
Tel: 0118 974 8300
Headmaster: Mr S G G Aiano MA(Cantab)
Type: Coeducational Boarding & Day
Age range: 0–18
No. of pupils: 426 VIth77
Fees: Day £12,846–£15,132 WB £22,527–£25,965
FB £22,527–£25,965

Luckley-Oakfield School

Luckley Road, Wokingham RG40 3EU
Tel: 0118 978 4175
Headmistress: Miss V A Davis BSc(London), ARCS
Type: Girls' Boarding & Day
Age range: 11–18
No. of pupils: 300 VIth50
Fees: Day £12,735 WB £20,109 FB £21,699

Specialist & Sixth Form Schools and Colleges

Key to symbols

(†) Boys' school

(♀) Girls' school

(††) Coeducational school

(🌐) International school

(16) Tutorial or sixth form college

(A) A levels

(⌂) Boarding accommodation

(£) Bursaries

(IB) International Baccalaureate

(✐) Learning support

(16) Entrance at 16+

(✿) Vocational qualifications

LONDON

CENTRAL LONDON

Accent International Consortium for Academic Programs Abroad
99-103 Great Russell Street, London WC1B 3LA
Tel: 020 7813 7723
Head: Natasa Blecic
Type: Coeducational

Cavendish College
35-37 Alfred Place, London WC1E 7DP
Tel: 020 7580 6043
Principal: Dr J Sanders BSc, MBA, PhD
Type: Coeducational Day

City Business College
178 Goswell Road, London EC1V 7DT
Tel: 020 7251 6473
Principal: Mr Munir Nowaz
Type: Coeducational Day

City Lit Centre & Speech Therapy
Keeley House, Keeley Street, London WC2B 4BA
Tel: 020 7492 2600
Principal: Mr G W Horgan
Type: Coeducational

College of Central London
73 Great Eastern Street, London EC2A 3HR
Tel: 020 7739 5555
Head: Mr Nicolas Kailides
Type: Coeducational

eCollege London
1-3 Rivington Street, London EC2A 3DT
Tel: 020 7729 9755
Head: Sheila Prendergast
Type: Coeducational

Financial Training Academy
4 Frederickís Place, Old Jewry, London EC2R 8AB
Tel: 0870 4232316/020 7397 1210
Head: Mr Rafi Ahmad
Type: Coeducational

Guildhall School of Music & Drama
Barbican, London EC2Y 8DT
Tel: 020 7382 7192
Principal: Barry Ife CBE, FKC, HonFRAM
Type: Coeducational Day

Hansard Society
40-43 Chancery Lane, London WC2A 1JA
Tel: 020 7438 1222
Head: Fiona Booth
Type: Coeducational

Holborn School of Finance & Management
25 Old Gloucester Street, Queen Square,
London WC1N 3AN
Tel: 020 7404 2422
Head: Felix Orogun
Type: Coeducational

HULT-International Business School
46-47 Russell Square, Bloomsbury, London WC1B 4JP
Tel: 020 7584 9696
Provost: Mr Ray Hilditch BA, MBA, PGCE, FRSA
Type: Coeducational Day
Age range: 17–60
No. of pupils: 300 B130 G170
Fees: Day £4000 FB £10,260

Italia Conti Academy of Theatre Arts
Italia Conti House, 23 Goswell Road, London EC1M 7AJ
Tel: 020 7608 0047
Principal: Anne Sheward
Type: Coeducational Day
Age range: 10–21

Kensington College
23 Bloomsbury Square, London WC1A 2PJ
Tel: 020 7580 1113
Type: Coeducational Day

Kensington College of Business
Wesley House, 4 Wild Court, Holborn, London WC2B 4AU
Tel: 020 7404 6330
Director: Ian Pirie MA(Oxon)
Type: Coeducational Day

London College of English & Advanced Studies Ltd
178 Goswell Road, London EC1V 7DT
Tel: 020 7250 0610
Type: Coeducational Day

London College of International Business Studies
14 Southampton Place, London WC1A 2AJ
Tel: 020 7242 1004
Heads: Mr Philip Moore & Ms Irene Chong
Type: Coeducational

London School of Accountancy & Management
3rd Floor, 12-20 Camomile Street, London EC3A 7PT
Tel: 020 7623 8777
Head: Mr Dak Patel
Type: Coeducational

London School of Business & Management
Central House, 14 Upper Woburn Place,
London WC1H 0NN
Tel: 020 7388 8877
Head: Mr Alistair Andrews
Type: Coeducational Day

LTC College London
15-17 Great Portland Street, London W1W 8QA
Tel: 020 7580 3659
Head: Mr Ashok Pattani
Type: Coeducational Day

National Council for Drama Training
1-7 Woburn Walk, London WC1H 0JJ
Tel: 020 7387 3650
Director: Adele Bailey
Type: Coeducational

Pitman Training Centre
Warnford Court, 29 Throgmorton Street,
London EC2N 2LT
Tel: 020 7256 6668
Principal: Mrs J Almond
Type: Coeducational Day

Sotheby's Institute of Art - London
30 Bedford Square, Bloomsbury, London WC1B 3EE
Tel: 020 7462 3232
Director: Ms Megan Aldrich
Type: Coeducational Day

The College of Central London
73 Great Eastern Street, London EC2A 3HR
Tel: 020 7739 5555
Director of Studies: Barry Culverwell
Type: Coeducational Day
Fees: Day £3300

The Courtauld Institute of Art
Somerset House, Strand, London WC2R 0RN
Tel: 020 7848 2777
Director: Dr Deborah Swallow
Type: Coeducational

The London Film School
24 Shelton Street, London WC2H 9UB
Tel: 020 7836 9642
Director: Ben Gibson
Type: Coeducational Day

The Method Studio London
Conway Hall, 25 Red Lion Square, London WC1R 4RL
Tel: 020 7831 7335
Type: Coeducational

The School of Computer Technology
73 Great Eastern Street, London EC2A 3HR
Tel: 020 7739 9002
Type: Coeducational Day

Tudor College London
1-6 Speedy Place, off Cromer Street, London WC1H 8BU
Tel: 020 7837 8382
Principal: Mr Timothy Bell
Type: Coeducational

Williams College
Thavies Inn House, 5 Holborn Circus, London EC1N 2HB
Tel: 020 7583 9222
Head: Mr Mujeeb Pathamanathan
Type: Coeducational Day

EAST LONDON

Building Crafts College
Kennard Road, Stratford, London E15 1AH
Tel: 020 8522 1705
Principal: Mr John Taylor
Type: Coeducational Day

City College of Technology

Unit 23, 1-13 Adler Street, London E1 1EG
Tel: 0870 0429615
Head: Mr Denis Akwara
Type: Coeducational

City of London College

71 Whitechapel High Street, London E1 7PL
Tel: 020 7247 2166
Head: Mr David Nixon
Type: Coeducational

City of London College

80 Backchurch Lane, London E1 1LX
Tel: 020 7247 2166
Head: Mr David Nixon
Type: Coeducational

College of Technology London

Bow House, 153-159 Bow Road, London E3 2SE
Tel: 020 8980 7888
Head: Nigel Hall
Type: Coeducational

East End Computing & Business College

149 Commercial Road, London E1 1PX
Tel: 020 7247 8447
Head: Anthony Wilkinson
Type: Coeducational

East London College

Panther House, 647-661 High Road, London E11 4RD
Tel: 020 8539 2224
Type: Coeducational

Guildhall College

60 Nelson Street, London E1 2DE
Tel: 020 7480 9000
Head: Mr Terence Moore
Type: Coeducational

Interlink College of Technology & Business

Interlink House, Unit 11, Unity Works, 22 Sutherland Road, Walthamstow, London E17 6JW
Tel: 0208 531 1118
Head: Mr Kanmi Alo
Type: Coeducational

Leyton College

15-17 Church Chambers, 11-12 Church Lane, London E11 1HG
Tel: 0208 9880368
Head: Nagaraju Chitrapu
Type: Coeducational

London Crown College

80-90 Mile End Road, London E1 4UN
Tel: 020 7790 3330
Head: Mr Firoz Hasan
Type: Coeducational

London Oriental Academy

Suite B, 1-3 Kempton Road, East Ham, London E6 2LD
Tel: 020 8470 9876
Head: Saraswathi Namasivayam
Type: Coeducational

London School of Commerce & IT

128 Commercial Road, London E1 1NL
Tel: 020 7702 2509
Head: Dr Abul Kalam
Type: Coeducational Day

London School of Computer Education

Second Floor, 1-3 Norton Folgate, London E1 6DB
Tel: 020 7392 9696
Head: Mr David Kohn
Type: Coeducational Day

Metropolitan College of London

22-27 The Oval, London E2 9DT
Tel: 020 7159 2601/7168 2024
Head: Mr Mazumdar Kumar
Type: Coeducational Day

Stratford College of Management

298 Romford Road, London E7 9HD
Tel: 020 8522 0060
Head: Dr Raza
Type: Coeducational Day

The Academy Drama School
189 Whitechapel Road, London E1 1DN
Tel: 020 7377 8735
Principal: T Reynolds RADA
Type: Coeducational Day
Age range: 17–40
No. of pupils: 66 B27 G39
Fees: Day £2850–£5985

Western Governors Graduate School
27-33 Bethnal Green Road, London E1 6LA
Tel: 020 7033 9596
Principal: Mark Chatlani
Type: Coeducational Day

Whitechapel College
1-13 Adler Street, London E1 1EG
Tel: 020 7377 8887
Principal: Luke Julias Maughan-Pawsey
Type: Coeducational Day

NORTH LONDON

5 E College of London
Selby Centre, Selby Road, London N17 8JL
Tel: 020 8885 3456/5454
Head: Mr Raj Doshi
Type: Coeducational Day

Academy of the Science of Acting & Directing
9-15 Elthorne Road, London N19 4AJ
Tel: 020 7272 0027
Principal: Helen Pierpoint BSc, PhD
Type: Coeducational

City of London Business College
Ebenezer House, 726-728 Seven Sisters Road,
London N15 5NH
Tel: 020 8800 6621
Head: Mr Kwateng
Type: Coeducational

City of London Business College
Gaunson House, Units 1 / 1A / 2, Markfield Road,
London N15 4QQ
Tel: 020 8808 2810
Head: Mr Kwateng
Type: Coeducational

Court Theatre Training Co
55 East Road, London N1 6AH
Tel: 020 7739 6868
Artistic Director: June Abbott
Type: Coeducational

Impact Factory
Suite 121, Business Design Centre, 52 Upper Street,
London N1 0QH
Tel: 020 7226 1877
Partners: Robin Chandler & Jo Ellen Grzyb
Type: Coeducational

London School of Business & Computing
Business Design Centre, 52 Upper Street, London N1 0QH
Tel: 020 7288 6307/8
Head: Dr Viramouttou
Type: Coeducational Day

London Studio Centre
42-50 York Way, Kings Cross, London N1 9AB
Tel: 020 7837 7741
Directors: Mr Nicholas Espinosa & Ms Nikki Espinosa
Type: Coeducational
Age range: 18+

One-Tech (UK) Ltd
1st Floor, 12 Cheapside, High Road, London N22 6HH
Tel: 020 8889 0707
Head: Mr Len Sutherland
Type: Coeducational Day

The City College
University House, 55 East Road, London N1 6AH
Tel: 020 7253 1133
Principal: A Andrews MCMI
Type: Coeducational Day
Age range: 18–40
No. of pupils: B130 G42

The Dance Studio
843-845 Green Lanes, London N21 2RX
Tel: 020 8360 5700
Type: Coeducational

The Institute - Hampstead Garden Suburb
The Institute Office, 11 High Road, London N2 8LL
Tel: 020 8829 4141
Institute Principal: Fay Naylor
Type: Coeducational

The London Academy of Health & Beauty
53 Alkham Road, Stoke Newington, London N16 7AA
Tel: 020 8806 1135
Type: Coeducational Day
🚹 16⁺

The Poor School & Workhouse Theatre
242 Pentonville Road, Islington, London N1 9JY
Tel: 020 7837 6030
Director: Paul Caister
Type: Coeducational
🚹 16⁺

Vista Training
107-115 Stamford Hill, London N16 5RP
Tel: 020 8802 8772
Type: Coeducational
🚹 16⁺

NORTH-WEST LONDON

Brampton College
Lodge House, Lodge Road, Hendon, London NW4 4DQ
Tel: 020 8203 5025
Principal: Bernard Canetti BA(Hons), MSc
Type: Coeducational Day
Age range: 16–18
No. of pupils: 250
🚹 16⁺ Ⓐ 16⁺

British American Drama Academy
14 Gloucester Gate, London NW1 4HG
Tel: 020 7487 0730
Head: Paul Costello
Type: Coeducational
🚹 16⁺

Hampstead College of Fine Arts & Humanities
24 Lambolle Place, Belsize Park, London NW3 4PG
Tel: 020 7586 0312
Co Principals: Candida Cave CFA(Oxon) & Nicholas Cochrane CFA(Oxon)
Type: Coeducational Day
Age range: 13–19
No. of pupils: 115
Fees: Day £5700–£14,850
🚹 16⁺ Ⓐ £ 16⁺

Hendon Secretarial College
15 Watford Way, Hendon, London NW4 3JL
Tel: 020 8202 3677
Type: Coeducational
🚹 16⁺

Lakefield Catering & Educational Centre
Maresfield Gardens, Hampstead, London NW3 5RY
Tel: 020 7794 5669
Course Director: Mrs Maria Brown
Type: Girls' Boarding & Day
Age range: 16–24
No. of pupils: 16
Fees: FB £1160

London Academy of Dressmaking and Design
18 Dobree Avenue, Willesden, London NW10 2AE
Tel: 020 8451 7174
Principal: Mrs P A Parkinson MA
Type: Coeducational Day
Age range: 13+
Fees: Day £2650
🚹 16⁺ 🖊 16⁺ 🌀

London Thames College
Crown House, North Circular Road, Park Royal, London NW10 7PN
Tel: 020 8961 9003
Head: Dr Archana Raheja
Type: Coeducational Day
🚹 16⁺

Maria Montessori Institute
26 Lyndhurst Gardens, Hampstead, London NW3 5NW
Tel: 020 7435 3646
Director of Training & School: Mrs Lynne Lawrence BA, Mont Int Dip(AMI)
Type: Coeducational/Montessori teacher training
Age range: 18+
No. of pupils: 50
Fees: Day £7100
🚹 16⁺

NW5 Theatre School
14 Fortess Road, London NW5 2EU
Tel: 020 7482 3236
Founder: George O'Gorman
Type: Coeducational
Age range: 16–30
Fees: Day £3600
🚹 16⁺ 16⁺

Sue Nieto Theatre School
19 Parkside, London NW7 2LJ
Tel: 020 8201 1500
Principal: Sue Nieto
Type: Coeducational
Age range: 3–18
🚹 16⁺

Sylvia Young Theatre School

Rossmore Road, Marylebone, London NW1 6NJ
Tel: 020 7402 0673
Headteacher: Ms Frances Chave BSc, PGCE, NPQH
Type: Coeducational Day
Age range: 10–16
No. of pupils: B69 G128
Fees: Day £7650–£10,620 WB £13,800–£14,500
FB £16,300–£17,500

The Brampton College

Lodge House, Lodge Road, Hendon, London NW4 4DQ
Tel: 020 8203 5025
Principal: B Canetti BA(Hons), MSc
Type: Independent Sixth Form College
Age range: 15–20
No. of pupils: B143 G102
Fees: Day £2735–£12,470

The Central School of Speech and Drama

Embassy Theatre, Eton Avenue, London NW3 3HY
Tel: 020 7722 8183
Principal & CEO: Professor Gary Crossley
Type: Coeducational Day

The Interior Design School

22 Lonsdale Road, Queens Park, London NW6 6RD
Tel: 020 7372 2811
Principal: Ms Iris Dunbar
Type: Coeducational Day

Theatretrain

69 Great North Way, London NW4 1HS
Tel: 020 8202 2006
Director: Kevin Dowsett CertEd, AdvDip(Drama in Education)
Type: Coeducational
Age range: 6–18

Wentworth Tutorial College

6-10 Brentmead Place, London NW11 9LH
Tel: 020 8458 8524/5
Principal: Alan Davies BSc, MSc
Type: Coeducational Day
Age range: 14–19
No. of pupils: 115 B82 G33

SOUTH-EAST LONDON

Alpha Meridian Colleges

Meridian House, Greenwich High Road, Greenwich, London SE10 8TL
Tel: 020 8853 4111
Head: Mr Kudsi Tuluoglu
Type: Coeducational

Bellerbys College

Bounty House, Greenwich, London SE8 3DE
Tel: 020 8694 7000
Head: Mr Andy Quin
Type: Coeducational Boarding & Day
Age range: 15–19
No. of pupils: B150 G150
Fees: Day £9600–£13,800 FB £16,730–£20,930

Blake Hall College

10-11 Dock Offices, Surrey Quays Road, London SE16 2XU
Tel: 020 7252 2033
Head: Mr Brink Gardner
Type: Coeducational

Goldsmith International Business School

N107 (North Building), Westminster Business Square, 45 Durham Street, London SE11 5JH
Tel: 020 7820 8212
Head: Mr Emman Aluko
Type: Coeducational

Greenwich School of Management

Meridian House, Royal Hill, Greenwich, London SE10 8RD
Tel: 020 8516 7800
Head: Dr W G Hunt
Type: Coeducational

Hamilton College

9 Albert Embankment, London SE1 7SP
Tel: 020 7820 1133/020 7793 9801
Head: Mr Zubair Ahmad
Type: Coeducational

Holborn College

Woolwich Road, London SE7 8LN
Tel: 020 8317 6000
Principal: Mr Mohamed Maladwala
Type: Coeducational Day

Kaplan Financial (London)
179-191 Borough High Street, London SE1 1HR
Tel: 020 7407 5000
Head: Mr Vinod Siyani
Type: Coeducational

Kings Langley College of Management
Astra House, 23-25 Arklow Road, London SE14 6EB
Tel: 020 8694 2200
Head: Anthony Ward
Type: Coeducational

Laban
Creekside, London SE8 3DZ
Tel: 020 8691 8600
Principal & Chief Executive: Mr Anthony Bowne
Type: Coeducational Day
No. of pupils: 350

London Bridge Business Academy
7-13 Melior Street, London SE1 3QP
Tel: 020 7378 1000
Head: Shmina Mandal
Type: Coeducational

London City College
Royal Waterloo House, 51-55 Waterloo Road,
London SE1 8TX
Tel: 020 7928 0029
Principal: Dr N Kyritsis MA, DMS, MCIM
Type: Coeducational

London College of Accountancy
200 Great Dover Street, London SE1 4YB
Tel: 020 7407 1119
Head: Mr Ravi Gill
Type: Coeducational

London College of Computing & Management
Atrium Suite, The Hop Exchange, 24 Southwark Street,
London SE1 1TY
Tel: 020 7378 6333
Head: Dr Waheed Iqbal
Type: Coeducational

London College of Engineering & Management
18-36 Wellington Street, London SE18 6PF
Tel: 020 8854 6158
Head: Mr Shakhar Sharman
Type: Coeducational

London Institute of Shipping and Transport
51-55 Waterloo Road, London SE1 8TX
Tel: 020 7928 0029
Head: Dr N Kyritsis
Type: Coeducational

Maritime Greenwich College
4th Floor, Royal Sovereign House, 40 Beresford Street,
London SE18 6BF
Tel: 0208 305 8508
Head: Mr N Kandel
Type: Coeducational Day

McAlpine Dance Studio
Longfield Hall, 50 Knatchbull Road, London SE5 9QY
Tel: 020 8673 4992
Type: Coeducational

The British School of Osteopathy
275 Borough High Street, London SE1 1JE
Tel: 020 7407 0222
Principal & Chief Executive: Martin Collins BSc(Hons), PhD,
MSc, Cbiol, MIBiol, FRSH, DO, ILTM
Type: Coeducational Day

SOUTH-WEST LONDON

360 GSP College
6th Floor, Wembley Point, 1 Harrow Road,
London HA9 6DE
Tel: 020 8672 4151/0845 6034709
Head: Mr Yassin Sayfoo
Type: Coeducational Day

Abbey College - London
22 Grosvenor Gardens, Belgravia, London SW1W 0DH
Tel: 020 7824 7300
Principal: Mr Mark Love BEd
Type: Coeducational Day & Boarding
Age range: 14–19
No. of pupils: 150 B70 G80 VIth150
Fees: Day £5950–£16,400 FB £30,200

Academy of Live & Recorded Arts

Studio1, Royal Victoria Patriotic Building, John Archer Way, London SW18 3SX
Tel: 020 8870 6475
Principal: Anthony Castro
Type: Coeducational Day
Age range: 18+
No. of pupils: 108 B46 G62
Fees: Day £3000–£9888

Chelsea Independent College

517-523 Fulham Road, London SW6 1HD
Tel: 020 7610 1114
Principal: Mr Paul Hunt
Type: Coeducational Day
Age range: 16–18
Fees: Day £7500–£14,700

Collingham

23 Collingham Gardens, London SW5 0HL
Tel: 020 7244 7414
Principal: Mr G Hattee MA(Oxon), DipEd
Type: Coeducational Day
Age range: 14–19
No. of pupils: B130 G110 VIth200
Fees: Day £4140–£11,850

DUFF MILLER COLLEGE

For further details see p. 109

59 Queen's Gate, South Kensington, London SW7 5JP
Tel: 020 7225 0577
Email: enqs@duffmiller.com
Website: www.duffmiller.com
Principals: C Denning BSc, PGCE & C Kraft BSc, BPS
Type: Coeducational Day
Age range: 14–19
No. of pupils: 260
Fees: Day £10,000–£16,000

First Steps School of Dance & Drama

234 Lillie Road, London SW6 7QA
Tel: 020 7381 5224
Type: Coeducational
Age range: 3–17
No. of pupils: B50 G450
Fees: Day £2700

Fulham & Chelsea College

Eden House, 59 Fulham High Street, London SW6 3JJ
Tel: 020 7384 4500
Heads: Mr Xavier Amaladoss Arokiam & Ms Kristy Partridge
Type: Coeducational

Inchbald School of Design

Interior Design Faculty, 7 Eaton Gate, London SW1W 9BA
Tel: 020 7730 5508
Principal: Mrs Jacqueline Duncan FIIDA, FIDDA
Type: Coeducational Day
Age range: 18–50
No. of pupils: 120 B20 G100

JJAADA Interior Design Academy

28 Abbeville Mews, 88 Clapham Park Road, London SW4 7BX
Tel: 020 7494 3363

Judith Blacklock Flower School

4/5 Kinnerton Place South, London SW1X 8EH
Tel: 020 7235 6235
Head: Judith Blacklock
Type: Coeducational

London College of Business & Computer Studies

219 Clapham Road, London SW9 9BE
Tel: 020 7733 4868
Principal: Mr T Olarewaju
Type: Coeducational

London College Wimbledon

LCW House, 2A Mansel Road, London SW19 4AA
Tel: 020 8944 1134
Type: Coeducational

London Electronics College

20 Penywern Road, Earls Court, London SW5 9SU
Tel: 020 7373 8721
Principal: M D Spalding BSc(Hons), MSc, CEng, MIEE, PGCE, MCybSoc, FRSA, MIOD
Type: Coeducational Day
Age range: 21–65
Fees: Day £5100

London Film Academy
The Old Church, 52a Walham Grove, London SW6 1QR
Tel: 020 7386 7711
Founders & Joint Principals: Daisy Gili & Anna Macdonald
Type: Coeducational

Mander Portman Woodward - London
90-92 Queen's Gate, London SW7 5AB
Tel: 020 7835 1355
Principal: Matthew Judd BA, PGCE
Type: Coeducational Day
Age range: 14–19
No. of pupils: 434 B256 G178 VIth384
Fees: Day £7218–£17,973

Modern Montessori International Ltd (London)
MMI House, 142 Micham Lane London, London SW16 6SN
Tel: 020 8769 5555
Head: Mrs Marianne Burke
Type: Coeducational Day

Quest Business Training
5 Grosvenor Gardens, Belgravia, London SW1W 0BD
Tel: 020 7233 5957
Type: Coeducational Day
Age range: 16–45

Royal Academy of Dance
36 Battersea Square, London SW11 3RA
Tel: 020 7326 8000
Chief Executive: Luke Rittner
Type: Coeducational Day

Royal College of Art
Kensington Gore, London SW7 2EU
Tel: 020 7590 4444
Rector & Vice-Provost: Professor Christopher Frayling
Type: Coeducational

The Heatherley School of Fine Art
80 Upcerne Road, Chelsea, London SW10 0SH
Tel: 020 7351 4190
Head: John Walton RP, DFA(Lond)
Type: Coeducational Day
Age range: 17–80

Westminster Tutors
86 Old Brompton Road, South Kensington, London SW7 3LQ
Tel: 020 7584 1288
Principal: Virginia Maguire BA, MLitt
Type: Coeducational Day
Age range: 14–mature
No. of pupils: B25 G25 VIth40
Fees: Day £5500–£18,500

Wimbledon School of Art
Merton Hall Road, London SW19 3QA
Tel: 020 8408 5000
Principal: Professor Roderick Bugg
Type: Coeducational

WEST LONDON

Acton Training Centre
296 High Street, Acton, London W3 9BJ
Tel: 020 8992 4144
Head: Mr Sukhev Virdi
Type: Coeducational

Alan D Education
61-62 East Castle Street, London W1W 8NQ
Tel: 020 7580 1030
Director of Education: Alan Hemmings
Type: Coeducational Day
Fees: Day £200 FB £12,400

Albemarle Independent College
18 Dunraven Street, London W1K 7FE
Tel: 020 7409 7273
Co-Principals: Beverley Mellon & James Eytle
Type: Coeducational Day
Age range: 16–19
No. of pupils: 160 B85 G75
Fees: Day £12,500–£14,500

American InterContinental University (AIU) - London
110 Marylebone High Street, London W1U 4RY
Tel: 020 7467 5600
Dean: Dr Allan Plath
Type: Coeducational Day
Age range: 16+

Arts Educational Schools London

Cone Ripman House, 14 Bath Road, Chiswick,
London W4 1LY
Tel: 020 8987 6666
Headmaster: Mr Oliver Price
Type: Independent Vocational Day
Age range: 11–18
No. of pupils: 200
Fees: Day £11,100

ASHBOURNE INDEPENDENT SIXTH FORM COLLEGE
For further details see p. 107

17 Old Court Place, Kensington, London W8 4PL
Tel: 020 7937 3858
Email: admin@ashbournecollege.co.uk
Website: www.ashbournecollege.co.uk
Principal: M J Kirby MSc, BApSc
Type: Independent Sixth Form College
Age range: 16–19
No. of pupils: 170 B80 G90
Fees: Day £19,725 FB £21,500

Bales College

742 Harrow Road, Kensal Town, London W10 4AA
Tel: 020 8960 5899
Principal: William Moore
Type: Coeducational Independent Secondary
Age range: 11–19
No. of pupils: 90 B60 G30
Fees: Day £7950–£8550 FB £16,050

Barbara Speake Stage School

East Acton Lane, East Acton, London W3 7EG
Tel: 020 8743 1306
Principal: Miss B M Speake MBE, ARAD, MISTD, MIDTA
Type: Coeducational Day
Age range: 3½–16
No. of pupils: 125 B45 G80
Fees: Day £5400–£5700

Bickenhall College of Computing

126-134 Baker Street, First Floor, London W1U 6UE
Tel: 020 7486 0707/1574
Head: Mr David Kohn
Type: Coeducational

Blake College

162 New Cavendish Street, London W1W 6YS
Tel: 020 7636 0658
Course Director: D A J Cluckie BA, BSc
Type: Coeducational Day
Fees: Day £4720–£5310

Boston College of London

15 Leeland Road, West Ealing, London W13 9HH
Tel: 020 8810 1888
Head: Dr Dag Dandashi
Type: Coeducational

BPP Professional Education

142-144 Uxbridge Road, London W12 8AA
Tel: 020 8740 2222
Head: Martin Taylor
Type: Coeducational Day

Campbell Harris Tutors

185 Kensington High Street, London W8 6SH
Tel: 020 7937 0032
Principals: Mark Harris & Ms Claire Campbell
Type: Coeducational Day
Age range: 13+
No. of pupils: B30 G30
Fees: Day £4000–£9000

Christie's Education

153 Great Titchfield Street, London W1W 5BD
Tel: 020 7665 4350
Academic Director: Jon Waldon
Type: Coeducational Day

College of Naturopathic & Complementary Medicine Ltd

41 Riding House Street, London W1W 7BE
Tel: 01342 410 505
Head: Hermann Keppler
Type: Coeducational

David Game College

David Game House, 69 Notting Hill Gate, London W11 3JS
Tel: 020 7221 6665
Principal: D T P Game MA, MPhil
Type: Coeducational Day
Age range: 15–25
No. of pupils: 450 B200 G250
Fees: Day £5000–£8500

Davies, Laing & Dick Independent College

100 Marylebone Lane, London W1U 2QB
Tel: 020 7935 8411
Principal: Mr David Lowe MA(Cantab), FRSA
Type: Coeducational Day
Age range: 15+
No. of pupils: 320 B170 G150 VIth280
Fees: Day £15,000–£16,900 FB £30,000

Ealing Independent College

83 New Broadway, Ealing, London W5 5AL
Tel: 020 8579 6668
Principal: Dr Ian Moores
Type: Coeducational Day
Age range: 13–20
No. of pupils: 100 B70 G30 VIth70
Fees: Day £3865–£12,600

Edgware Academy of Languages & Computer Science

Tigris House, 256 Edgware Road, London W2 1ES
Tel: 020 7224 9722
Head: Mr Kanat Ayyildiz
Type: Coeducational

Hammersmith Management College

80-90 King Street, Hammersmith, London W6 0QW
Tel: 020 8748 7481
Head: Mr J Nizami
Type: Coeducational

Happy Child Training Centre

109 Uxbridge Road, Ealing, London W5 5TL
Tel: 020 8579 3955
Type: Coeducational Day

Hotel and Catering Training Company

2nd Floor, South Wing, 26-28 Hammersmith Grove, London W6 7HT
Tel: 020 8735 9700

Lansdowne College

40-44 Bark Place, London W2 4AT
Tel: 020 7616 4400
Principal: Mr Hugh Templeton FCCA
Type: Coeducational Day
Age range: 14–19
No. of pupils: 235 B120 G115 VIth200
Fees: Day £15,500

Le Cordon Bleu Culinary Academy

114 Marylebone Lane, London W1U 2HH
Tel: 020 7935 3503
Type: Coeducational Day
Age range: 18+

Leiths School of Food & Wine

16-20 Wendell Road, London W12 9RT
Tel: 020 8749 6400
Managing Director: Camilla Schneideman
Type: Coeducational Day
Age range: 17–99
No. of pupils: 96
Fees: Day £16,500

London Academy of Music & Dramatic Art

155 Talgarth Road, London W14 9DA
Tel: 020 8834 0500
Head of Examinations: Dawn Postans
Type: Coeducational Day
Age range: 17+

London College

1st Floor, 23-25 Eastcastle Street, London W1W 8DF
Tel: 020 7580 7552
Head: Mr David Kohn
Type: Coeducational

London College of Professional Training Ltd

The Opportunities Centre, 370-376 Uxbridge Road, London W12 7LL
Tel: 020 8746 2120
Head: Mrs Margaret Arokiasamy
Type: Coeducational

London Hotel School

Springvale Terrace, West Kensington, London W14 0AE
Tel: 020 7665 0000
Head: Mr Rod Hardingham
Type: Coeducational

London International College

147 Oxford Street, London W1D 2JE
Tel: 020 7734 6420
Principal: Mr T Ktorides
Type: Coeducational Day

London School of Management Ltd
43-47 New Broadway, Ealing, London W5 5AH
Tel: 020 8567 4355
Head: Mr R S Rupal
Type: Coeducational Day
(♦♦) (16+)

London Skills Academy
123 Godolphin Road, London W12 8JN
Tel: 020 8749 6711
Head: Dr Tunde Idowu
Type: Coeducational Day
(♦♦) (16+)

Montessori Centre International
18 Balderton Street, London W1K 6TG
Tel: 020 7493 0165
Director: Ms Barbara Isaacs
Type: Coeducational Day
Age range: 17–60
(♦♦) (16+)

Oxford House College - London
30 Oxford Street, London W1W 8AW
Tel: 020 7580 9785
Principal: Ms Muberra Orme
Type: Coeducational Day
(♦♦) (16+)

Ravenscourt Tutorial College
28 Studland Street, Ravenscourt Park, London W6 0JS
Tel: 020 8741 2577
Principal: Miss P M Saw
Type: Coeducational Day
(♦♦) (16+)

RAY COCHRANE BEAUTY SCHOOL
For further details see p. 112
118 Baker Street, London W1U 6TT
Tel: 020 7486 6291
Email: email@raycochrane.co.uk
Website: www.raycochrane.co.uk
Principal: Miss Baljeet Suri CIDESCO, CIBTAC, FETC, IFA
Type: Private Vocational
Age range: 16–50
No. of pupils: 40
Fees: Day £2195–£8995
(16+) (16+)

Sassoon Academy
56 Davies Mews, London W1K 5AA
Tel: 020 7399 6902
Education Manager: Peter Crossfield
Type: Full time private education
Age range: 16–45
Fees: Day £13,500
(♦♦) (16+) (⚘)

Scott's College London
47-49 Oxford Street, London W1D 2EB
Tel: 020 7437 5611
Head: Dr Michael Sonny-Ijoma
Type: Coeducational Day
(♦♦) (16+)

St Patrick's International College
24 Great Chapel Street, London W1F 8FS
Tel: 020 7287 6664
Principal: Mr Girish Chandra
Type: Coeducational Day
(♦♦) (16+)

West London College
Parliament House, 35 North Row, Mayfair,
London W1K 6DB
Tel: 020 7491 1841
Principal: Paul S Smith BA(Hons), FRSA
Type: Coeducational Day
(♦♦) (16+)

West London School of Management & Technology
99-103 St James Annexe, The Broadway, West Ealing,
London W13 9BP
Tel: 020 8840 1177
Principal: Mr Syed Raza Gilani
Type: Coeducational Day
(♦♦) (16+)

GREATER LONDON

Acorn Independent College
39-47 High Street, Southall, Middlesex UB1 3HF
Tel: 020 8571 9900
Principal: Mrs Gladys Watt
Type: Independent GCSE & Sixth Form Coeducational Day
Age range: 13–19
No. of pupils: 115
Fees: Day £9500–£12,950
(♦♦) (16+) (A)

Beckenham College
The Clockhouse Business Centre, Unit 2, Thayers Farm
Road, Beckenham, Kent BR3 4LZ
Tel: 020 8650 3321
Principal: Mrs E Wakeling
Type: Coeducational Day
Age range: 16+
Fees: Day £100–£3500
(♦♦) (16+) (16+) (⚘)

Bird College

The Centre, 27 Station Road, Sidcup, Kent DA15 7EE
Tel: 020 8300 6004/3031
Principal & Chief Executive: Ms Shirley Coen BA(Hons), FSRA
Type: Coeducational Day
(�) (16·)

Cambridge Tutors College

Water Tower Hill, Croydon, Surrey CR0 5SX
Tel: 020 8688 5284/7363
Principal: Mr M Di Clemente
Type: Coeducational Day & Boarding
Age range: 15–22
No. of pupils: 280 B140 G140 VIth280
Fees: Day £14,400 FB £18,300
(♦) (16·) (A) (⚖) (£) (16·)

College of Accountancy & Management Studies

1276 Greenford Road, Greenford, Middlesex UB6 0HH
Tel: 020 8426 4555
Head: Dr Errol Mathura
Type: Coeducational
(♦) (16·)

Harrow Secretarial College & Computer Training Centre

68 Station Road, Harrow, Middlesex HA1 2SQ
Tel: 020 8424 9900
Type: Coeducational Day
(♦) (16·) (16·) (🕸)

International School of Business Studies

204-226 Imperial Drive, Rayners Lane, Harrow, Middlesex HA2 7HH
Tel: 020 8872 4103
Head: Mr Dawar Aziz
Type: Coeducational
(♦) (16·)

New London College

1 Martindale Road, Hounslow, Middlesex TW4 7EW
Tel: 020 8570 7766
Head: Mr Vikram R Kolagatla
Type: Coeducational Day
(♦) (16·)

Purley Language College Ltd

34 Brighton Road, Purley, Surrey CR8 3AD
Tel: 020 8660 5060
Type: Language School
(♦) (16·)

Rambert School of Ballet & Contemporary Dance

Clifton Lodge, St Margaret's Drive, Twickenham, Middlesex TW1 1QN
Tel: 020 8892 9960
Principal: R McKim
Type: Coeducational Day
Age range: 16+
(♦) (16·)

Regal International College

542B High Road, Wembley, Middlesex HA0 2AA
Tel: 020 8795 5335
Head: Mr S Sivakumar
Type: Coeducational Day
(♦) (16·)

REGENT COLLEGE

For further details see p. 110

Sai House, 167 Imperial Drive, Harrow, Middlesex HA2 7HD
Tel: 020 8966 9900
Email: application@regentcollege.uk.com
Website: www.regentcollege.uk.com
Principal: Mr Selva Pankaj MBA, FCMA
Type: Coeducational Day
Age range: 11–19
No. of pupils: 151 B93 G58
Fees: Day £9000
(♦) (16·) (A) (16·)

Richmond The American International University in London

Queen's Road, Richmond, Surrey TW10 6JP
Tel: 020 8332 8200
President & CEO: Dr Norman Smith
Type: Coeducational Day
(♦) (16·)

Royal Botanic Gardens

School of Horticulture, Kew, Richmond, Surrey TW9 3AB
Tel: 020 8332 5545
Principal: Emma Fox BEd(Hons), DipHort(Kew)(Hons)
Type: Coeducational Day
(♦) (16·)

The Secretary College

123 South End, Croydon, Surrey CR0 1BJ
Tel: 0208 688 4440
Principal: Mr J E K Safo
Type: Coeducational Day
(♦) (16·)

SOUTH-EAST

BRIGHTON & HOVE

Bartholomews Tutorial College

22-23 Prince Albert Street, Brighton,
Brighton & Hove BN1 1HF
Tel: 01273 205965/205141
Governor: W A Duncombe BSc
Type: Coeducational Boarding & Day
Age range: 14+
No. of pupils: 40 B20 G20 VIth30
Fees: Day £15,700–£18,700 WB £20,000–£23,000
FB £20,000–£23,000

Bellerbys College

44 Cromwell Road, Hove, Brighton & Hove BN3 3EU
Tel: 01273 339373
Principal: N Addison
Type: Coeducational Day & Boarding
Age range: 14–20
No. of pupils: 700 VIth610
Fees: FB £17,500–£21,000

European School of Animal Osteopathy

25 Old Steine, Brighton, Brighton & Hove BN1 1EL
Tel: 01273 673332
Head: Jean-Yves Girard
Type: Coeducational

Hove College

48 Cromwell Road, Hove, Brighton & Hove BN3 3ER
Tel: 01273 772577
Director: Mr John Veale
Type: Coeducational Day

Portslade Music Academy

5b Station Road, Portslade, Brighton,
Brighton & Hove BN41 1GA
Tel: 01273 422227

CAMBRIDGESHIRE

Abbey College - Cambridge

17 Station Road, Cambridge, Cambridgeshire CB1 2JB
Tel: 01223 578280
Principal: Dr Julian Davies
Type: Coeducational Boarding
Age range: 16–24
No. of pupils: B102 G111
Fees: Day £5950–£15,250

Bellerbys College

Queens Campus, Bateman Street, Cambridge,
Cambridgeshire CB2 1LU
Tel: 01223 363159
Principal: John Rushton
Type: Coeducational Day
Age range: 15–25
No. of pupils: B163 G181
Fees: FB £15,300

Cambridge Centre for Sixth-form Studies

1 Salisbury Villas, Station Road, Cambridge,
Cambridgeshire CB1 2JF
Tel: 01223 716890
Principal: Mr Stuart Nicholson MA(Oxon), MBA, PGCE,
NPQH, CPhys
Type: Independent Sixth Form College
Age range: 15–19
No. of pupils: 202 B108 G94
Fees: Day £6285–£16,014 FB £9477

Cambridge School of Beauty Therapy

94 High Street, Sawston, Cambridge,
Cambridgeshire CB2 4HJ
Tel: 01223 832228
Principal: Mrs P Keyte
Type: Coeducational Day

Cambridge Seminars Tutorial College

Logic House, 143-147 Newmarket Road, Cambridge,
Cambridgeshire CB5 8HA
Tel: 01223 313464
Principal: M R Minhas BSc, CEng
Type: Independent Sixth Form College
Age range: 16–20
Fees: Day £12,000

CATS Cambridge

13-15 Round Church Street, Cambridge,
Cambridgeshire CB5 8AD
Tel: 01223 314431
Principal: Dr Glenn Hawkins
Type: Coeducational Boarding & Day
Age range: 14–19+
No. of pupils: 352
Fees: Day £14,480–£23,850 FB £20,270–£33,150

Mander Portman Woodward - Cambridge

3-4 Brookside, Cambridge, Cambridgeshire CB2 1JE
Tel: 01223 350158
Principal: Dr Nick Marriott
Type: Coeducational Day & Boarding
Age range: 15–19
No. of pupils: 130 B65 G65 VIth100
Fees: Day £2925–£15,975 FB £7425–£20,475

(♣) (16) (A) (♠) (£) (✎)

Queen's Marlborough College

Bateman Street, Cambridge, Cambridgeshire CB2 1LU
Tel: 01223 367016
Principal: Mrs C Bickford
Type: Coeducational Day

(♣) (16)

St Andrew's Cambridge

2A Free School Lane, Cambridge,
Cambridgeshire CB2 3QA
Tel: 01223 360040
Principal: Mrs A Collins
Type: Coeducational Day & Boarding
Age range: 14–20
No. of pupils: B67 G63 VIth130
Fees: FB £15,000–£17,000

(♣) (16) (A) (♠)

EAST SUSSEX

Buckswood St George's

36 Pevensey Road, St Leonards-on-Sea,
East Sussex TN35 4LT
Tel: 01424 813696
Type: Coeducational Boarding
Age range: 16+
Fees: FB £13,350–£26,700

(♣) (16) (A) (♠) (16+)

Windmill Hill Tennis and Golf Academy

Windmill Hill, Hailsham, East Sussex BN27 4RZ
Tel: 08700 339 997
Managing Director: Steven P Jones
Type: Coeducational Day

(♣) (16)

ESSEX

Bliss College

211 Olympic House, 28-42 Clements Road, Ilford,
Essex IG1 1BA
Tel: 020 8553 7975
Head: Mrs Shani Varghese
Type: Coeducational

(♣) (16)

East 15 Acting School

Hatfields, Rectory Lane, Loughton, Essex IG10 3RY
Tel: 020 8508 5983
Director: John Baraldi
Type: Coeducational Day

(♣) (16)

Empire College London

Forest House, 16-20 Clements Road, Ilford, Essex IG1 1BA
Tel: 020 8553 2683
Head: Ms Aaiesha Tak
Type: Coeducational

(♣) (16)

London Academy of Management Sciences

9th Floor Wentworth House, 350 Eastern Avenue, Ilford,
Essex
Tel: 020 8554 9169
Head: Mr Asif Siddiqui
Type: Coeducational

(♣) (16)

London College of Business

6A Monteagle Court, Wakering Road, Barking,
Essex IG11 8PD
Tel: 020 8591 2222
Head: Mr Zenon Adamek
Type: Coeducational

(♣) (16)

London College of Business & Finance

8th Floor, Crown House, Cambridge Road, Barking,
Essex IG11 8NW
Tel: 020 8507 8883
Head: Mr Sandeep Jethwa
Type: Coeducational

(♣) (16)

Paragon School of Furniture Restoration

11-13 Town Street, Thaxted, Dunmow, Essex CM6 2LD
Tel: 01371 832032

(♣) (16)

HERTFORDSHIRE

Champneys International College of Health & Beauty

Chesham Road, Wigginton, Tring, Hertfordshire HP23 6HY
Tel: 01442 291333
College Principal: Ms Pam Clegg
Type: Coeducational Day
Age range: 16+
No. of pupils: 61
Fees: Day £3000–£9050

(♣) (16) (£) (✎) (16+)

Justin Craig Education

Craig House, 13 High Street, Colney Heath, St Albans,
Hertfordshire AL4 0NS
Tel: 01727 827000
Director of Courses: Mrs M Craig
Type: Coeducational Day & Boarding
Age range: 15+

St Albans Tutors

69 London Road, St Albans, Hertfordshire AL1 1LN
Tel: 01727 842348
Joint Principals: Assim Jemal BA(Hons) & Lucy Webster
BA(Hons), PGCE
Type: Coeducational Day
Age range: 15+
No. of pupils: B28 G16
Fees: Day £3400

KENT

CATS Canterbury

68 New Dover Road, Canterbury, Kent CT1 3LQ
Tel: +44 (0)1223 345698
Principal: Marie-Louise Banning
Type: Coeducational Day & Boarding
Age range: 15–22
No. of pupils: 275

European School of Osteopathy

Boxley House, The Street, Boxley, Maidstone,
Kent ME14 3DZ
Tel: 01622 671 558
Principal: Mr Renzo Molinari DO

MEDWAY

Rochester Independent College

Star Hill, Rochester, Medway ME1 1XF
Tel: 01634 828115
Principals: Alistair Brownlow, Brian Pain, Pauline Bailey
Type: Independent, Mixed, Boarding and Day
Age range: 11 upwards
No. of pupils: 200
Fees: Day £12,750 FB £21,750

READING

Chiltern College

16 Peppard Road, Caversham, Reading RG4 8JZ
Tel: 0118 947 1847
Head: Christine Lawrence
Type: Coeducational Day

Impact International College

81 London Street, Reading RG1 4QA
Tel: 0118 956 0610
Head: Mr Alan Loveridge
Type: Coeducational

Queensland College London

Reading Campus, 80 London Street, Reading RG1 4SJ
Tel: 0118 956 9111
Head: Alan McColm
Type: Coeducational Day

University Tutorial College

12 Friar Street, Reading RG1 1DB
Tel: 0118 951 1990
Principal: Mr Avtar Nazren
Type: Coeducational Day

SOUTHAMPTON

Wessex Tutors

44 Shirley Road, Southampton SO15 3EU
Tel: 023 8033 4719
Principal: Mrs J E White BA(London)
Type: Coeducational Day
Age range: 14–21
No. of pupils: B20 G20
Fees: Day £800–£7000

SOUTHEND-ON-SEA

Crown College

121-129 North Road, Westcliff-on-Sea, Southend-on-
Sea SS0 7AH
Tel: 01702 341169
Principal: Ms T Corsiwi
Type: Coeducational Day

SURREY

Cambridge Management College
4-8 Castle Street, Oakington, Kingston-Upon-Thames,
Surrey KT11SS
Tel: 08003166282
Principal: Dr Peter Holmes
Type: Coeducational
(�♦) (16)

Guildford Secretarial & Business College
17 Chapel Street, Guildford, Surrey GU1 3UL
Tel: 01483 564885
Corporate Training Manager: Mrs V Alexander
Type: Coeducational Day
(♦♦) (16)

Hurtwood House
Holmbury St Mary, Dorking, Surrey RH5 6NU
Tel: 01483 279000
Principal: Mr Cosmo Jackson
Type: Coeducational Boarding
Age range: 16–18
No. of pupils: 300 B150 G150
Fees: FB £30,600–£35,100
(♦♦) (16) (A) (⚜)

London Academy of Administrative Studies
3rd Floor, Sycamore House, 799 London Road, Thornton
Heath, Surrey CR7 6AW
Tel: 020 8689 5912
Principal: Mr O Filani
Type: Coeducational Day
(♦♦) (16)

Royal School of Needlework
Apartment 12A, Hampton Court Palace, East Molesey,
Surrey KT8 9AU
Tel: 020 8943 1432
Principal: Mrs E Elvin
Type: Coeducational Day
Age range: 17–30
No. of pupils: 24
(♦♦) (16)

Tante Marie School of Cookery
Woodham House, Carlton Road, Woking,
Surrey GU21 4HF
Tel: 01483 726957
Principal: Mrs Marcella O'Donovan
Type: Coeducational Day
Age range: 16–60
No. of pupils: 72 B29 G43
Fees: Day £13,995
(♦♦) (16) (✎) (16)

WEST BERKSHIRE

The Royal Berkshire Academy of Performing Arts
42 Pembroke, Bracknell, West Berkshire RG12 7RD
Tel: 020 7193 9485
Type: Coeducational
Age range: 8–19
(♦♦) (16)

WEST SUSSEX

West Dean College
West Dean, Chichester, West Sussex PO18 0QZ
Tel: 01243 811301
Principal: Mr Robert Pulley
Type: Coeducational Day
(♦♦) (16)

WINDSOR & MAIDENHEAD

Redroofs
Littlewick Green, Maidenhead,
Windsor & Maidenhead SL6 3QY
Tel: 01628 822982
Principal: June Rose
Type: Coeducational Day
Age range: 8–16+
No. of pupils: B32 G50
Fees: Day £3192
(♦♦) (16) (16) (♣)

Examinations & qualifications

Common Entrance

The Common Entrance examinations are used for transfer from junior to senior schools at the ages of 11+ and 13–. The papers are set centrally but the answers are marked by the senior school for which a candidate is entered. Candidates normally take the examination in their own junior or preparatory schools, either in the UK or overseas.

Common Entrance is not a public examination as, for example, GCSE, and candidates may normally be entered only in one of the following circumstances:

a) they have been offered a place at a senior school subject to their passing the examination, or

b) they are required to take the examination as a preliminary to sitting the scholarship examination, or

c) they are entered as a 'trial run', in which case the papers are corrected by the junior school concerned.

At 11+ the examination consists of English, mathematics and science. The 11+ examination is designed so that it can be taken by candidates either from independent preparatory schools or by candidates from schools in the maintained sector who have had no special preparation. At 13+ most candidates come from independent preparatory schools, and the compulsory subjects are English, mathematics and science. Papers in French, geography, German, Greek, history, Latin, religious studies and Spanish are also available and candidates offer as many subjects as they can.

The 13+ examination came into being in the early part of this century, and has for many years been used by the majority of boys' and coeducational senior schools admitting pupils at that age. The 11+ examination dates from 1947, when the Common Entrance Examination for Girls' Schools Ltd was founded by a group of headmistresses with the object of 'improving the standard of secondary education by the establishment of an accepted standard of attainment for the admission of pupils to girls' senior schools'. In recent years the distinction between the 'girls' and the 'boys' examinations has blurred, with a large number of girls taking the 13+ examination and some boys taking 11+. This blurring of distinctions has been accelerated by the increase in the number of co-educational preparatory and senior schools. In 1989 the Common Entrance Examination Committee (Boys) and the Board of Common Entrance Examination for Girls' Schools Ltd joined forces to form the Common Entrance Board and subsequently the Independent Schools Examinations Board. The Board consists of members of the Headmasters' and Headmistresses' Conference, the Girls' Schools Association and the Independent Association of Preparatory Schools. All the examinations are nowadays available both to girls and to boys.

Rapid changes in education nationally have resulted in regular reviews of the syllabuses for all the examinations. The introduction of GCSE and then the National Curriculum brought about a number of changes. Since preparation for GCSE starts at 11, and work for the National Curriculum Key Stage 3 starts at the same age, it is a guiding principle that Common Entrance should be part of the natural progression from 11-16, and not a diversion from it.

In the light of the requirements of the National Curriculum, the Independent Schools Examinations Board has adapted its syllabuses to be in line with the appropriate levels of the National Curriculum.

The Independent Schools Examinations Board is very much aware that one of the strengths of the independent sector has been its insistence on high standards, and many of the Board's senior school customers have stringent entry requirements. At the same time, in its framing of both syllabuses and examinations, the Independent Schools Examinations Board endeavours to cater for the full wide range of ability to be found in the independent sector.

Details of the Common Entrance examinations are obtainable from the General Secretary at the address below. Copies of past papers and other publications are obtainable from CE Publications at the same address.

Independent Schools Examinations Board
Jordan House
Christchurch Road
New Milton
Hampshire BH25 6QJ

Tel: 01425 621111
Fax: 01425 620044

Email: enquiries@iseb.co.uk
Website: www.iseb.co.uk

The General Certificate of Secondary Education (GCSE)

Information supplied by the Qualifications and Curriculum Authority

What are the GCSE qualifications?

GCSEs qualifications were first introduced in 1986 and are the principal means of assessing Key Stage 4 and a range of other subjects. They command respect and have status not only in the UK but worldwide. New syllabuses (now called specifications), matched to the revised National Curriculum that was implemented in September 2000, were introduced in September 2001.

Main features of the GCSE

There are three unitary awarding bodies for the GCSE in England (see 'Examination boards and Awarding Bodies' section, **p562**). WJEC and CCEA also offer GCSE qualifications in Wales and Northern Ireland as well as England. Each examining group designs its own specifications but they are required to conform to criteria laid down by the Qualifications and Curriculum Authority (QCA), the Welsh Assembly Government's Department for Education, Lifelong Learning and Skills (DELLS) and the Northern Ireland Council for the Curriculum, Examinations and Assessment (CCEA) (collectively called the regulatory authorities) which set out the rules and principles for all examinations in all subjects. The award of a grade is intended to indicate that a candidate has met the level of knowledge or skill laid down by the criteria.

A flexible approach to assessment is one of the main features of GCSE. Candidates have the chance to demonstrate what they know and can do in a variety of ways. Many specifications give credit for assignments set and marked by the teacher, with some external moderation, and the marks awarded form a contribution towards the final grade achieved. This is in addition to more traditional examinations at the end of the course. The proportion of credit obtained from coursework is subject to limits laid down by the regulatory authorities.

Grading

Candidate performance at GCSE is graded from A* to G.

There are 'differentiated' examination papers in many subjects. The scheme of GCSE assessment may involve two papers targeted at either grades A*-D or grades C-G. The higher tiered paper (graded A*-D) will also provide for an exceptional grade E on the higher tier, so that candidates who just miss a D grade are not disadvantaged. Mathematics uses three tiers; some subjects – such as history and art – use one.

Can anyone take GCSE qualifications?

GCSEs are intended mainly for 16-year-old pupils, but are open to anyone of any age, whether studying full time or part time at a school, college or privately. There are no formal entry requirements.

GCSEs are available in a wide range of humanities, sciences, arts, languages, maths and technology subjects. Students normally study up to ten subjects over a two-year period. Short course GCSEs are available in some subjects (including ICT and religious studies) – these include half the content of a full GCSE, so two short course GCSEs are equivalent to one full GCSE.

Vocational GCSEs

GCSEs in vocational subjects are also now available in:

- Applied art and design
- Applied business
- Applied ICT
- Applied science
- Engineering
- Health and social care
- Leisure and tourism
- Manufacturing

General Qualifications at Advanced Level, General Certificate of Education (GCE), General Certificate of Education (GCE) in applied subjects, and Advanced Extension Award (AEA)

Information supplied by the Qualifications and Curriculum Authority.

Typically, you will study advanced level qualifications over a two-year period. There are no lower or upper age limits. Schools and colleges usually expect students aged 16-18 to have obtained grades A*-C in five subjects at GCSE level before taking an advanced level course. This requirement may vary between centres and according to which specific subjects are to be studied. Mature students may be assessed on different criteria as to their suitability to embark on the course.

All these qualifications consist of a number of units. They can be assessed in stages, using opportunities in January and June, or at the end of the course.

GCE Qualifications

GCE qualifications are available at two levels. The Advanced Subsidiary (AS) is the two-unit General Certificate of Education (GCE). It provides progression between GCSE at level 2 and the full A level. It is both the first half of an A level and a qualification in its own right. All A level specifications include an AS. There are currently five free-standing AS qualifications that do not lead to a full A level, namely critical thinking, European studies, science for public understanding, social science: citizenship and world development.

The A level is the four- to six-unit GCE. It consists of the AS and a further three units called the A2, usually studied in the second year. Nearly 70 titles are available, covering a wide range of subject areas, including humanities, sciences, language, business, arts, mathematics and technology.

GCE AS and A levels normally contain a proportion of coursework up to 30 per cent, (though some practical or creative subjects have more). All GCE A levels contain in one or more of the A2 units an assessment that tests students' understanding of the whole specification (synoptic assessment). GCE AS and A levels are graded A-E. Students generally take four or five subjects at AS level in the first year of advanced level study. In the second year, they generally study A2 units in two or three subjects, thereby completing A levels in those subjects.

Revised A level specifications were introduced in September 2008, with a new A* grade awarded from 2010 to those students who have achieved both of the following:

• Grade A overall (that is 80 per cent of the maximum uniform marks for the whole A level qualification).

• 90 per cent of the maximum uniform marks on the aggregate of the A2 unit scores. The A* grade is awarded for the A level qualification only and not for the AS qualification or for individual units.

GCEs in applied subjects

Following extensive consultation, the Vocational Certificate of Education (VCE) has now been restructured along the lines of the General Certificate of Education (GCE). The new qualifications have an AS/A2 structure, comparable to existing GCEs. They are no longer known as vocational A levels, but are called GCEs/A levels in applied subjects. The revised qualifications were introduced for first teaching in September 2005.

The new qualifications continue to provide a broad introduction to a vocational area and to encourage distinctive teaching and assessment approaches, using work-related contexts. As with current specifications, opportunities for the development and assessment of key skills will be signposted in the new specifications.

Qualifications available

There are four qualifications available, with the following structure:

- Advanced Subsidiary General Certificate of Education: three AS units, one of which is externally tested, the remainder internally assessed; graded A-E.
- Advanced Subsidiary General Certificate of Education (double award): six AS units, typically two of which are externally tested, the remainder internally assessed; graded AA, AB-EE.
- Advanced General Certificate of Education: six units (three AS units plus three A2 units), typically two of which are externally tested, the remainder internally assessed; graded A-E.
- Advanced General Certificate of Education (double award): 12 units (six AS units plus six A2 units), typically four of which are externally tested, the remainder internally assessed; graded AA, AB-EE.

Vocational areas

New specifications have been developed in the ten vocational areas listed below. The specifications are available at AS, AS (double award), A level and A level (double award) unless otherwise indicated.

Applied art and design

Applied business

Applied ICT

Applied science

Engineering (available only as AS and A level awards)

Health and social care

Leisure studies

Media: communication and production (available only as AS and A level awards)

Performing arts (available only as AS and A level awards)

Travel and tourism

Advanced Extension Awards

The Advanced Extension Award (AEA) is intended to challenge the most able advanced level students. It assesses candidates' abilities to apply and communicate effectively their understanding of the subject using the skills of critical analysis, evaluation and synthesis. It was first available in summer 2002 in 17 subjects and is awarded at merit and distinction grades.

Guidance on these qualifications is available to schools and colleges on the QCA's main website (www.qca.org.uk) but in particular on its new 14-19 Learning website (www.qcda.gov.uk/20891.aspx).

Functional Skills

Information supplied by the WJEC

Functional skills are freestanding qualifications offered at Entry Level, Level 1 and Level 2, which may be taken alongside GCSEs or vocational qualifications. The aim of functional skills at Entry Level and Levels 1 and 2 is to encourage learners to demonstrate their skills in a range of contexts and for various purposes. These skills are of vital importance in many areas as they are essential in many careers and can add immeasurably to an individual's general quality of life.

Since September 2008, functional skills have been part of the generic learning for Diplomas and are expected to be incorporated in the GCSE specification revisions for 2010. The assessment structure for the functional skills qualifications follows the WJEC's well-established structure at GCSE and Entry Level.

The final evaluation of the pilots will take place in summer 2010, but assessments and awards will run through to 2011 before the first examination of the revised specifications take place, and will be fully supported by WJEC.

Key Skills Qualifications

The key skills qualifications are available in:

• Communication
• Information technology
• Application of number

These are considered to be essential for all areas of work and are available at levels 1-4.

Key skills are increasingly popular with employers and higher education institutions because they demonstrate that your skills are at the level they require. These skills help to ensure that when you begin working you will be effective in your job role straight away. The qualifications may be taken alongside the qualifications described in this section.

There are three further key skills units:

• Improving own learning and performance
• Working with others
• Problem solving

These wider key skills develop your personal skills and are valued highly by employers.

Entry Level Qualifications

If you want to take GCSE or NVQ Level 1 but have not yet reached the level required, then Entry Level qualifications are for you. These qualifications are designed to get you started on the qualifications ladder.

Entry level qualifications are available in a wide range of areas. You can take an Entry Level certificate in most subjects where a similar GCSE exists. There are also vocational Entry Level qualifications - some in specific areas like retail or catering and others where you can take units in different work-related subjects to get a taster of a number of career areas. There are also Entry Level certificates in life skills and the basic skills of literacy and numeracy.

Anyone can take an Entry Level qualification - your school or college will help you decide which qualification is right for you.

Entry Level qualifications are flexible programmes so the time it takes to complete will vary according to where you study and how long you need to take the qualification.

National Vocational Qualifications – NVQs

NVQs reward those who demonstrate skills gained at work. They relate to particular jobs and are usefully taken while you are working. There are five levels of NVQ and they are usually in specialised areas such as customer service, hairdressing or sales supervision.

Within reason, NVQs do not have to be completed in a specified amount of time. They can be taken by full-time employees or by school and college students with a work placement or part-time job that enables them to develop the appropriate skills.

There are no age limits and no special entry requirements.

NVQs are organised into five levels, based on the competencies required. Levels 1-3 are the levels most applicable to learners within the 14-19 phase. Achievement of level 4 within this age group will be rare.

There are over 1300 different NVQs to choose from.

Further guidance on NVQs is available on :
www.direct.gov.uk/en/EducationAndLearning/QualificationsExplained/DG_10039029

BTECs

Information supplied by Edexcel

BTEC First Diplomas

BTEC First Diplomas are introductory work-related programmes covering a wide range of vocational areas including business, engineering, information technology, health & care, media, travel & tourism and public services.

Programmes usually last one year and may be taken full or part time.

They are practical programmes that provide a foundation for the knowledge and skills you will need in work. Alternatively, you can progress onto a BTEC National qualification, vocational A level or equivalent.

There are no formal entry requirements but you may need some GCSEs at grades D-G in order to study BTEC First Diploma.

BTEC National Diplomas, Certificates and Awards

BTEC National Diploma and Certificate programmes are long-established vocational programmes.

BTEC Nationals are practical programmes that are highly valued by employers. They enable you to gain the knowledge and skills that you will need in work, or give you the choice to progress onto a BTEC Higher National or a degree.

BTEC Nationals cover a range of vocationally specialist sectors including early years, construction, fine art, aerospace, engineering, information technology, business, media, performing arts, public services, sport, IT practitioners and applied science.

The programmes may be taken full or part time, and can be taken in conjunction with appropriate NVQs and/or Key Skills units at an appropriate level.

There are no formal entry requirements, but if you have any of the following you are likely to be at the right level to study a BTEC National qualification.

• GNVQ Intermediate
• BTEC First qualification
• GCSEs – At grades A* to C in several subjects
• Relevant work experience

There are also, in some areas, very specialist BTEC National Awards (*eg* Airline and Airport Operations).

BTEC Higher National Diplomas & Certificates – HNDs & HNCs

BTEC HNDs and HNCs are further and higher education qualifications which offer a balance of education and vocational training.

They are available in a wide range of work-related areas such as design, business, health & care, computing, engineering, hospitality & leisure management and public services.

BTEC Higher National courses combine study with hands-on work experience during your course. Once completed, you can use the skills you learn to begin your career, or continue onto a related degree course.

HNDs are often taken as a full-time course over two years but can also be followed part-time in some cases.

HNCs are usually for people who are working and take two years to complete on a part-time study basis by day release, evenings, or a combination of the two. Some HNC courses are done on a full-time basis.

There are no formal entry requirements, but if you have any of the following you are likely to be at the right academic level:

- At least one A level
- A VCE (formerly Advanced GNVQ)
- A BTEC National Certificate or Diploma
- A level 3 NVQ

Diploma

The Diploma is a composite qualification made up of:

- Principal Learning
- Generic Learning
- Additional and Specialist Learning (ASL).

Studying a Diploma enables learners to demonstrate skills, knowledge and understanding across a varied programme of learning.

Learners who complete the full requirements of the Diploma will be informed of their results and their overall grade, on 27 August. They will receive their certificates in October.

Should the need arise learners can resit any of the constituent qualifications of the Diploma. Although there are no limits to most unit resits, the availability of these depends upon the component awarding body; you should contact them directly to check. For ASL there is a range of different qualifications available and so the limits to and availability of resits will depend upon the qualification as well as the awarding body.

For more information see:
www.direct.gov.uk/en/EducationAndLearning/QualificationsExplained/DG_070676

Scottish Qualifications

Information supplied by Scottish Qualifications Authority

The qualifications system in Scotland is unique within the UK. It is based on three main qualification 'types': National Qualifications, taken at school and college; Higher National Certificates (HNCs) and Higher National Diplomas (HNDs), taken at college; and Scottish

Vocational Qualifications (SVQs), designed for the workplace. Most of the qualifications are made up of units and are developed and awarded by the Scottish Qualifications Authority.

National Qualifications

The counterpart in Scotland of the GCSE/GCE are National Qualifications. In addition to Standard Grade, taken in the fourth year of secondary education, there are five levels of National Qualifications: Access, Intermediate 1, Intermediate 2, Higher and Advanced Higher. Four or five passes at Higher is the most common entry requirement for higher education.

Both academic and vocational areas of study are represented in the NQ framework – some are job orientated, such as travel and tourism, and others are along more traditional lines, such as history, maths and English.

The building blocks

The Post-16 National Qualifications framework is built up of units, courses and group awards. With the exception of Standard Grade courses, these are all offered at five levels:

• National Units

The smallest element is called a unit and the majority require 40 hours of study. Units are internally assessed

• Courses

Standard Grades are usually done in S4, at one of three levels: Foundation, General and Credit. Awards are made in terms of a seven-point scale one to seven, where one is the highest award. Most Standard Grades are assessed on the basis of examination and an internally assessed element, such as a project or investigation. National Courses are made up of three units plus up to an additional 40 hours extra study. Each unit is internally assessed and in addition there is an exam which informs the grade awarded for the course – A, B, or D – with A being the highest award.

• Scottish Group Awards (SGAs)

SGAs are coherent programmes of courses and units which cover a particular subject area. There are 16 broad areas of study, such as art and design, computing and information technology, or land and environment. An SGA can be attained within one year, or worked towards over a longer period of study. Previous achievements, such as Standard Grades, can also be credited towards an SGA.

Core Skills

Similar to key skills in England and Wales, these are the skills we need to do well in education and training, to succeed in work and to get on in life:

- Problem solving
- Communication
- Numeracy
- Information technology
- Working with others

All National Qualifications have core skills embedded in them, but it is also possible to take stand-alone units.

Higher National Qualifications

Higher National Certificates (HNCs) and Higher National Diplomas (HNDs) are generally taken in colleges. They are vocational qualifications developed in consultation with industry to ensure their quality and relevance, and are recognised by employers as good evidence of ability.

All the courses are made up of Higher National Unit credits (one credit represents roughly 40 hours of timetabled learning). The design rules for HNCs and HNDs are under review, but the current course format is as follows:

- HNCs are made up of 12 credits and usually take one year to complete
- HNDs are made up of 30 credits and usually take two years to complete.

As well as being relevant entry qualifications to the world of work, some HNCs allow direct entry into the second year of a degree programme, and some HNDs allow direct entry to third year. Higher National Qualifications will also provide the knowledge and understanding required for Scottish Vocational Qualifications (SVQs), the work-based qualification that many companies use for training and development. Possessing an HNC or HND can also allow entry to a number of professional bodies.

Scottish Vocational Qualifications (SVQs)

These are the Scottish equivalent of NVQs and are designed to be assessed in the workplace. Available in five levels, they cover almost every type of occupation, and prove competence to a national standard.

Skillseekers is a way for young people in Scotland to start work straight from school and get a qualification at the same time. School leavers are given Skillseeker 'credits' which will pay for training, and allow them to work towards an SVQ.

Another option through Skillseekers is to do a **Modern Apprenticeship**. A Modern Apprenticeship delivers training as a craftsman, technician or manager in a particular industry or business and successful apprentices also gain an SVQ at level 3.

Certification

The Scottish Qualifications Certificate is a cumulative record of all the qualifications a candidate has achieved to date, including a core skills profile.

Next steps

For more information about:

- SQA qualifications – call the SQA on 0845 279 1000
- Subject choices at school – talk to your Guidance Teacher or Careers Advisor
- College programmes, HNC/HND courses and career information – call Learndirect Scotland on 0800 100 9000 or visit their website on: www.learndirectscotland.com; or contact your local college.

The International Baccalaureate

Information supplied by the IB

The International Baccalaureate (IB) offers three challenging and high quality educational programmes for a worldwide community of schools, aiming to develop internationally minded people who, recognizing their common humanity and shared guardianship of the planet, help to create a better, more peaceful world.

The IB works with schools around the world (both state and privately funded) that share the commitment to international education to deliver these programmes.

Schools that have achieved the high standards required for authorization to offer one or more of the IB programmes are known as 'IB World Schools'. There are over half a million students attending more than 2300 IB World Schools in 128 countries and this number is growing annually.

IB World Schools:

• share the mission and commitment of the IB to quality international education;
• play an active and supporting role in the worldwide community of IB schools;
• share their knowledge and experience in the development of IB programmes;
• are committed to the professional development of teachers.

IB Programmes

The three IB programmes share a common philosophy and common characteristics. They develop the whole student, helping students to grow intellectually, socially, aesthetically and culturally. They provide a broad and balanced education that includes science and the humanities, languages and mathematics, technology and the arts. The programmes teach students to think critically, and encourage them to draw connections between areas of knowledge and to use problem-solving techniques and concepts from many disciplines. They instil in students a sense of responsibility towards others and towards the environment. Lastly, and perhaps most importantly, the programmes give students an awareness and understanding of their own culture and of other cultures, values and ways of life.

All three programmes:

• have a strong international dimension;
• draw on content from educational cultures around the world;
• require study across a broad range of subjects;
• include both individual subjects and trans-disciplinary areas;
• give special emphasis to learning languages;
• focus on developing the skills of learning;
• provide opportunities for individual and collaborative planning and research;
• encourage students to become responsible members of their community.

IB programmes include:

• a written curriculum or curriculum framework;
• student assessment appropriate to the age range;

- professional development and networking opportunities for teachers;
- support, authorization and programme evaluation for the school.

The IB Primary Years Programme

The IB Primary Years Programme, for students aged three to 12, focuses on the development of the whole child as an inquirer, both in the classroom and in the world outside. It is a framework consisting of five essential elements (concepts, knowledge, skills, attitude, action) and guided by six transdisciplinary themes of global significance, explored using knowledge and skills derived from six subject areas (language, social studies, mathematics, science and technology, arts, personal, social and physical education) with a powerful emphasis on inquiry-based learning.

The most significant and distinctive feature of the IB Primary Years Programme is the six transdisciplinary themes. These themes are about issues that have meaning for, and are important to, all of us. The programme offers a balance between learning about or through the subject areas, and learning beyond them. The six themes of global significance create a trans-disciplinary framework that allows students to 'step up' beyond the confines of learning within subject areas:

- Who we are.
- Where we are in place and time.
- How we express ourselves.
- How the world works.
- How we organize ourselves.
- Sharing the planet.

The IB Primary Years Programme exhibition is the culminating activity of the programme. It requires students to analyse and propose solutions to real-world issues, drawing on what they have learned through the programme. Evidence of student development and records of PYP exhibitions are reviewed by the IB as part of the programme evaluation process.

Assessment is an important part of each unit of inquiry as it both enhances learning and provides opportunities for students to reflect on what they know, understand and can do. The teacher's feedback to the students provides the guidance, the tools and the incentive for them to become more competent, more skilful and better at understanding how to learn.

Unique characteristics of the programme include the following:

- It encourages international-mindedness in IB students.
- It encourages a positive attitude to learning by engaging students in inquiries and developing their awareness of the process of learning so that they become lifelong learners.
- It reflects real life by encouraging learning beyond and through traditional subjects with meaningful, in-depth inquiries into real issues.
- Through the learner profile, it emphasizes the development of the whole student—physically, intellectually, emotionally and ethically.

The IB Middle Years Programme

The IB Middle Years Programme, for students aged 11 to 16, provides a framework of academic challenge that encourages students to embrace and understand the connections between traditional subjects and the real world, and to become critical and reflective thinkers. Students are required to study their mother tongue, a second language, humanities, sciences, mathematics, arts, physical education and technology. In the final year of the programme, students also engage in a personal project, which they will use to demonstrate the understandings and skills they have developed throughout the programme.

Students study subjects from each of the eight subject groups through the five areas of interaction: approaches to learning, community and service, human ingenuity (formally *homo faber*), environments, and health and social education.

- Approaches to learning is concerned with developing the intellectual discipline, attitudes, strategies and skills that will result in critical, coherent and independent thought and the capacity for problem solving and decision-making.

- Community and service starts in the classroom and extends beyond it, requiring students to participate in the communities in which they live. The emphasis is on developing community awareness and concern, a sense of responsibility, and the skills and attitudes needed to make an effective contribution to society.

- Human ingenuity allows students to focus on the evolution, processes and products of human creativity. It considers their impact on society and on the mind. Students learn to appreciate the human capacity to influence, transform, enjoy and improve the quality of life. This area of interaction encourages students to explore the relationships between science, aesthetics, technology and ethics.

- Environments aims to make students aware of their interdependence with the environment so that they become aware of their responsibility, and may take positive, responsible action for maintaining an environment fit for the future.

- Health and social education prepares students for a physically and mentally healthy life, aware of potential hazards and able to make informed choices. It develops in students a sense of responsibility for their own wellbeing and for the physical and social environment. Assessment is criterion referenced, so students around the world are measured against pre-specified criteria for each subject group. Teachers may modify these criteria to be age-appropriate in the earlier years of the programme.

Teachers set assessment tasks that are assessed internally in the school. External checks (either moderation or monitoring of assessment by IB examiners) are carried out on this internal assessment to ensure worldwide consistency of standards. For schools that require official IB certification for their students, moderation is carried out every year.

Unique characteristics of the programme include the following:

- It encourages international-mindedness in IB students, starting with a foundation in their own language and culture.

- It encourages a positive attitude to learning by challenging students to solve problems, show creativity and resourcefulness and participate actively in their communities.

- It reflects real life by providing a framework that allows students to see the connections among the subjects themselves, and between the subjects and real issues.

- It supports the development of communication skills to encourage inquiry, understanding, language acquisition, and to allow student reflection and expression.

- Through the learner profile, it emphasizes the development of the whole student - physically, intellectually, emotionally and ethically.

The IB Diploma Programme

The IB Diploma Programme, for students aged 16 to 19, is an academically challenging and balanced programme of education with final examinations that prepares students for success at university and life beyond.

IB Diploma Programme students study six courses at higher level or standard level. Students must choose one subject from each of groups 1 to 5, thus ensuring breadth of experience in languages, social studies, the experimental sciences and mathematics. The sixth subject may be an arts subject chosen from group 6, or the student may choose another subject from groups 1 to 5. At least three and not more than four subjects are taken at higher level (recommended 240 teaching hours), the others at standard level (150 teaching hours). Students can study these subjects, and be examined, in English, French or Spanish.

In addition, three core elements - the extended essay, theory of knowledge and creativity, action, service - are compulsory and central to the philosophy of the programme.

Students take written examinations at the end of the programme, which are marked by external IB examiners. Students also complete assessment tasks in the school, which are either initially marked by teachers and then moderated by external moderators or sent directly to external examiners.

The marks awarded for each course range from one (lowest) to seven (highest). Students can also be awarded up to three additional points for their combined results on theory of knowledge and the extended essay. The diploma is awarded to students who gain at least 24 points, subject to certain minimum levels of performance across the whole programme and to satisfactory participation in the creativity, action, and service requirement. The highest total that a Diploma Programme student can be awarded is 45 points.

Unique characteristics of the programme include the following:

- It provides a package of education that balances subject breadth and depth, and considers the mature of knowledge across disciplines through the unique theory of knowledge course.

- It encourages international-mindedness in IB students, starting with a foundation in their own language and culture.

- It develops a positive attitude to learning that prepares students for university education.

- It has gained a reputation for its rigorous external assessment with published global standards, making this a qualification welcomed by universities worldwide.

- It emphasizes the development of the whole student - physically, intellectually, emotionally and ethically.

For more information on IB programmes, visit www.ibo.org

The International Baccalaureate Organization
Peterson House
Malthouse Avenue
Cardiff Gate
Cardiff CF23 8GL

Tel: 029 2054 7777
Fax: 029 2054 7778
Email: communications@ibo.org

Schools authorised to offer the International Baccalaureate Organization's Diploma Programme in the United Kingdom

ENGLAND

Bedfordshire

Bedford High School for Girls
Bromham Road
Bedford MK40 2BS
Tel: 01234 360221
Fax: 01234 353552
Email: herrick.p@bedfordhigh.co.uk
IB coordinator: Philip Herrick

Bedford School
De Parys Avenue
Bedford MK40 2TU
Tel: 01234 362200
Fax: 01234 362283
Email: cmarsh@bedfordschool.org.uk
IB coordinator: Colin Marsh

Biddenham Upper School and Sports College
Biddenham Turn
Bedford MK40 4AZ
Tel: 01234 342521
Fax: 01234 334530
Email: rob.tomalin@biddenham.beds.sch.uk
IB coordinator: Robert Tomalin

Luton Sixth Form College
Bradgers Hill Road
Luton LU2 7EW
Tel: 01582 877500
Fax: 01582 877501
Email: cnh@lutonsfc.ac.uk
IB coordinator: Colin Hall

Berkshire

Leighton Park School
Shinfield Road
Reading RG2 7ED
Tel: 0118 987 9600
Fax: 0118 987 9625
Email: marjorymorris@leightonpark.com
IB coordinator: Marjory Morris

Pangbourne College
Pangbourne
Reading RG8 8LA
Tel: 0118 984 2101
Fax: 0118 984 1239
Email: robert.kirby@pangcoll.co.uk
IB coordinator: Robert Kirby

Ranelagh School
Ranelagh Drive
Bracknell RG12 9DA
Tel: 01344 421233
Fax: 01344 301811
Email:
ran_maw@ranelagh.bracknell-forest.sch.uk
IB coordinator: Mark Williams

Reading School
Erleigh Road
Reading RG1 5LW
Tel: 0118 966 2966
Fax: 0118 935 2755
Email: judyhonickberg
@readingschool.reading.sch.uk
IB coordinator: Judy Honickberg

The Abbey School
Kendrick Road
Reading RG1 5DZ
Tel: 0118 987 2256
Fax: 0118 987 1478
Email: robinsonli@theabbey.co.uk
IB coordinator: Liz Robinson

Waingels College
Denmark Avenue, Woodley
Reading RG5 4RF
Tel: 0118 969 0336
Fax: 0118 944 2843
Email: tiljt@waingels.wokingham.sch.uk
IB coordinator: Jean Tillyard

Wellington College
Dukes Ride
Crowthorne RG45 7PU
Tel: 01344 444 000
Fax: 01344 444 002
Email: daj@wellingtoncollege.org.uk
IB coordinator: David James

Blackpool

Blackpool Sixth Form College
Blackpool Old Road
Blackpool FY3 7LR
Tel: 01253 394911
Fax: 01253 300459
Email: pbenson@blackpoolsixth.ac.uk
IB coordinator: Philip Benson

Brighton & Hove

Varndean College
Surrenden Road
Brighton BN1 6WQ
Tel: 01273 508011
Fax: 01273 542950
Email: spm@varndean.ac.uk
IB coordinator: Sean McEvoy

Bristol

Merchants' Academy
Gatehouse Avenue, Withywood
Bristol BS13 9BL
Tel: 0121 2626091
Fax: 0121 2621994
Email: polly.higgins@merchantsacademy.org
IB coordinator: Polly Higgins

The Red Maids' School
Westbury-on-Trym
Bristol BS9 3AW
Tel: 0117 962 2641
Fax: 0117 962 1687
Email: r_cameron@redmaids.bristol.sch.uk
IB coordinator: Ross Cameron

The Ridings High School
High Street
Winterbourne
Bristol BS36 1JL
Tel: 01454 252 041
Email: lwoodward@ridingshigh.org
IB coordinator: Laura Woodward

Buckinghamshire

Slough Grammar School
Lascelles Road
Slough SL3 7PR
Tel: 01753 522892
Fax: 01753 538618
Email:
ibcoordinator@sloughgrammar.berks.sch.uk
IB coordinator: Ruth Symons

The Hazeley School
Emperor Drive, Hazeley
Milton Keynes MK8 0PT
Tel: 01908 555620
Fax: 01908 508357
Email: vstanley@hazeley.milton-keynes.sch.uk
IB coordinator: Vanessa Stanley

The Langley Academy
Langley Road, Langley
Slough SL3 7EF
Tel: 01753 214440
Fax: 01753 596321
Email: oliver.haden@langleyacademy.org
IB coordinator: Oliver Haden

Cambridgeshire

Impington Village College
New Road, Impington
Cambridge CB4 9LX
Tel: 01223 200400
Fax: 01223 200418
Email: sixthform@impington.cambs.sch.uk
IB coordinator: Sandra Morton

The Stephen Perse Sixth Form College
Shaftesbury Road
Cambridge CB2 8AA
Tel: 01223 488430
Fax: 01223 467420
Email: sda@stephenperse.com
IB coordinator: Simon Armitage

Cornwall

Callington Community College
Launceston Road, Callington PL17 7DR
Tel: 01579 383292
Fax: 01579 383562
Email: djkemp@callington-comm.cornwall.sch.uk
IB coordinator: Debs Kemp

The Bolitho School
Polwithen, Penzance TR18 4JR
Tel: 01736 363271
Fax: 01736 330960
Email: enquiries@bolitho.cornwall.sch.uk
IB coordinator: Peter Trythall

Truro College
College Road, Truro TR1 3XX
Tel: 01872 267000
Fax: 01872 267100
Email: andyw@trurocollege.ac.uk
IB coordinator: Andy Wildin

Cumbria

Dallam School
Haverflatts Lane, Milnthorpe LA7 7DD
Tel: 015395 65165
Fax: 015395 65175
Email: r.doyle@dallam.eu
IB coordinator: Richard Doyle

Windermere St Anne's School
Patterdale Road, Windermere LA23 1NW
Tel: 015394 46164
Fax: 015394 88414
Email: jdavey@wsaschool.com
IB coordinator: Jenny Davey

Devon

EF International Academy Torquay
EF House, Castle Road, Torquay TQ1 3BG
Tel: 01803 202932
Fax: 01803 202943
Email: gavin.nattrass@ef.com
IB coordinator: Gavin Nattrass

Exeter College
Hele Road, Exeter EX4 4JS
Tel: 0845 111 6000
Fax: 01392 279972
Email: bwoodfin@exe-coll.ac.uk
IB coordinator: Betty Woodfin

Ivybridge Community College
Harford Road, Ivybridge PL21 0JA
Tel: 01752 691000
Fax: 01752 691247
Email: sbeyer@ivybridge.devon.sch.uk
IB coordinator: Sönke Beyer

King Edward VI Community College
Ashburton Road, Totnes TQ9 5JX
Tel: 01803 869200
Fax: 01803 869201
Email: dtroake@kingedwardvi.devon.sch.uk
IB coordinator: David Troake

Plymouth College
Ford Park, Plymouth PL4 6RN
Tel: 01752 203300
Fax: 01752 203246
Email: jshields@plymouth-college.co.uk
IB coordinator: Jonathan Shields

Plymouth High School for Girls
St Lawrence Road, Plymouth PL4 6HT
Tel: 01752 208308
Fax: 01752 208309
Email: jironside@phsg.org
IB coordinator: Jacqueline Ironside

Torquay Boys' Grammar School
Shiphay Manor Drive, Torquay TQ2 7EL
Tel: 01803 615 501
Fax: 01803 614 613
Email: akosmacz@tbgs.torbay.sch.uk
IB coordinator: Andy Kosmaczewski

Dorset

Sherborne School
Abbey Road, Sherborne DT9 3AP
Tel: 01935 812249
Fax: 01935 810423
Email: pts@sherborne.org
IB coordinator: Peter Such

Sherborne Girls
Bradford Road, Sherborne DT9 3QN
Tel: 01935 818287
Fax: 01935 389445
Email: pd@sherborne.com
IB coordinator: Penny Deacon

Thomas Hardye School
Queens Avenue, Dorchester DT1 2ET
Tel: 01305 266064
Email:
kchittenden@thomas-hardye.dorset.sch.uk
IB coordinator: Kaye Chittenden

Essex

Anglo-European School
Willow Green, Ingatestone CM4 0DJ
Tel: 01277 354018
Fax: 01277 355623
Email: strachanj@aesessex.co.uk
IB coordinator: Jane Strachan

Brentwood School
Ingrave Road, Brentwood CM15 8AS
Tel: 01277 243243
Fax: 01277 243299
Email: twoffenden@brentwood.essex.sch.uk
IB coordinator: Timothy Woffenden

Chelmsford County High School for Girls
Broomfield Road, Chelmsford CM1 1RW
Tel: 01245 352 592
Fax: 01245 345746
Email: mpalmer@cchs.essex.sch.uk
IB coordinator: Michael Palmer

Felsted School
Felsted, Great Dunmow CM6 3LL
Tel: 01371 822600
Fax: 01371 822607
Email: psc@felsted.org
IB coordinator: Paul Clark

Havering Sixth Form College
Wingletye Lane, Hornchurch RM11 3TB
Tel: 01708 514400
Fax: 01708 514488
Email: jessicalawley@havering-sfc.ac.uk
IB coordinator: Jessica Lawley

Notley High School
Notley Road, Braintree CM7 1WY
Tel: 01376 556304
Fax: 01376 550991
Email: rory.fox@notleyhigh.com
IB coordinator: Rory Fox

Palmer's College
Chadwell Road, Grays RM17 5TD
Tel: 01375 370121
Fax: 01375 385479
Email: jdeath@palmers.ac.uk
IB coordinator: John Death

The Sixth Form College, Colchester
North Hill, Colchester CO1 1SN
Tel: 01206 500778
Fax: 01206 500770
Email: morrisseyj@colchsfc.ac.uk
IB coordinator: Jim Morrissey

Gloucestershire

Cheltenham Bournside School
Warden Hill Road, Cheltenham GL51 3EF
Tel: 01242 235555
Fax: 01242 226742
Email: kew@bournside.gloucs.sch.uk
IB coordinator: Kate Webster-Blythe

Cirencester College
Fosse Way Campus, Stroud Road
Cirencester GL7 1XA
Tel: 01285 640994
Fax: 01285 644171
Email: kba@cirencester.ac.uk
IB coordinator: Katy Albiston

Cleeve School
Two Hedges Road, Bishops Cleeve
Cheltenham GL52 8AE
Tel: 01242 672546
Fax: 01242 678604
Email: bas@cleeveschool.net
IB coordinator: Ben Slatter

The Cheltenham Ladies' College
Bayshill Road, Cheltenham GL50 3EP
Tel: 01242 520691
Fax: 01242 227882
Email: revellr@cheltladiescollege.org
IB coordinator: Rebecca Revell

Greater Manchester

Cheadle & Marple Sixth Form College
Hibbert Lane, Marple, Stockport SK6 7PA
Tel: 0161 484 6600
Fax: 0161 484 6601
Email: gillian.wilkinson@camsfc.ac.uk
IB coordinator: Gillian Wilkinson

Loreto Sixth Form College
Chichester Road, Manchester M15 5PB
Tel: 0161 226 5156
Fax: 0161 227 9174
Email: kblackburn@loreto.ac.uk
IB coordinator: Katie Blackburn

Manchester Grammar School
Old Hall Lane, Fallowfield
Manchester M13 0XT
Tel: 0161 224 7201
Fax: 0161 257 2446
Email: c.buckley@mgs.org
IB coordinator: Chris Buckley

Salford City College - Eccles Centre
Chatsworth Road, Eccles
Manchester M30 9FJ
Tel: 0161 789 5876
Fax: 0161 789 1123
Email: flawson@ecclescollege.ac.uk
IB coordinator: Francis Lawson

St Columba's Catholic School
Ripley Street, Bolton BL2 3AR
Tel: 01204 333421
Fax: 01204 333420

Tonge Moor Community Primary School
Stott Lane, Bolton BL2 2LR
Tel: 01204 333755
Fax: 01204 333756

Trafford College
Manchester Road, West Timperley
Altrincham WA14 5PQ
Tel: 0161 952 4600
Fax: 0161 952 4672
Email: enquiries@stcoll.ac.uk
IB coordinator: Claire Rawlinson

Hampshire

Alton College
Old Odiham Road, Alton GU34 2LX
Tel: 01420 592200
Fax: 01420 592253
Email: martin.savery@altoncollege.ac.uk
IB coordinator: Martin Savery

Brockenhurst College
Lyndhurst Road, Brockenhurst SO42 7ZE
Tel: 01590 625555
Fax: 01590 625526
Email: pharriss@brock.ac.uk
IB coordinator: Patricia Harriss

Havant College
New Road, Havant PO9 1QL
Tel: 023 9248 3856
Fax: 023 9247 0621
Email: james.mcinnes@havant.ac.uk
IB coordinator: James McInnes

Taunton's College
Hill Lane, Southampton SO15 5RL
Tel: 02380 511811
Fax: 02380 511991
Email: yatesc@tauntons.ac.uk
IB coordinator: Catharine Yates

The Portsmouth Grammar School
High Street, Portsmouth PO1 2LN
Tel: 02392 360036
Fax: 02392 364256
Email: s.taylor@pgs.org.uk
IB coordinator: Simon Taylor

Hertfordshire

Beaumont School (BeauSandVer)
Oakwood Drive, St Albans AL4 0XB
Tel: 01727 854 726
Fax: 01727 847 971
Email:
morag.mccrorie@beaumont.herts.sch.uk
IB coordinator: Morag McCrorie

Haileybury
Haileybury, Hertford SG13 7NU
Tel: 01992 462507
Fax: 01992 470663
IB coordinator: Laura Pugsley

Hockerill Anglo-European College
Dunmow Road,
Bishop's Stortford CM23 5HX
Tel: 01279 658451
Email: admin@hockerill.herts.sch.uk
IB coordinator: Vicki Worsnop

Sandringham School (BeauSandVer)
The Ridgeway, St Albans AL4 9NX
Tel: 01727 759 240
Fax: 01727 759 242
Email:
graeme.swann@sandringham.herts.sch.uk
IB coordinator: Graeme Swann

Stanborough School
Stanborough Park, Garston
Watford WD25 9JT
Tel: 01923 673268
Fax: 01923 893943
Email:
pmartin@stanboroughpark.herts.sch.uk
IB coordinator: Peter Martin

Verulam School (BeauSandVer)
Brampton Road, St Albans AL1 4PR
Tel: 01727 766100
Fax: 01727 766256
Email: sue.turner@verulam.herts.sch.uk
IB coordinator: Susan Turner

Isle of Wight

Medina High School
Fairlee Road, Newport PO30 2DX
Tel: 01983 526523
Fax: 01983 528791
Email: ckeith@medina.iow.sch.uk
IB coordinator: Crispin Keith

Kent

Barton Court Grammar School
Longport, Canterbury CT1 1PH
Tel: 01227 464600
Fax: 01227 781339
Email: mdriscoll@bartoncourt.org
IB coordinator: Moira Driscoll

Bexley Grammar School
Danson Lane, Welling DA16 2BL
Tel: 02083 048538
Fax: 02083 040248
Email: brown-k@bexleygs.co.uk
IB coordinator: Ken Brown

CATS Canterbury
68 New Dover Road, Canterbury CT1 3LQ
Tel: 01223 345698
Fax: 01227 866550
IB coordinator: Noel Ensoll

Chislehurst and Sidcup Grammar School
Hurst Road, Sidcup DA15 9AG
Tel: 0208 302 6511
Fax: 0208 309 6596
Email: joanne.king@csgrammar.com
IB coordinator: Joanne King

Cobham Hall School
Cobham, Gravesend DA12 3BL
Tel: 01474 823371
Fax: 01474 825906
Email: ibcoordinator@cobhamhall.com
IB coordinator: Andrew Owen

Dane Court Grammar School
Broadstairs Road, Broadstairs CT10 2RT
Tel: 01843 864941
Fax: 01843 608811
Email: sunderland@danecourt.kent.sch.uk
IB coordinator: Steven Sunderland

Dartford Grammar School
West Hill, Dartford DA1 2HW
Tel: 01322 223039
Fax: 01322 291426
Email:
pfidczuk@dartfordgrammar.kent.sch.uk
IB coordinator: Peter Fidczuk

Dover Grammar School for Boys
Astor Avenue, Dover CT17 0DQ
Tel: 01304 206117
Fax: 01304 206074
Email:
acruttenden@dovergramboys.kent.sch.uk
IB coordinator: Aidan Cruttenden

Maidstone Grammar School
Barton Road, Maidstone ME15 7BT
Tel: 01622 752101
Fax: 01622 753680
Email: keith.derrett@mgs-kent.org.uk
IB coordinator: Keith Derrett

Sevenoaks School
Sevenoaks TN13 1HU
Tel: 01732 455133
Fax: 01732 456143
Email: nsa@sevenoaksschool.org
IB coordinator: Mr Nick Alchin

The Leigh City Technology College
Green Street, Green Road
Dartford DA1 1QE
Tel: 01322 620 400
Email: can@leighctc.kent.sch.uk
IB coordinator: Colin Ankerson

The Norton Knatchbull School
Hythe Road, Ashford TN24 0QJ
Tel: 01233 620 045
Email:
roger.baker@norton-knatchbull.kent.sch.uk
IB coordinator: Roger Baker

The Rochester Grammar School
Maidstone Road, Rochester ME1 3BY
Tel: 01634 843049
Fax: 01634 818340
Email: saunp002@medway.org.uk
IB coordinator: Paul Saunders

Tonbridge Grammar School
Deakin Leas, Tonbridge TN9 2JR
Tel: 01732 365125
Fax: 01732 359417
Email: marionmiddleton@tgs.kent.sch.uk
IB coordinator: Marion Middleton

Lancashire

Lancaster and Morecambe College
Morecambe Road, Lancaster LA1 2TY
Tel: 01524 66215
Fax: 01524 843078
Email: t.jones@lmc.ac.uk
IB coordinator: Tessa Jones

Rossall School
Broadway, Fleetwood FY7 8JW
Tel: 01253 774260
Fax: 01253 772052
Email: ibatrossall@hotmail.com
IB coordinator: Doris Dohmen

St Mary's College
Shear Brow, Blackburn BB1 8DX
Tel: 01254 580464
Fax: 01254 665991
Email: s.flanagan@stmarysblackburn.ac.uk
IB coordinator: Sarah Flanagan

Leicestershire

Groby Community College
Ratby Road, Groby, Leicester LE6 0GE
Tel: 0116 287 9921
Fax: 0116 287 0189
Email: vevans@grobycoll.leics.sch.uk
IB coordinator: Viv Evans

Wyggeston & Queen Elizabeth I College
University Road, Leicester LE1 7RJ
Tel: 0116 223 1900
Fax: 0116 223 1999
Email: helen.bull@wqeic.ac.uk
IB coordinator: Helen Bull

Lincolnshire

Thomas Deacon Academy
Queen's Gardens, Peterborough PE1 2UW
Tel: 01733 426 060
Fax: 01733 426 061
Email: lhm@deacons.peterborough.sch.uk
IB coordinator: Louise Moir

Tollbar Business & Enterprise College
Station Road, New Waltham
Grimsby DN36 4RZ
Tel: 01472 500505
Fax: 01472 500506
Email: enquiries@tollbarbec.co.uk
IB coordinator: D Shelton

London

Christ the King Sixth Form College
Belmont Grove, Lewisham
London SE13 5GE
Tel: 020 8297 9433
Fax: 020 8297 1460
Email: ran@ctksfc.ac.uk
IB coordinator: Richard Anderson

Elthorne Park High School
Westlea Road, Hanwell
London W7 2AH
Tel: 0208 566 1166
Fax: 0208 566 1177
Email: agrant@ephs.ealing.sch.uk
IB coordinator: Alistair Grant

George Green's School
100 Manchester Road
Isle of Dogs, London E14 3WE
Tel: 0207 987 6032
Fax: 0207 538 2316
Email: gnaughten@georgegreen.com
IB coordinator: Geraldine Naughten

Highlands School
148 Worlds End Lane
London N21 1QQ
Tel: 0208 370 1100
Fax: 0208 370 1100
Email: tutonk@highlands.enfield.sch.uk
IB coordinator: Karl Tuton

International Community School
4 York Terrace East
Regent's Park, London NW1 4PT
Tel: 0207 935 1206
Fax: 0207 935 7915

International School of London
139 Gunnersbury Avenue
Acton, London W3 8LG
Tel: 0208 992 5823
Fax: 0208 993 7012
Email: huwbach@btopenworld.com
IB coordinator: Huw Davies

King Fahad Academy
Bromyard Avenue
Acton, London W3 7HD
Tel: 0208 743 0131
Fax: 0208 749 7085
Email: sue.austin@thekfa.org.uk
IB coordinator: Sue Austin

King's College School
Southside, Wimbledon Common
London SW19 4TT
Tel: 0208 255 5352
Fax: 0208 255 5357
IB coordinator: Neil Tetley

Southbank International School -
Hampstead
16 Netherhall Gardens
Hampstead, London NW3 5TH
Tel: 0207 243 3803
Fax: 0207 727 3290

Southbank International School -
Kensington
36-38 Kensington Park Road
Kensington, London W11 3BU
Tel: 0207 243 3803
Fax: 0207 727 3290

Southbank International School -
Westminster
63-65 Portland Place
Regent's Park, London W1B 1QR
Tel: 0207 243 3803
Fax: 0207 727 3290
Email: ppi@southbank.org
IB coordinator: Paul Pickering

St Dunstan's College
Stanstead Road, London SE6 4TY
Tel: 0208 516 7200
Fax: 0208 516 7300
Email: salgeo@sdmail.org.uk
IB coordinator: Sue Algeo

St Mary Magdalene Academy
Liverpool Road, London N7 8PG
Tel: 0207 697 0123
Fax: 0207 697 8430
Email: firstcontact@smmacademy.org
IB coordinator: Donna Critcher

The Godolphin and Latymer School
Iffley Road, Hammersmith
London, W6 0PG
Tel: 0208 741 1936
Fax: 0208 735 9520
Email:
ctrimming@godolphinandlatymer.com
IB coordinator: Caroline Trimming

The North London International School
Friern Barnet Lane
London N11 3LX
Tel: 0208 920 0600
Fax: 0208 211 4605
Email: edithvanderlinden@yahoo.co.uk
IB coordinator: Edith van der Linden

Westminster Academy
The Naim Dangoor Centre
255 Harrow Road
London W2 5EZ
Tel: 0207 121 0600
Email: owells@westminsteracademy.biz
IB coordinator: Oliver Wells

Merseyside

Broadgreen High School
Queens Drive
Liverpool L13 5UQ
Tel: 01512 28 6800
Fax: 01512 20 9256
Email: mhedges@broadgreenhigh.org.uk
IB coordinator: Martina Hedges

Calday Grange Grammar School
Grammar School Lane
West Kirby, Wirral CH48 8GG
Tel: 0151 625 2727
Fax: 0151 625 9851
Email: michael.skelly@calday.wirral.sch.uk
IB coordinator: Michael Skelly

Cowley Language College
Hard Lane
St Helens WA10 6LB
Tel: 01744 678 030
Email: cowley@sthelens.org.uk
IB coordinator: Matthew Hesketh

Formby High School
Freshfield Road, Formby
Liverpool L37 3HW
Tel: 01704 835 650
Fax: 01704 835 657
Email: nicola@davies168.freeserve.co.uk
IB coordinator: Nicola Davies

King George V College
Scarisbrick New Road
Southport PR8 6LR
Tel: 01704 530601
Fax: 01704 548656
Email: jcw@kgv.ac.uk
IB coordinator: Jane Wells

Liverpool College
Queen's Drive
Mossley Hill, Liverpool L18 8BG
Tel: 0151 724 4000
Fax: 0151 724 3154
Email: hlock@liverpoolcollege.org.uk
IB coordinator: Harry Lock

Range High School
Stapleton Road
Formby, Liverpool L37 2YN
Tel: 01704 879315
Fax: 01704 833470
Email: ga2@range.sefton.sch.uk
IB coordinator: Graham Aldridge

Middlesex

ACS Hillingdon International School
Hillingdon Court, 108 Vine Lane
Hillingdon, Uxbridge UB10 0BE
Tel: 01895 259771
Fax: 01895 818404
IB coordinator: Chris Green

Bishop Ramsey Church of England School
Hume Way, Ruislip HA4 8EE
Tel: 01895 639227
Fax: 01895 62242
Email: cwatson@hillingdongrid.org
IB coordinator: Carole Watson

Dormers Wells High School
Dormers Wells Lane, Southall UB1 3HZ
Tel: 0208 813 8671
Fax: 0208 813 8861
Email:
imccartney@dormers-wells.ealing.sch.uk
IB coordinator: Ian McCartney

North London Collegiate School
Canons, Canons Drive
Edgware HA8 7RJ
Tel: 0208 952 0912
Fax: 0208 951 1391
Email: mburke@nlcs.org.uk
IB coordinator: Michael Burke

Richmond upon Thames College
Egerton Road, Twickenham TW2 7SJ
Tel: 0208 607 8000
Fax: 0208 744 9738
Email: swinfield@rutc.ac.uk
IB coordinator: Stephen Winfield

St Helen's School
Eastbury Road, Northwood HA6 3AS
Tel: 01923 843210
Fax: 01923 843211
Email: mary.bowman@sthn.co.uk
IB coordinator: Mary Bowman

Villiers High School
Boyd Avenue, Southall UB1 3BT
Tel: 0208 813 8001
Fax: 0208 574 3071
IB coordinator: Amanda Sara

West London Academy
Compton Crescent
Northolt UB5 5LP
Tel: 0208 841 4511
Fax: 0208 841 4480
Email: cantyd@westlondonacademy.co.uk
IB coordinator: Dennis Canty

Norfolk

Gresham's School
Cromer Road, Holt NR25 6EA
Tel: 01263 714511
Fax: 01263 712028
Email: mseldon@greshams.com
IB coordinator: Mark Seldon

Notre Dame High School
Surrey Street, Norwich NR1 3PB
Tel: 01603 611431
Fax: 01603 763381
Email: pshort@notredamehigh.norfolk.sch.uk
IB coordinator: Paul Short

Nottinghamshire

Bilborough College
College Way, Nottingham NG8 4DQ
Tel: 0115 851 5000
Fax: 0115 851 5804
Email: david.shaw@bilborough.ac.uk
IB coordinator: David Shaw

South Wolds Community School
Church Drive, Keyworth
Nottingham NG12 5FF
Tel: 0115 937 3506
Fax: 0115 937 2905
Email: chughes@southwolds.notts.sch.uk
IB coordinator: Carole Hughes

Oxfordshire

Headington School
London Road, Oxford OX3 7TD
Tel: 01865 759100
Fax: 01865 760268
Email: jstephenson@headington.org
IB coordinator: James Stephenson

Henley College
Deanfield Avenue
Henley-on-Thames RG9 1UH
Tel: 01491 579 988
Fax: 01491 410 099
Email: bhug@henleycol.ac.uk
IB coordinator: Bridie Hughes

North Oxfordshire Academy
Drayton Road
Drayton, Banbury OX16 0UD
Tel: 01295 253181
Fax: 01295 279876
Email:
kaddy.beck@northoxfordshire-academy.org
IB coordinator: Kaddy Beck

St Clare's
139 Banbury Road, Oxford OX2 7AL
Tel: 01865 552031
Fax: 01865 513359
Email: nick.lee@stclares.ac.uk
IB coordinator: Nick Lee

St Edward's
Woodstock Road, Oxford OX2 7NN
Tel: 01865 319200
Fax: 01865 319202
Email: elzingaj@stedwards.oxon.sch.uk
IB coordinator: Jesse Elzinga

Rutland

Oakham School
Chapel Close, Oakham LE15 5DT
Tel: 01572 758 758
Fax: 01572 758 595
Email: slw@oakham.rutland.sch.uk
IB coordinator: Simone Lorenz-Weir

Shropshire

Ellesmere College
Birch Road, Ellesmere SY12 9AB
Tel: 01691 622321
Fax: 01691 623286
Email: isn.tompkins@ellesmere.com
IB coordinator: Ian G Tompkins

Somerset

Beechen Cliff School
Alexandra Park, Bath BA2 4RE
Tel: 01225 480466
Fax: 01225 314025
Email: judithowen@beechencliff.org.uk
IB coordinator: Judith Owen

Bridgwater College
Bath Road, Bridgwater TA6 4PZ
Tel: 01278 455464
Fax: 01278 444363
Email: aldridgem@bridgwater.ac.uk
IB coordinator: Martyn Aldridge

Hayesfield School Technology College
Upper Oldfield Park, Bath BA2 3LA
Tel: 01225 426151
Fax: 01225 427005
Email: c.trueman@hayesfield.com
IB coordinator: Catherine Trueman

Sidcot School
Oakridge Lane, Winscombe BS25 1PD
Tel: 01934 843102
Fax: 01934 844181
Email: philip.perkins@sidcot.org.uk
IB coordinator: Philip Perkins

Taunton School
Staplegrove Road, Taunton TA2 6AD
Tel: 01823 349 200
Fax: 01823 349 201
Email: ibcoordinator@tauntonschool.co.uk
IB coordinator: Martin Bluemel

The Royal High School GDST
Lansdown Road, Bath BA1 5SZ
Tel: 01225 313877
Fax: 01225 465446
Email: a.holloway@bat.gdst.net
IB coordinator: Angharad Holloway

Staffordshire

City of Stoke-on-Trent Sixth Form College
Victoria Road, Fenton
Stoke on Trent ST4 2RR
Tel: 01782 854222
Fax: 01782 747456
Email: mike.casey@stokesfc.ac.uk
IB coordinator: Michael Casey

De Ferrers Specialist Technology College
St Mary's Drive, Trent Campus
Burton upon Trent DE13 0LL
Tel: 01283 239936
Email: gallowayp@deferrers.mg4l.net
IB coordinator: Paul Galloway

Thomas Alleyne's High School
Dove Bank, Uttoxeter
Stafford ST14 8DU
Tel: 01889 561820
Fax: 01889 561850
Email: dodd@tahs.org.uk
IB coordinator: Carole Dodd

Surrey

ACS Cobham International School
Heywood, Portsmouth Road
Cobham KT11 1BL
Tel: 01932 867251
Fax: 01932 869789
Email: cworthington@acs-england.co.uk
IB coordinator: Craig Worthington

ACS Egham International School
Woodlee, London Road
Egham TW20 0HS
Tel: 01784 430800
Fax: 01784 430626
Email: kord@acs-england.co.uk
IB coordinator: Justin McCarthy

Box Hill School
Mickleham, Dorking RH5 6EA
Tel: 01372 373382
Fax: 01372 363942
Email: pengilleym@boxhillschool.org.uk
IB coordinator: Monica Pengilley

Coloma Convent Girls' School
Upper Shirley Road, Croydon CR9 5AS
Tel: 0208 654 6228
Fax: 0208 656 6485
Email: griffin@coloma.croydon.sch.uk
IB coordinator: Mary Griffin

King Edward's School Witley
Petworth Road, Wormley
Godalming GU8 5SG
Tel: 01428 686768
Fax: 01428 682850
Email: mehargc@kesw.surrey.sch.uk
IB coordinator: Ms Christine Meharg

Kings College for the Arts & Technology
Southway, Guildford GU2 8DU
Tel: 01483 458956
Fax: 01483 458957
Email: n.clay@kingscollegeguildford.com
IB coordinator: Nick Clay

Kings International College
Watchetts Drive, Camberley GU15 2PQ
Tel: 01276 683539
Fax: 01276 709503
Email:
a.reynolds@kings-international.co.uk
IB coordinator: Anne Reynolds

Marymount International School
George Road
Kingston upon Thames KT2 7PE
Tel: 0208 949 0571
Fax: 0208 336 2485
Email: acdean@marymount.kingston.sch.uk
IB coordinator: Brian Johnson

Overton Grange School
Stanley Road, Sutton SM2 6TQ
Tel: 0208 239 2383
Fax: 0208 239 2382
Email: mcachia@suttonlea.org
IB coordinator: Maria Cachia

TASIS The American International School
in England
Coldharbour Lane, Thorpe TW20 8TE
Tel: 01932 565252
Fax: 01932 564644
Email: cgordon@tasisengland.org
IB coordinator: Chantal Gordon

Whitgift School
Haling Park, South Croydon CR2 6YT
Tel: 0208 688 9222
Fax: 0208 760 0682
Email: ibcoordinator.whitgift@lgfl.net
IB coordinator: Stewart Cook

Sussex

Ardingly College
College Road, Ardingly
Haywards Heath RH17 6SQ
Tel: 01444 893000
Fax: 01444 893001
Email: widgetcat@hotmail.com
IB coordinator: John Langford

Bexhill College
Penland Road, Bexhill-on-Sea TN40 2JG
Tel: 01424 214545
Fax: 01424 215050
Email: ianmowat@bexhillcollege.ac.uk
IB coordinator: Ian Mowat

Chichester High Schools Sixth Form
Kingsham Road, Chichester PO19 8AE
Tel: 01243 832546
Fax: 01243 832580
Email: mmcguffin@wsgfl.org.uk
IB coordinator: Madeleine McGuffin

Hastings College of Arts & Technology
Archery Road
St Leonards-on-Sea TN38 0HX
Tel: 01424 442222
Fax: 01424 721763
Email: cmorrell@hastings.ac.uk
IB coordinator: Chris Morrell

Steyning Grammar School
Church Street, Steyning BN44 3LB
Tel: 01903 814786
Fax: 01903 879273
Email: rtunbridge@sgs.uk.net
IB coordinator: Richard Tunbridge

Worth School
Paddockhurst Road, Turners Hill
Crawley RH10 4SD
Tel: 01342 710200
Fax: 01342 710230
Email: ssmith@worth.org.uk
IB coordinator: Simon Smith

Tyne & Wear

Newcastle Sixth Form College
Parsons Building, Rye Hill
Scotswood Road
Newcastle upon Tyne NE4 7SA
Tel: 0191 200 4450
Fax: 0191 200 4541
Email: lynda.evans@ncl-coll.ac.uk
IB coordinator: Lynda Evans

South Tyneside College
St George's Avenue
South Shields NE34 6ET
Tel: 0191 427 3500
Fax: 0191 427 36548
Email: geoff.holmes@stc.ac.uk
IB coordinator: Geoff Holmes

Tyne Metropolitan College
Embleton Avenue, Wallsend
Newcastle upon Tyne NE28 9NJ
Tel: 0191 229 5000
Fax: 0191 229 5301
Email: adrian.shepherd@tynemet.ac.uk
IB coordinator: Adrian Shepherd

Warwickshire

Warwickshire College
Warwick New Road,
Leamington Spa CV32 5JE
Tel: 01926 318000
Fax: 01926 318111
Email: hadkins@warkscol.ac.uk
IB coordinator: Helen Adkins

West Midlands

City Technology College, Kingshurst
PO Box 1017
Cooks Lane, Kingshurst
Birmingham B37 6NZ
Tel: 0121 329 8300
Email: roz.trudgon@kingshurst.ac.uk
IB coordinator: Roz Trudgon

Finham Park School
Green Lane, Coventry CV3 6EA
Tel: 02476 418135
Fax: 02476 840803
Email: v.chandley@finhampark.co.uk
IB coordinator: Victoria Chandley

George Dixon International School & Sixth
Form Centre
City Road, Edgbaston
Birmingham B17 8LF
Tel: 0121 675 4488
Email: colinmac@gn.apc.org
IB coordinator: Colin McKenzie

Halesowen College
Whittingham Road, Halesowen B63 3NA
Tel: 0121 602 7777
Fax: 0121 585 0369
Email: mgrant@halesowen.ac.uk
IB coordinator: Mick Grant

The Sixth Form College, Solihull
Widney Manor Road
Solihull B91 3WR
Tel: 0121 704 2581
Fax: 0121 711 1598
Email: mjennings@solihullsfc.ac.uk
IB coordinator: Michael Jennings

Wiltshire

Marlborough College
Marlborough SN8 1PA
Tel: 01672 892 300
Fax: 01672 892 207
Emial: rtm@marlboroughcollege.org
IB coordinator: Richard Markham

New College Swindon
New College Drive
Swindon SN3 1AH
Tel: 0808 172 1721
Fax: 01793 436437
Emial: jayne.chaston@newcollege.ac.uk
IB coordinator: Jayne Chaston

St John's School and Community College
Orchard Road, Marlborough SN8 4AX
Tel: 01672 516 156
Fax: 01672 516 664
Emial: sround@stjohns.wilts.sch.uk
IB coordinator: Sue Round

Warminster School
Church Street, Warminster BA12 8PJ
Tel: 01985 210 160
Fax: 01985 210 154
Email: obourne@warminsterschool.org.uk
IB coordinator: Olivia Bourne

Wootton Bassett School
Lime Kiln, Wootton Bassett SN4 7HG
Tel: 01793 841 900
Fax: 01793 841 968
Email: MCU@woottonbassett.wilts.sch.uk
IB coordinator: Marian Curran

Worcestershire

Bromsgrove School
Worcester Road
Bromsgrove B61 7DU
Tel: 01527 579679
Fax: 01527 576177
Email:
mbowenjones@bromsgrove-school.co.uk
IB coordinator: Michael Bowen-Jones

Kingsley College
Woodrow Drive, Redditch B98 7UH
Tel: 01527 523088
Fax: 01527 514245
Email: gibbos@kingsley.worcs.sch.uk
IB coordinator: Sue Gibbons

Malvern College
College Road, Malvern WR14 3DF
Tel: 01684 581500
Fax: 01684 581617
Email: jpk@malcol.org
IB coordinator: John Knee

York

Easingwold School
York Road, Easingwold
York YO61 3EF
Tel: 01347 821451
Fax: 01347 823301
Email: k.shires@easingwold.n-yorks.sch.uk
IB coordinator: Karen Shires

Huntington School
Huntington Road, Huntington
York YO32 9WT
Tel: 01904 752100
Fax: 01904 752101
Email: jr.uttley@huntington-ed.org.uk
IB coordinator: Jonathan Uttley

Queen Ethelburga's College
Thorpe Underwood Hall
Ouseburn, York YO26 9SS
Tel: 01423 333330
Fax: 01423 331444
Email: dwillis@queenethelburgas.edu
IB coordinator: Denise Willis

Yorkshire, East

Hull College
Queen's Gardens, Hull HU1 3DG
Tel: 01482 329943
Email: kharding@hull-college.ac.uk
IB coordinator: Kate Harding

Yorkshire, North

Harrogate Grammar School
Arthurs Avenue, Harrogate HG2 0DZ
Tel: 01423 531127
Fax: 01423 521325
Email: ib@hgs.n-yorks.sch.uk
IB coordinator: Michael Bailey

Lady Lumley's School
Swainsea Lane, Pickering YO18 8NG
Tel: 01751 472846
Fax: 01751 477259
Email: phowell@ladylumleys.freeserve.co.uk
IB coordinator: Peter Howell

Prior Pursglove College
Church Walk, Guisborough TS14 6BU
Tel: 01287 280800
Fax: 01287 280280
Email: b.tailby@prior.pursglove.ac.uk
IB coordinator: Barbara Tailby

Scarborough College
Filey Road, Scarborough YO11 3BA
Tel: 01723 360620
Fax: 01723 377265
Email: aevirgen@scarboroughcollege.co.uk
IB coordinator: Amanda Evirgen

Yorkshire, South

Doncaster College
The Hub, Chapell Drive
Doncaster DN1 2RF
Tel: 01302 553553
Fax: 01302 553559
Email: jo.burgess@don.ac.uk
IB coordinator: Jo Burgess

High Storrs School
High Storrs Road, Sheffield S11 7LH
Tel: 0114 267 0000
Fax: 0114 266 8485
Email: b.plant@highstorrs.sheffield.sch.uk
IB coordinator: Barbara Plant

Yorkshire, West

Park Lane College
Park Lane, Leeds LS3 1AA
Tel: 0845 045 7275
Fax: 0113 216 2020
Email: j.parkinson@parklanecoll.ac.uk
IB coordinator: Jennifer Parkinson

The Grammar School at Leeds
Alwoodley Gates, Harrogate Road
Leeds LS17 8GS
Tel: 0113 229 1552
Fax: 0113 228 5111
Email: jmh@gsal.org.uk
IB coordinator: Mark Humphries

ISLE OF MAN

King William's College
Castletown, Isle of Man IM9 1TP
Tel: 01624 820428
Fax: 01624 820401
Email: rene.filho@kwc.sch.im
IB coordinator: Rene Filho

JERSEY

Hautlieu School
Wellington Road, St Saviour JE2 7TH
Tel: 01534 736 242
Fax: 01534 789 349
Email: p.wallacesims@hautlieu.sch.je
IB coordinator: Paul Wallace-Sims

SCOTLAND

Fettes College
Carrington Road, Edinburgh EH4 1QX
Tel: 0131 311 6744
Fax: 0131 311 6714
Email: jc.fern@fettes.com
IB coordinator: John Fern

International School of Aberdeen
296 North Deeside Road
Milltimber, Aberdeen AB13 0AB
Tel: 01224 732267
Fax: 01224 735648
Email: marybeth.kiley@isa.aberdeen.sch.uk
IB coordinator: Mary Beth Kiley

Motherwell College
Dalzell Drive, Motherwell ML1 2DD
Tel: 01698 232425
Fax: 01698 232527
Email: lcowan@motherwell.ac.uk
IB coordinator: Lorraine Cowan

St Leonards School
St Andrews, Fife KY16 9QJ
Tel: 01334 472126
Fax: 01334 476152
Email: k.wowk@stleonards-fife.org
IB coordinator: Karen Wowk

WALES

Coleg Llandrillo
Llandudno Road
Rhos-on-Sea LL28 4HZ
Tel: 01492 546666
Fax: 01492 543052
Email: m.monteith@llandrillo.ac.uk
IB coordinator: Melanie Monteith

Rydal Penrhos
Pwllycrochan Avenue
Colwyn Bay LL29 7BT
Tel: 01492 530155
Fax: 01492 531872
Email: info@rydal-penrhos.com
IB coordinator: Wyn Williams

Swansea College
Ty Coch Road, Swansea SA2 9EB
Tel: 01792 284000
Fax: 01792 284074
Email: s.phillips@swancoll.ac.uk
IB coordinator: Sue Phillips

United World College of the Atlantic
St Donat's Castle
Llantwit Major CF61 1WF
Tel: 01446 799000
Fax: 01446 799277
Email: mark.godwin@atlanticcollege.org
IB coordinator: Mark Godwin

Westbourne School
4 Hickman Road, Penarth CF6 2AJ
Tel: 029 2070 5705
Fax: 029 2070 9988
Email: garethjones@westbourneschool.com
IB coordinator: Gareth Jones

Whitchurch High School
Penlline Road, Whitchurch
Cardiff CF4 2XJ
Tel: 02920 629700
Fax: 02920 629701
Email: daviesjw@whitchurch.cardiff.sch.uk
IB coordinator: Jonathan Davies

Awarding bodies

Awarding bodies

In England there are three Unitary Awarding Bodies, each offering GCSE, including applied GCSEs, A level and applied A levels. There are separate Awarding Bodies in Wales (WJEC) and Northern Ireland (CCEA). The Awarding Body in Scotland (SQA) offers equivalent qualifications.

AQA - Assessment and Qualification Alliance

Qualifications offered:
GCSE
A level (AS and A2)
FCSE
FSMQ
Advanced Extension Award (AEA)
Entry Level Certificate (ELC)
Key Skills
Basic Skills
VRQ
Diploma (AQA City & Guilds Foundation, Higher & Advanced)
Project (AQA City & Guilds Foundation, Higher & Advanced)
AQA Baccalaureate
Functional Skills
Level 1 and 2 Certificate
Preparation for Working Life

Other assessment schemes:
Unit Award Scheme (UAS)
Access to Higher Education (AHE)

Contact:
Email: mailbox@aqa.org.uk   Website: www.aqa.org.uk

Devas Street, Manchester M15 6EX
Tel: 0161 953 1180   Fax: 0161 273 7572

Stag Hill House, Guildford, Surrey GU2 7XJ
Tel: 01483 506506   Fax: 01483 300152

31-33 Springfield Avenue, Harrogate, North Yorkshire HG1 2HW
Tel: 01423 840 015   Fax: 01423 523 678

CCEA - Council for the Curriculum, Examinations and Assessment

Qualifications offered:
GCSE
GCE AS/A2 Level
Key Skills (Levels 1-4)
Entry Level Qualifications
GOML
ACETS
BTECs
Essential Skills
Occupational Studies

Contact:

29 Clarendon Road, Clarendon Dock, Belfast, BT1 3BG

Tel: (028) 9026 1200   Fax: (028) 9026 1234

Edexcel

Qualifications offered:
Edexcel's qualifications are offered worldwide and include:
AEA
DiDA
Diploma
GCE AS/A2
GCSE
Adult Literacy and Numeracy (usually referred to as Adult Basic Skills), Skills for Life, Functional Skills, Foundation Learning, Key Skills, Entry Level Certificate, Project Qualifications and ESOL (Skills for Life)
BTEC Customised Qualifications
BTEC Foundation Diploma (art & design)
BTEC Introductory/Entry/Nationals
BTEC Higher National Certificate and Higher National Diploma (HNC/HND)
BTEC Foundation Degree
BTEC Firsts
IGCSE
NVQ
Contact: One90 High Holborn, London WC1V 7BH
Tel: 0870 240 9800; Fax: 020 7190 5700; Email: via online enquiries form at www.edexcel.org.uk
Website: www.edexcel.org.uk

IB - International Baccalaureate Organization

Qualifications offered:

IB Diploma

Contact:
The International Baccalaureate Organization
Peterson House, Malthouse Avenue, Cardiff Gate, Cardiff, CF23 8GL
Tel: 029 2054 7777
Fax: 029 2054 7778
Email: communications@ibc.org
Website: www.ibo.org

OCR - Oxford Cambridge and RSA Examinations

Qualifications offered:
GCSE
GCE AS/A2 Level
STEP - Sixth Term Examination Paper
OCR Nationals
NVQ
Basic Skills
Key Skills
Entry Level
FSMQ - Free Standing Maths Qualification
Diplomas
'Own brand' qualifications, including:
IT (CLAiT), iPRO, iTQ and iMedia, business, languages, teaching/training, admin, secretarial etc

Contact:
OCR, 1 Hills Road, Cambridge CB1 2EU
Website: www.ocr.org.uk

Vocational Qualifications, Customer Contact Centre
Tel: 02476 851509; Email: vocational.qualifications@ocr.org.uk

General Qualifications, Customer Contact Centre
Tel: 02476 851509; Email: general.qualifications@ocr.org.uk

SQA - Scottish Qualifications Authority

Qualifications offered:
National Qualifications:
> Access 1& 2
> Standard Grade
> Intermediate 1
> Intermediate 2
> Higher
> Advanced Higher

Higher National Qualifications:
> HNC
> HND

Vocational Qualifications:
> SVQ

Contact:
Glasgow - The Optima Building, 58 Robertson Street, Glasgow, G2 8DQ

Edinburgh - Ironmills Road, Dalkeith, Midlothian, EH22 1LE

Tel: 0845 279 1000
Email: customer@sqa.org.uk
Website: www.sqa.org.uk

WJEC

Qualifications offered:
GCSE
GCE A/AS/AEA
Functional Skills
Entry Level
Key Skills
Key Stage 3
Welsh Baccalaureate/Diploma
Foundation, HIgher & Extended Project

Contact:
245 Western Avenue
Cardiff, CF5 2YX
Tel: 029 2026 5000
Website: www.wjec.co.uk

Educational organisations

Educational Organisations

The Allied Schools (AS)
Providers of financial and administrative support services and advice to member schools, and is also secretariat to their governing bodies (registered charity No. 1051729):

Barnardiston Hall
Canford School
Harrogate Ladies' College
Highfield School
Old Hall School
Riddlesworth Hall Preparatory School
Rosehhill Westonbrit
Stowe School
Westonbirt School
Wrekin College

Membership is open to other schools.

General Manager, Michael Porter BA, MSc
Cross House, 38 High Street, Banbury
Oxfordshire OX16 5ET
Tel: 01295 222380
Fax: 01295 275350

Email: admin@alliedschools.org.uk
Website: www.alliedschools.org.uk

Artsmark
Arts Council England's Artsmark was set up in 2001, and rounds are held annually.

All schools in England can apply for an Artsmark – primary, middle, secondary, special and pupil referral units, maintained and independent – on a voluntary basis. An Artsmark award is made to schools showing commitment to the full range of arts – music, dance, drama and art and design.

Arts Council England
14 Great Peter Street
London SW1P 3NQ
Tel: 0800 0560 196
Email: artsmark@artscouncil.org.uk
Website: www.artscouncil.org.uk/artsmark

Association for the Education and Guardianship of International Students (AEGIS)

AEGIS brings together schools and guardianship organisations to promote the welfare of international students. AEGIS provides accreditation for all reputable guardianship organisations.

Secretary: Janet Bowman
AEGIS
66 Humphreys Close, Randwick
Stroud, Gloucestershire GL5 4NY
Tel/Fax: 01453 755160
Email: secretary@aegisuk.net   Website: www.aegisuk.net

The Association of American Study Abroad Programmes (AASAP)

Established in 1991 to represent American study programmes in the UK.

Staff Assistant: Corinne Cohen
AASAP/UK
Dilke House, Malet Street
London WC1E 7JN
Tel: 0207 636 0761
Email: info@aasapuk.org   Website: www.aasapuk.org

The Association of British Riding Schools (ABRS)

An independent body of proprietors and principals of riding establishments, aiming to look after their interests and those of the riding public and to raise standards of management, instruction and animal welfare.

General Secretary, Association of British Riding Schools
Queen's Chambers
38-40 Queen Street, Penzance
Cornwall TR18 4BH
Tel: 01736 369440   Fax: 01736 351390
Email: office@abrs-info.org   Website: www.abrs-info.org

Association of Colleges (AOC)

Created in 1996 to promote the interest of further education colleges in England and Wales.

Association of Colleges
2-5 Stedham Place
London WC1A 1HU
Tel: 0207 034 9900   Fax: 0207 034 9950
Email: enquiries@aoc.co.uk   Website: www.aoc.co.uk

Association of Governing Bodies of Independent Schools (AGBIS)

The objects of the Association are to advance education in independent schools. AGBIS promotes good governance and provides training, advice and appropriate documentation. (Registered charity No. 1108756)

Enquiries should be addressed to AGBIS General Secretary:
Shane Rutter-Jerome
AGBIS, Renshaw Barns, Upper Woodford
Salisbury, Wiltshire SP4 6FA
Tel: 01722 782 900   Fax: 05601 264 801
Email: admin@agbis.org.uk   Website: www.agbis.info

The Association of Heads of Independent Schools (AHIS)

Membership is open to all heads of girls' and of independent schools which are accredited by the ISC (Independent Schools Council).

Mrs A V Whatmough, Hon Secretary
St Nicholas' School
Redfields House, Redfields Lane
Church Crookham
Fleet
Hampshire GU52 CRF
Email: headspa@st-nicholas.hants.sch.uk

Association of Learning Providers (ALP)

ALP's purpose is to influence the education and training agenda. They are the voice of independent learning providers througout England.

ALP
Colenso House
46 Bath Hill
Keynsham
Bristol BS31 1HG
Tel: 0117 986 5389
Email: enquiries@learningproviders.org
Website: www.learningproviders.org.uk

The Association of School and Colleges Leaders (ASCL)

Formerly the Secondary Heads Association, the ASCL is a professional association for secondary school and college leaders.

General Secretary:
J E Dunford OBE, BSc, MEd, PhD, FRSA
130 Regent Road
Leicester LE1 7PG
Tel: 0116 299 1122   Fax: 0116 299 1123
Email: info@ascl.org.uk   Website: www.ascl.org.uk

The Association of Tutors

The professional body for independent private tutors. Members provide advice and individual tuition to students at all levels of education. The tutoring may be supplementary to full course provision or may be on a full course basis.

Enquiries to:
The Secretary
The Association of Tutors
63 King Edward Road
Northampton NN1 5LY
Tel: 01604 624171
Website: www.tutor.co.uk

Boarding Schools' Association (BSA)

For information on the BSA see editorial on page xxxv

The British Accreditation Council for Independent Further and Higher Education (BAC)

For information on the BAC see editorial on page xxxiii

The British Association for Early Childhood Education (Early Education)

Promotes quality provision for all children from birth to eight in whatever setting they are placed. Publishes booklets and organises conferences for those interested in early years education and care. (Registered charity Nos. 313082; SCO39472.)

Early Education
136 Cavell Street
London E1 2JA
Tel: 020 7539 5400   Fax: 020 7539 5409
Email: office@early-education.org.uk   Website: www.early-education.org.uk

The Choir Schools' Association (CSA)

Represents 44 schools attached to cathedrals, churches and college chapels, which educate cathedral and collegiate choristers.

The Information Officer
Windrush
Church Road
Martket Weston
Diss
Norfolk IP22 2NX
Tel: 01359 221333
Email: info@choirschools.org.uk   Website: www.choirschools.org.uk

The Council for Independent Education (CIFE)

CIFE is the professional association for independent sixth form and tutorial colleges accredited by the British Accreditation Council for Independent Further and Higher Education (BAC), the Independent Schools Council or the DCSF (OFSTED). Member colleges specialise in preparing students for GCSE and A level (AS and A2) in particular and university entrance in general.

The aim of the association is to provide a forum for the exchange of information and ideas, and for the promotion of best practice, and to safeguard adherence to strict standards of professional conduct and ethical propriety. Further information can be obtained from:

The Secretary, CIFE, 1 Knightsbridge Green, London SW1X 7NW
Tel: 0208 767 8666
Email: enquiries@cife.org.uk   Website: www.cife.org.uk

Council of British International Schools (COBIS)

COBIS is a membership association of British schools of quality worldwide and is committed to a stringent process of quality assurance for all its member schools. COBIS is a member of the Independent Schools Council (ISC) of the United Kingdom.

Dr Fiona Rogers, General Secretary, COBIS
Oxford Brookes University
Harcourt Hill Campus
Oxford OX2 9AT
Tel: 01865 488564   Fax: 01865 488666
Email: general.secretary@cobis.org.uk   Website: www.cobis.org.uk

Council of International Schools (CIS)

CIS is a not-for-profit organisation committed to supporting its member schools and colleges in achieving and delivering the highest standards of international education. CIS provides accreditation to schools, teacher and leader recruitment and best practice development. CIS Higher Education assists member colleges and universities in recruiting a diverse profile of qualified international students.

CIS
21A Lavant Street
Petersfield
Hampshire GU32 3EL
Tel: 01730 263131   Fax: 01730 268913
Email: cois@cois.org   Website: www.cois.org

Dyslexia Action (DA)

A registered, educational charity (No. 268502) which has established teaching and assessment centres and conducts teacher-training throughout the UK. The aim of the institute is to help people with dyslexia of all ages to overcome their difficulties in learning to read, write and spell and to achieve their potential.

Dyslexia Action
Park House
Wick Road
Egham
Surrey TW20 0HH
Tel: 01784 222300 Fax: 01784 222333
Email: info@dyslexiaaction.org.uk Website: www.dyslexiaaction.org.uk

European Association for International Education (EAIE)

A not-for-profit organisation aiming for internationalisation in higher education in Europe. It has a membership of over 1800.

EAIE
PO Box 11189
1001 GD Amsterdam
The Netherlands
Tel: +31 20 344 5100 Fax: +31 20 344 5119
Email: eaie@eaie.nl Website: www.eaie.org

European Council of International Schools (ECIS)

ECIS is a membership organisation which provides services to support professional development, good governance and leadership in international schools.

ECIS
21B Lavant Street
Petersfield
Hampshire GU32 3EL
Tel: 01730 268244 Fax: 01730 267914
Email: ecis@ecis.org Website: www.ecis.org

The Girls' Day School Trust (GDST)

The Girls' Day School Trust (GDST) is one of the largest, longest-established and most successful groups of independent schools in the UK, with 4000 staff and over 20,000 students between the ages of three and 18. As a charity that owns and runs a family of 29 schools in England and Wales, it reinvests all its income into its schools for the benefit of the pupils. With a long history of pioneering innovation in the education of girls, the GDST now also educates boys in some of its schools, and has two coeducational sixth form colleges. (Registered charity No. 306983.)

100 Rochester Row
London SW1P 1JP
Tel: 020 7393 6666 Fax: 020 7393 6789
Website: www.gdst.net

Girls' Schools Association (GSA)

For information on the GSA see editorial on page xxxvii

The Headmasters' and Headmistresses' Conference (HMC)

For information on the HMC see editorial on page xxxviii

Human Scale Education (HSE)

An educational reform movement aiming for small education communities based on democracy, fairness and respect. (Registered charity No. 1000400)

Human Scale Education
Unit 8, Fairseat Farm
Chew Stoke, Bristol BS40 8XF
Tel/Fax: 01275 332516
Email: info@hse.org.uk   Website: www.hse.org.uk

The Independent Association of Preparatory Schools (IAPS)

For further information about IAPS see editorial on page xl

The Independent Schools Association (ISA)

For further information about ISA see editorial on page xli

The Independent Schools' Bursars Association (ISBA)

Exists to support and advance financial and operational performance in independent schools. The ISBA is a charitable company limited by guarantee. (Company No. 1121757; registered charity No. 6410037.)

General Secretary: J R B Cock
ISBA, Unit 11-12 Manor Farm
Cliddesden
Basingstoke
Hampshire RG25 2JB
Tel: 01256 330369   Fax: 01256 330376
Email: office@theisba.org.uk   Website: www.theisba.org.uk

The Independent Schools Council (ISC)

The Independent Schools Council exists to promote choice, diversity and excellence in education; the development of talent at all levels of ability; and the widening of opportunity for children from all backgrounds to achieve their potential. Its 1280 member schools educate more than 500,000 children at all levels of ability and from all socio-economic classes. Nearly a third of children in ISC schools receive help with fees. The Governing Council of ISC contains representatives from each of the eight ISC constituent associations listed below.

Members:
Association of Governing Bodies of Independent Schools (AGBIS)
Council of British International Schools (COBIS)
Girls' Schools Association (GSA)
Headmasters' and Headmistresses' Conference (HMC)
Independent Association of Prep Schools (IAPS)
Independent Schools Association (ISA)
Independent Schools Bursars' Association (ISBA)
Society of Headmasters and Headmistresses of Independent Schools (SHMIS).

The council also has close relations with the BSA and the SCIS. See also page xlii

St Vincent House, 30 Orange Street, London WC2H 7HH
Tel: 020 7766 7070   Fax: 020 7766 7071
Website: www.isc.co.uk

The Independent Schools Examinations Board (ISEB)

Details of the Common Entrance examinations are obtainable from:

Independent Schools Examinations Board
Jordan House
Christchurch Road
New Milton
Hampshire BH25 6QJ
Tel: 01425 621111   Fax: 01425 620044
Email: enquiries@iseb.co.uk   Website: www.iseb.co.uk

Copies of past papers can be purchased from Galore Publishing Ltd:
Tel: 01580 764242
Email orders@galorepark.co.uk   Website: www.galorepark.co.uk

The Inspiring Futures Foundation (IFF)

The IFF provides careers education and guidance to schools and students. Professional support and training is available to school staff and our Futurewise programme provides individual, web based, support for students and their parents. Career/subject insight courses, gap-year fairs and an information service are additional elements of the service.

Andrew Airey, Chief Executive
The Inspiring Futures Foundation
St George's House, Knoll Road
Camberley, Surrey GU15 3SY
Tel: 01276 687500   Fax: 01276 28258
Website: www.inspiringfutures.org.uk

International Baccalaureate (IB)
For full information about the IB see full entry on page 290

International Schools Theatre Association (ISTA)
International body of teachers and students of theatre, run by teachers for teachers. Registered charity No. 1050103.

Del Hayton, Operations Manager
Watchbell
Old Hill
Helston,
Cornwall TR13 8HT
Tel: 01326 560398   Fax: 01326 561100
Website: www.ista.co.uk

The Joint Eductional Trust (JET)
A charity (No. 313218) which helps children who have suffered tragedy or trauma at home, or who are at risk, to attend independent day or boarding schools or state boarding schools.

JET
6-8 Fenchurch Buildings
London EC3M 5HT
Tel: 020 3217 1100   Fax: 020 3217 1110
Email: admin@jetcharity.org   Website: www.jetcharity.org

London International Schools Association (LISA)
LISA is a consortium of ECIS registered schools in the UK. For more information contact each school direct – see website: www.lisa.org.uk

Maria Montessori Institute (MMI)
Authorised by the Association Montessori Internationale (AMI) to run their training course in the UK. Further information is available from:

Maria Montessori Institute
26 Lyndhurst Gardens
Hampstead
London NW3 5NW
Tel: 020 7435 3646   Fax: 020 7431 8096
Email: info@mariamontessori.org   Website: www.mariamontessori.org

The National Association for Gifted Children (NAGC)
For over forty years the NAGC has been promoting that 'It's Alright To Be Bright'.

NAGC
Suite 14, Challenge House
Sherwood Drive
Bletchley
Milton Keynes
Buckinghamshire MK3 6DF
Tel: 0870 450 0295   Fax: 0870 770 3219
Email: amazingchildren@nagcbritain.org.uk   Website: www.nagcbritain.org.uk

**The National Association of Independent Schools
& Non-Maintained Schools (NASS)**
A membership organisation working with and for special schools in the voluntary and private
sectors within the UK. Registered charity No. 1083632.

Claire Dorer, Chief Executive Officer
NASS
PO Box 705
York YO30 6WW
Tel/Fax: 01904 621243
Email: cdorer@nasschools.org.uk
Website: www.nasschools.org.uk

National Day Nurseries Association (NDNA)
A national charity (No. 1078275) which aims to promote quality in early years.

NDNA
National Early Years Enterprise Centre
Longbow Close
Huddersfield
West Yorkshire HD2 1GQ
Tel: 01484 407070   Fax: 01484 407060
Email: info@ndna.org.uk   Website: www.ndna.org.uk

National Foundation for Educational Research (NFER)
NFER is the UK's largest independent provider of research, assessment and information
services for education, training and children's services. Its work enables policy makers and
practitioners to make better, more informed decisions, drawing on sound evidence and
accurate information.

NFER's purpose is to make a difference to learners of all ages, expecially to the lives of children
and young people, by ensuring that its work improves the practice and increases the
understanding of those who work with and for learners.
Its clients inlcude UK government departments and agencies at both national and local levels,
which benefit from NFER's full range of expert and professional services, including access to
international networks and data sources.
NFER is a not-for-profit organisation and a registered charity No. 313392.

Head Office
The Mere, Upton Park
Slough, Berkshire SL1 2DQ
Tel: 01753 574123   Fax: 01753 691632
Email: enquiries@nfer.ac.uk   Website: www.nfer.ac.uk

New England Association of Schools & Colleges (NEASC)

An association of schools in the New England area of the USA.

NEASC
Suite 201, 209 Burlington Road
Bedford
MA 01730-1433
USA
Tel: +1 781 541 5406   Fax: +1 781 271 0950
Email: kwillis@neasc.org   Website: www.neasc.org

The Round Square Schools (RSIS)

An international group of schools formed in 1967 following the principles of Dr Kurt Hahn, the founder of Salem School in Germany, and Gordonstoun in Scotland. The Round Square, named after Gordonstoun's 17th century circular building in the centre of the school, now has more than 70 member schools in 20 countries: Australia, Bangladesh, Bermuda, Canada, Colombia, England, France, Germany, India, Japan, Kenya, Oman, Peru, Scotland, Singapore, South Africa, Switzerland, Thailand, UAE and the United States. Registered charity No. 327117. The member schools in the United Kingdom are:

Girls
Cobham Hall, Kent   Westfield, Newcastle upon Tyne
Coeducational
Abbotsholme, Derbyshire   Box Hill, Surrey
Gordonstoun, Scotland   Wellington College, Berkshire
Windemere St Anne's, Cumbria

For more information about Round Square Schools, please contact:

Jane Howison Secretary & Treasurer
The Round Square
Braemar Lodge
Castle Hill
Hartley
Kent DA3 7BH
Tel: 01474 706927
Fax: 01737 217133
Email: jane@roundsquare.org
Website: www. roundsquare.org

School Fees Independent Advice (SFIA)

For further information about SFIA, see editorial page xxii

SFIA Educational Trust Ltd (SFIAET)

A registered charity (No. 270272) established for the furtherance of education. They have a grant fund which can be awarded to schools and organisations who comply with their set criteria.

SFIA Educational Trust Ltd
Tectonic Place
Holyport Road
Maidenhead
Berkshire SL6 2YE
Tel: 01628 502040
Fax: 01628 502049
Website: www.plans-ltd.co.uk/trusts

Schools Music Association of Great Britain (SMA)

The SMA is a national 'voice' for music in education. (Registered charity No. 313646.)

President: Sir Peter Maxwell Davies CBE
Hon Secretary: Maxwell Pryce MBE

SMA Registered Office
71 Margaret Road
New Barnet
Hertfordshire EN4 9NT
Tel/Fax: 020 8440 6919
Website: www.schoolsmusic.org.uk

Scottish Council of Independent Schools (SCIS)

Representing about 97% of the independent, fee-paying schools in Scotland, the Scottish Council of Independent Schools (SCIS) is the foremost authority on independent schools in Scotland and offers impartial information, advice and guidance to parents. Registered charity No. SC01803.

21 Melville Street
Edinburgh, Scotland EH3 7PE
Tel: 0131 220 2106   Fax: 0131 225 8594
Email: info@scis.org.uk   Website: www.scis.org.uk

Society of Education Consultants (SEC)

The Society is a professional membership organisation that supports management consultants who specialise in education and children's services. The society's membership includes consultants who work as individuals, in partnerships or in association with larger consultancies.

SEC Administrator
Floor 5, Amphenol Buisness Centre
Thanet Way
Whistable, Kent CT5 3JF
Tel: 0845 345 7932
Email: administration@sec.org.uk   Website: www.sec.org.uk

Society of Headmasters and Headmistresses of Independent Schools (SHMIS)
For full information about HMC see editorial on page xliv

The State Boarding Schools' Association (SBSA)
For full information about the SBSA see editorial on page xxxvi

Steiner Waldorf Schools Fellowship (SWSF)
Representing Steiner Waldorf Education in the UK and Ireland, the SWSF has member schools and early years centres in addition to interest groups and other affiliated organisations. Member schools offer education for children within the normal range of ability, aged three to 18. (Registered charity No. 295104.)

The Secretary,
Steiner Waldorf Schools Fellowship
Kidbrooke Park, Forest Row
Sussex RH18 5JA
Tel: 01342 822115
Email: mail@swsf.org.uk

Fax: 01342 826004
Website: www.steinerwaldorf.org.uk

Support and Training in Prep Schools (SATIPS)
SATIPS aims to support teachers in the independent and maintained sectors of education. (Registered charity No. 313699.)

SATIPS
Cherry Trees
Stebbing
Great Dunmow
Essex CM6 3ST
Website: www.satips.com

UCAS Universities and Colleges Admissions Service
UCAS is the organisation responsible for managing applications to higher education courses in England, Scotland, Wales and Northern Ireland. (Registered charity No. 1024741)

UCAS
PO Box 28
Cheltenham
Gloucestershire GL52 3LZ
Customer Service: 0871 468 0463
Email: enquiries@ucas.ac.uk

Website: www.ucas.com

UKCISA – The Council for International Student Affairs
UKCISA is the UK's national advisory body serving the interests of international students and those who work with them. (Registered charity No. 1095294)

UKCISA
9-17 St Albans Place
London N2 0NX
Tel: 020 7107 9922 (advice line)

Website: www.ukcisa.org.uk

United World Colleges (UWC)
UWC was founded in 1962 and their philosophy is based on the ideas of Dr Kurt Hahn (see Round Square Schools). Registered charity No. 313690.

The United World Colleges (International)
Second Floor
17-21 Emerald Street
London WC1N 3QN
Tel: 020 7269 7800   Fax: 020 7405 4374
Email: ukcio@uwc.orgWebsite: www.uwc.org

World-Wide Education Service of CfBT Education Trust (WES)
A leading independent service which provides home education courses worldwide.

WES World-wide Education Service
Waverley House, Penton, Carlisle
Cumbria CA6 5QU
Tel: 01228 577123
Fax: 01228 577333
Email: office@weshome.com
Website: www.weshome.com

Index